Diffusion of Gender Quotas in Latin America and Beyond

LATIN AMERICA
Interdisciplinary Studies

Gladys M. Varona-Lacey
General Editor

Vol. 19

PETER LANG
New York • Washington, D.C./Baltimore • Bern
Frankfurt • Berlin • Brussels • Vienna • Oxford

Diffusion of Gender Quotas in Latin America and Beyond

Advances and Setbacks in the Last Two Decades

EDITED BY Adriana Piatti-Crocker

PETER LANG
New York • Washington, D.C./Baltimore • Bern
Frankfurt • Berlin • Brussels • Vienna • Oxford

Library of Congress Cataloging-in-Publication Data

Diffusion of gender quotas in Latin America and beyond:
advances and setbacks in the last two decades / edited by Adriana Piatti-Crocker.
p. cm. — (Latin America: interdisciplinary studies; 19)
Includes bibliographical references and index.
1. Women—Legal status, laws, etc.—Latin America. 2. Women's rights—
Latin America. 3. Sex discrimination—Law and legislation—
Latin America. 4. Equality before the law—Latin America.
I. Piatti-Crocker, Adriana.
KG136.W64G46 346.801'34—dc22 2010014264
ISBN 978-1-4331-1087-0 (hardcover)
ISBN 978-1-4539-0247-9 (e-book)
ISSN 1524-7805

Bibliographic information published by **Die Deutsche Nationalbibliothek.**
Die Deutsche Nationalbibliothek lists this publication in the "Deutsche
Nationalbibliografie"; detailed bibliographic data is available
on the Internet at http://dnb.d-nb.de/.

29 Broadway, 18th floor, New York, NY 10006
www.peterlang.com

Contents

Introduction

ADRIANA PIATTI-CROCKER

During the 1990s, a growing number of countries made significant efforts to help reduce the gender gap in public posts of high ranking. Among a number of institutional devices, gender quotas have been one of the most popular and effective mechanisms for rapidly increasing the proportion of women in politics. Gender quotas provide women with a means to secure their participation in legislatures; they have been implemented in developed and developing countries, and have been influenced by both domestic and international phenomena (Crocker, 2007). Undoubtedly, research on gender quotas has become one of the fastest growing scholarships within the subfield of women and politics and deserves the attention of international relations scholars, students, and policy-makers. However, most studies on gender quotas have focused on country-cases (Baldez 2004, Beckwith 2003, Schmidt and Saunders 2004) or on several countries in a region (Dahlerup 2004, Kittilson 2006, Matland and Montgomery ed. 2003); yet, few scholars have examined sub-national or cross-national diffusion of gender quotas in Latin America, despite the fact that it was within this region where the legislative "quota wave" originated (Htun, 2002). This volume is an attempt to remedy that situation and provide for a rich comparative analysis of this policy proliferation in Latin America and beyond.

The appeal of this book is three-fold. First, it discusses the adoption of a legislative quota in Argentina and its diffusion to other Latin American countries, a process driven by external factors such as regional and international conferences and organizations, and by gender quota campaigns developed in each of the countries adopting the legislation. Second, this volume includes an in-depth examination of twelve case studies; Argentina and Mexico at both national and sub-national levels, Brazil, Peru, Costa Rica, Dominican Republic and Uruguay, and beyond Latin America, Chapter Ten analyzes the adoption of legislative quotas in the former communist and post-conflict countries of Armenia, Bosnia-Herzegovina and Serbia. These country-cases examine in detail the internal developments that led to the adoption of legislative quotas at national and sub-national levels in some cases. In addition, these chapters explore the factors that have constrained and facilitated policymaking in these countries, such as: legal systems, political culture (including religion), public opinion, institutional arrangements, political parties and political actors (politicians, NGOs). Finally, the last chapter of this volume argues that despite an increasing proportion of women legislators in the countries adopting gender quota legislation and other more general positive outcomes for women politicians, there is also another less auspicious trend for women in the region and beyond. Chapter Eleven summarizes the advances and setbacks that women politicians still face today in the countries studied in this volume and analyzes the apparent end of a quota wave in Latin America since the turn of the millennium.

Gender Quotas and their Merits

Gender quotas have been generally classified into three broad categories; reserved seats, party-level quotas, and legislative quotas (Piatti-Crocker and Kempton 2008, Krook 2009)[1]. Reserved seats were first introduced in the 1930s and have become more popular since the 2000s (Krook 2009). Reserved seats set aside a certain number of seats in parliament for women. They establish group-specific avenues of representation and circumvent the existing party and electoral systems. That is, instead of being elected by regular procedures, women are either appointed or nominated by the president, the elected parliament, or may be selected in another manner (Krook 2006, Piatti-Crocker and Kempton 2008). Reserved seats have become prevalent in a number of African and Middle Eastern countries, such as Rwanda, Uganda, and Afghanistan (Quota Project 2010).

Party-based quota systems appeared first in the 1970s. Party-level quotas are adopted by individual political parties willing to increase the proportion of women candidates in their elective posts. In this type of system, it is up to a given political party to adopt a gender quota. In addition, the percentage of women required by the quota and how these quotas are designed and implemented are left to the decision of a given political party. Party-based quota systems are prevalent in Western Europe, though many other countries in Latin America (such as Chile and Nicaragua)

Asia (Thailand, Philippines, etc.) and Africa (South Africa, Botswana, among others) have also implemented this type of quotas (Dahlerup 2006, Krook 2009).

Finally, legislative quotas appeared in the 1990s. This type of quotas mandates all parties presenting candidates for legislative elections to include a certain percentage of women in their candidate party-lists. Legislative quotas have been primarily a Latin American phenomenon. Starting with Argentina in 1991, quotas spread to twelve other Latin American countries in less than a decade: Bolivia, Brazil, Costa Rica, Dominican Republic, Ecuador, Honduras, Mexico, Panama, Paraguay, Peru, Colombia and Venezuela—though the last two, later revoked the legislation—and more recently, Uruguay adopted a legislative quota. Latin America has been traditionally considered to have a profound male-oriented legacy (*machismo*) and has generally shown little regard in attempting to close the gender gap. Thus, it is remarkable the fact that many Latin American countries have adopted such progressive legislation for women. Proponents of legislative quotas argue that these *newer* quotas are more effective than others because they involve *blanket mechanisms*, requiring all political parties to implement a quota regardless of their ideological stance. These proponents also favor national legislation because they believe that a country-wide policy tends to close the gender gap more rapidly (Quota Project 2010). Beyond Latin America, other countries including, Belgium and France in Western Europe and Armenia, Bosnia-Herzegovina and Serbia in Eurasia and Eastern Europe have adopted similar quotas.

Widespread adoption of gender quotas worldwide seems puzzling since these policies infringe on one of the most widely held assumptions of legislative behavior; the fact that elected officials seek to safeguard their positions (Baldez 2004). Providing women with a preferential quota may threaten political positions traditionally held by men. Conversely, women account for at least half of the population in most societies and adopting gender quota legislation could benefit the election of the party supporting a gender quota bill. Indeed, in Latin America, public opinion has favored the inclusion of women in highly-ranked political positions[2]. Finally, gender quotas have been regarded as an important component of a *real* participatory democracy in the region, where gender-based discrimination should be prevented or remedied.

Those opposed to gender quotas have generally based their arguments on the fact that they provide an advantage to women on biological grounds instead of merit. More broadly, opponents to gender quotas claim that such institutional mechanisms threaten principles of liberal democracies because they give women preferential treatment, instead of equality of opportunity. A more proper course of action, these arguments suggest, would require cultural changes within political parties, as men increasingly understand women's concerns (Bacchi 2006, Piatti-Crocker and Kempton 2008).

Proponents of quotas reply that one can invoke the illiberal nature of quotas only if men and women were equally present in positions of authority. Accordingly, the Inter-American Commission of Human Rights among other organizations, have claimed consistently that affirmative action measures are fully "in compliance with the principle of non-discrimination and the applicable provisions of human rights" (IACW 2004).

Much more contentious is the argument that quotas produce *second class politicians*, because women are elected on the grounds of their sex instead of their abilities, thus creating a separate—*less qualified*—pool of legislators. The counterargument is that merit itself may be gendered (Dahlerup 2006, Krook 2006, Lovenduski 2005, Murray 2010) and if women's merit is currently undermined, the inclusion of women would precisely serve to expand the pool of talent and diversity driven by quotas. Some recent works have also suggested that once elected in legislatures, women's parliamentary volume and activity do not seem to differ between *quota* women and other legislators, at least, in the case of France (Murray 2010). In sum, and despite their legal challenges, gender quota systems are crucial for the creation of a critical mass of women in traditionally male-dominated legislatures.[3]

Theoretical Approach

This book is written from the theoretical perspective of international diffusion and attempts to explain the spread of policy in Latin America and beyond, employing external and internal variables. In broad terms, diffusion refers to the process by which institutions, practices, behaviors, or norms are transmitted between individuals and/or between social systems (Starr 1991). The process "involves a set of assumptions about the nature of systems, how they interact, and how the environmental context will affect the units studied" (Starr 1991, 367). Diffusion models have been employed to interpret the spread of wars (Siverson and Starr 1991, Simowitz 1998, Diehl and Vasquez 2008), democratic regimes (Huntington 1991 , Schedler 1998, Bell and Staeheli 2001, Groshek 2010), free markets (Simmons et al. 2003, Pitlik 2007) and gender mainstreaming (True and Mintrom 2001). However, the nature, forms, and consequences of the diffusion of policy are complex subjects because they can be studied at several levels of analysis and may refer to distinctive processes. Most (1990, 938) asserts that diffusion models may be conceived in a general framework, "where there are linkages between some state's policy and other previously occurring factors, which are external to the state." The author also suggests that for diffusion "culture is embedded, substantially organized, regionally and worldwide, and particularly enhanced in the contemporary world by an increasing interdependence among states" (ibid). Interdependence has opened up the policy process within states to a broader array of groups, including groups that have been considered to be traditionally weak in both political and economic senses, such as those concerned with the advancement of gender issues (True and Mintrom 2001) Increasingly those perspectives also claim that states learn and become embedded in global norms that help shape their domestic behavior and more particularly, the conduct towards their citizens. Norms and practices are then transmitted "from one individual to another or from one state to another" (Florini 1996, 369).

Since the 1990s, networking among women through international and regional conferences and meetings has emerged with extraordinary force in Latin America and beyond. Increasing socialization among women's inter-governmental organizations and NGOs was driven primarily by the pre- and post-1995 Women's Conference in Beijing and rooted in international norms like the Convention on the Elimination of all Discrimination Against Women (CEDAW).

Chapter One shows that such efforts had a strong impact on the diffusion of gender quotas from Argentina to other twelve Latin American countries (Baldez 2004, Beckwith 2003, Krook 2006) and Chapter Ten examines the role of international norms and conferences in spreading the adoption of legislative gender quotas in former communist and post-conflict Eurasian and Eastern European countries.

As to the level of analysis, earlier works have been more inclined to emphasize external determinants to explain international diffusion. For example, Ross and Homer (1976, 29) suggest that "a model or approach that relies on the effects of internal characteristics of states, such as economic development or political organization, can be contrasted with one based on the external characteristics of the state or diffusion approaches." Yet, more recent scholarship suggests that a comprehensive approach to study diffusion of norms, values, and policy should include a combination of external and internal determinants, bridging the artificial gap between what occurs within a state and outside of it (True and Mintrom 2001, Mintrom and Vergari 1998, Berry and Berry 1990). Starr (1991, 377) claims that "in the contemporary world we must understand not only the internal context but the external as well and move onto the complex linkages between national and international systems," which according to the author, " is more relevant today than two decades ago because we live in an era of cascading interdependence." This volume will incorporate both external factors (women's conferences and organizations) and internal determinants (political parties, bureaucracies, politicians, women's organizations, etc.) to explain the diffusion of legislative quotas in Latin America and beyond. Certainly, this integrative approach has helped overcome significantly the analytical dichotomy between domestic and international realms in the diffusion of legislative quotas.

Organization of the Book

As briefly discussed above, this book analyzes the process of cross-national diffusion of gender quotas and examines the construction of policy adoption and its descriptive effects in several Latin American countries and beyond. The chapters are organized around the timing of policy adoption, beginning with an overview of the innovation-diffusion processes in Latin America and ending with an analysis of the adoption of gender quotas in three former communist and post-conflict Eurasian and Eastern European countries.

Chapter One, by Piatti-Crocker examines the innovation-diffusion of policy from Argentina to twelve other Latin American countries and analyzes how the "external" process of networking among women helped shape the internal process of policy adoption in Latin America. Following a brief discussion of innovation-diffusion approaches, Chapter One analyzes the adoption of the 1991 Argentine legislative quota, the first of its kind. As should be expected, since 1993—when the quota was first implemented—Argentina experienced a sharp increase in the proportion of women legislators; and this successful implementation had a significant "bandwagon" effect in the region. In addition, Chapter One examines the process of cross-national diffusion, which was encouraged by networking among women through international and regional conferences and meetings and the emergence of quota campaigners throughout the world, particularly as a result of the 1995 UN-sponsored Fourth World Women's Conference in Beijing (Htun and Jones 2002).

Chapter Two, by Archenti and Tula, analyzes quotas in Argentina, their diffusion and implementation at sub-national levels. Argentina has one of the highest percentages of women legislators in the Americas—third after Cuba and Costa Rica (IPU, 2010). However, at sub-national levels, laws regulating gender quotas have had varied effects. This chapter deals with the scope and limitations of electoral laws at sub-national levels in Argentina, including the City of Buenos Aires and four of its largest provinces (Buenos Aires, Córdoba, Mendoza, and Santa Fé). It discusses Argentina's diverse electoral systems at subnational levels and how such institutional mechanisms have influenced the implementation of gender quota laws. This chapter also examines political parties as main actors in the candidate-selection process and how a majority of the parties at sub-national levels have opted for a minimalist interpretation of the gender quota legislation.

Chapter Three, by Piscopo, analyzes the effect of Mexico's thirty percent gender quota law on the representation of women and its diffusion along the country's political institutions. The process of implementing and reforming the quota in Mexico spanned about two decades, effectively raising the proportion of women in its *Congreso de La Nacion* (National Legislature) from an average of thirteen percent in the 1990s to an average of twenty-two percent in the 2000s. However, and despite several reforms, legislative quotas have not reached the minimum thirty-percent required by law due to several legal loopholes and Mexico's electoral system. As a result of these shortcomings, female political elites—themselves party leaders and legislators—have become more focused about achieving "gender fairness" in politics and society. Apart from quotas, additional reforms such as the creation of a legislative commission on gender equity, a gender mainstreaming mechanism for the federal budget, national equality laws and equal opportunity plans, a national women's agency, and political parties' statutory commitments to equity in their nomination procedures and policy platforms have been also introduced, despite significant resistance. Thus, the norms of gender equity that underlie quotas can rapidly and positively, diffuse within countries and across institutions.

Chapter Four, by Zetterberg, analyzes Mexico's implementation of sub-national legislative quotas. Being structured as a federal state—much like the United States—in Mexico, each state has its own electoral code. Thus, following the national gender quota law, some states introduced legislative quotas, whereas others did not. This chapter first describes the diffusion of sub-national level quotas; it shows that a majority of the states have adopted some kind of quota policy, and that more than half of the policies were adopted either concurrently or soon after the 2002 revision of the national quota law. Chapter Four then analyzes the role of the national quota law for the adoption of quotas at the state level. By using the illustrative case study of the state of Zacatecas, this chapter shows that the national legislation was influential in the adoption of quotas at sub-national levels. Finally, Zetterberg's chapter assesses the numerical impacts of sub-national quota policies on women's representation in state legislatures and other far-reaching consequences for women. By reviewing the literature on quotas at sub-national level, this chapter intends to show that quota policies represent the single most important factor in explaining the variation of women representation across Mexico.

Chapter Five, by Araujo and Alves, examines the election of women legislators in Brazil's Federal Chamber of Deputies and the obstacles they experience. Despite the introduction of a quota policy in 1995, its reshaping in 1997 and 2009 and the election of its first female president in 2010, Brazilian legislatures are still dominated by men. This chapter includes an in-depth analysis of the 2002, 2006 and 2010 legislative elections and employs a multivariate analysis that incorporates a combination of both institutional and socioeconomic factors. The outcome of these elections in Brazil, illustrates both the obstacles that Brazilian female legislators must overcome in order to be elected and the weak implementation of quota policies in the country.

Chapter Six, by Schmidt, examines the origins and impacts of gender quotas in Peru within the context of Peru's weak and often volatile party system. Particular attention is paid to largely fortuitous interactions with two very different electoral systems: open list PR in the congressional elections of 2000, 2001, and 2006; and majoritarian block lists in the municipal elections of 1998, 2002, and 2006, as well as the regional elections of 2002 and 2006. These interactions were largely unanticipated by either the political elite or various feminist groups that have championed gender quotas. However, the unexpected success of gender quotas has also contributed to a large gender gap in rates of incumbent candidacies and re-election, particularly in local governments in the most backward parts of the country.

Chapter Seven, by García Quesada, examines the adoption of legislative quotas in Costa Rica, one of the few consolidated democracies in Latin America (Freedom House, 2011). Costa Rica has today, the second highest percentage of women legislators in Latin America (after Cuba). In world standards, the country ranked eleventh in 2010, with thirty-nine percent of women in its unicameral legislature (IPU, 2010). Following the adoption of a legislative gender quota in the mid-1990s by the end of the decade a forty percent quota—the highest percentage in the region—was adopted. More recently, Costa Rica adopted a gender parity clause that will be implemented beyond legislatures, to all public posts. This Chapter examines the factors that explain the evolving legislative quota in Costa Rica and the challenges in implementing the recent parity law, particularly in uninominal elections.

Chapter Eight, by Polanco, analyzes the adoption of legislative quotas in the Dominican Republic and their effects in the political representation of women for both the national and municipal elections of 1998, 2002, 2006, and 2010. The author examines the positive outcomes of the quota laws in gradually increasing the representation of women in the national Chamber of Deputies and in municipalities, but also explains the obstacles in implementing the legislation in the Senate. In addition, Chapter Eight analyzes the more recent changes in the country's party system and electoral laws, which combined with a traditional and male-oriented political culture, may impinge on the successful implementation of quotas in the country. Since, according to Polanco, the effective application of quotas depends on the existence of closed party-lists, a key question is whether it would be possible to maintain an effective implementation of quotas in the recently reformed open-lists multi-party system where major parties are experiencing rampant atomization and loss of credibility, and where the role of institutionalized political parties is being replaced by clientelistism and political corruption.

Chapter Nine, by Johnson and Pérez examines Uruguay's decline from being the region's most staunch defender of women's political rights in the early 1900s to having one of the worst performances in terms of women's access to political office a century later. In addition, Chapter Nine introduces an account of the repeated failed attempts to get legislative gender quota laws passed in the country's post-dictatorship period and an analysis of the process that finally led to the recent adoption of a gender quota law in 2009, its implementation in the 2009 primary elections, and its non-application during the national elections of October of the same year. The chapter ends with some final remarks on the prospects of quota implementation during the electoral cycle of 2014–2015 and for Uruguayan women's political representation in general.

Chapter Ten, by Tasch analyzes the adoption of legislative quotas in three former communist and post-conflict countries; Armenia, Bosnia-Herzegovina, and Serbia. This chapter examines the critical role of the United Nations in the adoption of legislative quotas in all three countries; first, through the Beijing Conference and its Platform for Action and later, through its Security Council resolution 1325. In addition, this chapter studies the significant role of the Organization of Security and Cooperation in Europe (OSCE) and other internal determinants in the process of policy adoption. The author argues that whereas, the adoption of gender quotas in Armenia, Bosnia-Herzegovina and Serbia has shown an increasing political participation and representation of women, the successful implementation of these policies was also influenced by several internal factors, including the countries' electoral systems, design of their quota laws, support of civil society organizations (particularly women's NGOs), willingness of political parties to enforce quotas, changes in their traditional male-oriented social values, and the role of other political forces willing to take gender issues seriously. Taking into consideration that there are many post-conflict countries in the world dealing with social and gender biases, this chapter's findings provide the reader with an interesting analysis of how gender quotas may both help close the gender gap and promote long-term peace.

The volume concludes with a chapter by Piatti-Crocker that examines the current status of gender quota laws in Latin America. Literature on the study of diffusion (Bernard and Killworth, 1978, Mintrom and Vergari 1997, and Rogers 1981 and 2003) argues that a given social network may follow a series of phases of development and that after a high rate of interaction where cliques grow together to form a connected network that increases the likelihood of diffusion; as the network matures there is gradually a decrease or change in the system's communication structure and diffusion may decrease or stall. This seems to have been the case of gender quota laws across Latin America. Whereas the adoption of gender quota legislation peaked in Latin America during the 1996–1998 periods, when ten Latin American countries adopted gender quota legislation and two more in the year 2000, since the turn of the millennium, this "wave" has stalled in Latin America. Efforts at both regional and domestic levels have only been sufficient to implement legislation in Uruguay despite several attempts in other countries, and policy adoption has even reversed in two of the thirteen original cases. Following reputable scholarship on diffusion, it seems very unlikely that a gender quota wave of the kind experienced in the 1990s will regain strength any time soon in Latin America. However, countries with legislative quotas have experienced sub-national diffusion following the national level legislation and several improvements in quota designs including the adoption of parity laws in some cases. Moreover, legislative quota policies have diffused beyond the region within the last decade as shown in Chapter Ten. In the end, future adoption of gender quotas beyond the countries currently with the legislation will depend significantly on whether internal structures are open to absorb political, institutional, and social changes shaped by the international or regional environments.

CHAPTER ONE

Jumping on the Bandwagon

Explaining Innovation and Diffusion of Gender Quota Laws in Latin America

ADRIANA PIATTI-CROCKER

In recent years, an increasing number of countries in Latin America and beyond have adopted legislative quotas for women by reforming their constitutions or electoral laws. Legislative gender quotas require political parties to include a minimum percentage of women among their candidates. Legislative quotas challenge the normative and traditional principle of equality of opportunity, include "sex" as a separate identity category, and are the newest types of gender quotas (Krook 2009:161).

In 1991, Argentina was the first country in the world to use legal means to ensure women's representation through a mandatory gender quota law for national legislators (Jones, 1998). This legislation surprised many scholars and policy-makers for its innovative nature, rapid adoption, and effective implementation. A more significant turn of events for the purpose of this chapter is the diffusion of gender quota legislation to twelve other Latin American countries in less than a decade. International and regional conferences and organizations, including the United Nations Conference in Beijing (1995), regional conferences preparatory of Beijing, and other governmental and non-governmental organizations helped shape the diffusion of quotas region-wide. Yet, domestic factors, such as women's campaigns, women legislators, and the role of bureaucracies and the president in a few cases, played a significant role in the adoption of legislative quotas in Latin America. Finally, whereas the adoption of legislative quotas has effectively increased the proportion of women in congress in all cases, the mere advent of quotas has not resulted in a uniform increase. Rather, the increase has occurred rapidly and effectively in some cases, even surpassing the minimum quota required, while in others, women still remain widely underrepresented.

Following a brief discussion of the prevailing literature on policy innovation and diffusion, this chapter makes the following major claims. First, after the passage of the innovative national legislation in Argentina, the adoption of gender quotas in twelve other Latin American countries was largely a consequence of diffusion, rather than parallel development. Second, whereas the process of socialization at both the global and regional levels played a key role in shaping internal preferences; the adoption of legislative quotas in twelve Latin American countries after Argentina was the result of several internal determinants. Finally, this chapter deals with the effectiveness of gender quota legislation in Latin America and the factors that have contributed to its successful or rather weak implementation. Overall, this chapter provides fresh insights concerning the internal and external dimensions of policy diffusion, and illustrates how the local and the global interact in politically significant ways.

Constructing Policy Innovation in Argentina: The 1991 Gender Quota Law

The vast scholarship dealing with social change can be traced back to the nineteenth century. However, literature on social change "does not offer a coherent view or a uniform set of assumptions. Instead, there has been pervasive disagreement in regard to both substantive arguments and the appropriate level of analysis "(Piatti-Crocker 2010). More recently, constructivist theorists claim that norms have lives of their own and that changes may occur when those norms evolve and spread according to circumstances of time and space (Piatti-Crocker, 2010).[1]

Innovation-diffusion approaches have been incorporated into constructivist perspectives for two reasons: first because innovation/diffusion like constructivism deal with social change, and second, because they both focus on how norms and preferences originate and disseminate among groups or social communities (Piatti Crocker, 2010). In Rogers (2003) view, an innovation is "an idea, practice, or policy that is perceived as new by an individual or other units of adoption," learned through communication channels or "the process by which participants create and share information with one another of a new idea" over time and within a social system or "a set of interrelated units with a common goal" (15–16). Accordingly, innovation indicates "where the stimulus for emulation comes from or the existence of a model or prototype" (12).

> However, newness in an innovation need not just to involve new knowledge. Someone may have known about an innovation for some time but may have not developed a favorable or unfavorable attitude towards it.

> Newness of an innovation may be expressed in terms of knowledge, persuasion, or a decision to adopt (Rogers 2003:12).

According to documented evidence and a number of interviews conducted for this purpose, Argentine women politicians were the main agents of policy innovation in the domestic realm and of policy diffusion to both the country's provinces and beyond the country's borders (Lubertino, 2003). Whereas, women politicians in Argentina did not embody a single ideological perspective, they shared a similar interest in advocating the adoption of gender quotas. María José Lubertino asserts that four factors contributed to the gender quota debate in Argentina: first the "feminization" of political women, which by the late 1980s developed into a rather cohesive group with a common understanding of the role of gender in politics; second, contacts with European women—particularly women from Spain and Germany's Socialist Parties—by using both informal and formal channels of communication; third, the coherent organization of Argentine political women from traditionally rival political parties. Fourth, the emergence of gender quota campaigns at both national and regional levels (Lubertino, 1992: 13). In addition, this more women-friendly environment was influenced by the return of democracy to Argentina in 1983, following seven years of repression during the *dirty war* (Crocker, 2005) and by Argentina becoming a party to the Convention on the Elimination of all Discrimination Against Women (CEDAW) in 1985.[2]

Even though the Partido Justicialista (PJ) had already experimented with gender quotas in Argentina during the early 1950s, only about four percent of the country's legislators in the lower chamber were women prior to 1991. The debate on gender quotas in Argentina emerged around 1985, first at party-level, within the two largest political parties in the country—the Radical Civic Union (UCR), and the Justicialist (PJ) Parties—and starting in 1988 at the national level and across political parties (Lubertino, 2003). Further, the number of women activists who were involved in the quota campaign was negligible compared to the number of women participating as candidates, volunteers, or occupying political posts within the parties. Yet, in measuring how influential a small group of women may be in producing radical change, the size of the group may not carry as much weight as the positions they occupy. Gender quota campaigners were leaders of influential bureaucracies, members of the national parliament, women councils in the city of Buenos Aires, or positioned in political posts of high ranking (Lipsciz, 2003).[3]

Significant legal precedents on behalf of quotas were the Western European experiences with quotas, particularly the Spanish and German cases of party-level quotas. In both countries their socialist parties had implemented quota legislation in the 1980s and through NGOs and regular communication between these parties and Argentine quota campaigners; the debate on gender quota adoption was brought to Argentina.[4] Maria Rigat Pflaum, president of the Women's Bureau of the Ebert Foundation in Argentina, claimed that before the gender quota law was introduced to the Argentine Senate, the Ebert Foundation drew on the experience of quotas in Germany's Social Democratic Party (SDP) and sponsored seminars and assemblies in the country's provinces (Rigat-Pflaum, 2003). The organization also published two booklets explaining the experiences with party-level gender quotas in Germany and Spain (Fundacion Ebert, 1990 and 1991). However, Argentina adopted legislative quotas, rather than party-level quotas, as is commonly the case in Europe.

On November 6, 1989 Senator Margarita Malharro de Torres of the Unión Cívica Radical Party (UCR) representing the province of Mendoza introduced a gender quota bill in the National Senate.[5] The bill had two requirements: a minimum thirty percent quota for legislative candidates in Argentina's closed list system and a requirement that a corresponding percentage of women be placed in "winnable" positions (Gallo and Giacobone 2001:7). On September 20, 1990 Malharro's bill was adopted by an overwhelming majority, with only two PJ senators opposing it. On November 6, 1991 and this time, backed by an extensive mobilization of women, the bill was adopted in the Chamber of Deputies by a majority of votes and only opposed by the Conservative (UCEDE) and Socialist Movement (MAS) parties.[6] At sub-national levels, the national quota law served as model for provincial-level legislation. For example, in May 1992, only a few months following the national law, Santa Fé approved its own thirty percent quota law for candidates to the provincial legislature. By 2000, twenty-two of the twenty-three provinces and the federal district had adopted gender quota laws (Crocker, 2005).

Following the adoption of legislative quotas, a new battle for women politicians emerged over the law's enforcement. First, since the law's placement mandate was rather ambiguous, in 1993 Regulatory Decree 379 incorporated the policy of including at least one woman for every two men candidates in party lists for the elections in the lower house (Gallo and Giacobone 2001:27). Second, even after the decree was adopted a majority of the candidate lists violated the required placement mandate. During the 1993 elections, when the law was first implemented, only a few of the nationwide 213 lists followed the legal requirements (Durrieu 1998:120). In addition, there was a shared concern among political women that the quota law could be declared unconstitutional by the Supreme Court; given that Article 16 of the 1853 Argentine Constitution establishes that all citizens are equal before the law. Hence, the supreme tribunal could interpret affirmative action as endorsing reverse discrimination. Such had been the case in previous rulings by the highest tribunals of Italy, France, Costa Rica, and Colombia. Thus, when in 1994 a Constitutional National Assembly gathered to introduce reforms to the 1853 Constitution, the inclusion of an affirmative action clause was one of the key successful demands made by its eighty female members (Crocker, 2007). In its final form, the constitutional reform of 1994 incorporates a clause that guarantees women affirmative action not only in the legislature but also in all "elective and political posts" (Constitución de la Nación Argentina, art. 37).

> This (Argentine) constitution seeks to put both *sexes on an equal footing* in both public and private lives, through positive action in politics and the workplace, and in private life, establishing equality in the exercise of sexual and reproductive rights and in the family. (Lubertino 2003:32)

Finally, Argentine president Fernando De La Rúa (Alianza Party) used Decree 1,246/2000 to extend the gender quota law to "all elective posts of deputies, senators, and national constituents" (Gallo and Giacobone 2002:170). Although placement mandate violations have become less frequent since the new decree was adopted, women politicians still act as watchdogs to prevent legal infringements at both the national and provincial levels.[7]

Diffusion of Innovations: Gender Quota Laws at Crossnational Levels

Most of the scholarship concerned with the study of diffusion has applied the approach to interpret the evolution of past events in a time-space context. Yet, the purpose of explaining diffusion is not merely to introduce a historical descriptive analysis, but also to analyze some aspects of the process by which new phenomena are communicated. A number of scholars identify this process as "socialization" (Crocker 2005, Florini 1996, Mintrom 2000, Rogers 2003).[8]

In broad terms, diffusion "refers to the process by which institutions, practices, behaviors, or norms are transmitted between individuals and/or between social systems" (Welsh 1984:12). The process "involves a set of assumptions about the nature of systems, how they interact, and how the environmental context will affect the units studied" (Starr 1991:367). However, the nature, forms, and consequences of the diffusion of policy and behavior are complex subjects because they can be studied at several levels of analysis and may refer to distinctive processes. In all cases, Emanuel Adler (1991: 43) observes that "there is a dynamic relationship between historical and structural forces that helps explain the nature of the diffusion of values." Adler (1993:50) identifies this dynamic process as "cognitive evolution." The author suggests that because "our ideas, beliefs, and behaviors are learned from other people," collective learning will be closely related to the ability of groups to convey their experiences to other groups. Yet, a given institutional framework will help shape how these beliefs are translated into action, how they are implemented and what makes some ideas possible or impossible to enforce. Adler claims that just as science progresses, social processes also evolve through what he calls an "inter-subjective consensus," or the unconscious agreement between relevant actors within a specific institutional framework (54).

Rogers (2003) suggests that an innovation can be communicated in a number of ways; however, socialization plays a critical role in facilitating its diffusion. In Rogers' view, socialization arises "within a web of places, people, physical, and communications links in which information, people, and goods flow play a key role in the diffusion of policy innovation." Thus, through socialization members of a diffusion network are exposed to new ideas or policies. Mintrom and Vergari (1998) claim that communication channels, including interpersonal exchanges or organizational networks increase significantly the chances of diffusion. In other words, the process of diffusion is contingent primarily on the "diffusion networks" or the socialization stage of the process and the extent to which such networks have the capacity to influence others to adopt innovations (Rogers 2003).

Harvey Starr (1991) posits that one of the key factors in the study of innovation-diffusion is "where the stimulus for emulation comes from, or the existence of a model or a prototype." The prototype "exhibits certain behavior and the observer," he adds, "matches that behavior" (359–360). John Kingdon (1995) calls this process the "bandwagon effect," by which people or groups of people first "speak of a growing realization, an increasing feeling, a lot of talk in the air, and coming to a conclusion," and then, after a certain degree of general acceptance there seems to be what Kingdon refers to as the "the take-off point", when many people begin to discuss the proposal or idea (140).

This consensus seems to be connected to frameworks on regionalism (Acharya 2001, Checkel 1999, Katzenstein 1996). Recent literature on regionalism no longer conceptualizes regions in terms of mere geographical contiguity, but rather in terms of purposeful social, political, cultural, and economic interaction among states (Calleya 1997). Theorists on regionalism argue that regional interactions can lead to the creation of a regional political culture and a regional "identity" that may have important political implications (Adler and Crawford 2002, Choi and Caporaso 2002). This regional context with frequent interactions of political women from all over Latin America helped shape the process of gender quota diffusion cross-nationally as it will be explained in the next sub-section.

Diffusion of Quotas: External Determinants

During the 1980s, the women's movement in Latin America embarked on a process of expansion in both qualitative and quantitative terms. Qualitatively, women's groups became more aware of the fact that traditional roles have kept them lagging behind men in the public life, including employment opportunities and involvement in key political posts. Maxine Molineux (2001:180) asserts that "those active in the women's movement followed a course which some participants have described as a shift, albeit hesitant and conditional, from the margins to the center." Quantitatively and due to a great extent, to a new wave of regional re-democratization, Latin America experienced the emergence of a significant number of interest groups, a process that Molineux citing Sonia Alvarez, describes as the "NGOization" of the Latin American women's movement (181). In addition, whereas an extensive number of NGOs emphasized development activism instead of egalitarianism, an even greater number of organizations dealt exclusively with women's rights (Lycklama et al., 1998).

Some of the women interviewed for this project observed that even though most women's NGOs rely on very limited budgets, socialization among them at national, regional, and global levels became increasingly popular because of the development of communications technology and more specifically, due to the significant role of the internet.[9] In sum, processes of political opening and democratization developed and offered women a more suitable setting in which an increasing number of women's organizations at different levels (local, national, and regional) emerged almost spontaneously. A revitalized civil society made room for the discussion of a variety of women's demands, particularly regarding political and social gains (Lycklama et al. 1998: 30).

Networking among women appeared to have had a strong impact on the diffusion of gender quotas (Baldez 2004, Beckwith 2003, and Krook 2006). Among some of the relevant organizations, the Friedrich Ebert Foundation held meetings with the purpose of discussing gender quotas in the Southern Cone countries. In 1990, women with liaisons to Ebert from the Southern Cone countries of Argentina, Brazil, Chile, Paraguay, and Uruguay, formed the *Foro de Mujeres del Cono Sur* (Women's Forum of the Southern Cone), one of the earlier regional women networks that debated the employment of gender quotas in Europe and Latin America. According to a report published by the Ebert Foundation, "the Argentine office created the Women's Forum for its twenty participants coming from the five Southern Cone countries in Latin America, all of them very involved in politics" (Ebert 2002:10). This organization began meeting annually in 1991 "and established since then, strong contacts among its participants through whom experiences are shared" (Ebert 2002:11). The report also suggests that the Forum's discussions focused on "questions related to equality of opportunities, integration with Mercosur, and legislation over gender quotas . . . ." (Ebert 2002:12).

Extending the discussion on quotas to other Latin American countries beyond the Southern Cone, the Women's Commission of the Latin American Parliament (PARLATINO) was an important source of regional socialization. Citing the

Brazilian legislator Marta Suplicy, Htun and Jones (2002: 34) claim that "Latin American legislators gathered at Parlatino in São Paolo to consider the experience in Argentina." Franganillo (2003) claims that "representatives from PARLATINO gathered from all over Latin America to participate at regional meetings." Marcela Durrieu (2003) and Cecilia Lipsciz (2003) shared with the author similar claims.[10]

Of particular interest was a 1994 conference organized by Economic Commission of Latin America and the Caribbean (ECLAC) in Mar del Plata, Argentina to prepare for the 1995 World Conference in Beijing at which the Commission of Women and Development (*Unidad Mujer y Desarrollo)* endorsed affirmative action for political women.[11] Although the report does not mention explicitly the Argentine experience with its gender quota law, the document identifies the new policy trend when it asserts that "some countries have been implementing mechanisms of affirmative action . . . through specific measures" (ECLAC 1994). In addition, a panel of Argentine women in Mar del Plata discussed the country's experience with its national gender quota legislation at the conference and also at other informal settings such as restaurants or coffee bars, where the subject was brought up by interested Latin American feminists (Franganillo 2003, Lipsicz 2003). Finally, women who had been involved in quota campaigns in Argentina were invited by NGOS, such as WEDO and the Women's Leadership Program (PROLEAD), and IGOs, such as the Inter-American Bank of Development (IBD) to share their experiences with quotas in Argentina.[12]

Yet, the regional mobilization was the result, to a great extent, of a global UN-sponsored agenda. More particularly, the 1995 Fourth World Women's Conference in Beijing was crucial in the diffusion of legislative quotas in Latin America in three main instances. First, during the pre-conference period, when a number of regional conferences organized by both IGOS and NGOs set the agenda and prepared proposals to be presented at the UN conference.[13] Second, during the conference itself, which "legitimized the idea of gender quotas" (Htun and Jones 2002). Indeed, "the resulting Beijing Declaration and Platform for Action, signed unanimously by all 189 states participating at the conference, called on governments to take measures to ensure women's equal access and full participation in power structures and decision-making, as well as to increase women's capacity to participate in decision-making leadership" (Krook 2009:3). More specifically, the conference provided crucial momentum for the diffusion of gender quotas across the region (Camacho Granados 1997, Htun and Jones 2002, Krook 2006). The National Document (*Informe Nacional*) presented by Argentina, included a report on the country's national and provincial-levels legislative quotas.[14] Finally, the process of diffusion was also shaped by the post-Beijing period, when organizations within the U.N. system sponsored the implementation and follow-up of gender-based policies. It recommended that governments prepare national plans for action by

1996, outlining implementation strategies in consultation with major institutions and civil society organizations.[15] It is noteworthy that most Latin American countries adopted legislative quotas within two years following the Beijing conference. This is another indicator of the U.N.'s influential role.[16]

Other sources appear to confirm that cross-national socialization such as conferences, meetings, and organizations played a very significant role in the diffusion of gender quota laws in Latin America. For example, in Honduras, Ménendez and Montesdeoca (2002:18) observe that women legislators gathered the necessary documentation and experiences abroad—particularly from Argentina, but later from Peru and Costa Rica—through meetings and conferences to submit a proposal in its legislature in 1998. In Costa Rica, the Argentine gender quota legislation was an important precedent for the country's 1996 law. In addition, Juliana Martinez a member of the feminist foundation *Acceso* of Costa Rica claims that the 1993 executive decree enacted in Argentina served as a model when Costa Rican women decided to include a similar placement mandate in their legislation (e-mail correspondence: October 11, 2004).

According to an alternative explanation, the adoption of mandatory gender quotas throughout Latin America was not the result of diffusion but instead a consequence of parallel developments and shared preferences. However, this alternative explanation seems inadequate for two reasons. First, the lapse of time between the innovator (Argentina) and the other Latin American countries was too great. Second, even if there might have been some discussion regarding gender quotas in other countries, there was no concrete action (i.e. adoption of new policy) before or concurrent with the Argentine national legislation, contradicting the logic of parallel development.

There was certainly a significant time period between the passage of the quota law in Argentina and the adoption of similar legislation in other Latin American countries. Following Argentina, the next countries to adopt similar gender quota legislation did so five years later. Even an earlier experience with gender quotas in Costa Rica does not contradict this thesis. In fact, in 1988 Costa Rica sought to introduce gender quotas but was not successful. The eventual passage of the Law of Real Equality (1990) included a requirement that political parties adopt measures to increase women's election (Jones 2004), but as discussed in Chapter Seven, it was not until 1996 and following several attempts that a gender quota law was finally adopted in Costa Rica (García Quesada 2003). Most Latin American countries adopted gender quota legislation between 1996 and 1998, and two in 2000. Certainly, much of the scholarship related to diffusion finds time to be an essential variable because the passage of time (at least initially) increases the likelihood of diffusion (Berry and Berry, 1990, Box-Steffensmeier and Jones 2001, Mintrom 2000, Mintrom and Vergari 1998, Starr 1991).

Although there was some discussion regarding gender quotas in other Latin American countries even before the passage of the Argentine gender quota law, this discourse is best categorized as "pre-diffusion" or, as Kingdon suggests, a situation in which there is some degree of internal political debate but no concrete action. In this case, there was some discussion supporting gender quota legislation in selected Latin American countries and during several regional meetings, yet none of the countries adopted the legislation.[17]

Overall, the regional and global developments of the mid-1990s, particularly the pre- and post-Beijing processes, were crucial in stimulating debate over gender quotas, which intensified from a mere ideological aspiration to a real phenomenon. Through socialization women had the opportunity to discuss their experiences with gender quotas at regional and global conferences and adopt key resolutions that pressured national governments to modify policy and behavior in favor of women.

The Internal Processes: Adoption of Legislative Gender Quotas in Latin America

As discussed in previous pages, after Argentina and in the short period of two years (1996~1998), ten Latin American countries adopted similar legislative quotas and two others did so in 2000. However, whereas "emulation" is central to diffusion, this does not imply that the "emulating" social group will adopt a given policy in an identical manner. Certainly, some similarity must be present, but in many cases, diffusion will experience a process of internal adaptation according to the receiving group's cultural or institutional circumstances. Rogers (2003, 17) calls this adjustment process *re-invention* and shows that most adopters tend to modify the emulated policy before adopting the innovation. Indeed, this rapid diffusion of legislative quotas in Latin America was a process that involved both external (regional and global conferences and organizations) and internal forces (national governmental mechanisms, legislators, or other members of government, NGOs, etc.) and as explained below, policies were adapted to fit a given country's institutional and cultural framework. In the previous pages we discussed the "external process," which helped shape ideas through socialization and the successful implementation of gender quotas in Argentina. In this subsection we will briefly discussed the "internal processes" of re-invention or how some of the Latin American countries adopting gender quotas translated ideas into action.[18]

For example, in 1996 Brazil adopted quota legislation. The Brazilian law implemented a quota system only to be enforced in Brazil's municipal elections of 1996. The regulation stated that in order to register for these elections parties had to fill at least twenty percent of the places on their lists with women. This law was accompanied by a campaign called "women unafraid of power" (mulheres sem medo do poder), encouraging women to venture into the world of politics. Between 1995–1997, national representatives introduced eight proposals to Congress. By the end of 1997, Brazil's National Congress was able to amend the country's electoral legislation, which required that at least twenty-five percent of state and federal representatives in parliament for the election of 1998 be women (ECLAC, 1998). The minimum percentage of the following elections would be raised to thirty percent for each sex. According to Clara Araujo (2003), the legislation was not debated intensely in the National Congress, it passed with some open objections, particularly from the right-wing parties, but without rejecting it.

In 1996, Paraguay adopted a twenty percent quota for both the lower and upper houses. The quota also established a placement mandate of at least one woman every five places. According to prominent feminist figures in Paraguay, the adoption of quota legislation in that country was the product of networking among women, especially the *Red de Mujeres Políticas*—Political Women's Web—and the *Secretaría de la Mujer de la Presidencia de la República*—Women's Secretariat (Bareiro and Soto, 1997). The law also established other non-discriminatory measures, such as the formation of separate lists for men and women in national elections and the separate tabulation of votes by women and men, but these dispositions are yet to be implemented.

In Bolivia, the discussion over the issue of quotas began around 1993, but it was not until a year later that the debate was taken seriously. According to Zabala Canedo (1998), the collaboration among the Subsecretaría de Asuntos de Género, the Foro Político de Mujeres, and the Latin American Parliament (PARLATINO) led to the submission of a quota bill for national legislators. The proposal was initially rejected in 1996, but reintroduced and adopted in 1997. The quota law established a thirty percent quota for the lower house and a twenty-five percent quota for the upper house. In addition, all political parties submitting a list of candidates were required to have at least thirty percent women candidates in the so-called "security zones" or priority representation in legislative elections. According to the legislation, the initial quota served as a reference, to be increased five percent in each subsequent election until it reached fifty percent (Quota Project, 2008). With Constitutional changes in 2009 favoring the representation of women, the proportion of female senators elected increased dramatically. These significant recent developments will be discussed in Chapter Eleven of this volume.

According to Gregory Schmidt (see Chapter Six), Peru's gender quotas were the product of pressure from the country's feminist movement, the efforts of congresswomen of various political parties, and decisive support from President Alberto Fujimori. Moreover, the international and regional momentum for quotas was strengthened by the Platform for Action adopted at the 1995 Beijing

Conference, which was attended by four Peruvian congresswomen and a 1997 inter-parliamentary meeting on gender equity in New Delhi. New codes for the national and municipal elections passed in 1997 required that women and men must each constitute at least twenty-five percent of each party's candidates. Quotas were implemented in municipal elections (1998) before national elections (2000). The quota was expanded to 30 percent in December 2000 (Schmidt, 2004).

Venezuelan women politicians demanded an increasing representation of women in governmental posts in a *Manifesto of United Women Leaders* published in 1988. The manifesto declared that "the parties and independent groups ought to know that we women are in condition and prepared to defend our right to share political power with men, who have exercised control over it permanently" (Friedman, 2000). However, the minimum goal of 30 percent quota mentioned in a previous document was not introduced in this occasion due to the Christian Democratic Party's (COPEI) objections (Friedman 2000, 218). Moreover, the 1990s saw "a decline in women's cojunctural coalition building" primarily as the result of one of the worst financial crisis in Venezuela. In 1998, the National Women's Council and some congresswomen formed the *Bicameral Commission for Women's Rights*, proposed the adoption of an article in the 1998 Suffrage and Participation Law to ensure that all parties' electoral lists, whatever the election, would have at least 30 percent female candidates. The proposed reform was initially adopted but repealed two years later (Jones & Htun, 2001).

Colombia adopted legislative quotas in 2000, and the first election under the law was held in March 2002. The Colombian gender quota law was also the product of women's networking through the *Redes de Mujeres Colombianas* (Colombian Women's Web) and the creation of the National Office of Equity of Women established after Beijing in 1995. Colombia's quota law, however, established a 30 percent gender quota for the very ambiguous "high level government positions" that led to controversy (Red Nacional de Mujeres, 2003). It was not until administrative regulations were issued that controversy subsided. The regulations required the presence of at least one woman for every three candidates or a minimum of thirty percent of women in all the party lists presenting candidates for the country's legislative elections.[19] However, the 2000 quota law was declared unconstitutional by Colombia's high court in 2001 and the law was later revoked (Lozano Eljure, 2003).

Honduras also adopted a legislative quota for women in the year 2000. According to Méndez and Montesdeoca (2002), during the period between 1994–1998 political women legislators developed strategies and set the agenda through the establishment of the Commission of Women in the country's legislature. For example, women legislators such as Alba Alonzo de Quesada, Norma Marina García, and Soad Salomón de Faccussé gathered the necessary documentation and experiences abroad through meetings and conferences and submitted a proposal in 1998. At the same time, other alternative bills, including one from the Governmental Office of Women (OGM) and Honduras' Liberal Party were proposed. Yet, the process before the adoption of the law was complicated: a male representative was required to be part of the Commission of Women to provide "legitimacy to the bill" and other unfortunate events, including Hurricane Mitch, postponed the adoption of the law. In May 2000, and with the support of women's NGOs and governmental organiza-

Table 1.1: Gender Quota Legislation in Latin America

COUNTRY	DATE	LEGISLATION
Argentina	1991	Law 24,012 (30%)
Bolivia	1997	Reform and Completion of the Electoral System Act (30%). A constitutional reform will include a parity law for the next legislative elections.
Brazil	1997	Law 9,504 (originally quota of 20%, expanded to 30% in 2000)
Colombia	2000	Law 581 was later overturned
Costa Rica	1996	Law 7653 (quota for parties and Assembly delegations, 40%). Parity law (50%) will be implemented in 2012
Dominican Republic	1997	Electoral Law 275/97 (25%); 33% since 2000.
Ecuador	1997	Labor Protection Act (20%). Reformed in 2000; 30% of candidates on electoral lists must be women, both for ordinary and supplementary seats
Honduras	2000	Ley de Igualdad de Oportunidades (30%)
Mexico	1996	Amendment to the Federal Code on Electoral Procedures and Institutions modified in 2002 (30%). In 2008 a 40% quota was adopted.
Panama	1997	30% for internal and general elections.
Paraguay	1996	Law 834 Electoral Code (20%).
Peru	1997	Law 26,859 for national elections (25%). Law 26,864 for municipal elections (25%). In 2000, gender quotas were raised to 30% at national, regional, municipal levels.
Venezuela	1998	Suffrage and Political Participation Act (30%). Law repealed in 2000
Uruguay	2009	30% minimum quota for both genders. The quota will be implemented during the 2014 national elections.

Source: ECLAC, 2010.

tions, the law was finally adopted. The law "For the Equality of Opportunity for Women" requires a 30 percent gender quota in all party lists for legislative candidates. In the 2001 national elections, Honduras' gender quota law was first implemented.[20]

Taken together, the *internal forces* that contributed to the adoption of gender quota legislation in Latin America were many and varied from country to country. A common factor, though, was the important role of women politicians, including governmental organizations such as the Paraguayan Women Secretariat or through the small group of women legislators. As it occurred in Honduras, even though women legislators represented a very small minority in the Houses, they were able to introduce gender quota bills and successfully convince male counterparts to adopt the legislation. Other important networking channels were women's non-governmental organizations, such as Colombian Women's Web or the various Peruvian feminist groups. Finally, Presidents Fujimori in Peru and Menem in Argentina played a key role in the process.

The Impacts of Gender Quota Legislation in Latin America

As should be expected, countries with legislative quotas have been generally successful in increasing the proportion of women legislators. One of the clearest examples of such success is Argentina. From 1993 (when the quota was first implemented) to 2001, there was an increase of seventeen percent of women legislators in the Argentine Chamber of Deputies. During the same period of time, the percentage of women legislators in the Senate increased by thirty percent. Between 2001 and the 2007 legislative elections, the percentage of women in the Chamber of Deputies increased by eleven percent, and by nine percent in the Senate during the same time-period. Currently, the percentage of women legislators in Argentina exceeds the minimum thirty percent quota in both chambers.

In Costa Rica, "the largest gain (in the percentage of women elected to Congress) was achieved by the adoption of quotas ..." but "the percentage of women legislators only reached (and actually surpassed) the minimum quotas threshold of forty percent with the addition of a placement mandate" during the 2002 elections (Jones 2004). Costa Rica adopted recently a gender parity clause, by which a fifty present quota, with strict alternation on lists also known as the "zipper system" will be enforced next during the 2014 national elections (see García Quesada's Chapter Seven).

Finally, in 2001 Bolivia approved a new electoral system of Mixed-Member PR for its Lower House and introduced a placement mandate of one woman for every three candidates but only in the PR election. In the uninominal plurality districts women still remain widely unrepresented. Following the reform of its Constitution in 2009, a parity-clause was introduced in its article nine, by which women and men should alternate candidate seats. However, during the last senate elections, the process was still governed by a temporary law and did not fully incorporate the new constitutional clause in the area of gender equality. Therefore, an umbrella organization that linked a number of women's groups mobilized with the slogan, *Women Ready for the Ballot, Women Protagonists*. The effective women's campaign and the support of President Evo Morales led to a temporary gender parity mechanism that required an equal number of men and women in all parties presenting candidate lists for the election of senators. This measure contributed to an increase in the proportion of women elected to the Bolivian Senate from 3.7 percent (after the 2005 elections) to forty-seven percent of senators in 2009 (Quota Project 2010).

As seen on the tables below and despite an increasing percentage of women in all the national legislatures where quotas have been introduced, some quotas have been more effective than others. Leading scholarship on quotas has debated over the factors that influence more positively on the election of women, such as the type of electoral system (Matland and Studlar 1996, Schmidt and Saunders 2004); district and party magnitude (Norris 2004, Jones 2004); effective quotas and relative magnitude of largest party (Gallo, Sample and Schmidt 2008, and Schmidt, Chapter Six) and whether placement mandates are incorporated (Jones 1998, Krook 2009).[22] Going beyond this scholarship, Krook (2009,39) asserts that whereas "details of individual provisions shape implementation ... measures that appear similar sometimes have distinct effects on women's representation—and at the same time provisions that seem dissimilar have comparable results." Krook notes that specific quota campaigns interact with "numerous existing institutional measures" and emphasizes the importance on how those campaigns intersect with the reform or non-reform of other institutions (54–55). The author claims that when quota campaigns mutually reinforce other institutions (harmonizing sequences) they are expected to experience a dramatic success; such that they "fit together over time" as they "complement institutional reform with institutional configurational change." On the other hand, under disjointed sequences "quota campaigns clash with institutions, they produce conflicts and tensions that undermine efforts to promote change" (210). Krook shows that Argentina's successful implementation of legislative quotas was due to its quota campaigns' "harmonizing" sequences.[23]

Finally and despite the gender quota "wave" that spread to Latin America quite rapidly and effectively during the 1990s, there seems to be another, less auspicious trend in the region. As it will be discussed in Chapter Eleven, since the turn of the century, efforts at both regional and domestic levels have been only sufficient to adopt legislative quotas in Uruguay and two of the thirteen original cases (Colombia and Venezuela) have rejected the legislation. Indeed, following reputable scholarship on diffusion, it seems very unlikely that a gender quota wave of the kind experienced in the 1990s will regain strength any time soon in Latin America.

Figure 1.1: Impact of Quota Legislation: Lower Chambers and Unicameral Congresses*

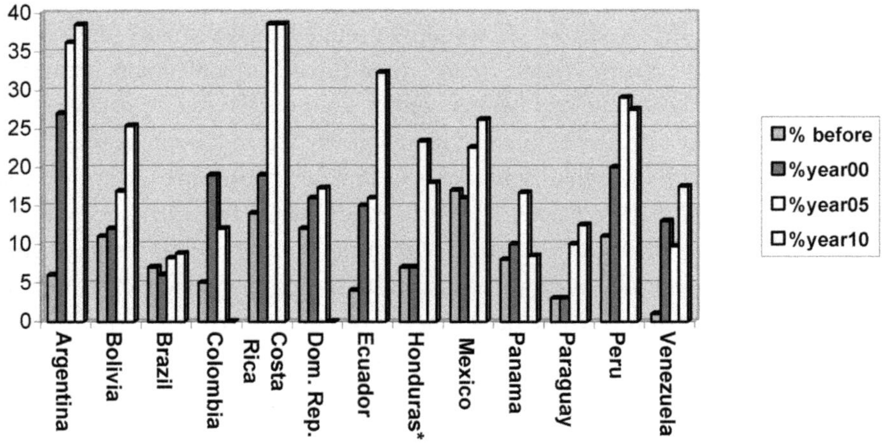

* Data from Inter-Parliamentary Union retrieved on May 25, 2010 from http://www.ipu.org/wmn-e/classif.htmt

Figure 1.2: Impact of Quota Legislation: Senate

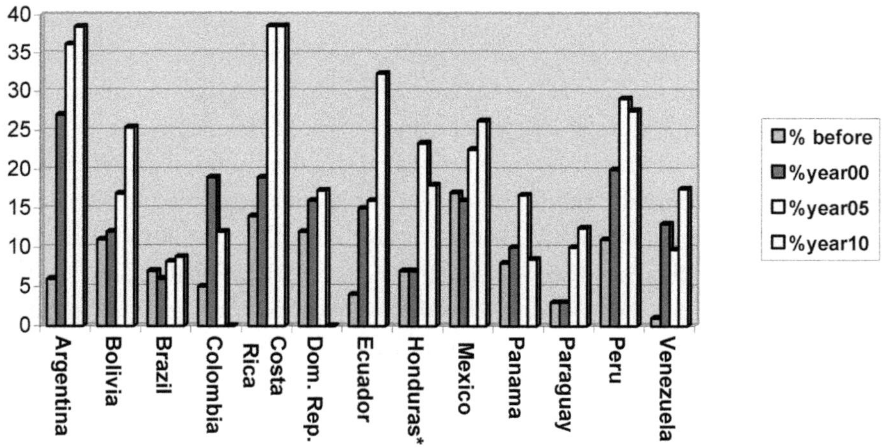

* No Data Available for Colombia (Lower and Upper Houses) and the Dominican Republic (Upper House).

Conclusion

Diffusion may be seen logically both as an international process where external factors influence the domestic affairs of a state, and also as one subfield of linkage politics, where both internal and external events interact within a state (Starr 1991, Berry and Berry 1990, True and Mintrom 2001). Thus, an appropriate explanation of diffusion should be given in terms both of the unit of analysis (e.g. states, individuals, or groups of individuals) and the social structures in which these units are embedded (e.g. world or regional systems). This chapter dealt with both dimensions by emphasizing processes of international diffusion through global and regional socialization, and briefly describing the internal factors that led some countries to adopt legislative quotas successfully.

This chapter argued that the adoption of legislation in Argentina in 1991 initiated a trend at cross-national levels. Although political parties in many European countries and the PJ in Argentina had adopted gender quotas earlier and some regional debate was evident at the time, the mandatory countrywide legislation adopted in 1991 by Argentina was the first of its kind. The adoption of the Argentine gender quota legislation in 1991 was precisely the "take-off point" for the sort of "bandwagon effect" (John Kingdon 1995). It gave rise to a gender quota movement in the region that was successful in passing similar legislation in twelve other Latin American countries.

The diffusion process was instigated by transnational organizations and conferences also referred in this chapter as the process of socialization, where women discussed the need to implement gender quota laws in their countries and Argentine politicians were invited to share the country's experiences with the innovative legislation. In addition, various domestic factors, including the demands of feminist organizations, women legislators, and women's governmental organizations among other factors, were critical in shaping the internal processes and in re-inventing the emulating policy to fit the institutional and cultural frameworks of the Latin American countries adopting the legislation. Yet, despite an increasing percentage of women in parliament in all countries, legislative quotas have been more effective in some cases than in others due to particular institutional mechanisms or other factors.

Overall, the integrative approach employed in this chapter helped to overcome significantly the analytical dichotomy between what occurs within a state (the domestic realm) and what occurs outside of it (the international realm). Certainly, such an integrative methodology has helped analyze more adequately the factors that led to a wave of legislative gender quotas in Latin America in less than a decade.

CHAPTER TWO

Candidate Selection as Political Barriers for Gender Quotas

The Case of Argentina at Subnational Levels

NÉLIDA ARCHENTI AND MARÍA INÉS TULA
TRANSLATED BY HORACIO ABELEDO

Argentina was the first country in the world to adopt a gender quota law for legislators at the national level in 1991. Law 24012, included in the National Electoral Code (article 60) is a legislated quota and is therefore mandatory for all political parties participating in general elections. The Argentine law was later expanded with the adoption of three regulatory decrees issued between 1993 and 2005. These regulations had the purpose of strengthening the legal provisions and achieving a real inclusion of women in representative bodies. The decrees expanded gender quotas to the national senate and sought to curb the deeply rooted practices among political parties of violating the legal quota requirements.

In contrast to other Latin American countries, Argentina's political parties monopolize their candidates' nomination process (Law 23298). Therefore, it is crucial that women are included during the candidate selection process since is it at this time when party lists and internal agreements (e.g. political, territorial, gender agreements) are consolidated. In general the process of candidate selection is carried out "behind closed doors" between party leaders and without the participation of women. Party elites are mostly composed by men, who are mainly in charge of consolidating the list of candidates. Hence, the implementation of gender quotas may challenge male control in the parties' decision-making process.

Party resistance against the inclusion of women derives both from strategic options and adaptive conducts. Each seat obtained by a woman as a result of the legal provisions is regarded as a lost seat for men, so men had been reticent to follow the legal provisions (Krook 2008). For example, during the first election held under the quota law in 1993, most of the political parties did not obey the law and others obeyed it only symbolically, placing women candidates in the last places of the list, or only as stand-in candidates. One of the most important measures of later regulatory decrees was a placement mandate, which since then, requires parties to place women in precise positions on the party lists, either by a rule of alternation or indicating certain specified positions. This measure then, prevented parties from including women as tokens, without real chances of being elected.

After the adoption of the national quota law; between 1992 and 2000, the Argentine provinces introduced similar laws, with the exception of the Autonomous City of Buenos Aires (where the national law was enforced) and in the Province of Jujuy. The provincial quota laws either replicate or surpass the minimum thirty percent gender quota required by the national law. This minimum percentage varies from district to district, according to the political dynamics and the particular correlation of forces in each province. In general, subnational quotas have tended to emulate the original national legislation. Thus, the regulatory decrees that were introduced later to the national legislation were not included in many subnational laws. For example, placement mandates or substitution mechanisms for replacing legislators were not adopted in some provinces.

Scholarship has examined the impact of gender quotas in the Argentine National Congress (Jones 1997; Archenti 2002, 2004; Tula 2002; Marx et al 2007; Archenti and Tula 2008). These studies indicate a significant increase of women legislators in both houses. Between 1991 and 2005 there was an increase of 5.4 to 35.4 percent in the Chamber of Deputies and from 36.1 in 2001 (when the quotas were first applied) to 43.5 percent in 2005 in the Senate (Archenti and Tula, 2008). This increase not only showed a more equitable representation of women in both chambers but it also promoted social, political and cultural recognition of gender differences because women became more visible and occupied political spaces traditionally held by men. Moreover, an increasing women's presence permitted a greater communication between women legislators and women NGOs, and brought more diversity to parliamentary and public agendas that included new areas of concern (Archenti and Tula 2008).

There is a general consensus on the types of electoral mechanisms that may favor the access of women to the legislative chambers, such as large multi-member districts, and closed and blocked lists (Jones 2000, Marx et al 2007, Archenti and Tula 2008, Krook 2009). The Argentine electoral system has been regarded as beneficial to women, resulting in an effective implementation of quota laws, particularly when compared to other Latin American countries. In contrast, there is no much work on the implementation of quotas at provincial levels. The most recent references are the quantitative comparative analyses of Jones (1997), and Archenti and

Tula (2008), which include all of the country's twenty-four electoral districts. There are also case studies for the provinces of Misiones (Martín 2010), Buenos Aires (Colotta 2010), and Salta (Ramos and Spaventa 2010). In spite of the considerable heterogeneity of these studies, they all show a positive impact of gender quotas in subnational legislatures.

However, in recent years the increase of women representatives has stalled. The explanation lies mainly in the fact that political parties tend to observe the strict minimum quota required by the law. Thus, there seems to be a glass ceiling for women, where the minimum percentage of women that quota laws impose has been taken as a maximum percentage by political parties (Archenti and Tula 2008).

Selection of Candidates: Key Components for an Increasing Representation of Women

As we have noted in the previous section, the selection of candidates for elections is one of the most meaningful party-level decisions (Norris 2006). Not only because this is the time when candidates are selected by their parties, but also because it is an opportunity to either climb up the ladder of party structure or lose control of significant power resources (Shattschneider 1941, Ranney 1981). Therefore, obtaining a place in the ballot becomes a key component of power in the party structure; especially when winning elections becomes the main goal of party members, and becoming a candidate entails the prospect of access to elective offices (Kirchheimer, 1965). As Hazan and Rahat (2009) suggest, the selection processes not only affect party politics, they can also reflect party politics since they bring into evidence the modes of recruitment in an organization (Epstein 1967, Gallagher 1988); may serve as evidence of the low proportion of women in their nominations (Baldez 2007); link party elites to the candidates and connect voters together (Taylor 2000); shed light on the relation between leaders and activists regarding internal rules (whether they are committed to their observance or they transgress them systematically); and may show the level of the pary's internal cohesion (Gallagher 1988; Billie 2001).

Although the legal framework and formal institutions create incentives for the adoption of more inclusive selection procedures, not all parties react in the same way. These dissimilar responses may be due to the diverse interactions between formal institutional rules, such as the electoral system and federalism; certain particular contextual situations, such as competition structures inside the parties; and party-level variables, like ideological cohesion and leadership fragmentation (Siavelis and Morgenstern 2008). Candidate selection procedures have also an impact on the elected candidates and on their representativity, taking into account the degree of significant social cleavages (Gallagher 1988; Norris 1993, 1996 and 1997). This refers to variables like age, ethnicity, and gender, but also refers to the amount and the kind of political or professional experience, as well as ideological identity (Katz 2001). Norris (1993) finds that affirmative gender mechanisms work much better in political parties with formal and localized recruitment processes.

Argentina is a presidential republic with a bicameral Congress, and a federal organization in which the twenty-four subnational governments (twenty-three provinces and the capital city) have substantial autonomy. The 257 members of the national Chamber of Deputies are elected in closed multi-member party lists in districts of variable magnitude (the median magnitude is three, the average is five), and uses D'Hondt system for allocation of seats. The chamber is renewed by halves (127 or 130 deputies) every two years. In each election all districts renew part of their delegation by halves, or as close to that as possible. Because of Argentina's federal organization, each province and municipality can devise its own legislative design, choose its electoral system for the election of authorities, and establish rules of operation for political parties as long as they do not clash with the prescriptions of the national constitution and national laws.

In Argentina candidates to elective offices are selected either through internal elections, through the sole decision of a leader, the party elite or in a small number of cases, through competitive vote in party congresses. Political parties, not government officials, are in charge of the provisions (such as electoral rolls and ballot papers) for the carrying out of the internal elections of party authorities as well as for candidates to national, provincial, and municipal offices. The internal organization of political parties is governed by a *Carta Orgânica*, the fundamental law of the party, which establishes the duties and rights of the members, the forms of election of party authorities and of candidates for public offices. It also regulates the party's internal discipline. In this institutional context, the features of the electoral system combined with the internal organization of each party, make up the general institutional framework to be considered when analyzing women's access to parliament.

Party Lists and Gender Distribution

The selection of women candidates and their positions in party-lists are strongly conditioned by the behavior of political parties and depend largely on agreements reached by the party leadership, or by the main coalition within political organizations. In this selection process, most parties have been reluctant to incorporate women candidates above the minimum percentages required by law. This attitude has become a serious obstacle for a more equitable gender distribution in the legislative chambers. In this respect, the electoral performance of women is subordinated to the ways in which parties interpret and apply gender quotas. A mere glance at general election results will show that political parties adopt a minimalist attitude towards this legislation (Jones 1997).

An analysis of the candidate lists reveals that parties tend to choose a certain gender configuration and repeat it throughout the list, or at least for those places that have a chance of winning seats. This research shows that in most cases, the gender configuration of party lists coincides with the minimum percentage required by the gender quota laws. However, the gender configuration of party lists is not necessarily associated with the party's ideology. These findings undermine previous scholarship showing that left-wing political parties have more positive attitudes towards women candidates. Indeed, several studies on European parliaments claim that the adoption of gender quotas reflects demands for equality and representation, traditionally associated with left wing parties and feminist proposals (Norris and Lovedunski 1993, Martínez Ten 1998, Krook 2008). However, in this study we observe that among those parties that obtained seats, left wing parties are no exception to the general tendency of a minimalist application of the law.

Gender Composition of Candidate-lists in Five Subnational Districts

An analysis of gender configuration in Argentina's subnational level party-lists includes a combination of different electoral systems, gender quota laws, and their effects regarding women political representation. This analysis shows the behavior of party elites when the lists are assembled. Subnational districts operate as launching platforms for politicians willing to access to new political careers at the national level (Jones 2004). Due to an absence of comparative research, this study is relevant since it explores the political dynamics of five subnational districts—Autonomous City of Buenos Aires (*Ciudad Autónoma de Buenos Aires,* CABA) and the provinces of Buenos Aires, Córdoba, Mendoza and Santa Fe—and analyzes the gender configurations of party lists for subnational legislators during the legislative elections of 2007.

Table 2.1 shows a significant increase in the proportion of women legislators after gender quota laws were implemented in these five districts. On average, the percentage of women in these chambers rose from six percent in 1991 (before the quota law was passed) to thirty-two percent in 2005.

A slight decrease in women's representation is observed after the 2007 legislative elections. This may be due to reforms in electoral laws such as a decrease in CABA and Mendoza's district magnitude due to partial renewal of their legisla-

Table 2.1: Women in Chambers of Deputies (1991–2005 and 2007)

DISTRICT	LS 1991	WOMEN IN 1991 (PRE-QUOTAS)	WOMEN AS % OF LS	LS 2005	WOMEN IN 2005 (POST-QUOTAS)	WOMEN AS % OF LS	LS 2007	WOMEN IN 2007	WOMEN AS % OF LS
Buenos Aires	92	7	**8**	92	28	**30**	92	26	**28**
Ciudad de Buenos Aires (CABA)	--	--	--	60	22	**37**	60	21	**35**
Córdoba	66	5	**8**	70	24	**34**	70	19	**27**
Mendoza	48	2	**4**	48	12	**25**	48	11	**23**
Santa Fe	50	2	**4**	50	17	**34**	50	16	**32**

Source: Archenti y Tula (2008), Chambers of Deputies and Electoral Courts of the provinces.
Note: 1) In Santa Fe, the data of 2005 correspond to the period 2003–2007, 2) CABA legislature was created in 1996.
Acronyms: LS: Legislature size.

tors; Córdoba's reforms in 2000 that reduced the size of its legislature; the alternation of electoral sections that hampered comparison between successive election years in the Province of Buenos Aires; and the number of political parties that reached the legal threshold for representation in Santa Fe. The greatest decrease is observed in the province of Córdoba even though this is the only district with a parity law. The electoral design of this district has resulted in an inefficient application of its parity clause, which affects only a sixty-three percent of the seats being contested.

Another factor that can become an obstacle for women candidates trying to gain legislative seats is the design of party lists. As already mentioned, party lists are the result of a complex candidate selection process, the features of which are not the same in all parties. In this sense, the configuration of the lists is a valid indicator of the ways quota laws were applied in each of the districts, as a result of party behavior combined with the limits established by their electoral systems.

The five districts selected are the most important ones in terms of the number of voters and they represent different types of electoral systems. Whereas the City of Buenos Aires (CABA) and Santa Fe districts are multi-member with a large district magnitude, Buenos Aires and Mendoza have electoral districts with variable magnitude, and Córdoba has a segmented system. Besides, CABA, Buenos Aires, and Mendoza possess proportional distribution formulas, whereas Santa Fe has a majoritarian system and Córdoba, due to its design, applies simultaneously a

Table 2.2: Chamber of Deputies and Representation (Electoral Regulations, October 2007)

DISTRICT	LEGISLATURE SIZE	RENEWAL	FORM OF REPRESENTATION	DISTRICT MAGNITUDE	ELECTORAL FORMULA	LEGAL THRESHOLD	TYPE OF LIST
Ciudad de Buenos Aires (CABA)	60	Partial	Multimember District	30/1	D'Hondt	No threshold	CyB
Buenos Aires	92	Partial	By Section (8)	6/2, 11/3, 14/1, 15/1, 18/1	*Cociente* (electoral quota)	No threshold	CyB
Córdoba	70	Total	Segmented				CyB
Mendoza	48	Partial	By Section	8/1, 6/1, 5/2	D'Hondt	3%	CyB
Santa Fe	50	Total	Multimember District	50/1	PS	3%	CyB

Source: Archenti y Tula (2008)
Acronyms: PS: Plurality System that rewards winners, CyB: Closed and Blocked.

proportional and a majority formula. In addition, gender quota laws in each of these districts differ in their basic regulations.

It should be noted that for comparative purposes, only the data for the general elections of 2007 were considered because in that election all districts renewed representatives. Not all districts renew their legislatures in the same manner and at the same time. For example, Córdoba and Santa Fe renew their legislatures completely every four years. The Province of Buenos Aires has a peculiar mode of partial renovation. In contrast to the majority of subnational districts, where the number of seats to be renewed is determined on the basis of the total number of seats, in Buenos Aires the renewal alternates electoral sections (one group of sections renews all representatives on an election year, the remaining sections on the next election year) and each section has a fixed number of deputies and senators. This method ensures that partial renewals do not result in a decrease of the district magnitude in each electoral section. For example, in 2007 only deputies from sections I, IV, V, and VII were elected. Finally, these districts provide a sample of the political parties that are relevant in the Argentine political scenario: the traditional nationwide parties—Partido Justicialista (PJ) and Unión Cívica Radical (UCR)—emergent political organizations—Coalición Cívica and Propuesta Republicana (PRO)—and others of subnational character like the Partido Demócrata in Mendoza and the Partido Nuevo in Córdoba. These data is intended to show, how the combination of electoral systems and party strategies in the design of party lists influences the chances of women gaining legislative seats.

Political Parties and Gender Quotas in the Argentine Provinces

The Autonomous City of Buenos Aires (CABA)

In 1996 the first constitution of CABA was approved. Since then, the legislative branch is a single chamber legislature, composed of sixty members, who are partially renewed every two years. The legislators are elected in multi-member districts of large magnitude through direct vote; the distribution system is proportional (Articles 68 and 69).

CABA does not possess a special law regulating affirmative action for political women, though it contemplates them in its constitution. Since 1993 (when the city was not yet autonomous) up to the present, national law 24012 has been in force in the city, together with its regulatory decrees (379/93, 1246/00, and 451/05). This legislation establishes that candidate lists must include a minimum of thirty percent of women or they will not be admitted, and it includes a placement mandate through which women are guaranteed places in positions with chances of being elected. Upon renewal of one, two or more seats, percentage computations must proceed starting from the first position, and women must occupy one out of every three successive places on the list.[1]

In addition, the constitution of CABA establishes in its ninth chapter, several provisions with strong gender content, directed at guaranteeing real equality of opportunity and treatment between men and women in their exercise of civil, political, economic, social and cultural rights. This constitution also provides a gender quota for elective office and determines that they "cannot include more than seventy percent of candidates of the same sex with the probability of being elected. Nor may three candidates of the same sex be included in consecutive order" (Article 36). Table 2.3 shows the gender configuration of the lists of parties that won seats in the legislative elections of the CABA in 2007.

As may be observed, two dominant gender configurations appear repeatedly: "Man, Man, Woman" (MMW) and "Woman, Man, Man" (WMM). The rank-order MMW complies strictly with the legal minimum of "one woman for every two men" or third, sixth, ninth, places and so on. The second configuration (WMM) is more favorable to women, since they are placed in positions with bet-

Table 2.3: Gender Configuration of the Party Lists that Won Seats City of Buenos Aires, Chamber of Deputies, 2007. District Magnitude=30

POSITION	PROPUESTA RE-PUBLICANA	DIÁLOGO POR BUENOS AIRES	FRENTE PARA LA VICTORIA	FRENTE MÁS BUENOS AIRES	COALICIÓN CÍVICA	MOVIMIENTO SOCIALISTA DE LOS TRABAJADORES	PARTIDO BUENOS AIRES PARA TODOS
1	M	M	M	W	W	W	M
2	M	M	M	M	M	M	M
3	W	W	W	M	W	M	W
4	M	M	M	W	M	W	M
5	M	M	W	M	W	M	M
6	W	W	W	M	M	M	W
7	M	M	M	W	M	W	M
8	M	M	M	M	W	M	M
9	W	W	W	M	M	W	W
10	M	M	M	W	W	M	M
11	M	M	M	M	W	M	W
12	W	W	W	M	M	W	M
13	M	M	M	W	M	M	M
14	M	M	M		W	M	W
15	W	W	W	M	M	W	M
Women elected	5	1	1	1	1	1	0
Seats won	15	5	3	3	2	1	1

Source: Author's elaboration of data provided by the Tribunal Superior de Justicia de la Ciudad de Buenos Aires.

Note: The table shows data corresponding to the first fifteen places, which is the highest number of seats obtained by a party in that election (PRO 2007)

ter chances of being elected (first, fourth, seventh, and so on). Notwithstanding its advantages, when the configuration is maintained throughout the list, (or at least in those positions with chances of being elected) it reproduces in quantitative terms the minimum required by the gender quota law: one woman for every three candidates.

The Province of Buenos Aires

The Province of Buenos Aires has a bicameral legislature. The Chamber of Deputies has ninety-two members and the Senate has forty-six. The legislators have a four-year mandate, each chamber being renewed by halves every two years (arts. 70 and 80 of the 1994 PCo). Deputies and senators are elected directly by PR and the district is divided into eight electoral multi-member sections of variable magnitude.[2] The quota law (11733) modified article thirty-two of the province's electoral law (5109). This clause establishes that candidate lists must have a minimum of thirty percent gender quota for women and an equal percentage of male candidates in all categories, who must be placed proportionally in winnable positions. These percentages are applied to the totality of the lists and are rejected if they do not comply with the required quota. Regulatory decree 429/97 establishes

Table 2.4: Gender Configuration of Party Lists that Won Seats. Province of Buenos Aires, Chamber of Deputies, 2007. Electoral Sections and Parties in each Section

	SECTION I DM=15				SECTION IV DM=14			SECTION V DM=11				SECTION VII DM=6	
Position	FPV	CC	UNA	PRO	FPV	CC	UCR	FPV	CC	UNA	PRO	FPV	CC
1	M	W	M	M	M	M	M	M	M	M	M	M	M
2	M	M	W	M	M	W	M	M	M	M	W	M	M
3	W	M	M	W	W	M	W	W	W	W	M	W	W
4	M	M	M	M	M	M	W	M	M	M	M	M	W
5	M	M	W	M	M	W	M	M	W	W	M	M	M
6	W	W	M	W	W	M	W	W	M	M	W	W	M
7	M	W	M	M	M	M	M	M	M	W	M		
8	M	W	W	M	M	W	W	M	W	M	M		
9	W	M	M	M	W	M	M	W	M	M	W		
10	M	W	M	W	M	M	M	M	W	W	W		
Women Elected	2	1	1	0	3	1	0	1	1	0	0	1	0
Seats Won	8	3	2	2	9	3	2	5	3	2	1	4	2

Source: Authors' elaboration of data provided by the Junta Electoral of the province of Buenos Aires
Note: The table shows data corresponding to the first ten positions, except in the case of section VII where 6 seats are contested.

a placement mandate, by which the first position of the candidate lists may be filled by either a man or a woman, but the following positions must be filled by no more than two consecutive candidates of the same gender. In other words, the minimum legal requirement is "one woman for every two men."

Table 2.4 shows the gender configuration of political lists presented by political parties during the 2007 legislative elections for all four electoral sections that renewed deputy seats. This data is important because, since there are several sections (in contrast with other provinces), the configuration of the candidate lists must be adapted to the conditions of each electoral section and to political negotiations each party carries out in order to win votes. Therefore, even within one political party the gender configuration of its lists may vary from section to section.

Frente para la Victoria won in all four sections and obtained twenty-six seats, of which only seven were women. In their lists the configuration is the same for the four sections: Man, Man, Woman (MMW), the third, sixth, and ninth place being reserved for women. Thus, women were placed within the minimum positions legally required.

In the remaining political parties and in compliance with the law, female candidates occupied one of the first three positions of the party lists. Still, since in most cases women were relegated to the third position, in parties that won one or two seats, women had no chances of being elected. Indeed, of the thirteen lists winning seats in this election, nine of them carried a woman in the third position (sixty-nine percent), three placed them in the second position (twenty-three percent), and only one (CC-section I) had a woman in the first place as "head of the list" (eight percent). The more women-friendly behavior of *Coalición Cívica* in these elections is easily explained since this party has a strong female leadership.

The Province of Mendoza

In the province of Mendoza the legislative is also bicameral (Deputies and Senate), whose members are elected directly in four electoral sections. None of these sections can elect less than eight deputies and six senators. Law 2551, in force in Mendoza since 1959, establishes that in each electoral section a PR system is applied for both categories, using the D'Hondt system for the allocation of seats and a minimum threshold of three percent. Legislators are elected for four years and can be reelected. Both chambers are renewed by halves every two years.

Law 6831/ 2000 modified the province's quota system, which establishes that candidate lists must contain a minimum of thirty percent of women and that "this shall come into effect by dividing each list in thirds and ensuring a minimum of one woman in each third of the lists." The law has been interpreted as re-

Table 2.5: Gender Configuration Party Lists Winning Seats in the Chamber of Deputies of the Province of Mendoza, 2007. Electoral Sections and Parties in Each Section

	SECTION I DM= 8					SECTION II DM= 6		SECTION III DM= 5			SECTION IV DM= 5		
Position	PJ	PV	Cc	PD	UCR	PJ	Cc	Cc	PJ	PD	PJ	PV	Cc
1	M	M	M	M	M	M	W	M	M	M	M	M	M
2	M	M	M	M	M	M	M	M	W	M	M	M	M
3	W	W	W	W	W	W	M	W	M	W	W	W	W
4	M	M	M	M	M	M	M	M	M	M	M	W	M
5	W	M	M	M	M	M	W	M	M	W	W	M	M
6	W	M	W	W	W	W	M						
7	W	W	M	M	W								
8	M	W	M	M	M								
Women elected	1	0	0	0	0	1	1	0	1	0	0	0	0
Seats won	3	2	1	1	1	4	2	2	2	1	2	2	1

Source: Authors' elaboration of data provided by the Junta Electoral of the province of Mendoza.
Note: The table shows data corresponding to the district magnitude of each electoral section.

quiring a minimum of "one woman for every two men." The law also establishes that the penalty for non-compliance is the rejection of the lists.

Table 2.5 shows that women candidates tend to be placed by most parties in the third and sixth places, regardless of the political or ideological tendency of the party. On the other hand, with the exception of *Concertación Ciudadana* (Cc) in the second electoral section, no list was headed by a woman, and only the *Partido Justicialista* (PJ) in the third section carried a woman in the second position of the list. Also, with the exception of the *Partido Justicialista* in the first section, no party exceeded the minimum placement mandate for women established by law.

The result of this ordering can be observed on the table above. Only the PJ in three sections, and the Cc in one, incorporated a woman in Mendoza's legislature during the 2007 legislative elections. A high level of party fragmentation due to the division of sections within districts, together with the placement on the third place of the lists (the number of seats won being in most cases less than three) constitutes a dramatic scenario for women politicians in this province.

The Province of Santa Fe

In Santa Fe, the legislative is also bicameral. The Chamber of Deputies is composed of fifty members with four year mandates and eligible for reelection. Twenty-eight deputies are assigned to the party with the largest number of votes, and twenty-two to the rest of the parties, in proportion to the votes obtained (article 32 of the constitution and article 16 of province law 12367/2004). The D'Hondt method is employed for the allocation of seats with an additional threshold of three percent of the electoral rolls of the district (Province Law 9280/1983). Political parties, fronts, or alliances must include a minimum of one candidate for each department.[3] Both chambers are renewed every four years.

In turn, the provincial gender quota legislation requires that every candidate list presented at both provincial and local levels, and/or for the election of Constitutional Conventions must be composed of a minimum of one third of women candidates. In addition, women must be placed alternately and/or successively for all the electable positions whether principal or substitute, whichever the electoral system might be (Law 10802/92). Party lists not complying with these requirements are rejected by the provincial Electoral Court. Regulatory decree 358/93 stipulated the minimum number of women the parties must include in their lists. The party obtaining twenty-eight seats must include a minimum of nine women, and if any party wins twenty-two seats the party must have a minimum of seven women. In turn, regulatory decree 1745/93 required that when a political party presents a list for the first time, or must renew a single seat (or no seat) the number of seats shall be considered equal to one and, in this case, it may be filled by either a man or a woman. But in the following positions a minimum of one woman for every two men must be included in the list to ensure a one-third of women candidates. If the party renews two seats, at least one of the two candidates must be a woman.

The inclusion of women in party lists during Santa Fe 2007 legislative elections complies merely with the minimum quota legally required. In this case, the placement mandate loses relevance, since the electoral system assigns a fixed number of seats to the first and second parties provided no other political party or parties exceed the threshold. The placement mandate is only important when other smaller parties achieve the threshold and compete for the twenty-two seats, since in this case, the distribution of seats follows the proportional representation system, taking as a base the votes obtained by each party. In addition, when second and third forces compete for the twenty-two remaining seats, the likelihood of women winning seats will depend of their placement on the lists; the closer to the top, the greater the chances women candidates will win a seat.

In the last provincial legislative elections, only two political forces won seats in the Chamber of Deputies. The *Frente Progresista Cívico y Social* (FPCyS) with 44.57 percent of the vote, *Frente para la Victoria* (FPV) with 37.21 percent, and far behind, the *Unión Cívica Radical*, with 2.71 percent, but the latter could not satisfy the minimum legal threshold to win a seat. As a result twenty-eight seats went to the FPCyS and twenty-two to the FPV. As for women, the parties winning seats complied only with the minimum percentages required by law. Thus, just nine women from the FPCyS and seven from the FPV won seats in Santa Fé's legislature during the 2007 election.

The Province of Córdoba

In Córdoba, the constitutional reform of 2001 abrogated the Senate. The legislative branch is now unicameral with seventy members. Deputies are elected through a segmented representation system. Twenty-six members are elected in uninominal districts (one for each department in the province). This representation is based on territorial divisions and representatives are elected by a plurality formula. The remaining forty-four legislators are elected through a PR system and seats are allocated implementing the D'Hondt system, in a large multi-member district with closed and blocked lists.

The gender quota in this province is different from other provincial districts in the country. Since the adoption of the "Law of Equivalent Gender Participation" (Law 8901/00), all candidate lists for public office must obey the principle of gender parity. This means that all candidate lists elected in any of the constitutionally or legally created departmental bodies (executive, deliberative, control, selection, professional or disciplinary bodies), must guarantee that candidates of both genders be placed in equitable positions. Both national and provincial judicial authorities, supervising the election process must dismiss lists that do not satisfy this requirement. In case of non-compliance (if and when the number of candidates of each gender makes it possible), the judiciary may rearrange the lists so that they satisfy the legal requirements. Article 5 of the provincial quota law specifies the following order that must be satisfied; first, when an even number of seats must be contested, the lists of candidates, including substitutes, must alternate genders, one of each gender for every two consecutive candidates; second, when the number of seats is odd, the lists of principal candidates must satisfy the above mentioned order, and the last position may be occupied by either a male or female candidate; third, the order of the substitutes must be the inverse of the order of principal candidates, so that if there is a greater number of candidates of one gender, there must be greater number of substitute candidates of the other gender; finally, when only one seat must be filled, the genders of principal and substitute candidates must be different.

In case of vacancy the law establishes a mechanism of replacement. The vacant seat shall be replaced immediately, first by a candidate of the same gender according to the order of the official list. When replacements of the same gender

Table 2.6: Gender Configuration of Party Lists that Won Seats (Chamber of Deputies of the Province of Córdoba, 2007) Uninominal Member Districts (1/26)

DEPARTMENT	PJ	UCR	ALIANZA FRENTE CÍVICO
Capital	M	M	M*
Calamuchita	M*	M	M
Colón	M	M	M*
Cruz del Eje	M*	M	M
General Roca	M*	M	M
San Martín	M*	W	M
Ischilín	M*	M	M
Juárez Celman	M*	M	M
Marcos Juárez	M*	W	M
Minas	M*	M	M
Pocho	M*	M	M
Punilla	M	M	M*
Río Cuarto	M*	M	W
Río Primero	M	M*	No candidate was presented
Río Seco	M*	M	M
Río Segundo	M*	W	M
Roque Sáenz Peña	M*	W	M
San Alberto	M*	M	M
San Javier	M	M*	W
San Justo	M*	M	M
Santa María	M*	M	M
Sobremonte	M*	M	W
Totoral	M	M*	M
Tulumba	M*	W	M
Unión	M*	M	M
Tercero Arriba	M*	M	M
Seats won	20	3	3
Women who won seats	0	0	0

Table 2.6 cont.

DEPARTMENT	PJ	UCR	ALIANZA FRENTE CÍVICO
Men who won seats	20	3	3
Women candidates	0	5	3
Men candidates	26	21	22

Source: Authors' elaboration of data provided by Electoral Court of the Province of Córdoba
* Won seats.

are exhausted, the succession may continue with substitutes of the opposite gender according to the order of the list. The law also provides a limit on the parity clause in the case of parties whose registered members of one gender do not exceed thirty percent of the total number of voters in the electoral roll. In this case, the lists must adapt the nomination of candidates keeping the proportions of the electoral roll. As to the gender configuration adopted for multimember party lists, with forty-four members, the law clearly establishes the positions occupied by each gender, indicating the alternation of one and one for every two places. It is noteworthy that out of fourteen parties winning seats through PR, twelve of them (eighty-six percent) submitted lists headed by men.

The results varied according to the electoral system implemented. In the twenty-six uninominal districts women did not win any seats in 2007. Men thus, obtained thirty-seven percent of the total number of seats in the province's legislature. The parties did not show the political will to include women in these first-past the post elections. The *Partido Justicialista* did not present women in any of the departments, the *Unión Cívica Radical* only in five and the *Alianza Frente Cívico* in three. The PR multi-member election was more beneficial for women. Twenty-five men and nineteen women were elected. Yet, despite the parity law, male candidates obtained fifty-seven percent of the seats compared to forty-three percent of women. Most parties placed male candidates in the top position on the party lists and many parties won only a single seat. Thus, women did not win an equal number of seats because parties opted once again, for a minimalist implementation of the law.

Córdoba is an interesting case, because whereas the parity clause should benefit women in theory; its electoral system and the ways that parties and alliances select their candidates have a negative effect on women actually winning seats. Large, multi-member districts with closed and blocked lists and a parity quota system should guarantee a sustainable representation of women, however, during the elections of 2007 only twenty-seven percent of women won seats in the province's legislature.

Conclusion

The gender quota laws adopted in Argentina during the 1990s at both national and subnational levels have proven to be efficient mechanisms in increasing the percentage of women legislators. The combination of gender quotas with different institutional arrangements, such as electoral systems with large multimember lists, proportional electoral formulas, closed and blocked lists, and placement mandates have been beneficial for the election of women.

However, Argentina presents in its institutional and electoral legal structure two features that condition the efficacy of the quota laws; the federal organization of the country and the control of political parties in the candidate selection process. Federalism allows each province and each municipality to design its own political and electoral system generating diverse institutional scenarios. A subnational level comparative analysis allows for a better understanding of which combination of mechanisms tend to be more or less successful. The country's political parties in control of the selection of candidates make them leading and unavoidable actors in these analyses.

Although there are several studies on the impact of quota laws in Latin America and a few on Argentina's subnational districts, these refer mainly to the descriptive and substantive impacts of the laws in their legislatures. Yet, there are no studies that analyze the consequences of enforcing these laws within political parties during the candidate selection process, or regarding strategic and adaptive responses developed by the parties since the adoption of gender quotas. The main consequences of the quota laws for political parties are the changes produced in the dynamics of internal competition. On the one hand, they generate new rivalries between female members, by opening slots for their candidacies. On the other hand, they create rivalries between men and women who are eager to be placed in the top positions of the candidate lists. In the first case, the struggle between women weakens the possibility that female candidates will organize collectively and strengthens their dependency on party gatekeepers. In the second case, the confrontation between genders creates competition between sectors or factions within the party and affects the traditional practices in the candidate selection procedures. This is an unevenly matched struggle since men have historically controlled all the reins of party power, and women have tried unsuccessfully to participate in this exercise of power.

Broadly speaking, political parties have not perceived the quota laws as a road to renovation, a way of increasing internal democracy, guided by the values of equality and fairness. Nor have they interpreted them as a new scenario for the encouragement of preferences. Their basic answer was resistance to these measures. The reasons for this blunt opposition include a political culture based on patriarchy, pragmatic reasons based on electoral speculation, and mainly political reasons related to the struggle for spheres of power and decision-making linked to a differential access for the control of resources and positions. In this study, we have taken the gender configuration of party lists as an indicator of how quota laws are implemented. The manner in which parties distribute their candidacies has a significant effect on whether women will win seats. An analysis of the composition of party lists shows whether parties merely comply with the minimum legal requirements, or they are committed to establish a more balanced gender distribution for the top list positions.

The cases in this chapter show that after many years since the adoption of the national gender quota law, political parties still adopt a minimalist interpretation of the quota provisions and favor a bureaucratic observance of the law. In this research, diverse gender configurations for the design of party lists have been found. In general, party lists tend to place women candidates in the lowest legal position. In cases of low district magnitudes (for example when the district is divided into electoral sections) or of high party fragmentation, a third place is not enough to win a seat. Thus, the lists tend to reproduce the minimum legal gender formula both in quantitative terms and in terms of ordering.

Perhaps the most interesting case is that of Córdoba, where the quota law establishes a parity structure for the lists. Yet, in the 2007 elections, eighty-eight percent of the single-member party lists of two of the three political parties that won seats were led by men. No female candidate had access to the legislature through this system. In the case of multimember districts, only twelve of fourteen lists were led by women. Due to high party fragmentation combined with proportional distribution of seats, ten parties obtained a single parliamentary seat, thus, the parity law operated in practice only for the four remaining parties.

In sum, candidate selection led in most cases by party elites tend to favor a gender order in their lists, which expresses a policy of restricted incorporation of women candidates in both quantitative and positional terms. In the first case, quantitative restrictions are formulated through the minimalist interpretation of the quota law. In the second case, a positional restriction is seen merely as a bureaucratic compliance with the quota laws and placement mandates. The tensions generated by the application of the quota laws within political parties, diversifying the competition for candidacies have provoked changes in political strategies, loyalties, complicities and pressures, since new female actors burst into the scene of this competition The development of these rivalries within each of the parties in the various districts, and their implications should be the subject for further research.

Chapter Three

Gender Quotas and Equity Promotion in Mexico

Jennifer M. Piscopo

Mexico stands out as an important gender quota innovator in Latin America. Argentina typically receives the spotlight, as the first country in Latin America—and the world—to adopt a legislative gender quota in 1991. In the Argentine case, the statutory fiat rapidly and effectively changed candidate selection procedures for all political parties. Yet, a quota *also* appeared in Mexico in 1991. This party-level quota was voluntarily adopted by the left-wing *Partido de la Revolución Democrática* (PRD) and applied to their internal candidate nomination practices. Over the next two decades, quotas in Mexico evolved from unreliable party-level rules to effective national-level mandates. This chapter argues that the lengthy battle to implement strong quota laws in Mexico—when compared to the overnight change in other Latin American countries—has actually helped the broader cause of women's equality.

Observers and theorists have often treated the connection between gender quotas, on the one hand, and policies benefiting women's well-being, on the other hand, as sequential. In other words, first countries pass quotas, and then female legislators—now elected in greater numbers—advocate for policies that protect women's rights. Mexico, however, underwent a protracted process to adopt and reform its legislative quota. (In this chapter, "legislative quota" denotes a quota rule implemented via parliamentary statute.) This process began and continued because female elites—meaning female party activists and female legislators—lobbied tirelessly to increase women's political participation in the parties and the Congress.

These indefatigable quota proponents ensured that questions of women's representation and women's rights remained in the political spotlight. As a result, quotas became folded into a larger package of equality-promoting and discrimination-ending reforms, the passage of which has characterized Mexican politics since the mid-1990s. The Mexican case demonstrates that quotas can be adopted, implemented, and reformed under conditions of extreme activist pressure, and that the measures cannot be divorced from proponents' other efforts to set policies that benefit women.

Political Institutions in Mexico

In Mexico, political parties structure all aspects of political life. Each of the three principal parties—the PRI (*Partido Revolucionario Institucional*), the PAN (*Partido Acción Nacional*), and the PRD—have organizational structures that parallel the federal system of government.[1] The rank-and-file are referred to as *militantes,* meaning party militants or activists. The *militantes'* work is controlled by the CEN, the *Comité Ejecutivo Nacional* (National Executive Committee), which oversees the 32 state-level committees, the *Comités Directivos Estatales* (CDEs, or State Directing Committees) and numerous municipal committees. The committees are organized into offices and secretariats, which have policy remits akin to cabinet portfolios in the executive branch (i.e., youth, international relations). Through these branches, the committees manage myriad tasks within the party, from running leadership training to directing get-out-the-vote drives. Thus, most members holding positions in the CEN, the CDEs, and the municipal committees are full-time, remunerated leaders. At all levels, the committees constitute the center of party life, with the CEN managing its subsidiaries in a tightly-controlled, centralized fashion.[2] When the party controls the federal or state executive branch, the Mexican president and the governors are the national and state party presidents, respectively; when the party is out of power, the national and state party presidents are the future candidates for these offices. Terms such as "the party leadership" or the "the party directorate" refer to the CEN, the CDEs, the party president and vice-president, and the governors.

The parties are programmatically and ideologically coherent. They differ principally in their approach to economic governance and religion, with the PAN on the neoliberal, conservative, Catholic "right" side of the spectrum and the PRD on the social justice, welfare-oriented, and secular "left" side of the spectrum. The PRI, historically a populist-style party representing workers, peasants, and myriad citizen groups, positions itself in the center or center-left.[3] In the Congress, voting follows party lines. Legislators enjoy substantial autonomy when introducing initiatives,[4] as parties focus on disciplining committee work and floor votes, leaving bill authorship largely untouched.[5] The Mexican Constitution prohibits reelection. This proscription, combined with the prevalence of party posts within the CEN and the CDEs, gives the party directorate extensive control over legislators' careers and thus their behavior.[6]

The Mexican Congress employs a mixed electoral system. The five hundred members of the lower house, known as the Chamber of Deputies, are elected from majoritarian, single-member districts (three hundred *diputados*) and closed-list proportional representation (PR) districts (two hundred *diputados*). The PR districts are known as *circunscripciones*, and five *circunscripciones* elect forty deputies each. The upper house, the Senate, has 128 members. Ninety-six of these Senators are elected at the state level through a "majoritarian list system": the party whose lists garners the most votes in that state wins two senate seats, and the party whose lists receives the second-most votes wins one seat. The remaining thirty-two senators are elected from a single, nation-wide PR list. All candidates are dual pairs of *proprietarios* (primaries) and *suplentes* (substitutes), the latter of whom have no duties following the election unless the *priorietario* resigns. The Mexican Constitution prohibits citizen candidates, which means that aspirants must run beneath the party label. While the degree of centralization in the parties' candidate selection procedures varies, the party leadership essentially controls nominations and loyalty is the driving criterion.[7] The reelection prohibition, the absence of citizen candidacies, and the institutional depth of the CEN and CDEs means that Mexico's political parties control their members' *entire* political careers.

Origins of Demands for Quotas

The formidable nature of Mexican party politics explains why female activists first demanded quotas not in the Congress but within the political parties. By the early 1990s, female elites in Mexico had recognized that attaining positions of power within the Congress would allow them to make consequential changes to the laws and policies governing women's lives. Yet, they also acknowledged the widespread gender discrimination that kept them out of the parties' candidate selection pools.

First, during the 1988–1991 legislative periods, female legislators successfully introduced and passed a revised penal code for the treatment of sex crimes. During this process, it became apparent that women's presence in the congress "was essential for the advocating for gender quality and women's issues."[8] Second, this legislative achievement—which marked a notable first in terms of a statutory change that explicitly dealt with gender interests—was itself possible because of Mexico's changing political system. For six decades, the PRI controlled the legislative and executive branches: the president, also head of the party, introduced all key statutory initiatives, and the party leaders ensured these initiatives passed through a pliant bicameral congress.[9] Growing electoral competition in the 1980s, however, was gradually shifting the balance of power from the executive to the legislature. The fractionalization of the Congress created space for legislators to introduce proposals that could succeed, provided that these proposed statutory changes—like the sex crimes bill—underwent a process of coalition-building among legislators and between ministers and lawmakers. If female elites were to harness this balance-of-power shift to further benefit female constituents, then they needed to guarantee their future election.

Yet, in Latin America and elsewhere, increasing democratization and electoral competition have meant the marginalization of women, whose candidatures become perceived as too risky and unconventional.[10] In Mexico, the PRI did not lose its legislative majority until the 1997 mid-term elections. Nonetheless, the opposition parties were making substantial inroads by the early 1980s; their electoral successes demonstrated that non-*Priístas* could attain political power, making careers in the PAN and the PRD more viable and attractive to politicians.[11] The tenuous but growing power of the opposition meant business as usual among the political elite, a traditional operating mode that privileges male candidacies. Competition for votes did *not* incentivize parties to appeal to female voters by presenting sex-balanced tickets. Rather, as spots became more valuable, few female politicians occupied the highly-coveted electoral berths.[12] The barriers for Mexican women were clearly at the candidate selection phase.[13]

Indeed, as shown in Table 3.1, the representation of women from opposition parties and from the PRI *fell* precipitously in the 1991 elections, particularly in the

Table 3.1: Percentage of Women in the Mexican Congress

ELECTION YEAR	CHAMBER OF DEPUTIES	ELECTION YEAR	SENATE
1982	10.5	1982	15.6
1985	10.5		
1988	11.8	1988	10.9
1991	8.8	1991	4.7
1994	14.1	1994	10.9
1997	17.4	1997	7.8
2000	16.0	2000	31.25
2003	24.0		
2006	23.4	2006	19.5
2009	28.2		

Source: Center for the Study of the Advancement of Women and Gender Equity, Mexico Congress.

Senate. In the 1980s, women's representation reached a high of almost sixteen percent in the Senate and nearly twelve percent in the Chamber of Deputies, falling to five and nine percent in 1991, respectively. This decline occurred at precisely the moment when competition among the PRI, the PAN, and the newly-formed PRD increased. This setback galvanized female party members in their demand for affirmative action measures.

Quotas in Mexico's Political Parties

As Bruhn explains, "quotas resulted from activism by party women who believed party leaders would not include women without a requirement."[14] Indeed, female party members had good evidence for their belief, as nominating conventions held by all parties in the late 1980s and early 1990s failed to extend candidacies to female members. These same "party women" were simultaneously participating in national, non-partisan meetings that established forums of interchange among female politicians, activists, feminists, and academics. For instance, the attendees at the 1991 National Convention of Women for Democracy demanded quotas to end women's underrepresentation in the legislature, and several affirmed their intention to seek nominations from their parties.[15]

This demand had been most voluble within the PRD and the PRI. The PRD, founded in 1989 by former communists and leftist PRI defectors, was institutionalizing its structure at the precise moment that quotas were demanded. Bruhn describes the PRD as "semi-anarchic, relatively decentralized and porous," with a commitment to internal as well as external democracy.[16] These features allowed female delegates to the 1991 convention to extract a prior promise from the PRD leadership: the electoral lists formulated at the convention would include twenty-five percent women. When the leadership reneged on the agreement—due largely to cutthroat competition for nominations—the women sought the formal adoption of a quota.[17] At the 1993 party convention, female delegates demanded a public vote, which ended in the successful reformation of the party's internal statutes. The PRD adopted a twenty percent candidate quota for the PR lists, which was raised to thirty percent in 1996 and extended to party leadership positions. As Claudia Corichi of the PRD noted, "It was largely women who drove the implementation of quotas."[18] Party women's elation notwithstanding, none of these measures were extensively publicized outside the party.

The PRI followed the PRD, adopting its thirty percent quota in 1996. Yet, women's struggles for gender equality had a longer history in this older, centralized, and institutionalized party. PRI presidents Miguel de la Madrid (elected 1982) and Carlos Salinas (elected 1988) had implemented a limited, informal array of affirmative action measures within the party. The greater advocate was de la Madrid, who believed that "to change México, you needed women."[19] De la Madrid collaborated with a highly-regarded female campaign aide to develop short lists that identified competent and qualified female *militantes.* These short lists were then distributed to upper-tier PRI leaders, with de la Madrid's firm instructions that leaders were to select women to serve in the party's secretariats as well as *suplente* candidates for federal and local offices. His successor, Salinas, mandated that meetings on different policy themes include at least twenty-five percent women.[20] These informal policies were never incorporated into the party's charter, but did constitute a limited form of "affirmative action" sought and implemented by female aides and supported by the party president.[21] In 1994, *Priísta* women managed to convince the party's presidential candidate, Ernesto Zedillo, to double the number of women candidates from 1988 elections. This promise, as with his predecessors' actions to promote women's leadership, was never publicized outside the party.

The PRI president clearly manages a top-down, hierarchical, and authoritarian organization. Unlike in the PRD, female quota proponents needed to convince only the president and his governors,[22] who control the selection of candidates and impose their choices via undemocratic, state and national conventions.[23] Female party advocates, organized in their party's *rama femenina* [women's wing], formed a Council for the Integration of Women and a Congress of Women for Change. They continued to press for formal measures to promote women's participation throughout the early 1990s, even as the PRI faced heightened competition, candidacies became important commodities, and party leaders became reluctant to follow affirmative action measures. At the same time, however, the first woman was appointed head of the CEN. She supported quotas, explicitly intervening in leadership decisions to appoint qualified women over qualified men. She remembers that when the men protested about placing women in important positions, she responded, "And how many men are there in important positions?"[24] Her actions contributed to the PRI directorate's 1996 decision to apply a thirty percent internal quota for federal candidates.

The right-leaning PAN resisted quotas until 1999. Candidate selection in the PAN is driven more by the party's militant base rather than by convention delegates (as in the PRD) or by party leaders (as in the PRI). In the PAN, any militant can attend a party convention and vote for candidates.[25] Changes to these and other selection rules—such as a quota—must be approved by the party assembly, which consists of the militant base as well as the party directorate.

Perhaps paradoxically, the female rank-and-file in the PAN did not perceive the same gender discrimination during the 1990s as did their counterparts in the PRI and the PRD. This difference can only be partly attributed to the PAN's conservative approach to gender roles and principal emphasis on merit-based selection. The party *also* faced a longstanding problem of recruiting any willing candidates, male or female. The PAN was the PRI's longtime opposition party, founded in 1939; for decades, the PAN struggled to recruit qualified members, precisely because PRI dominance meant that *Panistas* would never have dramatically successful and distinguished careers.[26] Consequently, those women who entered the PAN had little trouble rising to leadership positions. A longtime *Panista* woman explained, "We were very few [women] and it was easy to rise through the ranks; we thought we already had space within the party, we understood politics, and we obtained the positions we wanted and participated when we wanted." Yet, as the PAN began to actually win—and as *Panista* careers became correspondingly more valuable—female militants realized that women were becoming "more isolated" as the party became "more competitive."[27] In 1999, they persuaded the party to stipulate that each candidate pairing of primary-substitute contain one man and one woman.[28]

When parties adopt quotas in succession, the quota literature has typically favored the competition-diffusion model.[29] In this version, quotas signal a commitment to gender equality more consistent with the founding principles of left parties; leftist parties thus adopt quotas first, followed by competitor parties who cannot risk losing the electoral advantage of seeming more "women friendly." Yet, these models presume that quotas receive publicity. In the Mexican case, the PRD's leftist orientation helped justify female members' demands for quotas. What the PRD *and* the PRI failed to do was publicize the quota—neither among its wider membership nor to the mass public.[30] This silence shows that the parties perceived *no* electoral advantage to adopting a quota. The measures may have been important for appeasing female militants and thus maintaining internal unity, but were not essential for attracting votes.

Thus, as Caul finds for Europe, the intra- and inter-party activism of female politicians drove parties to implement internal quotas.[31] Women from all the Mexican parties met regularly during the 1990s, in order to "exchange strategies and opinions about a variety of topics, including how to advance women candidates."[32] For instance, in 1992 female politicians formed the campaign *Ganando Espacios* (Gaining Spaces) to undergird their demands for quotas. The following year, women from the PRI and the PRD formed a working group entitled "From A to Z" that focused on women's equality. In 1996 and 1997, female legislators and ex-legislators from all three parties convened conferences whose agendas emphasized women's participation in social, economic, and political life.[33] A former PRI president and longtime legislator explained that, in terms of women's advancement, "The ideologies and the programs of the parties are based on women's actions in each organization."[34] As such, it was party women's strategies and not the electoral incentive that diffused across the parties.

Further, the quota entrepreneurs in each party became constituencies committed to quotas' normative importance and actual success. At the time of the 1994 congressional elections, only the PRD applied a gender quota; the election of 11.4 percent women from the PRD lists, and 14.1 percent women overall, constituted a disappointment for party women. In 1997, when both the PRD and the PRI applied quotas, women constituted twenty-four percent of the PRD delegates elected, 15.1 percent of the PRI delegates, and 12.4 percent of the PAN delegates, yielding an overall total of 17.4 percent.[35] These low proportions occurred for several reasons. First, neither the PRI quota nor the PRD quota stipulated the *placement* of female candidates on the PR lists, allowing parties to cluster female candidates in the bottom, unelectable positions. Moreover, these quotas applied only to PR candidacies. Second, the PAN leadership claimed that affirmative action was antithetical to its meritocratic nomination practices.[36] In this context, female elites also sought statutory measures that would bind parties to nominate women. Quota laws would protect women's future nominations and help institutionalize a women's policy agenda.

Looking for Legislative Quotas

In the Congress, the quota lobby benefited from the constitutional prohibition on immediate reelection as well as the parties' ability to control politicians' appointments. Legislators finishing their congressional term return to their parties; they typically attain a leadership position in the CEN or the CDEs, and await re-nomination to either the lower or upper house. This rotation in office means that party women accumulate experience lobbying both *within* their parties and *from* the legislature. The female politicians simply press for their demands in whatever institution they currently occupy. By the mid-1990s, many women from all three major parties had gained strategically important positions in both forums, and these women—whom Rodríguez refers to as *las planas mayores* (the heavy hitters)[37]—were seeking legislative quotas that would "lock-in" their gains party level quotas.

Quotas were also gaining attention outside the parties. In 1995, the United Nations' Fourth World Conference on Women was held in Beijing. Female delegates from Mexico introduced the topic of quotas at the convention, and the Beijing Conference's *Platform for Action* endorsed the mechanisms as necessary for boosting women's political participation. The following year, quotas were endorsed at Mexico's 1996 conference *Asamblea de las Mujeres para la Transición Democrática* [Assembly of Women for the Democratic Transition], which was attended not only by party women, but by women from feminist non-governmental organizations. The "top item on the agenda" at this meeting was developing strategies for increasing the number of women in office.[38] Female activists in civil society were becoming important allies in the fight for women's equality, in which gender quotas became one of the many measures recommended by delegates attending international and domestic conferences.

The growing electoral competition also became important. While the parties failed to perceive the vote-getting appeal of quotas, they were seeking general reforms to Mexico's federal electoral code, the *Código Federal de Instituciones y Procedimientos Electorales* (COFIPE). The parties all had stakes in bargaining over such reforms, as the PRI needed to make concessions that would help them retain power, and the PAN and the PRD wanted changes that would make competition more fair and elections more transparent.[39] These reforms included procedural changes that affected campaign finance, proportionality rules (the translation of votes into seats), and voting oversight and certification. Congressional bargaining over electoral rules signaled moments of institutional flexibility, in which female legislators could introduce quotas to the discussion.[40]

Thus, as part of the 1993 electoral reforms, the Mexican Congress modified the COFIPE to state, "The political parties should promote, according to their own internal rules, the greater participation of women in the political life of the country, particularly through encouraging them to run for popularly-elected positions."[41] While this reform simply declared support for the principle of women's participation, it nonetheless marked the first appearance of a federal-level norm on this topic.[42] In 1996, the PRI-dominated Congress approved a sweeping package of electoral reforms. In addition to granting opposition parties access to state-funded media and campaign coffers, the new electoral rules *recommended* a thirty percent quota for PR and SMD candidacies in the upper and lower houses. This recommendation, though stronger than the 1993 statement, was unenforceable by definition. Further, the reform failed to suggest placement procedures for the PR lists, and failed to distinguish between *proprietario* and *suplente* candidates.[43] Yet neither of these reforms passed easily, and female deputies and senators had to lean strongly on their male colleagues for these concessions. A then-senator from the PRI recalled that, in 1996, the "angry debate raged for four hours, and only for a recommendation!"[44]

This process illustrates three important features about quotas in Latin America. First, moments of institutional flux help quota proponents introduce the question of women's underrepresentation. Second, quotas' initial forms are weak and non-binding.[45] On the one hand, both the normative declaration and the quota recommendation were costless for the Mexican parties to adopt. Unlike changes to territorial proportionality and campaign finance, symbolic commitments to promoting women's legislative representation would not materially or substantively affect parties' practices. On the other hand, the party leadership initially resisted even non-binding measures, which reveals the quotas' third feature: their normative importance. Quotas signal a reordering of the public sphere to include women, their perspectives, and their concerns.[46]

Practically, however, norms do not translate into seats. The number of women elected by *all* the political parties fell in the 2000 elections (see Table 3.1). This loss occurred despite internal pressure from party women, many of whom were now prominent congressional leaders or party directors, and notwithstanding the brightening international and domestic spotlights on gender equality. Party leaders consistently clustered women at the bottom of the PR lists, nominated them as *suplentes*, or nominated them as *proprietarios* in unwinnable plurality districts. This shirking occurred despite the decision of the Federal Electoral Institute, IFE (*Instituto Federal Electoral*) to "demand" the parties' compliance with the thirty percent recommendation for the 2000 elections. None of the parties perceived an electoral advantage to publicly promoting women. Rather, the tight competition—the very real, and ultimately realized, possibility of a PRI loss—meant that parties simply "could not risk" female candidates in 2000.[47]

Legislative Quotas and Gender Equality Policy: The First Generation

In this context, female politicians realized that a recommendation however interpreted and supported by the IFE, would be insufficient to guarantee women's election. Female legislators entering the 2000–2003 Congress made strengthening the electoral quota one of their principal goals—and they achieved it. Importantly, these parliamentarians could work within a gender equality apparatus erected by their predecessors in the previous congressional term.

Las planas mayores seated in the 1997–2000 term had laid important groundwork for addressing women's interests in the Congress. First, in 1997, the feminist non-governmental organization *Diversa* convened a conference entitled *"Avancemos un Trecho: por un compromiso de los partidos políticos a favor de las mujeres"* (We Advance a Little Way: Towards the political parties' promises to benefit women). At the conference, female legislators and representatives from eight political parties, including the PAN, committed themselves to collaboratively ensuring the placement of women's shared concerns on the congressional agenda.[48] Second, fifteen PRI legislators, six PRD legislators, and seven PAN legislators created a *Comisión Bicameral para la Equidad y Género* (Bicameral Commission on Equity and Gender). This commission promptly introduced a bill that would elevate the quota recommendation to legal requirement. The commission also helped secure the passage of the Law against Family Violence, which compelled criminal courts to penalize perpetrators.[49] Third, women from all the parties and women form civil society organizations convened the first *Parlamento de Mujeres* (Women's Parliament) in 1998. The *Parlamento de Mujeres* was officially endorsed by the Congress, and permitted female legislators and their citizen guests to host a "mini-parliament" in the plenary. The women met alone—that is, with no male colleagues present—to hear speeches about, participate in roundtables on, and establish a shared vision for women's policy agenda. The *Parlamento* met again in 1999 and 2000.

The female deputies and senators in the 2000–2003 congressional terms built on the momentum to address women's concerns. In June 2000, the women—while they were still candidates—signed a *Pacto Entre Mujeres* (Pact Among Women), which was subtitled "Towards a Government and Legislative Agenda." This document contained thirteen points, among which were the following: greater budgetary appropriations for women's programs, combating violence against women, promoting sexual and reproductive rights (without explicitly mentioning abortion), ending discrimination, ensuring the equitable distribution of family responsibilities, and, of course, ensuring women's political participation through quotas.[50] While the PAN declined to sign the *Pacto*, they did participate alongside PRI and PRD women, as well as civil society women, in the 2000 *Congreso Nacional de Mujeres hacia la Reforma del Estado* (National Congress of Women Seeking the Reform of the State). The *Congreso*, held in September at the beginning of the 200–2003 term, was convened in a manner similar to the *Parlmento* and discussed the policy areas itemized in the *Pacto Entre Mujeres*. Following the *Congreso*, one female legislator from the PRI, PAN, and the PRD summarized the accords before the Mexican Congress. Speaking for the PAN, the deputy Silvia América López Escoffie committed her party to supporting expanded labor rights for women, creating social programs to benefit women, and "endorsing all efforts made by women to work in favor of their greater development and equal integration into national life."[51]

Thus, both the pre-election Pact Among Women and the post-election National Congress of Women created "great expectations" for what the women legislators of the 2000–2003 Congress could achieve.[52] First, the legislators reached one of their agenda items by introducing and passing a statute that created the *Instituto Nacional de Mujeres* (National Institute of Women). This executive agency, known as InMujeres, received a mandate to "promote and encourage the conditions that facilitate the absence of discrimination, the equality of opportunities, and the equal treatment of the sexes" in Mexico.[53] Subsequently, President Vicente Fox of the PAN implemented *PROEQUIDAD* (Pro-Equity), a National Program for the Equality of Opportunities and End of Discrimination Against Women. *PROEQUIDAD* committed all branches of the public administration, in coordination with federal, state, and municipal governments, to "guarantee women access and participation to all structures of power and decision-making." Further, *PROEQUIDAD* explicitly authorized affirmative action measures as one strategy to reach this—and other—equality goals.[54]

Second, in 2002, the Gender and Equity Commission, jointly with the Governance Commission, introduced a bill to make the thirty percent quota mandatory. In the words of a then-deputy for the PRD, the consensus to introduce this measure had existed "for a long time" and been reaffirmed by the *Pacto* and the *Congreso*.[55] Critical was the changed attitude among *Panista* women, who were now more willing to recognize gender discrimination within their own party and within society. A prominent PAN woman noted that, as they began to win elections, "Automatically the men began to become the candidates and the women always the substitutes; the party was now much more *machista* than before."[56] Women from the PAN consequently reversed their earlier opposition to quotas, realizing that "there was no other way" to increase the number of women elected.[57]

Yet, *Panista* women's newfound commitment to quotas was not necessarily reflected in the party as a whole. The PAN had triumphed in the 2000 elections, ending the seven-decade electoral dominance of the PRI. The previous year, the PAN had agreed on the internal measure wherein each pair of *proprietario/suplente* candidates would contain one man and one woman. Yet, the PAN's stance on quotas was inconsistent. While Fox's *Panista* government was endorsing affirmative action measures within *PROEQUIDAD,* the PAN filed suit in the Supreme Court to contest the constitutionality of a subnational quota passed by the Coahuila state legislature. Women from the PAN and civil society were outraged, publicly embarrassing the party so much that the leadership sought to withdraw their lawsuit. This backpedaling was denied by the Mexican Supreme Court, which ruled against the PAN and upheld the constitutionality of quotas in 2002.[58] *Panista* women thus felt encouraged to break ranks and support the quota mandate, particularly given that the "quotas-are-unconstitutional" argument was no longer valid. They also "went public," building on growing civil society awareness of, and support for, quota measures. For instance, one longtime female PAN leader published an op-ed in Mexico's main newspapers, entitled "Quotas are Necessary to Guarantee the Participation of Women in the Political Parties."[59]

Importantly, female *Panistas*—as well as female *PRD-istas* and *Priístas*—had to advocate for quotas without jeopardizing their future political careers. Female legislators could not risk offending the party leadership, especially given these leaders' control over their future appointments and nominations. Thus, the women developed a two-tiered lobbying strategy. First, female legislators not seated on the Commission of Equity and Gender would participate in the lobby, demonstrating that support for the quota law transcended committee ties. Second, female legislators would always speak with male opponents from outside their party: no deputy or senator would face-off against a deputy or senator from her own party. As a then-PRD deputy explained, this strategy ensured "that men would never get angry with the women from their own party." She added that male legislators treat women from other parties with more respect than they treat women from their own parties. Since gentlemanly norms of courtly behavior take precedence over intra-party squabbling, "men listened to the women from other parties more carefully."[60] This strategy combined with public pressure to ensure the success of the bill, and the quota recommendation became law in April 2002.

Scholars frequently wonder why national legislatures would pass quota laws, particularly when such laws mean party leaders essentially agree to curb their own power. In the Mexican case, three factors were critical. First was the effect of negative publicity on the governing PAN, particularly given the newfound and vocal support from *Panista* women. Second was the potential or actual strengthening of party quotas. Women from both the PRD and the PRI had attempted to increase the internal nomination quotas from thirty percent to fifty percent, raising the matter at each party's national assembly in 2001. While the vote in the PRD failed, the vote in the PRI succeeded.[61] The PRI thus approved a fifty percent gender quota for PR and SMD candidates, a surprising outcome that sent "shock waves" through the party.[62] Given these proposed or actual changes to party quotas, a legislative quota of thirty percent was attractive to the party directorates because it would *reduce* their commitments to implementing the higher percentage. Third was that the 2002 quota law contained an essential loophole that would continue to facilitate parties' shirking behavior.[63] While the law specified that quotas apply to *proprietario* candidates, included a placement mandate for the PR lists, and provided censure for noncompliant parties, the law also stipulated that *parties choosing candidates via direct primaries were exempt from the quota.* Unintentionally, the 2002 quota law encouraged parties to democratize their candidate nomination procedures without necessarily compelling them to include more women.[64]

The Mexican case demonstrates how quotas are adopted with exceptions or reservations that limit their effectiveness. Since the 2003 elections—the first instance in which the legislative quota applied—the IFE has classified party primaries rather liberally, mostly because its lacks protocols that would verify parties' assertions that candidate selection indeed occurred via primaries.[65] The IFE's complacent certification of primaries has allowed Mexican parties to maintain extensive control over candidate selection without filling the quota.[66] Parties also deliberately run female candidates in throwaway races, that is, in those single-member districts which they already expect to lose.

Nonetheless, the percentage of women elected to the Congress rose to twenty-four percent in 2003 and fell only slightly to 23.4 percent in 2006. For the 2003 elections, female candidates competing from eight of the eleven parties formed a "Front for the Defense of Women's Political Rights," which worked to ensure that the IFE appropriately censured parties and demanded the reordering of lists so as to respect the quota.[67] Overall, the mobilization of party women on the broad theme of gender equality throughout the late 1990s and early 2000s provided a critical backdrop for the transformation of the quota statute. On the party side, female politicians had not only learned to formulate and deploy persuasive arguments for gender quotas, but they had successfully communicated across party lines about the status of women and the importance of equity. On the congressional side, beginning in 1997, female legislators achieved reforms to the budgetary process that would allocate greater resources to women's programs, as well as reforms that extended greater protections to victims of domestic violence, female prisoners, patients with gynecological cancers, and working mothers.

The Second Generation of Reforms

The 2002 Mexican quota law generally succeeded in facilitating the election of women. The vast majority of female legislators attribute their electoral success to the quota. As one PRD senator explained that "I was elected on the PR list, as the party is obligated by the federal electoral code to leave spaces for women."[68] Her co-partisan in the lower-chamber stated, "As a young, handicapped woman, I received a very high position on the PR list."[69] Moreover, party women manipulate the legislative quota to their advantage. One female *Panista* describes how she wished to enter the Senate in 2006. She knew her best chance lay in securing a high position on the PR list used to select thirty-two senators from a nationwide district. She also knew that the thirty percent quota, combined with the placement requirement, would force the PAN to run a woman candidate at minimum in the third-spot. Thus, during the internal primary, she needed to be merely the *woman* with the most votes, and not the *candidate* with the most votes. Her prediction proved correct. She emerged seventh in the overall primary, ahead of all other female contenders; this success elevated her to the third position on the PAN's list, and she safely won her Senate seat.[70]

These comments reveal the electoral security contained in receiving a nomination to the PR lists versus the uncertainty of running in SMDs under plurality rules. Indeed, most parties do not shirk the quota on the PR lists, as these spots have always been prizes doled out to loyalists, rewarding women as well as men. For instance, one PRI deputy explained that she could not compete in an SMD race in 2000: she remained outside of the governor's inner-circle, unpopular and thus unelectable. She appealed to the party president, who rewarded her "years of party service" with a slot on the PR list.[71] As such, parties thus typically apply their primary exemption to SMDs and not the PR lists.[72] Not only does the 2002 law permit this exemption, but none of the parties' internal quotas—with the exception of the PRI—apply to the SMD races. As one female PRD leader explained, "We have no problem with the PR districts, but we have to make a great effort to run women in the single-member districts."[73]

Given these concerns, female legislators and party militants in Mexico have refused to treat the 2002 legislative quota as the final reform. They continued to seek greater protections within their parties. For instance, PAN women have persuaded their party to adopt a forty percent internal quota for municipal councilors, a decision which addressed *Panistas'* most common argument against quotas—that women are unprepared for federal office. By nominating more women at the local level, the party hopes to train female *militantes* and avoid the situation where "you take the woman from her house so she can be a candidate, but she isn't prepared and you lose the election."[74] In 2005, the PRI extended the internal quota of fifty percent to include all positions on the CEN, the CDEs, and the municipal committees. A female PRI leader recalled the victory at the party's national assembly:

> It was a terrible fight; the women poured into the auditorium and denounced the men seated there, calling them backwards.... The men said we would take their spaces from them, but we asked whether they hadn't already taken the spaces from us.... They had always thought of us as timid and passive, docile loyalists who toed the party line, but when they saw how we fought, how we took the microphone, and how committed we were, they changed their minds.[75]

These words show the deep, and often fearless, commitment of party women to advancing their equitable participation within the parties. By 1997, the PRD had also moved forward, expanding the party quota to fifty percent for candidates for the federal PR and SMD districts and the municipal level councils.

Displaying the same dedication, the female legislators seated in the 2006–2009 Congress sought a stronger legislative quota. Women deputies and senators from the PRI and the PAN asked for fifty percent to match the quotas they had achieved internally. Women from the PAN, however, balked, asking "Does it have to be parity or can it be a percentage that better reflects the reality of our country?" *Panista* women argued that forty percent would be more palatable to their male colleagues, especially given objections that women were "not competitive enough" to fill half of the Congress.[76] For this reason, women legislators from the PAN negotiated their female colleagues from the PRI and the PRD down from fifty percent to forty percent.

The measure passed in 2008. The final bill mandated a forty percent quota for federal posts and for the political parties' directorate committees at *all* levels, as well as mandated the allocation of 2.3 percent of the parties operating budget to training programs for female leaders. Success occurred because the female legislators had won the grudging support of the PAN, and because the PRI and the PRD were incentivized to support a legislative quota whose forty percent threshold was lower than the fifty percent benchmark their female members had secured internally. As one female PRI leader noted, "Women's political participation always depends on party directors' political decision to allow it."[77]

Yet the 2008 revision reflected only part of female legislators' ongoing and far-reaching ability to win concessions from party directors. The 2003–2006 Congress, which occurred in between the 2002 and 2008 quota laws, continued the pattern of collaborating across parties to advance a shared women's agenda. In 2003, the legislators-elect signed a second *Pacto Entre Mujeres,* this one subtitled "A little way more for the full citizenship of women in Mexico." Working through the Gender and Equity Commission, female legislators then created a parliamentary research center entitled the *Centro de Estudios para el Adelanto de las Mujeres y la Equidad de Género* (Center for the Study of Women's Adancement and Gender Equity) and passed the General Law for Equality Between Men and Women. The commission also introduced and won statutory changes that encouraged executive officials to select women for posts in the public administration and that ended discrimination in the judicial branch and the Mexican Armed Forces.

Subsequently, women in the 2006–2009 Congress, in addition to winning a new legislative quota, passed two laws dedicated to ending violence against women. The first created a national response system to "prevent, protect, assist, and eradicate" violence against women, and the second reformed the judicial, penal, and health sectors to "ensure women's rights to be free from violence." The female legislators seated on the Commission of Equity and Gender also successfully altered line-item budget allocations to create programs that assisted women with AIDS, distributed the HPV vaccine in public hospitals, trained teachers about gender equity in the classroom, and provided scholarships to teenage mothers. The executive branch, under PAN president Felipe Calderón, supported these initiatives. In 2007, representatives from the federal, judicial, and executive branches at the national, state, and municipal level signed the *Acuerdo Nacional para la Igualdad entre Mujeres y Hombres* (National Plan for Equality between Men and Women). This plan committed state and government agents to introduce the principles of equality and empowerment, rights and non-discrimination, and a life free from violence in all institutions and programs.[78]

Despite this wealth of reform, the legitimacy of the gender quota and the recognition of gender equality are far from settled matters in Mexican politics. Five days after the 2009 elections, eight female legislators-elect—including women from the leftist PRD—renounced their seats in order that their male *suplentes* could enter the Congress. By the first three months into the 2009–2012 term, a total of sixteen *diputadas* had delivered their seats to male substitutes.[79] The actions of these women, termed "*Las Juanas,*" have prompted a widespread outcry among politicians, civil society, and the media. Female elites have accused *Las Juanas* of betraying their hard-won fight for gender equality. A PAN senator called their actions "a fraudulent violation of the quota law" and a PRD leader called the situation "supremely embarrassing" and "a complete step backwards."[80] Female legislators seated on the Commission of Equity and Gender, particularly women from the PAN and the PRD, have responded by introducing another quota reform, which would stipulate that *proprietario* and *suplente* candidates be of the same sex. As of July 2010, this initiative remained pending. These developments show that, nineteen years after the PRD's promise to nominate twenty-five percent women for federal elections, the question of women's equality remains at the forefront of Mexican politics.

Conclusion

This overview of quotas' adoption and implementation in Mexico provides important lessons for the history of gender quotas in Latin America and elsewhere. First, politicians adopt quotas even in the absence of an electoral incentive. The Mexican parties did not perceive an electoral advantage in implementing quotas, silencing news about these decisions in the 1990s. Rather, pressure from within drove the imposition of quotas from above. A female *Prísista* commented that, "when parties resist quotas, they are playing with fire."[81] Likewise, a male PRD leader stated, "I comply with the quota because, if I didn't, the women of my party would rise up against me. Of course, it is also useful if my party is seen to support women."[82] Even the PAN, which came under public pressure to support legislative quotas in the 2000s, did not perceive nominating women to be electorally advantageous. Rather, being seen to *hold women back* is an electoral *disadvantage.* All else equal, however, the political parties would prefer that quotas did not exist. As one *Panista* female firmly states, "If the quota were not in place, it would not be followed."[83] Mexico's parties capitalize on the positive publicity associated with quotas only after they become compelled to adopt them.

Second, gender quotas are not simply mechanisms used by conniving politicians to secure their electoral futures. Mexico prohibits reelection, meaning that women's legislative careers do not immediately benefit from the revised statutes. Female elites recognized that women's participation in political life was instrumental for achieving not simply congressional seats, but for advancing gender equality. Party women elected under gender quotas were instrumental in passing other reforms, from criminalizing marital rape to allocating money for maternity hospitals and domestic violence shelters. Female elites interviewed frequently cautioned that not all women elected under quotas will adopt a gender perspective; nonetheless, they all recognized how female legislators work collaboratively and successfully to not just win quotas, but to transform myriad policies to benefit female citizens. For Mexican women, quotas are both an ends and a means. As a PRD interviewee said, "When women begin advancing, men feel terribly threatened; but we are organized. We are not stopping now; we are going forward."[84]

CHAPTER FOUR

The Diffusion of Sub-National Gender Quotas in Mexico and Their Impacts

PÄR ZETTERBERG

Introduction

Four decades after the introduction of universal suffrage in Mexico, the share of female legislators was less than ten percent. In 1993, women's lack of political power was therefore put on the political agenda—two years after Argentina introduced the first electoral gender quota law in Latin America. Mexico's federal electoral law (*COFIPE*) was modified, and established that political parties should promote an increasing proportion of women in decision-making posts. One of the opposition parties, the Democratic Revolutionary Party (PRD), took an additional step and adopted the first quota provision in Mexico: the party included in its party statutes a thirty percent gender quota for committees and candidate lists (Bruhn 2003). Three years later, the Institutional Revolutionary Party (PRI)—Mexico's ruling party for almost seventy years—approved a recommendation to field no more than seventy percent of candidates of the same sex on its candidate lists. The same year, in 1996, the PRI-dominated Congress revised the *COFIPE* and wrote this measure into law (Baldez 2004).

The 1996 federal gender quota law, however, was not the first law in Mexico that specified that a share of the candidates had to be women. Because of the country's federal character, each of the thirty-one states as well as the Federal District of Mexico City has its constitution, electoral law, and local congress, respectively. As a consequence, the state of Chihuahua introduced the first quota law in Mexico, in 1994. The law required political parties to field no more than seventy percent of the same-sex candidates on their lists (Reynoso and D'Angelo 2006). Since then, a large number of states (but not all of them) has introduced gender quotas into their electoral code.

This chapter examines the adoption of gender quota policies at sub-national levels in Mexico. Hitherto, most research on gender quotas in Mexico (as elsewhere) have examined the federal (i.e. national) level (e.g. Baldez 2004, 2007; Bruhn 2003). A closer focus on sub-national quotas in Mexico, however, is warranted for various reasons: Empirically, neither the development of quotas at the state level nor the relationship between quotas at different levels of government has received sufficient scholarly attention; thus, we simply lack knowledge about the adoption of sub-national quotas. Methodologically, a comparative state-level analysis has an advantage over a cross-national approach (c.f. Jones 1998); it enables a comparison of different quota provisions within political systems that largely share key features; political culture, party system (after the completion of the democratic transition in 2000; mainly a three-party system,[1] and a mixed electoral system (i.e. a system that uses both a "first past the post" system of single member districts and proportional representation).

More specifically, the chapter sheds light on the diffusion of sub-national quotas in Mexico as well as their impacts. This is done in three steps: First, it describes the diffusion of sub-national quotas; when and where they were adopted as well as their main characteristics. Second, by using an illustrative case study (the state of Zacatecas), the chapter examines the role of federal quota reforms in the adoption of state-level quotas. Third, the chapter assesses the numerical impacts of sub-national quota policies on women's representation in state legislatures as well as their possible more far-reaching consequences.

The evidence consists mainly of secondary data drawn from previous research. The illustrative case study, however, uses data from a field trip to Mexico from September to December 2006. In Zacatecas, I interviewed legislators, local government officials, and women's rights activists who were involved in the quota reform process in 2003. Overall, twenty-six interviews were carried out in Zacatecas (for more information on the interviews, see Zetterberg 2009a).

The next section examines the development of sub-national gender quotas in Mexico. Subsequently, this chapter assesses the role of federal quota reforms on quota adoption at the state level, with the help of the illustrative case study. Then, it analyzes the impacts of quotas on women's political representation. This chapter concludes with a summary of the findings and discusses the challenges of gender quotas and women's political representation in Mexican politics.

The Diffusion of Sub-national Gender Quotas in Mexico

Since the introduction of gender quotas in Chihuahua in 1994, all states but two (Nayarit and Nuevo León) have adopted some kind of quota policy. A quota has been defined as "an affirmative action measure that establishes a percentage or number for the representation of a specific group" (Dahlerup 2007, 78).[2] However, in the text of a specific law, gender quota provisions may be expressed in gender-neutral terms (a maximum-minimum representation for both sexes). Of the twenty-nine states (and the Federal District) that have adopted gender quotas, most of them carried through a quota reform after *COFIPE* was modified in 2002. In the 2002 revision of *COFIPE*, political parties were no longer recommended to field at least thirty percent female candidates; they were required to do so. Rank order specifications were also included as well as sanctions for non-compliance (see Piscopo in this volume for a more comprehensive presentation of the 2002 federal quota law).

Roughly speaking, the development of quota adoption at the state level could be characterized by three different *waves*. The time period of 1994 to 2001 represents the *first wave*, which is characterized by the pioneer Mexican work on quota policies, mostly by the state of Chihuahua at the state level and by the revision of *COFIPE* in 1996 at the federal level. Chihuahua was not only the first state to adopt any kind of quota policy; it was also the first state (in 1997) to include a combination of the specific provisions (rank order specifications and sanctions for non-compliance) that later were widely adopted to make quotas more effective. Chihuahua had a few immediate followers—Oaxaca (also in 1997) and the Federal District (in 1999)—that included similar requirements in their respective quota law. The less strict federal quota law, on the other hand, also inspired some states to adopt quotas. Durango (in 2000) and Michoacán (in 2001) included a recommendation in their electoral codes to field at least thirty percent women on their candidate lists. However, in general there were only a few quota reforms during the initial wave of quota policies in the Mexican states (see Table 4.1). Thus, at this stage quota policies at the state level have not been institutionalized. Different quota provisions were tested during this wave, but none of them became a dominant policy.

The first real expansion—and institutionalization—of quota policies in Mexico comes in the *second wave*, from 2002 to 2007. In a three-year period, 2002–2004, more states (twelve of them) adopted quotas than during the eight-year time period (1994–2001) during the previous wave. I suggest that the 2002 revision of *COFIPE* represents the starting point of this wave. The main characteristic of the *COFIPE* revision, and of the wave, is a closer attention given to the enforceability

Table 4.1: Three *Waves* of Quota Policies in Mexico, Over Time

LATE 1990S: PIONEERS AND FEDERAL STATE FOLLOWERS	EARLY 2000S: THIRTY PERCENT "STRICT QUOTA"	LATE 2000S: INCREASING THE PERCENTAGE
Chihuahua (1994)	COFIPE (2002): Sanctions + rank order	Federal District (2008): 54% (PR) / 30% (MS)
Sonora (1996): Sanctions	Campeche (2002): Sanctions	COFIPE (2008): 40%
COFIPE (1996): Only recommendation	Quintana Roo (2002)	Baja California (2008): 40%
Chihuahua (1997): Sanctions + rank order	San Luis Potosí (2002)	Campeche (2008): 50%
Oaxaca (1997): Sanctions + rank order	Puebla (2002)	Durango (2008): Sanctions + rank order
Guerrero (1998)	Guanajuato (2002): Rank order	Jalisco (2008): Rank order
Federal District (1999): Sanctions + rank order	Tamaulipas (2003): Sanctions + rank order	Mexico (state): 40%
Colima (1999): Sanctions	Yucatán (2003): Rank order	Oaxaca (2008): 40%
Mexico (state) (1999)	Zacatecas (2003): Sanctions + rank order	San Luis Potosí (2008): Rank order
Jalisco (2000)	Aguascalientes (2003): Sanctions	Sonora (2008): 50%
Durango (2000): Only recommendation	Baja California Sur (2003)	Tabasco (2008): 40%
Coahuila (2001)	Chiapas (2004): Sanctions + rank order	Tamaulipas (2008): 40%
Michoacán (2001): Only recommendation	Guerrero (2004): Rank order	Tlaxcala (2008): 50%
	Querétaro (2005): 40% quota	Aguascalientes (2009): 40%
	Sinaloa (2006)	Coahuila (2009): 40%
	Veracruz (2006): Rank order	Colima (2009): 50% (PR) / (30% (MS)
	Hidalgo (2007): Sanctions + rank order	Zacatecas (2009): 40%

Sources: Author's elaboration, with information from INMUJERES 2010, Zaremberg 2009, Reynoso and D Angelo 2006, and the specific electoral codes of the states.

and effectiveness of the quota policy. During this wave, no state introduces a "soft" recommendation in its electoral code; in contrast, a majority includes specific provisions (rank order specifications and/or sanctions for non-compliance) to make the quota effective (see Table 4.1).

The *third wave* is characterized by a greater focus on percentages. Already in the year 2005, the state of Querétaro adopted a forty percent quota policy. However, I suggest that the wave starts in January 2008, when the Federal District increased their thirty percent quota to fifty-four percent for proportional seats and when the Federal Congress revised *COFIPE* and raised the quota to forty percent (for both majority and proportional seats). In the following two years, as many as fifteen states introduced quotas, or revised their previous laws. As Table 4.1 shows, almost all of them went beyond the previous requirement of thirty percent. Most of the states followed the *COFIPE* requirement and adopted a forty percent quota policy; however, a few states (e.g. Campeche and Tlaxcala) included parity clauses (fifty percent).

Thus, a rough sketch of the quota diffusion in Mexico shows that the development of quotas has been a dynamic process lasting at least fifteen years. Various quota provisions were developed in the 1990s, but they were not very effective: From the late 1990s to the first years of the 21st century, the average number of women in local congresses increased by less than one percent, from 13.9 percent to 14.8 percent (Reynoso and D'Angelo 2006). Therefore, quota advocates in the different states learned from the experiences (both good and bad) of other states—and from the federal quota law; as a consequence, the adoption of quotas or its revision during the *third wave* appears to follow a similar trend.

An increased homogeneity in the wording of new quota policies, however, does not imply that quota laws in Mexican states are the same. As Table 4.2 shows, there is a substantial difference in quota provisions across the states. First, the quota requirements range from twenty-five percent to fifty-four percent, with a slight majority having a requirement of forty percent or more. Second, about half of the quota laws at the state level include enforcement mechanisms (i.e. strict sanctions for non-compliance), in order to ensure that the policy is implemented by political parties. About the same number of quota policies specify that the quota should apply to the *main candidate* and not to the substitute. Third, approximately two of three quota policies at state levels have ranked order mechanisms to ensure that women are placed on electable slots and not simply at the bottom of the lists. Finally, one of three quota laws do not have exception clauses, that is, tin they do not allow political parties to bypass quota requirements during the candidate selection process.[3]

Table 4.2: Gender Quota Policies in Mexican States

STATE	QUOTA	YEAR	PERCENT	SANCTION (NO REGISTER)	RANK ORDER	APPLY TO MAIN CANDIDATE *(PROPIETARIA)*	EXCEPTIONS
Aguascalientes	Yes*	2003/2009	40[4]	Yes	No	No	No
Baja California	Yes	2008[2]	40	Yes	No	No	Yes (MS)
Baja California Sur	Yes	2003	33	No	No	Yes	No
Campeche	Yes	2002[2]/2008[2]	50[4]	Yes	Yes	Yes	Yes (MS)
Chiapas	Yes	2004	30	Yes	Yes	Yes	No
Chihuahua	Yes	1994/1997	30	Yes	Yes[5]	Yes	No
Coahuila	Yes	2001/2009	404	Yes	Yes	Yes	Yes (MS)
Colima	Yes	1999/2009	50 (PR)[4]; 30 (MS)	Yes	Yes[5]	No	No
Federal District (Mexico City)	Yes	1999/2008	54 (PR)[4]; 30 (MS)	Yes	Yes	Yes	Yes (MS)
Durango	Yes	2000[3]/2008[2]	30	Yes	Yes	No	Yes (MS)
Guanajuato	Yes*	2002[2]	N.a.	No1	Yes	Yes	Yes
Guerrero	Yes	1998/2004	30	No2	Yes[5]	Yes	Yes (MS)
Hidalgo	Yes	2007	30	Yes	Yes	Yes	Yes (MS)
Jalisco	Yes*	2000/2008[2]	30	No	Yes[5]	No	No
Mexico (state)	Yes	1999/2008[2]	404	No	No	No	Yes
Michoacán	Yes3	2001	30	No	No	No	No
Morelos	Yes	2008[2]	50 (PR); 33 (MS)	Yes	Yes	Yes	Yes (MS)
Nayarit	No	-	-	-	-	-	-
Nuevo León	No	-	-	-	-	-	-
Oaxaca	Yes	1997/2008[2]	40[4]	No	No	Yes	Yes (MS)
Puebla	Yes	2002	25	No	No	Yes	No
Querétaro	Yes	2005	40	No	No	No	Yes
Quintana Roo	Yes	2002[2]	30	No	No	No	Yes
San Luis Potosí	Yes	2002[2]/2008[2]	30	Yes	Yes[5]	Yes	Yes (MS)
Sinaloa	Yes	1998/2006	30	No	No	Yes	No
Sonora	Yes	1996/2008[2]	50 ("paridad")	No	Yes	No	Yes (MS)

Table 4.2 cont.

STATE	QUOTA	YEAR	PERCENT	SANCTION (NO REGISTER)	RANK ORDER	APPLY TO MAIN CANDIDATE *(PROPIETARIA)*	EXCEPTIONS
Tabasco	Yes	2008[2]	40	No	No	No	Yes (MS)
Tamaulipas	Yes	2003/2008[2]	40[4]	Yes	Yes	Yes	Yes (MS)
Tlaxcala	Yes	2008[2]	50	No	Yes	No	Yes
Veracruz	Yes	2006	30	No	Yes	Yes	Yes (MS)
Yucatán	Yes	2003	30	No	Yes	No	No
Zacatecas	Yes	2003/2009	40[4]	Yes	Yes	Yes	Yes (MS)

Notes: * = The quota applies only to proportional representation. 3 = There is only a financial sanction. 2 = The reform took place after the revision of COFIPE in the same year. 3 = Only a recommendation. 4 = Before the revision of the law, there was a 30 percent quota. 5 = No rank order specification before the revision. MS = Majority seats.

Sources: Author's elaboration, with information from INMUJERES 2010, Zaremberg 2009, Reynoso and D Angelo 2006, and the specific electoral codes of the states.

The inclusion of enforcement mechanisms, exception clauses, and specifications about to which positions the quota applies (the main candidates or the substitutes) highlights the tension, or controversies, that characterize the quota debate in Mexico—at both national and subnational levels. Quota advocates have criticized political parties for lacking true commitment to the gender quotas. For instance, an exception clause is not only included in two-thirds of the quota policies at state levels, but also in the federal quota law (Baldez 2007). Moreover, enforcement mechanisms have been included as a response to a predominantly male reluctance of party gatekeepers to comply with quota requirements. By strictly regulating quota policies, decision-makers, who support quotas, try to make it difficult for political parties to bypass the requirements. Although quota policies at the state level in Mexico have been adopted by male-dominated legislatures, there are also critical voices to quotas among (mostly male) party activists within the major political parties (c.f. Zetterberg 2008). The next section examines the controversies that surrounded the adoption of quotas in the Mexican state of Zacatecas. The main focus is on the role that the federal quota law has played for the introduction of gender quotas at state levels.

Federal and Sub-National Quotas

In the literature on public policy, it is commonly held that there is a "federalism advantage" at the policy adoption stage: policies adopted at one level of government may be diffused to another level. So-called "diffusion effects" can work from the federal unit to the sub-national level, or the other way around (Franceschet, Forthcoming). The previous section puts the introduction of state-level gender quotas in relation to the development of federal quota policies (as stated in *COFIPE*). It is shown that the federal gender quota law was not the first quota policy in Mexico; nor was the wording of the 2002 and 2008 federal quota laws a novelty in Mexico. Thus, federal legislators should not be regarded as policy entrepeneurs nor quota policies should be seen mainly as a top-down process.

However, the federal quota law accelerated the adoption of state-level quota policies. Indeed, there was a major diffusion of state-level quota legislation after the passing or revision of the federal quota law. This is perhaps most evident after the 2008 revision of the federal quota law, when a large number of states, in a short period of time, made similar kinds of reforms by adopting a forty percent (or greater) gender quota. In addition, the 2002 federal quota revision provided a fairly large number of followers. In some of these cases, the similarities in the wording of the laws are striking.[4] Thus, the diffusion of quota policies in Mexico appears to go in both directions: in the early stages of the policy's lifecycle, there is more of a bottom-up process from a few states to the federal level; in the later stages it becomes more of a top-down process—from federal to state levels.

However, it is not evident in which specific ways the federal quota law could accelerate the process of quota expansion at the state level. Here, I make the argument that the federal quota policy has had an impact in at least two specific ways: First, the federal quota law provided quota advocates with a good argument as to why a state-level quota should be adopted in the first place. Thus, the adoption of a federal quota law created a momentum for activists at sub-national levels who wish to adopt quota policies. This sort of new opportunity structure might be especially important in a country like Mexico, which traditionally has had a centralized power structure (during the PRI hegemony), with a limited de facto power in the hands of states (Hecock 2006). Second, the specific formulations in the federal quota law are a key point of reference for quota advocates, who pressed for reforms in a specific state. Thus, the federal quota law provides women activists with an example of how a quota law more specifically could, and perhaps should, look like.

An Illustrative Case: The 2003 Quota Reform in Zacatecas

To support the argument stated above, I use the reform process in the State of Zacatecas. Zacatecas introduced legislative gender quotas in 2003 (the quota law was then revised in 2009), that is, a year after the revision of *COFIPE*. In line with the *COFIPE* revision, the quota was part of a larger electoral reform package. In close contact with the governor Ricardo Monreal (PRD), the Commission on Electoral

Affairs had been working since 2001 on a proposal to reform the electoral code; however, in the first months of 2003 the commission had not yet reached an agreement. Feminist activists, some of them also active in the governing PRD party of Zacatecas, received information in March 2003 that there was a silent agreement in the commission to exclude gender quotas from the reform package; "In the commission, they said within parenthesis that they should not discuss issues of gender equality: 'we shoud leave that out.'"[5] As a result, quota advocates mobilized under the label, The Plural Network of Women (*La Red Plural de Mujeres*) to press for the inclusion of gender quotas in the reform package. The network made an *iniciativa popular* (a bill proposal by a non-representative) in which they requested that a gender quota should be included in the electoral code. The network needed 500 signatures to be able to hand in the bill proposal; they got approximately 10,000 signatures.

The *Network* included party activists within women's branches of all the major political parties in the state—the PRD, the PRI, the PAN, and the PT (the Workers' Party/*el Partido de Trabajo*)—as well as women's organizations and a branch of the local government: the Women's agency (*INMUZA—Instituto para la mujer zacatecana*). Already in 2002, *INMUZA* and the Commission on gender equality organized forums about gender equality issues, where women's organizations and others could come up with suggestions on gender equality reforms. The adoption of gender quotas was one of the topics on these forums.

It is evident that the major revision of the federal quota law in 2002 provided quota advocates in Zacatecas with new ideas and expectations. Both the PRD and the PRI had adopted gender quotas in their party statutes. However, these were not always adhered to by party gatekeepers at the local level, but to some extent they changed the political discourse regarding the role of women in politics. Women's rights activists across Mexico gained a new momentum following the 2002 federal quota revision. After the battle at the federal level, they wished to adopt new quota policies also at the state level; "after getting something adopted at the federal level, you go for the state level too."[6] Thus, in short, the quota revision at the federal level provided women's rights activists in Zacatecas and other states with an argument as to why a new electoral code should include a quota provision.

The broad opposition to gender quotas in the Commission on Electoral Affairs might appear paradoxical, given the recently revised federal quota law as well as the quota provisions included in the PRI and PRD party statutes, respectively. However, to its very nature, quotas in Mexico are mainly a threat to party activists at the local level, not the federal level; nomination procedures and battles over candidacies take place mostly within the state structures of political party organizations (see also Zetterberg 2008). Moreover, the *silent* agreement within the commission appears to have been rational; an increasingly women-friendly discourse had raised the political price for publicly opposing quotas. As a male member of the Commission on Gender Equality puts it; "no political party was stupid enough to confront women."[7] As a result, once the women's network had presented its bill proposal and put the quota issue on the reform agenda, the network did not face open resistance. Rather, resistance to quotas was subtle.

The *Network* used several tactics to get the quota adopted. For instance, already in the construction of the bill proposal, the women's network took the potential opposition into consideration. There were some women in the network that wanted a fifty percent quota. A majority of the women were opposed to this idea, because they expected that a seventy/thirty percent quota would be more negotiable. Moreover, the network of women contacted politicians at the federal level to get support for its proposal. Among others, Mexico's First Lady supported the network's cause, and so did the president of the Committee on Gender Equality in the Federal Congress. Women in the PRD also approached national party leaders to ask for support. They wanted the national leadership to criticize the governor for violating the internal party statutes of PRD by not pushing the issue forward.

In addition, the *Network* mobilized within and outside of the state legislature. First, within the legislature, they gathered the support of the Committee on Gender Equality. This committee was the body within the legislature that formally elaborated and approved the quota proposal, before sending it to the plenary session for a final decision. During the negotiations within the committee, there were some minor disagreements between the members. For instance, a female PAN Representative opposed the *Network*'s idea of mandating political parties to reserve the same districts to only female contestants. She wanted to give each political party the freedom to choose which districts should have a female candidate. As a result, activists had to compromise in this and some other issues, and this specific suggestion was dropped from the final proposal. Outside the legislature, the *Network* organized a two-month permanent (twenty-four hours, seven days a week) protest to support the proposal and challenge the resistance to quotas. The protest reached the headlines also of national media, which put pressure on the main political parties and the governor.

On September 30 2003, the issue of gender quotas was finally debated in plenary session. After months of negotiations, resistance and protests, the proposal to introduce gender quotas in the electoral code passed unanimously. The new law was strict; candidate lists having more than seventy percent of the same sex were not going to be accepted for registration. The requirements applied both to candidates for proportional and majority seats. On proportional lists, it was not permitted to put two candidates of the same sex on the top of the list. However, there was one exception to the law: the parties did not have to comply with the law whenever women to majority seats were elected through internal voting (*elección interna*) within the political parties (c.f. Baldez 2007).

The similarities between the quota provision in Zacatecas and the 2002 federal quota law are striking. Both policies have a thirty percent minimum of female candidates; both include the same enforcement mechanism (no-registration); they have the same rank-order specifications; and they have an escape clause for lists to majority seats. The similarities between the provisions put emphasis on the impact of the federal quota law on the *wording* of the Zacatecan quota policy. As the analysis has shown, quota advocates had to make various compromises to have the bill passed. For pragmatic reasons, they initially compromised within themselves and presented a thirty percent quota rather than a proposal of parity. During the reform process, they had to relinquish some of their proposals, especially attempts to make the quota to majority seats more effective. Consequently, the proposal became more similar to the wording of the federal quota law. Thus, it seems as if the federal quota law became a point of reference during the process and a politically viable outcome. Concerned about the public image of the PRD, national party leaders followed the development in Zacatecas, and the governor's behavior, with increased care. Thus, the governor and party colleagues were influenced not only by the *Network*, but also by national party representatives. However, the governor and his party colleagues would not go beyond the minimum requirements of the federal quota law. The *Network*, on the other hand, was strengthened by the massive mobilization and popular support for their proposal, and was therefore not satisfied with less than the wording of the quota provisions in *COFIPE*. At the same time, they realized that they were unlikely to get more.

In sum, quota advocates at the state level could use the federal quota law as a tool in their attempts to push forward for a (new) quota law. The *Network* in Zacatecas used the federal quota law as an argument for why quotas should be introduced also in their specific state. It also used the wording of the federal quota law as a point of reference in the negotiations with male representatives. Despite being a single case study, it is not unlikely that other Mexican states behaved similarly, where a united women's movement pushed for quota reforms. The issue therefore deserves further empirical scrutiny, to get a broader picture of how one level of government impacts the adoption of a similar policy at another level.

Impacts of Gender Quotas on Women's Political Representation in the Mexican States

In the normative debate, at least four arguments have been presented to justify the introduction of quotas; one emphasizing reasons of justice, another focusing on women's specific experiences and resources for legislative politics, a third paying attention to women's particular interests, and a final argument focusing on the possibility that gender quotas provide female constituents with new political role models (see e.g. Bacchi 2006). These arguments are related to distinct forms of representation (see e.g. Zetterberg 2009a); hence, this section examines the impact of quotas on descriptive, substantive, and symbolic representation, respectively (see e.g. Pitkin 1967). Descriptive representation emphasizes the composition of the legislature and the extent to which the legislature is a portrait of the people at large. Here, descriptive representation refers strictly to the numerical representation of women (c.f. Krook et al. 2009). Substantive representation focuses on the work that representatives carry through within the legislature, once they are elected, and the extent to which they act in the interests of the represented. Symbolic representation , finally, emphasizes how representatives are regarded or perceived by those they represent, and how representatives' appearance might affect the self-image of the represented (see e.g. Goodin 1977).

Descriptive Representation

In general, research on the effects of quota policies at the state level is fairly limited. Among the empirical analyses on the topic, most attention has been paid to the issue of descriptive (or numerical) representation (see e.g. Reynoso and D'Angelo 2006; Zapata Morales 2008; Zaremberg 2009). Researchers have addressed the issue of whether quotas are effective in increasing the number of women in state legislatures. To address the question properly, they moved beyond a comparison of the percentage of women in state legislatures before and after the introduction of a quota. Rather, they have included various competing factors in longitudinal analyses, in an attempt to single out the specific effect of quotas on the proportion of women in state legislatures.

Perhaps, the most comprehensive analysis on the topic is a study by Reynoso and D'Angelo (2006). They analyze state-level elections (elections to the Federal District included) in Mexico from 1991 to February 2005, or a total of 160 elections. In the study, they examine the relative impact of specific quota provisions on women's representation in state legislatures, taking socio-economic and historical factors into account: the living conditions of women (life expectancy), the average level of education among women, the level of social development, and the number of female legislators in the previous term. By comparing the effects of quotas with other factors such as women's level of education, the authors are able to identify the impact of both episodic changes (quota policies) and continuous changes (socio-economic development, etc.) (c.f. Hughes and Paxton 2008).

Reynoso and D'Angelo find that quotas, along with the percentage of female legislators in the previous term, are the best predictors of women's political representation in Mexico's state legislatures. The socio-economic factors included in the analysis, on the other hand, appear not to be of much significance. The findings point at the ways in which a sudden change in the rules of the game could rapidly place women in politics on a new (and fast) track (c.f. Dahlerup and Freidenvall 2005). Whenever political parties have no choice but to nominate a certain share of women, large leaps in women's presence in legislative bodies are possible.

Two comments should be made in relation to the findings; first, not all quota provisions produce the same leaps. One factor appears to be of particular importance, namely whether or not it is explicitly specified that the quota should apply to the main candidate (*candidaturas propietarias*). Whenever there is no such specification, political parties have tended to comply with the quota largely by nominating female substitutes (*suplentes*). Second, the positive effects of quotas on women's political representation do not hide the fact that there are on average less than thirty percent women in the state legislatures. Thus, quota policies have contributed to reduce the gender gap of women in politics, but there is still a gap (Reynoso and D'Angelo 2006).

The findings of the Reynoso and D'Angelo study have been supported by more recent analyses on the impact that quotas have had on the presence of women in Mexico's state legislatures (e.g. Zapata Morales 2008). Thus, it could be concluded that gender quotas, mainly those with specific provisions, appear to have had the desired effects on women's descriptive representation in the Mexican states. The varying impacts of quota designs point at the importance of the wording of the law for its successful implementation.

Substantive Representation

Empirical analyses on the impact of quotas on substantive representation are scarce. One of the reasons for the lack of empirical studies relates to the relative difficulties in collecting empirical data. Whereas an analysis on descriptive representation presupposes the compilation of quota policies and data on the number of women in state legislatures (control factors excluded), an empirical analysis on the impact of quotas on substantive representation is likely to be more time-consuming. Written material on bill proposals and laws, and perhaps also transcripts of parliamentary debates, should be collected for more than one legislature or time period (in order to compare the actions of women elected via a specific quota design with those elected on another quota provision and/or "non-quotas"); or legislators should be interviewed or asked to fill in a survey questionnaire to get information about their parliamentary work.

One of the few analyses that touch on the topic of substantive representation is a study that examines the *prerequisites* for female legislators to act on women's behalf and thus for gender equal policy output to occur. By comparing the institutional constraints that female legislators face in Zacatecas (which has a strict quota law) with those in Michoacán (which has only a recommendation), Zetterberg (2008) tests the hypothesis that women elected via quotas are more likely to suffer from institutional constraints, and thus have a more circumscribed manoeuvrability in the legislature, than women who are not elected via quotas. The data consists of written material such as bill proposals as well as interviews with male and female legislators, party representatives at the state level, and state officials.

The analysis examines three institutional constraints—or obstacles—to women legislators' performance: tokenism ("externally controlled legislator", i.e. party leaderships select candidates that they could control), marginalization (legislator is kept outside leadership positions in the legislature), and invisibilization (legislator is ignored in decision-making). The findings give no support to the hypothesis that women elected via quotas suffer more from institutional constraints than other female representatives. Thus, in contrast to what has been suggested in the political debate on quotas, there is no evidence that the adoption of quotas generate second-class legislators who lack the possibility to push through policy reforms (see also Murray 2010). The lack of support for the hypothesis, however, does not mean that there are no tendencies of tokenism, marginalization, and invisibilization; it simply means that women elected via strict quota laws are not more likely to suffer from institutional constraints than any other woman. However, this analysis suggests that quotas might intensify problems of marginalization and invisibilization in one political sphere, namely within the internal processes of political parties. Quotas alter the rules of the game within political parties, forcing party gatekeepers to nominate women. This is likely to challenge male dominance within the parties and intensify the struggles over political power and control over the political agenda (see also Zetterberg 2008).

A *positive* interpretation of the pioneer analysis is that the adoption of quotas has not diminished the possibility for female legislators to represent the interests that women share as a group (however these interests are defined). On the other hand, reforms have changed the internal dynamics of political parties that might generate new struggles between men and women. Yet, this topic is under-researched and empirical analyses on more Mexican states are necessary in order to get a clearer picture of the broader consequences of Mexican quota policies.

Symbolic Representation

The possible far-reaching consequences of quotas, beyond the elite level, have rarely been analyzed. This is not surprising, given the relative newness of the reform. However, it has been suggested that quotas might generate new political role models, and consequently show female constituents that not only men, but also women may play an active role in politics.

There is some anecdotal evidence suggesting that quotas bring about a change on women's mindset. For instance, feminist activists in Zacatecas have argued that the increased presence of women representatives gives young women new ideas about their future careers. For example, in an interview, María Luisa Sosa de la Torre told the author that "today you hear girls saying that they want to be a politician when they get older—you never heard such things before."[8] According to activists, this new mentality among women is attributed to the increased number of women that hold political office. Women see that it is possible for a woman to become a legislator; thus, it is an achievable objective.

Yet, empirical analysis does not support the idea that quotas increase women's political inclusion. In a comparative analysis on more than 1,000 women citizens in sixteen Mexican states (and the Federal District), of which some states use quotas and others do not, there is no systematic difference in women's interest in politics, after controlling for other relevant factors (level of socio-economic development, etc.). In other words, women who live in a state with a quota law are not more likely to be politically engaged than other women. Nor do they trust their politicians to a greater extent than others (Zetterberg 2009b).

The lack of empirical support, however, does not rule out the possibility that quotas might have a positive impact on women citizens. It is possible that the measures used for the analyses do not fully capture the various impacts that quotas could have on female constituents. For instance, any impact of quotas on the attitudes and behaviour of non-elite women might first be visible among those who are already politically engaged. To give an example, quotas in Brazil have been known to strengthen the mobilization among organized women (Sacchet 2008). This chapter indicates that a similar pattern might exist in Mexico: the introduction of quotas at one level of government, or in one state, has created a momentum for activists at other levels or in other states. Thus, the adoption of quotas appears to have strengthened women at mid-levels—in political parties and/or in women's organizations. In sum, the lack of systematic evidence for any impacts of quotas on women's symbolic representation is not an argument for dismissing the idea that quotas could have impacts beyond the elite level; rather, it is an argument for paying closer attention to this issue, preferably by applying methodologically innovative research designs. Thereby, it is possible to scrutinize if quotas are able to impact not only the numerical representation of women, but also the broader society.

Conclusion

This chapter has examined the diffusion of quotas in Mexican states as well as their impacts. The analysis showed that quotas have diffused rapidly at subnational levels ever since the state of Chihuahua adopted the first quota policy in Mexico in 1994. Today, all states but two have some kind of gender quota policy. Although Chihuahua is the pioneer when it comes to quota policies in Mexico, a majority of the states adopted quotas after the revision of the federal quota law in 2002. Thus, the diffusion of quota policies has been directed at two levels: first a largely bottom-up process (from the sub-national level to the federal level) and later a top-down level (from the federal level to sub-national units). To understand the role of the federal quota law for the expansion of sub-national quotas, I have used the state of Zacatecas as an illustrative case. I argue that the federal quota law was influential in two specific ways; first, it provided quota advocates with a good argument as to why a state-level quota should be adopted. Thus, the adoption of a federal quota law created momentum for activists at sub-national levels. Second, the specific formulations in the federal quota law served as reference for quota advocates. In other words, the federal quota law provided women activists with an example of how a quota law should look like.

As to the impact of gender quotas at sub-national levels, the chapter has shown that there is a positive impact of quotas on women's descriptive (numerical) representation. However, some quota specifications seem to be more effective than others, generating relatively large leaps. As for substantive and symbolic representation, respectively, the lack of empirical analyses makes it difficult to draw any general conclusions. Hitherto, pioneer empirical work give little support to the idea that quotas in Mexico are beneficial not only for elite women, but for women in general and their beliefs about politics. However, initial empirical analyses on the institutional constraints for women elected via quotas suggest that this new group of legislators is not seen as inferior to others. Thus, there is a potential for women elected via quotas to be effective legislators and, if they choose to do so, to act for the benefit of women as a group.

To conclude, the adoption of quotas in Mexican states has been largely a positive process: within a fifteen years' time-span, twenty-nine of thirty-one states (as well as the Federal District) have introduced quotas; and these quotas were later improved to become increasingly effective. Quota policies have altered the rules of the game for candidate selection and provided women with increased possibilities to participate in public decision-making.

However, a final word of caution is necessary when referring to the substantive effect of quotas in reducing Mexico's gender gap. The repeated need to revise the quotas, and the loopholes that exist to circumscribe the provisions, reveal a problem with Mexican quota policies; that political parties are unwilling to implement them. The adoption of quotas may have increased women's likelihood to be elected to public office, but the quota policies have not eradicated the patriarchal structures within political parties, nor have they made the selection of female candidates a natural part of their work. In far too many cases, political parties have nominated a woman that shortly after the election resigned to leave her position to a man (see e.g. Salinas 2009). And too often political parties use public funds earmarked for women's capacity building to cover other expenses, rather than spending them on the designated purpose (see e.g. Román 2010). These actions contribute to limit the benefits—and perhaps also the legitimacy—of quota policies. Thus, a major challenge for advocates of women's political agency (especially advocates operating within the political parties) is to push for reforms that make the internal functioning of political parties more gender-equal and that circumscribe the power of a few (predominantly male) party bosses over candidate selection. Thereby, it is possible to strengthen women's positions within the parties as well as their power over the parties' political agenda. Moreover, such reforms may provide women new avenues to run for public office. Given the Mexican political parties' tradition to nominate women that they could control (see e.g. Baldez 2006), such a shift in power balance might be positive not only for women's numerical representation, but for women's overall situation in Mexican society. By democratizing political parties, female political actors are likely to have better opportunities to carry through policy reforms that increase gender equality and improve Mexican women's political agency and well-being.

Chapter Five

Participation of Women in the Elections of 2002, 2006 and 2010

The Quota Policy and the Brazilian Electoral System

Clara Araújo and José Eustáquio Diniz Alves[1]

In 2010, the Brazilian electorate consisted of approximately 135 million eligible voters of which seventy million were women and sixty-five million were men.[2] Together with the election of the President, there were also elections for governors of the twenty-six states of the Brazilian Federation plus the Federal District of Brasilia and fifty-seven senators, or the equivalent to two-thirds of the Upper House, 513 Federal Deputies and all State Deputies, or 1,036 regional representatives.[3] It can be stated, without fear of trepidation, that it is one of the most comprehensive and democratic electoral processes in the world.

In 2010, Brazil elected the first woman President and she does not conform to the traditional stereotype. Dilma Rousseff became a militant in left-wing organizations while studying economics at the Federal University of the state of Minas Gerais. Her resumé includes a history of political activism against the ruling military dictatorship, when she was a young woman, and subsequently the building of a career in administrative and political posts at municipal, state, and national levels. For six years during the two mandates of President Lula, she was the federal government's Chief of Staff, the principal vehicle for political dialogue and the policy-maker of main governmental programs.

Following the election of a woman in Brazil, Latin America became the region with the largest proportion of national level top leadership jobs in the hands of women. The region is also one where female presence in the Lower Houses has increased, as can be seen from the IPU ranking. At the present time Cuba, Argentina and Costa Rica are ranked at the top of the list. Quotas have been a big driving force in these rankings. In the 2010 presidential elections, two women—Dilma Rousseff of the Workers Party *(PT)* and Marina Silva of the Green Party *(PV)*—obtained a combined of almost two-thirds of the Brazilian electorate votes.

Despite these results in the latest presidential elections, Brazilian women have not had a great deal of success in overcoming the obstacles for a more egalitarian presence in politics. Women account for just 9.1 percent of mayors, 12.5 percent of councilors, 13.6 percent of state deputies and fifteen percent of senators. Among the existing areas of representation, the Federal Chamber of Deputies, with 8.8 percent of women, remains the area that is most difficult and/or resistant to female participation.

Indeed, notwithstanding the many advances highlighted above and the fact that today, women make up forty-three percent of the active workforce in the country; there is still a significant conservative streak with regard to the values of the Brazilian people. This dual perception, defined by the traditional role of men—the public person and the provider—and women—private and the *caregiver*—are still prevailing values in Brazil.[4] This conservative streak is not just related to traditional gender roles. Brazilians are still widely receptive to conservative moral and religious values, especially with regard to topics such as the decriminalization of abortion and same-sex marriage. These topics were included on the agenda for the televised debates held prior to the 2010 presidential election runoff. Critics focused on candidate Dilma Rousseff, who was associated with the legalization of abortion since she has, for some time, been supporting its decriminalization. Another focus of the campaign against presidential candidate Dilma Rousseff was the attempt to picture her as someone incapable of thinking for herself or acting on her own volition. At times authoritarian, at times inexperienced, her political biography and her declarations were always reinterpreted from a perspective of gender prejudice. This political culture is perhaps one of the factors that helps explain why women still experience so many difficulties when it comes to occupying positions of power in the country. However, this is not a characteristic peculiar to Brazil. It permeates a large part of the countries in Latin America and therefore only explains a small part of the process.

This chapter rehashes briefly the discussion about gender, representation and factors related to the electoral and party systems. It includes an in-depth analysis of the 2002, 2006 and 2010 general elections and employs a multivariate analysis that includes a combination of both institutional and socioeconomic factors. This research relies on data provided by the Supreme Electoral Court (TSE).

Institutional Dimensions of the Gender Gap

The outcome of the latest elections in Brazil, illustrates both the difficulty in overcoming the gender gap in politics and the weak implementation of quota policies in the country (Law 9504/1997). These policies, as elsewhere, constitute a mechanism that seeks to promote a more balanced representation between men and women at all levels of the legislative branch. In Brazil, however, there are constraints of differing magnitudes. Loopholes in legislation make it possible for the parties to create a reserve of at least thirty percent of the posts in candidate lists, but without the requirement to fill them, thus negating the obligation to select female candidacies. When it was created, the population of total candidacies from each party was also enlarged (rising from 100 to 150 percent of the vacant seats).

Given the abject results, the proposed new law approved in September 2009 (Law 12034) and valid for the 2010 elections, replaced the verb *to reserve* with the verb *to fill*. However, in the electoral process, the TSE resisted its enforcement, to make it mandatory to fill a minimum of thirty percent for either sex of the candidate lists, or to make it a condition that the parties could only run if these were fulfilled. The *TSE* allowed several parties to run without achieving the minimum quota. Moreover, it was unable to come to a decision in time when the appeals were lodged to correct this distortion. The number of women candidacies grew in 2010, in comparison with previous years, but the figure did not reach the minimum of thirty percent. At the same time, there was an increase in the percentage of *orange candidates* or formal candidacies without the knowledge or consent of the individuals concerned.

The issue of electoral quotas is just one aspect of the problem with the poor competitiveness of women in politics. There are countries that do not employ quotas and which, even with a similar cultural background, demonstrate rates of female participation in politics that are far more favorable than those seen in Brazil. We believe, therefore, that it is only possible to understand election outcomes and the quota experiment in Brazil from a multiple causal perspective, which has already been discussed by several authors involving other contexts (Norris 1993 and 1996, Htun 2002, Matland 2002). In short, socioeconomic and cultural aspects blend with aspects of institutional politics related to the system of political and electoral representation. It is under this prism that we shall discuss the following sub-sections.

The Electoral System and the Democratic Gender Gap: Factors for Consideration

Based on the referenced literature, we shall highlight below the aspects that we believe are most relevant in analyzing the Brazilian case.[5] These factors have been examined before, but this chapter will ascertain their significance for Brazil's 2002, 2006, and 2010 elections. We have made an assumption here of *multiple causality*: the interaction between different orders of factors that influences the current picture of the representation of women in politics.

The *type of electoral list* is a significant institutional variable. The basis of the Brazilian electoral system is open list PR, and this has been regarded as unfavorable to women since the individualized nature of the campaign increases the cost of elections, which mainly impacts female politicians. Successful examples of other quota experiments, such as in Argentina, Costa Rica and other countries in the region, serve to reinforce the proposal for switching to a closed list. However, this topic is very controversial in the political and academic arenas. Much of the link between closed lists and the success of women has been based on studies of countries that already have quotas. However, there is not even consensus in this case (Mateo 2002, Marx et al 2007, Htun and Jones 2002).

Another significant institutional mechanism discussed in the literature is the *size of constituencies*. Accordingly, there seems to be a significant link between large constituencies and greater chances for women to be elected. Large constituencies have a greater number of candidates, thus there is a tendency of proportionality, diversification of candidates, and inclusion of *outsiders*. However, in Brazil, the behavior of electoral constituencies is in direct contrast to what has been held dear, namely the positive relationship between larger constituencies and the greater electability of women.[6]

These results may be reinforced by the under-representation of the electorate in those states with higher populations and an over-representation of the smaller states.[7] For example, in 2000, the state of Roraima had a population of 324,397 which accounted for 0.2 percent of the Brazilian population. The state of São Paulo, with 37,032,403 inhabitants, represented 21.8 percent of the population of Brazil [Brazilian Institute of Geography and Statistics (IBGE), 2001]. However, Roraima had eight deputies, which represented 1.6 percent of the total number of 513 members of parliament in the Federal Chamber, while São Paulo had seventy deputies, representing a mere 13.6 percent of the total. This also defines something of a variation on the principle of "one man, one vote". There exists therefore a *positive discrimination* in regional terms in the Brazilian electoral system that favors the electorate in the small states to the detriment of the electorate in the larger—and more prosperous—states.[8]

In addition to the type of list and the size of the constituency, the *Party Size* is another variable considered to be important (Matland, 2002; and Schmidt, 2003; 2006).[9] In this case, knowing who the women candidates are and which parties they represent are important factors in determining their chances of being elected. In general, studies of this nature make comparisons between different countries. One way to evaluate if these factors are indeed important is to compare these variables between states in the federation.[10]

Dimensions internal to the party context may also play an important role in the electoral recruitment process and in whether women become electable candidates, especially their ideology and the party organization. Left-wing parties tend to encourage greater participation and enhance the chances of women being elected (Lovenduski 1993, Norris 1996, 2003, IPU 2000, Matland 2002, Katz and Mair 1992). The Brazilian model approximates to some of the trends identified in the literature; multi-party system, a reasonable number of small-to-medium sized parties and a certain tendency towards the greater absorption of women amongst small-to-medium sized parties and/or parties of the left.

Various authors also highlight factors such as *political culture* and certain *socioeconomic characteristics*, as being relevant (Norris and Inglehart, 2003; Diaz, 2002). Some of these socioeconomic features will be tested later. In Brazil, there are many differences in terms of the rates of female participation among states, even though they are all subject to the same national electoral legislation. On the other hand, the assumption that greater socioeconomic development would result in greater equality of political power is debatable.

Lastly, another aspect discussed in the literature, though still largely untested in statistical terms, is the relationship between *outsiders*—who are not yet deputies—and *insiders*—who are already in parliament, or the *influence of mandate on the chances of election*.[11] In a study on Costa Rica, Studlar and Shugart (2005) advanced the hypothesis that reelection could be decisive to the entry and to the broadening of political access for women. For his part, Chapman (1993) also analyzed this dimension as being relevant for the entry of women into politics, since it dealt with the usurping of individuals already *in situ*. In general, whoever is already firmly entrenched in these areas tends to have a certain political capital which is important in assuring permanence. Norris and Inglehart (2003) drew attention to the trend towards inertia in the process of recruitment and political access, a trend mediated by certain requisites that become guarantees of election. These requisites might occur as a consequence of the reproduction or a guarantee of the profile of a candidate who has already been submitted to the test of the ballot box and finds himself running. Thus, a variable for testing the chances of election, whether or not the candidate is running for *reelection* has been included in this analysis.

Therefore a number of hypotheses are examined in this chapter; 1) an increase in parliamentary participation by women in Brazil is not directly associated with the degree of socioeconomic development in the Regions and the States; 2) institutional variables linked to the electoral system influence and interfere with the chances of women achieving access to legislative positions; 3) political capital, in its diverse forms, is a decisive factor for being elected and, in turn, is more easily reproduced if the individual is already a member of parliament; 4) lastly, the outcome of the quota policy in Brazil needs to include a comprehensive understanding of the legislation and of its interaction with these other *multiple causal* factors, that have indirect impacts on quotas.

Table 5.1: Women Elected and the Percentage of Women Candidates and Women Elected Per State Chamber of Deputies—2002, 2006 and 2010

STATES (UF)	2002 ELECTIONS			2006 ELECTIONS			2010 ELECTIONS		
	% OF WOMEN CANDIDATES	NUMBER OF WOMEN ELECTED	% OF WOMEN ELECTED	% OF WOMEN CANDIDATES	NUMBER OF WOMEN ELECTED	% OF WOMEN ELECTED	% OF WOMEN CANDIDATES	NUMBER OF WOMEN ELECTED	% OF WOMEN ELECTED
AC	14.5	1	12.5	15.7	1	12.5	21.6	2	25.0
AL	14.7	0	0.0	11.8	0	0.0	18.5	2	22.2
AP	14.9	1	12.5	14.7	4	50.0	27.6	3	37.5
AM	7.3	1	12.5	12.7	2	25.0	23.6	1	12.5
BA	3.0	2	5.1	7.3	4	10.3	11.5	1	2.6
CE	13.9	0	0.0	8.2	1	4.6	20.7	1	4.5
DF	8.6	1	12.5	14.7	0	0.0	22.0	2	25.0
ES	13.0	2	20.0	20.2	4	40.0	16.7	4	40.0
GO	12.8	2	11.8	6.8	2	11.8	9.0	2	11.8
MA	11.5	2	11.1	11.4	1	5.6	12.5	1	5.6
MT	19.1	2	25.0	17.7	1	12.5	26.0	0	0.0
MS	21.8	0	0.0	21.6	0	0.0	32.9	0	0.0
MG	9.9	1	1.9	10.2	3	5.7	13.0	1	1.9
PA	13.8	1	5.9	15.1	2	11.8	17.6	1	5.9
PB	8.0	1	8.3	6.7	0	0.0	16.5	1	8.3
PR	7.6	1	3.3	9.8	0	0.0	21.1	2	6.7
PE	8.6	0	0.0	11.8	1	4.0	7.9	2	8.0
PI	10.2	1	10.0	4.8	0	0.0	24.7	1	10.0
RJ	13.6	6	13.0	13.6	6	13.0	25.0	4	8.7
RN	13.8	2	25.0	11.3	2	25.0	15.1	2	25.0
RS	10.5	4	12.9	11.4	3	9.7	23.3	1	3.2
RO	15.7	1	12.5	16.4	1	12.5	24.7	1	12.5
RR	13.9	2	25.0	15.7	2	25.0	24.2	2	25.0

Table 5.1 cont.

STATES (UF)	2002 ELECTIONS			2006 ELECTIONS			2010 ELECTIONS		
	% OF WOMEN CANDIDATES	NUMBER OF WOMEN ELECTED	% OF WOMEN ELECTED	% OF WOMEN CANDIDATES	NUMBER OF WOMEN ELECTED	% OF WOMEN ELECTED	% OF WOMEN CANDIDATES	NUMBER OF WOMEN ELECTED	% OF WOMEN ELECTED
SC	9.7	1	6.3	10.5	1	6.3	24.8	1	6.3
SP	9.9	6	8.6	14.4	3	4.3	19.5	6	8.6
SE	15.3	0	0.0	24.5	0	0.0	13.8	0	0.0
TO	22.6	1	12.5	22.2	1	12.5	25.0	1	12.5
Brazil	11.5	42	8.2	12.7	45	8.8	19.4	45	8.8

Source: Supreme Electoral Court, 2002, 2006 and 2010

Outcome of the Elections in the Federal Chamber—2002, 2006 and 2010

Having described the institutional factors that help explain the under-representation of women in politics, this sub-section interprets the results of the last three elections in Brazil's Federal Chamber of Deputies.

Table 5.1 shows the number of seats (column 2) that each state has the right to elect to the Chamber of Deputies, as well as the percentage of women candidates and women elected, by state, in the 2002, 2006 and 2010 elections. It should be noted that there is a significant variance in the size of the constituencies in Brazil—ranging from eight to seventy vacancies. Moreover, under the same affirmative action legislation, there are also large variations in each state between the various elections. The state of Amapá elected a woman in 2002, representing twelve percent of the vacancies; four women in 2006, representing fifty percent of vacant seats; and three women in 2010, representing 37.5 percent of the bloc of federal deputies in the state. In the state of São Paulo, the largest state in the federation, six women were elected in 2002 (8.6 percent of the total). This fell to three women in 2006, representing only 4.3 percent of the Sáo Paulo bloc in the Chamber of Deputies. In the 2010 elections, it went back to the previous level of six deputies elected, representing 8.6 percent of the total available seats. In general terms, larger states tend to present more modest results than smaller ones, with the exception of Rio de Janeiro. In addition, there are states with an identical number of seats where women are systematically elected; whereas other states elect none. This suggests that other factors connected with the local scenario and the political culture may be also influential.

Scholars and policy-makers claim that the quota system has not worked in Brazil due, partly, to a shortage of women candidates, but this is debatable. The existence of a larger *supply* of candidates in the electoral marketplace could theoretically enhance the possibility of women being elected. Although Brazil has an open list system, this is one of the grounds for employing quotas. There is, without doubt, a difference between the voter who has the chance to choose between two women or between ten women, even when one considers the size of the population, but the election of a greater number of women is in fact conditioned by a combination of factors, including the existence of more competitive female candidates. In other words, it is not simply a question of number. As can be seen from the table above, the total percentage of women candidates moved from a little over seven percent to nearly eleven percent during the first year of quotas—1998—and at the same time, the percentage of women elected fell. In 2006, women candidates represented 12.7 percent of the total and in 2010 this percentage rose to 19.4 percent. The percentage of elected women deputies, however, remained flat at 8.8 percent in the last two elections.

As discussed earlier in this chapter, it is evident that a relationship of cause and effect, between the number of women candidates and the number of women elected, cannot be expected. This leads us to play down our expectations of quotas. The quota policy, as it is formulated in Brazil, has not been effective in reversing the under-representation of women in Parliament. If this is the case, as we expect to be able to demonstrate, it may be necessary to include a broad interpretation of why women are under-represented, rather than relying on a narrow analysis. To make quotas more effective and beyond changing aspects of the current electoral system—such as the list system—it would be appropriate to analyze other factors that may have a positive impact on women's electability.

It is also important to identify the chances of women becoming political candidates as compared to men. In other words, it is a question of finding out to what degree, isolating these other factors and making observations purely on constituency size, or the degree of proportionality, the chances of women in comparison with the chances of men are mediated by the relationship between the universe of competitors and individuals elected. A number of descriptive analyses might enrich the hypotheses previously tested. We decided to analyze the relative impact of candidacies on the electability of women, from a descriptive and also comparative approach.

To this end, we employed the Relative Success Rate, a form of aggregation used in other studies, in which the period from 1994 to 2002 was analyzed and at the same time considering the *constituency size* factor.[12] A further aim was to evaluate if the Relative Success Rates tracked the variance observed for the types of electoral constituencies. The 1994 elections were the last to be held prior to the introduction of quotas. The advantage of this formula is that it permits (ignoring all other factors) the smoothing of the relationship between candidacies and election, between men and women.

In the table below the results are grouped according to constituency size.[13] In terms of the last five elections, the data show that, in proportional terms, women have better chances of being elected more often in smaller constituencies than in larger ones, as can be seen in table 5.2. Moreover, during the 1994 election, before quotas were implemented, more women were elected in all types of constituencies than in the other four elections that followed.

The data helps explain that: 1) women candidates were less successful than men in terms of electability (=100); 2) there is a certain relationship between the population of female candidates and the chances of success, but this relationship matters only up to a certain point and varies between types of constituencies; 3) women chances of being elected are greater in smaller constituencies, followed by large constituencies and finally medium-sized constituencies. In other words, in the case of Brazil, the thesis that women have better chances to be elected in larger constituencies due to an increase in proportionality does not hold true. The relationship is important up to a certain point, but it is not a direct relationship and is dependent on other variables.

However, another revealing factor is observing these constituencies in the light of their respective HDIs. In Brazil, the highest HDIs are also concentrated in larger constituencies. Similarly, this is where we find greater political organization and a larger number of parties. However it was especially in these constituencies where, systematically, a low level of performance was found with women candidates. An identical situation can be found in some of the medium-sized constituencies. Therefore, studies have concentrated on this institutional challenge. However, this does not necessarily mean that the smaller constituen-

Table 5.2: Relative Success Rate of Women Candidates for Federal Deputy 1994–2010

	1994	1998	2002	2006	2010
CONSTITUENCIES	SUCCESS RATE	SUCCESS RATE	SUCCESS RATE	SUCCESS RATE	SUCCESS RATE
Large	106.84	49.93	74.23	60.38	26.38
Medium	64.84	39.07	47.80	46.39	38.39
Small	117.41	68.05	86.41	98.29	69.80
Total	98.35	52.01	69.32	64.84	40.63

Source: Data of the Supreme Electoral Court 1994–2010

cies and constituencies with high percentages of candidacies will always return positive results.

By shifting the focus onto constituencies and observing the parties, the data of the three elections under study confirm what has been asserted by a majority of the literature. In ideological terms, and considering *in rough terms* the three large political blocks in Brazil, left-leaning parties tend to elect a larger percentage of women, as we can see from table 5.3.[14] In fact, the left systematically elects almost one half of women members of parliament. It can also be observed that the variance in the number of women elected in the last three campaigns was very small, both numerically and in terms of the distribution according to ideological groupings.

As part of the exploration of these interactions and with the focus still on the parties, we analyzed the 2010 results based on what we define as the Relative Success Rate to ascertain the relationship between their potential to attract women as candidates and to elect them.[15]

We sought to observe the behavior of these parties in relation to the proportion of candidacies and women elected. At the same time, we attempted to observe how these parties were positioned in the ideological spectrum noted above. Here, we have considered both the relationship with the ideological profile and studies that propose that the size of the party in which women stand could be a variable that is decisive to their chances. The Rate simply describes the success of women standing for elections relative to that of men within a particular party; it does not define the causes of this success. From the start, it should be noted that: a) not all of the parties presenting candidates, elected deputies;[16] b) among those that did not elect deputies, the percentages of women among their candidates varied greatly; c) of the twenty-one represented in the Chamber, thirteen parties elected women.

Table 5.3: Ideological Profile of the Parties that Elected Women Federal Chamber 2002–2010

	WOMEN ELECTED IN 2002		WOMEN ELECTED IN 2006		WOMEN ELECTED IN 2010	
IDEOLOGICAL PROFILE	NUMBER	%	NUMBER	%	NUMBER	%
Left	21	50.0	22	49.0	22	48.9
Center	13	31.0	13	29.0	13	28.9
Right	8	19.0	10	20.0	10	20.0
Total	42	100.0	45	100.0	45	100.0

Source: Supreme Electoral Court 2002–2010

Table 5.4, below shows that the highest Success Rates occurred among the small or very small parties and it confirms the two aspects highlighted by dominant literature: smaller parties and/or parties of the left tend to embrace women as candidates more often. Moreover they were parties with high rates of elected deputies. Their blocs, however, are very small and the number of women elected also tends to be small. The Brazilian Communist Party (*PCdoB*) is the only party on the left to be within the three that have positive rates. It is a small party, but more women were proportionately elected.

A look at the distribution of elected women by *party* and by *state* allows us to claim that: a) the parties of the left have a more scattered distribution in the states,

Table 5.4: Relative Success Rate of Parties that Elected Women Deputies to the Federal Chamber (2010)

PARTY	IDEOLOGICAL PROFILE	SUCCESS RATE	ABSOLUTE NO. OF WOMEN ELECTED	WOMEN ELECTED AS % OF TOTAL ELECTED IN PARTY	WOMEN CANDIDATES AS % OF TOTAL IN THE PARTY	% RANKING WOMEN CANDIDATES AMONGST THE PARTIES	% RANKING WOMEN ELECTED AMONGST THE PARTIES
PT do B (T)*	Right	250.0	1	33.33	16.67	22nd	12th
PC do B (S)	Left	195.6	6	40.00	25.42	2nd	3rd
PMN(T)	Right	100.7	1	25.00	24.88	3rd	11th
PSC (S)	Right	64.6	2	11.76	17.10	18th	10th
PSB (M)	Left	49.2	4	11.76	21.31	7th	5th
PP (M)	Right	49.1	4	9.76	18.04	16th	4th
PMDB (L)	Center	48.4	7	8.97	16.91	19th	2nd
PT (L)	Left	42.2	9	10.23	21.26	8th	1st
DEM (M)	Right	39.5	2	4.65	10.99	26th	7th
PDT (M)	Left	37.9	2	7.14	16.86	20th	8th
PV (S)	Left	28.8	1	6.67	19.89	14th	14th
PSDB (L)	Center	23.3	3	5.56	20.15	12th	6th
PR (M)	Center	19.6	2	4.88	20.73	9th	9th
PTB (M)	Center	16.6	1	4.76	23.16	4th	13th

Source: Supreme Electoral Court—Accessed on November 12, 2010. *T= "tiny" or very small parties, with less than 10 candidates elected. S = Small, between 10 and 20 candidates elected; M= Medium, between 21 and 50 candidates elected; and L = Large, more than 50 candidates elected.

while among the parties of the Center and the Right, the distribution is more concentrated; b) the electoral map of where women are elected also accompanies the logic of alliances in the states and the strength of the parties in these disputes and in the states.

However, inasmuch as the Relative Rate permits a more comparative view, it should be emphasized that forty-two percent of women elected in 2010 belong to the three big parties.[17] In 2006, when there was less fragmentation, four of the then considered large parties and fifty percent of the women elected in 2006 belonged to these four big parties. Besides the three named above, the DEM was considered a large party and the largest of right-leaning ones.[18] In this election, for the first time since it was formed, the DEM was relegated to the population of parties defined as medium-sized. With forty-three candidates elected, it is the largest in this category. The data suggest therefore that, in addition to the factors already discussed, other factors related to party fragmentation and size of the party also play an important role in this analysis.

Multivariate Analysis

To interpret the 2002, 2006 and 2010 elections of federal deputies, we sought to incorporate the variables evaluated by prevalent literature and observed the significance and interactions between these factors. The multivariate statistical employed in this study was prepared using the variables available in the *TSE* database. For the assessment of the level of development of the State, a number of variables were tested, such as the degree of urbanization, population density and the Human Development Index (HDI), provided by the Atlas of Human Development in Brazil (UNDP 2004).

The choice of the logistical regression model is down to the binary nature of the response variable, in other words, the chance of any one candidate (either male or female) to be elected. The model employs two types of covariables: a) those based on the *personal attributes* of the candidates: sex, education, age, marital status, party for which he/she is running and reelection, and b) those characteristics peculiar to the state in which the dispute is taking place, including: socioeconomic aspects and variables associated with the electoral system—degree of urbanization, population density and the Human Development Index (HDI); and those associated with the electoral system, including: the size of the "constituency" (number of vacant seats for federal deputies that each state possesses); and the size of the parties (number of candidates that one party elects in relation to the total number of seats available in the State). The variable *percentage of women candidates* in each state was tested, but was not statistically significant.

We have included the variables that are both available and deemed to be relevant according to the literature. Marital status has been a systematically, distinct profile for each sex and it tells us a lot about how gender permeates the building of careers and trajectories according to sex. The age grouping illustrates a little about the paths to building a career; the level of schooling has acted as a filter in the majority of countries. In the area of institutional variables associated with the electoral and party systems, our intention was to measure them in comparison with other variables, following the multidimensional perspective already discussed. We decided to keep the DEM as one of the big parties so that we could make comparisons with 2002 and 2006. Therefore four of the parties were regarded as big.

Four models were tested for both elections: two for either sex (men and women). One (table 5.5) without the variable of *reelection* and another (table 5.6) including the variable *reelection*. A third model (table 5.7) includes only men and a fourth (table 5.8) with only women. Table 5.5 shows the results of the variables that were statistically significant (to a level of 97 percent) in the first model, for the elections of 2002, 2006 and 2010: sex, education, age, marital status, parties, *constituency size*, population density and the HDI. Assuming the chance of a man being elected to be equal to 1, women had a lower chance, i.e. 0.67, in the elections of 2002 and 2006. In 2010, the chance of a woman being elected dropped to 0.45.

A higher level of school achievement increases the chances of being elected, irrespective of sex. The probability of victory is even greater for those candidates with a degree. In comparison with those educated at lower levels, the more highly educated had three times more chance (3.11) of election in 2002, over four times more chance (4.37) in 2006 and one and a half times more chance (1.59) in 2010. In 2010, the best chances of victory fell to candidacies with "degree course incomplete and High School completed" (4.37 times). In a recent study, Schutz *et al* (2006) conducted a survey and comparison of the level of education of female Argentinean and Brazilian deputies and found that a university education predominated in both scenarios. However, the proportion of Brazilian women in the legislature in 2002 with a university degree and/or post-graduation was as high as seventy-three percent and was greater than that of Argentineans. This is relevant because the average level of schooling for Argentine people is higher than for Brazilians. In other words, there is a greater correlation between the level of schooling and members of parliament in Brazil than in Argentina.

In the case of Brazil, where only 6.9 percent of the population over twenty-five years of age has a university degree, according to the demographic census of 2000 (*IBGE*, 2002), the population of potential competitors for the role of federal deputy is very limited. In this regard it is noteworthy that in 2006, 52.85 percent of candidates for the position of Federal Deputies in Brazil, stated that they were college educated, but of those elected, the percentages rose to 80.5 percent. In other words,

Table 5.5: Likelihood for a Federal Deputy to be Elected (Logistical Model for Both Sexes). Brazil, 2002, 2006 and 2010

	CO-EFFICIENTS	PR > CHISQ	RATIO OF PROB.	CO-EFFICIENTS	PR > CHISQ	RATIO OF PROB.	CO-EFFICIENTS	PR > CHISQ	RATIO OF PROB.
VARIABLES	2002			2006			2010		
SEX									
Male			1			1			1
Female	-0.4	0.0264	0.67	-0.41	0.0175	0.67	-0.80	<.0001	0.45
EDUCATION									
High school incomplete or lower			1			1			1
Degree course incomplete or High School completed	0.69	0.0005	1.99	0.61	0.0051	1.84	1.47	<.0001	4.37
Bachelor's Degree	1.13	<.0001	3.11	1.48	<.0001	4.37	0.46	0.053	1.59
AGE									
Under 35			1			1			1.00
35 +	0.59	0.0026	1.81	0.12	0.4955	1.13	0.18	0.2959	1.20
MARITAL SITUATION									
Unmarried			1			1			1
Married	0.32	0.0048	1.38	0.34	0.0027	1.4	0.57	<.0001	1.77
PARTIES									
Other Parties			1			1			1
PFL/DEM	1.94	<.0001	6.95	1.66	<.0001	5.26	1.22	<.0001	3.40
PMDB	1.37	<.0001	3.94	1.61	<.0001	5.03	1.25	<.0001	3.49
PSDB	1.44	<.0001	4.2	1.24	<.0001	3.47	1.03	<.0001	2.81
PT	1.3	<.0001	3.69	1.49	<.0001	4.44	1.46	<.0001	4.32
"CONSTITUENCY" SIZE									
Small (8 to 10 seats)			1			1			1
Medium (11 to 30 seats)	0.55	0.0002	1.4	0.2	0.1532	1.22	-0.08	0.5911	0,93
Large (31 +)	0.33	0.0162	1.73	0.27	0.059	1.32	0.06	0.6923	1,06

Table 5.5 cont.

VARIABLES	CO-EFFICIENTS	PR > CHISQ	RATIO OF PROB.	CO-EFFICIENTS	PR > CHISQ	RATIO OF PROB.	CO-EFFICIENTS	PR > CHISQ	RATIO OF PROB.
	2002			2006			2010		
POPULATION DENSITY OF STATE	0	0.0253	0.99	0	0.0647	1	0.00	0.0291	1,00
HDI OF THE STATE	-2.66	0.0152	0.07	-3.96	0.0002	0.02	-2.70	0.0094	0,07
INTERCEPT	-2.32	0.0042		-1.14	0.1449		-1.91	0.0169	
-2 Log L	2,691.57			2,790.77			2,868.22		
-2 Log L- null model	3,143.07			3,295.83			3,338.30		
N	4,298			4,946			5,144		
ANALYSIS OF EFFECTS - TYPE 3 Effects	DEGREE OF FREEDOM	WALD CHI-SQUARE	PR > CHISQ	DEGREE OF FREEDOM	WALD CHI-SQUARE	PR > CHISQ	DEGREE OF FREEDOM	WALD CHI-SQUARE	PR > CHISQ
Sex	1	4.93	0.0264	1	5.64	0.0175	1	22.22	<.0001
Education	2	75.93	<.0001	2	115.87	<.0001	2	98.35	<.0001
Age	1	9.07	0.0026	1	0.46	0.4955	1	1.09	0.2959
Marital status	1	7.94	0.0048	1	8.99	0.0027	1	25.39	<.0001
Parties	4	222.31	<.0001	4	226.48	<.0001	4	165.21	<.0001
"Constituency" size	2	14.05	0.0009	2	3.78	0.1508	2	0.99	0.6088
Population Density of state	1	5	0.0253	1	3.41	0.0647	1	4.76	0.0291
HDI of state	1	5.9	0.0152	1	13.61	0.0002	1	6.74	0.0094

Source: Supreme Electoral Court, 2002, 2006 and 2010

the route that leads to candidacy and then election shows that access to political posts of high-ranking is quite limited in Brazil.

Regarding age, candidates older than thirty-five have the greatest chances of being elected (1.81, 1.13 and 1.20 in the three elections, respectively). As previously discussed, this may be explained by the need to build a political career that requires a certain trajectory or accumulation of political capital and resources. Excepted from this age factor are "famous" people, and those who have inherited family capital and, consequently, do not need to take the long route, which is not uncommon in Brazilian politics. Age has a big influence on the rate of probability according to marital status, since married candidates had a 1.38 times greater rate of probability in 2002, 1.4 in 2006 and 1.77 in 2010, than those who were unmarried (single, separated, widows/widowers etc.). In the oldest age brackets, it tends to be more common for people to be married (bear in mind that the data indicate marital status and not the actual conjugal situation). Moreover, the force of cultural traditionalism favors candidacies which fit the mold of heterosexual and monogamous family life.

In terms of institutional factors, the variable *party* has a statistical significant weight in this model, as the parties achieving the most significant results were the four big parties. In other words, they were precisely those that elected the largest blocs in the Chamber of Deputies, particularly in 2002 and 2006, but also in 2010. Taking all the other parties as a benchmark, *PFL/DEM*, *PSDB*, *PMDB* and *PT* presented higher rates of probability of electing both men and women. Note that the chances of *PMDB* and *PT* candidates being elected increased in 2006 in comparison with the prior election, but fell in 2010, due to greater party fragmentation. Also note that the variance in probability reflects the alignments and the weight of the parties in the majority elections. As can be seen, in 2010 the *PT* , followed by the *PMDB* and coalition parties and those that won in the election for President, were also the ones where women had the best chances.

Regarding *constituency size*, Table 5.5 shows that when both men and women are considered in the model, the largest states have the highest rates of probability, in 2002 and 2006, but had no influence in 2010. The variable *Population Density* did not have an influence on the outcome, although it is statistically significant in the model. Once all of these variables are in check, the HDI produced a negative coefficient and a rate of probability of 0.07 in 2002, 0.02 in 2006 and 0.07 in 2010, showing that the probability of a candidate being elected diminishes as the state's HDI increases. The Wald test shows that the variables *Party* and *Education* are those that best explain the variation in data.[19] Therefore, they have a greater effect on the chances of victory of men and women, not only in 2002, but also in 2006 and 2010.

By adding the covariable *Reelection* to the previous model, the results change significantly, as is verified in table 5.6. The variables *sociodemographics*, *population density* and *HDI* lose their statistical weight, particularly for 2002. In this fresh adjustment to the model for 2002, 2006 and 2010, the only statistically significant variables were *Education, Party Size* and *Reelection* (at a level of ninety-seven percent), with *reelection* being the variable that takes on the greatest statistical weight (see Wald test value). The significance of *reelection* in 2010 was even more decisive. In 2002, a deputy seeking reelection had a 25.57 times greater chance of being elected. In 2006, this dropped to 16.2 times, indicating greater rejuvenation. In 2010,

Table 5.6: Likelihood for a Federal Deputy to be Elected According to a Number of Selected Covariables, Including Reelection (Logistical Analysis—Both Sexes). Brazil, 2002, 2006 and 2010

	CO-EFFICIENTS	PR > CHISQ	RATIO OF PROB.	CO-EFFICIENTS	PR > CHISQ	RATIO OF PROB.	CO-EFFICIENTS	PR > CHISQ	RATIO OF PROB.
VARIABLES	2002			2006			2010		
SEX									
Male			1			1			1
Female	-0.19	0.3855	0.83	-0.23	0.2188	0.79	-0.60	0.0017	0.549
EDUCATION									
High school incomplete or lower			1			1			1
Degree course incomplete or High School completed	0.5	0.034	1.66	0.42	0.0745	1.53	1.00	<.0001	2.717
Bachelor's Degree	0.81	<.0001	2.26	1.21	<.0001	3.36	0.29	0.275	1.335
AGE									
Under 35			1			1			1
35 +	0.02	0.091	1.03	-0.28	0.1471	0.76	-0.25	0.1987	0.782
MARITAL SITUATION									
Unmarried			1			1			1
Married	0.28	0.0456	1.32	0.11	0.3712	1.12	0.58	<.0001	1.785
PARTIES									
Other Parties			1			1			1
PFL/DEM	1.04	<.0001	2.84	1.44	<.0001	4.24	0.74	0.0032	2.092
PMDB	0.59	0.0042	1.81	1.35	<.0001	3.85	0.80	<.0001	2.229
PSDB	0.62	0.0033	1.87	1.18	<.0001	3.26	0.62	0.0041	1.861
PT	1.38	<.0001	3.97	1.12	<.0001	3.07	1.22	<.0001	3.376
"CONSTITUENCY" SIZE									
Small (8 to 10 seats)			1			1			1
Medium (11 to 30 seats)	0.19	0.261	1.21	0.01	0.9307	1.01	-0.29	0.0938	0.751

Table 5.6 cont.

	CO-EFFICIENTS	PR > CHISQ	RATIO OF PROB.	CO-EFFICIENTS	PR > CHISQ	RATIO OF PROB.	CO-EFFICIENTS	PR > CHISQ	RATIO OF PROB.
VARIABLES	2002			2006			2010		
Large (31 +)	0.14	0.4257	1.15	0.08	0.6046	1.09	-0.07	0.6563	0.928
POPULATION DENSITY OF STATE	0	0.0388	0.99	0	0.3935	1	0.00	0.6027	1
HDI OF THE STATE	-0.07	0.9614	0.94	-3.1	0.0116	0.05	-2.44	0.0545	0.087
INTERCEPT	-3.89	0.0001		-1.54	0.0868		-1.92	0.0467	
-2 Log L	1892.44			2275.73			2138.78		
-2 Log L- null model	2915.57			3295.83			3338.30		
N	3.864			4.946			5.144		
ANALYSIS OF EFFECTS - TYPE 3 Effects	DEGREE OF FREEDOM	WALD CHI-SQUARE	PR > CHISQ	DEGREE OF FREEDOM	WALD CHI-SQUARE	PR > CHISQ	DEGREE OF FREEDOM	WALD CHI-SQUARE	PR > CHISQ
Sex	1	0.75	0.3855	1	1.51	0.2188	1	9.84	0.0017
Education	2	27.51	<.0001	2	68.8	<.0001	2	35.45	<.0001
Age	1	0.01	0.91	1	2.1	0.1471	1	1.65	0.1987
Marital status	1	4	0.0456	1	0.8	0.3712	1	18.59	<.0001
Parties	4	76.37	<.0001	4	124.71	<.0001	4	60.22	<.0001
"Constituency" size	2	1.32	0.5158	2	0.32	0.8534	2	3.09	0.2132
Population Density of state	1	4.27	0.0388	1	0.73	0.3935	1	0.27	0.6027
HDI of state	1	0	0.9614	1	6.37	0.0116	1	3.70	0.0545
Candidates for reelection	1	544.63	<.0001	1	501.04	<.0001	1	644.68	<.0001

Source: Supreme Electoral Court, 2002, 2006 and 2010

the chances doubled—32.13 times—in relation to 2006. In other words, one-third of the election results tend to be explained by this variable.

The significance of *reelection* suggests a scenario of electoral inertia, that is to say, those deputies that make up the legislative body have greater chances of continuing in parliament. Clearly, reelection benefits men as they are the majority in the Chamber of Deputies and is disadvantageous to women who are seeking to change the status quo in the Legislative Branch. It suggests moreover three other aspects to be investigated further: the importance of a mandate as the *window shop* for consolidating electoral capital through parliamentary involvement; the possibility that the mandate will also serve for indirect forms of accumulation of non-financial resources, such as infrastructure for contact with the electorate, for the construction of channels of communication via the media, among others; and a growing difficulty for *outsiders* or those with little or no resources.[20]

Indeed the data show that, among the various factors causing female underrepresentation in politics, the significance of *reelection* works unfavorably for whoever wishes to join the elite. The high percentage of reelected candidates tends to maintain the current gender composition and makes it difficult for new candidates to gain seats in Parliament.[21] Reelection seems to be a trend that has become more significant in recent elections. Accordingly, it is possible to state that women, despite their increasing political involvement, are coming up against more adverse scenarios, although other factors may carry more weight for potential elections in the future.[22]

Tables 5.7 and 5.8 show the results of the adjusted models, separately for men and for women. In the case of men, as in the previous model, only the variables *Education, Party* and *Reelection* are statistically significant (at a level of 99 percent). For women, only *Reelection* was statistically significant (at a level of 99 percent). The increased significance of this variable was, in turn, far greater for women than for men. However, there are several important differences when comparing men and women candidates and their chances of being elected. As we already stated, age is also related to the different paths taken by men and women in the public arena and their responsibilities in the domestic area. Ignoring the variable *reelection,* it is possible to claim that, whereas for men the chances of being elected are slightly higher until thirty-five years of age, in the case of women the chances increased after thirty-five. This probably reveals a later entry into politics for women, possible career interruptions due to having small children or other family obligations and the need to accumulate greater political capital than men. So, only four members of parliament elected to the Chamber of Deputies were under thirty years of age while eighty one percent were between thirty-one and sixty years of age. By observing the distribution of the percentages of candidacies for federal deputies, according to sex and age range, we can confirm what this and other studies had already identified and suggested: women take longer than men to begin or build a political career, as among women, fifty-two percent were in the forty-five to fifty-nine age range, while the equivalent percentage for men was forty-eight percent.

One interesting new fact is that 1.8 percent of women candidates were in the eighteen to twenty-four age groups, versus 0.9 percent for men. This suggests that among

Table 5.7: Likelihood of Federal Deputies to be Elected According to A Number of Selected Covariables (Logistical Model, Only for Males). Brazil, 2002, 2006 and 2010

	CO-EFFICIENTS	PR > CHISQ	RATIO OF PROB.	CO-EFFICIENTS	PR > CHISQ	RATIO OF PROB.	CO-EFFICIENTS	PR > CHISQ	RATIO OF PROB.
VARIABLES	2002			2006			2010		
EDUCATION									
High school incomplete or lower			1			1			1
Degree course incomplete or High School completed	0.43	0.0869	1.54	0.3	0.2481	1.35	1.00	0.0001	2.71
Bachelor's Degree	0.83	<.0001	2.3	1.24	<.0001	3.45	0.36	0.1977	1.43
AGE									
Under 35			1			1			1
35 +	0.09	0.6808	0.91	-0.22	<.0001	0.8	-0.41	0.0401	0.66
MARITAL STATUS									
Unmarried			1			1			1
Married	0.24	0.1004	1.28	0.09	0.4838	1.1	0.65	<.0001	1.92
PARTIES									
Other Parties			1			1			1
PFL/DEM	0.99	<.0001	2.7	1.46	<.0001	4.29	0.75	0.0036	2.12
PMDB	0.65	0.0029	1.91	1.33	<.0001	3.76	0.80	<.0001	2.22
PSDB	0.56	0.0125	1.75	1.28	<.0001	3.61	0.65	0.0039	1.92
PT	1.32	<.0001	3.75	1.24	<.0001	3.46	1.26	<.0001	3.51
"CONSTITUENCY" SIZE									
Small (8 to 10 seats)			1			1			1
Medium (11 to 30 seats)	0.24	0.1827	1.27	0.1	0.5686	1.1	0.00	0.2507	1.0
Large (31 +)	0.17	0.3731	1.19	0.1	0.5881	1.1	-2.75	0.0721	0.06
POPULATION DENSITY OF STATE	0	0.0374	1	0	0.5057	1	-0.08	0.7333	0.93

Table 5.7 cont.

VARIABLES	CO-EFFICIENTS (2002)	PR > CHISQ (2002)	RATIO OF PROB. (2002)	CO-EFFICIENTS (2006)	PR > CHISQ (2006)	RATIO OF PROB. (2006)	CO-EFFICIENTS (2010)	PR > CHISQ (2010)	RATIO OF PROB. (2010)
HDI OF THE STATE	0.16	0.9131	1.17	-2.65	0.0398	0.07	0.03	0.8668	1.04
CANDIDATES FOR REELECTION	3.29	<.0001	26.93	2.8	<.0001	16.43	3.42	<.0001	30.51
INTERCEPT	-3.93	0.0002		-1.99	0.0349		-1.89	0.0685	
-2 Log L	1.698.56			2013.83			1894.9		
-2 Log L- null model	2.651.55			2963.43			2926.8		
N	3.432			4.319			4.145		
ANALYSIS OF EFFECTS - TYPE 3 Effects	DEGREE OF FREEDOM	WALD CHI-SQUARE	PR > CHISQ	DEGREE OF FREEDOM	WALD CHI-SQUARE	PR > CHISQ	DEGREE OF FREEDOM	WALD CHI-SQUARE	PR > CHISQ
Education	2	26.67	<.0001	2	67.28	<.0001	2	27.90	<.0001
Age	1	0.17	0.6808	1	1.13	0.2877	1	4.22	0.0401
Marital status	1	2.7	0.1004	1	0.49	0.4838	1	20.26	<.0001
Parties	4	62.07	<.0001	4	119.52	<.0001	4	56.35	<.0001
"Constituency" size	2	1.82	0.4033	2	0.4	0.8191	1	1.32	0.2507
Population Density of state	1	4.33	0.0374	1	0.44	0.5057	1	3.23	0.0721
HDI of state	1	0.01	0.9131	1	4.23	0.0398	2	0.41	0.8137
Candidates for reelection	1	507.95	<.0001	1	460.22	<.0001	1	563.60	<.0001

Source: Supreme Electoral Court, 2002, 2006 and 2010

younger candidates, women may be more inclined to begin a political career. Once again, the difference in the variable *marriage* also tends to be explained by the profile and universe of those entering, although when we look at the attributes of those elected, we see that there are far more women who are single, separated or divorced than their male counterparts. Even the variable *education* shows a slight difference, suggesting that it is still more important for women to hold a degree than it is for men.

Table 5.8: Likelihood for Federal Deputies to be Elected According to a Number of Selected Covariables (Logistical Model, Female Only). Brazil, 2002, 2006 and 2010

	CO-EFFICIENTS	PR > CHISQ	RATIO OF PROB.	CO-EFFICIENTS	PR > CHISQ	RATIO OF PROB.	CO-EFFICIENTS	PR > CHISQ	RATIO OF PROB.
VARIABLES	2002			2006			2010		
EDUCATION									
High school incom-plete or lower			1			1			1
Degree course in-complete or High School completed	0.43	0.4326	1.53	0.99	0.1221	2.68	0.67	0.3825	1.96
Bachelor's Degree	1.06	0.1575	2.89	0.95	0.0634	2.59	-0.66	0.4503	1.52
AGE									
Under 35			1			1			1
35 +	1.48	0.166	4.39	-0.38	0.4791	0.68	1.03	0.1791	2.79
MARITAL STATUS									
Unmarried			1			1			1
Married	0.48	0.2458	1.62	0.12	0.7341	1.13	0.00	0.9933	1.00
PARTIES									
Other Parties			1			1			1
PFL/DEM	1.72	0.0264	5.6	1.56	0.0155	1.35	0.20	0.8472	1.23
PMDB	0.04	0.9572	1.04	1.51	0.0045	4.54	0.53	0.402	1.70
PSDB	1.27	0.0602	3.55	0.23	0.7323	1.26	0.21	0.7952	1.23
PT	1.92	0.0002	6.83	0.3	0.6152	4.76	0.83	0.1384	2.29
"CONSTITUENCY" SIZE									
Small (8 to 10 seats)			1			1			1
Medium (11 to 30 seats)	-0.33	0.5554	0.72	-0.76	0.1426	0.91	-1.53	0.0042	0.22
Large (31 +)	-0.25	0.6443	0.78	0.27	0.5724	0.47	-0.05	0.9234	0.95
POPULATION DEN-SITY OF STATE	0	0.9252	1	0	0.4542	1	0.00	0.0829	1.00

Table 5.8 cont.

	CO-EFFICIENTS	PR > CHISQ	RATIO OF PROB.	CO-EFFICIENTS	PR > CHISQ	RATIO OF PROB.	CO-EFFICIENTS	PR > CHISQ	RATIO OF PROB.
VARIABLES	2002			2006			2010		
HDI OF THE STATE	-0.49	0.9189	0.62	-7.46	0.0756	0.01	-4.31	0.2861	0.01
CANDIDATES FOR REELECTION	2.82	<.0001	16.75	2.91	<.0001	18.42	4.38	<.0001	79.55
INTERCEPT	-4.98	0.1733		2.08	0.4883		-1.5027	0.6333	
-2 Log L	183.08			247.14			223.58		
-2 Log L- null model	257.3			323.78			360.82		
N	432			627			999		
ANALYSIS OF EFFECTS - TYPE 3 Effects	DEGREE OF FREEDOM	WALD CHI-SQUARE	PR > CHISQ	DEGREE OF FREEDOM	WALD CHI-SQUARE	PR > CHISQ	DEGREE OF FREEDOM	WALD CHI-SQUARE	PR > CHISQ
Education	2	2	0.3681	2	3.74	0.1538	2	7.34	0.0254
Age	1	1.92	0.166	1	0.5	0.4791	1	1.81	0.1791
Marital status	1	1.35	0.2458	1	0.12	0.7341	1	0.00	0.9933
Parties	4	16.96	0.002	4	12.08	0.0168	4	2.52	0.6415
"Constituency" size	2	0.44	0.8045	2	3.28	0.1936	2	8.65	0.0133
Population Density of state	1	0.01	0.9252	1	0.56	0.4542	1	3.01	0.0829
HDI of state	1	0.01	0.9189	1	3.16	0.0756	1	1.14	0.2861
Candidates for reelection	1	32.07	<.0001	1	38.21	<.0001	1	72.81	<.0001

Source: Supreme Electoral Court, 2002, 2006 and 2010

Finally, the chances of women being elected in states with lower HDIs tend to be higher. In other words, the correlation that is very much evident in the literature between greater socioeconomic development and greater equality, in the case of legislative politics does not hold ground. In this case, we believe that possible explanations would lie in the interaction between electoral and party systems. Smaller states with lower HDIs also tend to rely on a cruder, associative and political participation, with a greater role of the oligarchies and the more limited and well-defined electoral markets. Rather than based on gender, competition is sustained by traditional capital—family or economic—for electoral success.

If we now consider the so called *institutional variables* for a disaggregated analysis by sex, the previously discussed multiple cause perspective has a tendency to become more conspicuous. At the same time, not all the data confirm the trends discussed by the literature. In the case of the variable *constituency size*, Brazil's results point in the opposite direction. The data in table 5.7 also show that, in the case of the adjustment of the model just for the female candidacies, the size of the *constituency* works in the opposite direction to what happens with male candidacies. In other words, women have a better chance of being elected in smaller states, while men have better chances in medium-sized constituencies, followed by large constituencies (which also concentrate the majority of the states with the highest HDI rates), and fewer chances in small constituencies.

On the other hand, *party size* was relevant both before and after including the variable *reelection*, thereby corroborating an inverse direction to that usually enshrined in the literature (Matland 2002, Schmidt 2003, Araújo 2009). If we just look at women, we can see that the four big parties continue to exert greater weight in elections, i.e. the size and/or profile of the parties for which the women are standing is not immaterial. This impacts their chances of being elected, as indeed it does in the race to win a vacancy in the more competitive parties. In 2002, the likelihood of women being elected are far greater in the big four parties compared to the others. At the same time, when we look at the chances between these big four parties, we see that female candidates of the *PT* have a better chance: 6.83 times in 2002, 4.76 times in 2006 and 2.29 times in 2010. This confirms one of the factors discussed and already noted by the literature, namely that women tend to have a better chance in the parties of the left. Once again it should be remembered that this variable is also conditional upon other variables and that the very weight of the party tends to be important in determining these chances. The higher level of party fragmentation in 2010 increased the chances of women being elected for other parties.

When we introduce reelection, this becomes the most important variable, but the rate of probability of success for candidacies to reelection is higher for men—26.93 times in 2002, 16.43 in 2006 and 30.51 in 2010—than for women—16.65 times in 2002, 18.42 in 2006 and 79.55 in 2010. In the elections of 2002 and 2006, those women who were elected to the Chamber of Deputies, had fewer chances of being re-elected. However, in 2010, women had better chances of reelection than men, probably due to a greater number of women candidates. In other words, as the percentage of women candidates increases—with a heavy reliance on orange candidatures—the chances of reelection also increase.

Conclusions

Brazilian women have made great social progress in recent decades. They make up the majority of the population, the female electorate has surpassed the male electorate by five million people, eclipsed males at all levels of education (including doctorates), have a higher life expectancy, represent the majority of the economically active population (EAP) and have an average of over eleven years of formal education (Alves and Correa, 2009). Moreover, for the first time, a woman has been elected president. However, Brazilian women continue to be underrepresented in the legislature and, specifically, in the Federal Chamber. The introduction of the quota policy in 1995 (Law 9100) and its reshaping in 1997 (Law 9504) and 2009 (Law 12034) was not enough to improve the representation of political women.

The rate of rejuvenation of members of parliament has been steadily falling. This demonstrates reluctance to change at the Federal Chamber. Employing a multivariate analysis, it was possible to demonstrate in this study that the main variable explaining the electoral victory of a candidate in the 2002, 2006 and 2010 elections was *reelection*. This signifies the predominance of an entry dynamic with little rotation and defined by requisites that are difficult to be gained by *outsiders*. For example, a member of parliament has a public infrastructure in support of political action that is far greater than the majority of other individuals who enjoy some kind of political participation. Men have an advantage that has been in existence since the very creation of parliament. It is difficult for women to break this hegemony. Add to this all the other factors of gender injustice which have been already widely discussed.[23] Moreover, the quota policy has loopholes that make it unable to disrupt traditional male domination in terms of numbers and economic power of the candidates. This brings us to the need to understand *if and how* these trajectories have been modified at the party level; ranging from the age at which men and women have been joining parties, the time spent waiting from the moment of affiliation to their entry into the world of competition, as well as the rules and strategies relating to the distribution of funding.

The data also confirm a number of different patterns for men and women described in the literature that define the trajectories and the time taken to be accepted as political candidates. The former relates to the pattern of election in accordance with constituency size. *Constituency size* (number of seats up for grabs) does not seem to bear a relationship to *dispute density (candidate/seat relationship)*. Small and large states may vary in this relationship and between different election campaigns. However, other characteristics of the dispute should be highlighted. The first tends to contradict the predominant findings of literature: it is in the smaller constituencies with a smaller number of seats at stake that women tend to benefit. In turn, the largest proportion of the population is concentrated in bigger constituencies; there is a greater party fragmentation in the electoral dispute, i.e. there is a larger number of parties running and electing; and the parties tend to elect proportionally smaller blocs, by virtue of the greater dispersal of votes. Indeed, it is possible to assume the possibility that, in these states, due to the diversification of the supply of candidacies and parties (and not on account of density); greater investment becomes necessary on the part of the candidates and parties. This may occur either in the form of financial capital, or other forms of capital such as support networks and the party nexus. This context could in part explain the reasons why women might tend to stand less in these constituencies than in smaller constituencies and similarly, to be elected less proportionally.

HDI has been employed as an indicator and has acquired a significance that goes far beyond socioeconomic development—since it also refers to more egalitarian, social situations. We find that in Brazil, women's chances of election to the post of federal deputy are significantly reduced, precisely in those states where HDI is the highest. This prompts us to formulate potential hypotheses to be explored at a later date. One of these would be the relationship between larger constituencies and high HDIs, democratic participation, conservative values and the building of career paths. We might examine the degree of politicization, civic participation and the elitist nature of electoral politics in the country as factors with significant impact. In this case, by reducing or keeping stable the entry and preparation of new players on the political stage, the patterns of association would end up reducing the chances of expanding new leaderships. Along the same lines, it could be said that, in the states with lower HDIs, the types of requisites, resources and skills of candidates through which political trajectories are built, tend to be based more on family capital, political patronage and affiliations to the big parties particularly, in some states and regions. As for the very large constituencies, one issue to be explored is whether solid political trajectories would add more weight and, thus, greater accountability or expectations for the candidate on abilities not mentioned above. In other words, once women candidates find themselves at a disadvantage, the biggest impact would attach to them. We believe this line of interpretation should be explored further in future studies.

However, the data presented above allow us to reject the principle that women are apathetic to politics. If there were any grounds for this, it would be less likely that it would occur in the more developed states, with higher rates of association, where men and women enjoy better education, and women have financial independence and benefit from the labor market. If not just in relation to gender equality, but to values in general, the level of education and financial independence tend to have an indirect influence on people's perceptions. Therefore it is difficult to explain away female apathy in these states. If the low rates of candidacy and women elected are also explained by the "prejudice against women"; how can we explain that his occurs in those states which are theoretically more transparent and developed rather than in less developed states? And how should we connect "prejudice" to other variables?

Also important is the relationship between quotas, other institutional factors, the building of self-image, and the relative independence of the players in the definition of their actions. Factors that point at self-selection of women candidates by virtue of structural impediments are mentioned in the literature. Bourdieu (1999) suggested self-selection is required from women in various environments. This kind of pre-selection was also noted by Matland (2002), more specifically in the domain of political representation. Similarly, this involves again a discussion of "male prejudice", which needs to be placed in a better context and analyzed in greater depth through a multiple causal perspective.

Further analysis should also focus on political parties and their interactions with the types of constituency and electoral logic in Brazilian states. As observed in this chapter and according to previous literature left-leaning parties elect more women. Moreover, in Brazil's more recent elections, the more traditional, so-called large and medium-sized parties, which generally tend to be more resistant to the participation of women, also registered a positive female electoral performance as shown in this chapter. This leads us to assume that an analysis regarding "party resistance" merits closer examination.

Thus, the weight and the role of the parties in each state and the context of alliances seem very relevant for a study of women candidates. Where do women do best in the parties? What are the main trajectories that have led to their electoral success? The role of proportional elections, together with majority elections for federal and state levels of representation combined with the diverse nature and size of the constituencies/states, tend to establish close relationships with the voting logic encountered at both state and federal levels. As we indicated earlier, the distribution of women elected maintains a certain logic with the types of capital used in the different states/regions between the types of party and also with the local voting logic.

An opinion pollster conducted by *IBOPE* in February 2009 for the Special Department for Women's Policies (*SPM*, 2009), showed that the majority of the population of Brazil (seventy-five percent) is in favor of a quota policy for women in politics and supports punishment for political parties (eighty-six percent) that flout the legislation. The poll also shows that the electorate has a positive view of women's participation in politics. This was confirmed in the first round of the 2010 presidential elections, when the women candidates Dilma Rousseff and Marina Silva obtained sixty-six percent of the valid votes. The Regional Conferences on Women in Latin America and the Caribbean, held in Quito in 2007 and Brasília in 2010 reinforced the need for countries in the region to adopt affirmative actions to encourage women to participate in politics.[23]

The 2010 general elections were notable for two paradoxical occurrences: on the one hand, Brazil elected its first woman president; on the other, the low female representation in the Federal Chamber was left unchanged. It still remains to see whether the election of a woman president will increase the participation of women in other areas of political representation.

CHAPTER SIX

Gender Quotas in Peru

Origins, Interactions with Electoral Rules, and Re-Election

GREGORY D. SCHMIDT

Peru is an especially interesting case of gender quotas in Latin America and the world for several reasons. First, Albert Fujimori, Peru's authoritarian president of the 1990s, played a decisive role in the adoption of gender quotas, even though social trends and international diffusion probably would have led to the same result at some later date. Second, despite a very fragmented and volatile party system, quotas have been relatively successful in Peru under two quite different types of electoral systems: majoritarian block lists, which are used in municipal and regional elections; and a variant of open list proportional representation (PR) that is used in the country's congressional elections. Third, whereas most of the literature suggests that quotas are likely to be most successful in conjunction with closed list PR and placement mandates in electoral districts of high magnitude, both of the electoral systems used in Peru deviate from this prescription; indeed, their logics of inclusion are different. Fourth, although quotas have helped women to achieve increasing electoral success in Peru, female officeholders are considerably less likely to run for and win re-election.

The initial sections of this chapter discuss the origin of gender quotas in Peru and the political discourse that accompanied their adoption. Next, the chapter examines the impacts and logics of quotas in the different types of systems used in subnational and congressional elections and then analyzes the gender gap in re-election. A brief conclusion places the major findings in comparative perspective.

The Origin of Gender Quotas

During the 1990s the adoption of gender quotas in Peru—and more generally the breakthrough of women in electoral politics—were rooted in longstanding social trends, championed by the country's feminist movement, reinforced by international diffusion, accelerated by an authoritarian president, Alberto Fujimori, and eventually accepted by Peruvian society.

Following World War II, the Peruvian educational system had expanded rapidly and become accessible to women, while modernization and migration were opening up new employment opportunities in an increasingly urban society. These social trends and the growing availability of modern forms of contraception began to transform traditional gender roles, though progress was uneven across the economic and ethnic fault lines of a very stratified society. Several distinct types of female activists emerged during the late 1970s and 1980s, when women became involved in social movements, feminist groups, political parties, NGOs, self-help organizations, and other associations in civil society. During the 1980s a new generation of female university graduates began to make its mark in professions that had been dominated by men. The feminization of the professions continued in the 1990s. For example, by 1998 a majority of accountants and almost a third of economists were women (Webb and Fernández Baca 2000, 265).

Progress towards gender equity in electoral politics lagged behind trends towards equality in Peruvian society for many years. Although women were elected to Congress in 1956, the first year of female suffrage, they never filled more than 7.2 percent of the seats in either house of Peru's bicameral legislature. Moreover, women played only nominal and largely symbolic roles in Congress and the political parties before the 1990s. Absent from the cabinet until 1987, women enjoyed their greatest successes at the local level, primarily in Lima.[1] Behind the scenes, however, the new generation of female professionals was beginning to work its way up the bureaucratic ladders of the public sector (Blondet and Montero 1994, 20–21, 131–33, 147–49).

During the 1990 presidential run-off campaign, *Foro Mujer*, a group of feminist non-governmental organizations (NGOs), requested that various issues of concern to women—including gender quotas for governmental and public institutions—be discussed in the televised debate between Mario Vargas Llosa and Alberto Fujimori, a political outsider who won an overwhelming victory. The two candidates, however, ignored this proposed agenda, and the issue of gender quotas had little public resonance for the next several years. Nevertheless, Argentina's adoption of gender quotas in 1991 greatly encouraged feminists throughout Latin America. On International Women's Day in 1994, *Foro Mujer* formally proposed a female quota of thirty percent for candidates in national, regional, and municipal elections, as well as for intra-party contests (Yáñez 1998, 15–18). The momentum for quotas was strengthened by the Platform for Action adopted at the 1995 World Conference on Women in Beijing, which was attended by four Peruvian congresswomen: Martha Chávez, Martha Hildebrandt, and Luz Salgado from the pro-Fujimori majority, and Beatriz Merino from the opposition. A February 1997 inter-parliamentary meeting on gender equity in New Delhi, attended by Hildebrandt and Salgado, provided additional reinforcement.

Meanwhile, Fujimori had made gender equity a major theme of his second term. The president emphasized the importance of family planning in his second inaugural address in late July 1995. He reiterated this theme in mid-September as the only male head of state to address the Beijing Conference. An official web page "*Mujer en el Perú*" soon displayed the president's Beijing address, and topics of special concern to women began to be featured regularly in his speeches. During Fujimori's second term, the Ministry for the Promotion of Women and Human Development (PROMUDEH), a Committee on Women in Congress, a special women's division in the new Ombudsman's Office (*Defensoría del Pueblo*), and a bank devoted to mostly female microenterprise owners were established. Prominent women served as presidents of Congress, cabinet ministers,[2] chief prosecutor, heads of key autonomous agencies, and ambassadors, as well as in other important posts during Fujimori's second and abortive third terms.

Various factors explain the president's tilt toward women. The emergence of Susana Higuchi, the president's wife until 1996, as his most effective critic and brief rival for the presidency probably provided the initial impetus. Moreover, women had been almost totally absent among the leaders of the traditional parties that Fujimori so vociferously attacked, and popular stereotypes portrayed them as being more honest and virtuous than men. The presence of women in key positions gave the government useful ammunition against foreign and domestic critics who questioned the regime's commitment to democracy against the backdrop of the 1992 *autogolpe,* continuing human rights abuses, the increasingly public role of spymaster Vladimiro Montesinos, and the president's quest for a third term. Fujimori's most passionate defenders were women—such as Chávez, Hildebrandt, and Luisa María Cuculiza—whom the opposition was often reluctant to attack, out of deference to their gender. It also appears that the president viewed the empowerment of women as critical to family planning and poverty alleviation. Even some women who were not supporters of the president became convinced of his commitment to gender equity (*Caretas*, August 17, 2000, 47).

The issue of gender quotas once again became politically salient when Congress considered new electoral legislation in 1997. Martha Chávez was the chief author of the government's proposal, but she was skeptical of quotas[3] and did not include any provision for gender equity in the majority's bill. Nor did quotas appear in comprehensive alternative proposals drafted by a leading member of the opposition and the National Board of Elections (JNE). The Constitution Committee, however, also considered some three dozen bills that addressed more specific aspects of the electoral system. One of these bills, sponsored by opposition Congresswoman Lourdes Flores Nano, required that at least thirty percent of congressional candidates be of each gender. Another specific bill, authored by pro-Fujimori Congresswomen Martha Hildebrandt and Luz Salgado, proposed a twenty-five percent quota for female candidates only.

Flores Nano made the case for quotas before the Constitution Committee, but the majority of its members considered quotas to be unnecessary, and her proposal was rejected. "They almost beat me!" exclaimed Flores Nano, who, as one of Fujimori's leading critics, was no stranger to political confrontation (Gonzáles Arica 1997). When the newly created Committee on Women took up the issue later, Flores Nano deferred to women from the majority, and the twenty-five percent formula proposed by Hildebrandt and Salgado was endorsed.[4] The fledgling committee, however, did not yet have the authority to report a bill to the floor.

At this point, Fujimori intervened decisively by stating publicly that he would send a quota bill to Congress.[5] Whereas most members of Congress had been against quotas and had even ridiculed the idea, the majority immediately reversed its position and applauded the president's initiative (Yáñez 1998, 20). Once the passage of quotas became a foregone conclusion, only several congressmen—all from opposition parties—raised philosophical objections in a largely perfunctory floor debate (Congreso de la República 1997b). In order to counter charges that quotas were discriminatory and thus violated Article Two of the 1993 Constitution, gender-neutral language similar to that in Flores Nano's proposal was used in the final legislation. Law 26,859, a new basic statute on national elections passed in September 1997, stipulated that women and men must each comprise at least twenty-five percent of party lists for Congress. Similar language was soon incorporated into the new statute on municipal elections (Law 26,864) after a limited debate that once again focused on normative issues (Congreso de la República 1997a).

Although public knowledge of quotas was initially limited, by February 2000 over fourth-fifths of respondents to a national survey (82.9 percent of women and 78.9 percent of men) expressed support for the legislation (Calandria 2000, 21). This support did not dissipate once Fujimori fled Peru in November 2000. Indeed, the following month quotas were raised to thirty percent for congressional elections, and they would later be increased to thirty percent for municipal and regional elections (see Laws 27,387, 27,683, and 27,734). The Law of Political Parties, passed in 2003, reiterated the thirty percent gender quotas for lists of candidates established by previous legislation and extended them to lists for party offices (Law 28,094, Article 26). Thus, Fujimori is best viewed as an accelerator of gender quotas, rather than their fundamental cause. Had he not been an early champion of quotas, it is highly likely that trends in gender relations and feminist political activism would have eventually produced this reform, as in other Latin American countries.

Once quota legislation was passed, feminist organizations sought favorable legal interpretations and helped women to take advantage of quotas. The JNE has generally adopted interpretations of quota legislation that favor women. Moreover, informed observers agree that the JNE and regional electoral boards have generally enforced quotas. Lists that do not comply with the prescribed minimum number of female (or male) candidates are rejected.

The Discourse of Quotas

The normative arguments for and against quotas in Peru were similar to those made regarding affirmative action in the United States and other countries. Indeed, many of the arguments were borrowed or adapted from the U.S. context. Proponents of quotas argued that gender is a relevant criterion for differential treatment and that some affirmative action measures are needed to compensate for social and institutional biases that work against the participation of women (Villanueva Flores 1998, 23). Moreover, gender quotas for political candidates give women political opportunities but do not guarantee election and, therefore, do not discriminate against the rights of voters (Bermúdez Valdivia 1998, 25–55). Less evident in the pro-quota discourse were arguments justifying affirmative action on the basis of its positive impact on the political system.

Opponents of quotas argued that they violated the constitutional provision of equality and the voter's right to choose (Gonzáles Arica 1998, 23, 25–26). Congressman Jorge del Castillo maintained that quotas were especially objectionable in municipal elections, in which a closed list format does not allow voters to select specific candidates (Congreso de la República, 1997a). Moreover, as one male congressman argued, if women deserve special treatment, why not other marginalized groups, such as ethnic minorities?[6] Several congressmen also contended that women were capable of individual achievement on the basis of their own merits (Gonzáles Arica 1998, 23; Congreso de la República 1997a and 1997b). This also appeared to be a position held by some prominent women, such as Martha Chávez and Beatriz Boza[7] In addition, questions were raised about the qualifications of women in the poorer and more rural areas of Peru, a concern that was even shared by some proponents of quotas.

The congressional debate over quotas had a "bipolar" quality. In its initial stages there was a lively, normative debate in which men from the pro-Fujimori parties and some opposition parties tended to argue against quotas. Most, but not all, women defended quotas, with support from some progressive men, such as Javier

Diez Canseco and Henry Pease. Sadly, the debate was not always principled: some men were openly derisive towards women who supported quotas. However, once Fujimori came out in favor of quotas, his male supporters toed the party line and the debate became sterile.

The debate was conducted almost exclusively in normative terms, with virtually no attention to practical detail. Indeed, in talking to legislators, feminist political activists, and political analysts, this author found no evidence that any attention was paid to how quotas would actually work in conjunction with the very different rules that are used in congressional and regional/municipal elections in Peru. Given the relatively strong, but largely unanticipated, impacts of gender quotas in Peru, perhaps this lack of attention to detail was a blessing in disguise.

Quotas in Municipal and Regional Elections

The unitary Peruvian state is divided into twenty-five regions, 195 provinces, and 1,832 districts[8] Since 1983 municipal elections at the provincial and district levels have been held under a majoritarian, closed list format. The 2002 and 2006 elections in the newly established regions[9] also used the same system. However, a new system was adopted for the 2010 regional elections, as discussed at the end of this section. The intervening text describes the system used in municipal elections and in the 2002 and 2006 regional elections.

All voters cast separate ballots for regional and provincial councils. The capital districts of each province are governed by their respective provincial councils, but voters elsewhere also elect 1,637 district councils. Voters cast separate ballots for each tier of subnational government, but the votes for executive and legislative offices are fused at each level. In other words, before 2010 voters could not split their ballots between a slate for regional president and vice-president from one party and a list for the regional council from another party. Similarly, voters choose among lists for both mayor and municipal councilors at the provincial and district levels.

The number of candidates on the lists nominated by political parties or electoral alliances is equal to the number of members on the respective council (district magnitude). The number of municipal councilors varies according to population under a standard formula. The size of provincial councils ranges from five to fifteen members, except for Lima, which has thirty-nine councilors. About ninety-five percent of district councils have only five members, but a few have seven, nine, or even eleven councilors. Before 2010 the number of regional councilors was largely determined by the number of provinces in the region; however, population was also used in regions with less than seven provinces[10] Regional councils, including those to be elected in 2010, have ranged from seven to twenty members.

The party with the most votes wins the regional presidency or municipal mayoralty and at least a "majority plus one" of the seats on the regional or municipal council.[11] Thus, the winning list is awarded more than a minimum majority: at least four of five seats, five of seven seats, six of nine seats, seven of eleven seats, and so on.[12] The remainder of the seats is allocated to the other lists by the d'Hondt formula. In rare instances when the wining list scores a landslide victory, it can be awarded more than a "majority plus one" of the seats under the d'Hondt formula. The council seats won by a party or electoral alliance are filled by candidates in the order that they appear on the party's list.

Table 6.1 displays the percentage of council seats filled by women at the regional, provincial, and district levels since 1995, when the last elections without gender quotas were held. The district level is disaggregated between metropolitan Lima—the most affluent city in Peru, where women had enjoyed considerable electoral success even before quotas—and the rest of the country. Beginning in 1998, subnational elections have been held every four years.

With the introduction of a twenty-five percent gender quota in 1998, the female percentage of councilors in the districts of Lima increased by more than one-third to 29.70 percent from already high levels. The proportion of councilwomen at the provincial level almost doubled, from 10.81 percent to 21.54 percent. The most spectacular increases, however, occurred in districts outside of the capital, where the female share of council members more than tripled from only 6.96 percent to 23.50 percent.

When the quota was increased to thirty percent in 2002, the percentage of female councilors increased at the provincial level and in districts outside of Lima to

Table 6.1: Women Elected to Municipal and Regional Councils

PERCENTAGE FEMALE					
	1995	1998	2002	2006	2010
(Legal Quota)	(None)	(25%)	(30%)	(30%)	(30%)
Regional Councils			22.37	27.63	28.13
Provincial Councils	10.81	21.54	23.41	25.04	23.87
District Councils					
In Metropolitan Lima	21.82	29.70	25.75	31.76	30.88
Rest of Peru	6.96	23.50	26.87	28.16	27.86

Elaborated by author from data in JNE (1997, 1999, 2006b, 2006c, 2006d, 2006e), El Comercio and Movimiento Manuela Ramos (1999), PROMUJER (1998, 78–131; 1999, 7), and data provided by Zoila I. Cruz Molina of International IDEA.

23.41 percent and 26.87 percent respectively. Women filled only a slightly lower percentage of seats on the newly created regional councils (22.37 percent) than on provincial councils. However, the female share of district council seats in Lima actually fell from 29.7 percent in 1998 to 25.75 percent in 2002. In 2006 women made gains on councils at all levels.

Overall, women have fared best in Lima's district councils, with the notable exception of 2002. Reduced political activism probably explains their diminished success in the capital that year. In 1998 feminist activists—who had been energized by the recent passage of quota legislation—successfully put pressure on leaders of various parties to exceed the quota. In particular, PROMUJER, a joint project of five Lima-based NGOs encouraged women to become candidates, provided training, and helped them to negotiate places on the list. The gains in seats won by women between 1995 and 1998 in the capital were made on lists that exceeded the quota. Moreover, the female percentage of candidates, their placement on lists, and their electoral success were notably better in the districts where PROMUJER concentrated its efforts than in non-priority districts (Schmidt 2003a, 44–45). By 2002, however, this wave of political activism had dissipated, and the PROMUJER project had been completed. A difference of means test, using disaggregated data from sources in Table 6.1, shows that the decline in the female percentage of seats in 2002 was significantly greater at the .01 level in districts where PROMUJER had concentrated its efforts in 1998.

Women have comprised a higher percentage of district councils outside of Lima than of provincial councils since 1998 and of regional councils in 2002 and 2006. The female presence on these district councils was even greater than those in the capital in 2002. This pattern is remarkable because the districts outside of Lima include the least developed and most rural parts of the country where women contemplating candidacies have feared rejection by their husbands and public ridicule (Yáñez 1999, 108). Indeed, in rural areas, the political parties often have had difficulty in meeting their gender quotas because women are reluctant to run for office.[13]

Two factors—effective quotas and the relative magnitude of the largest party—were critical to the extraordinary success of women in districts outside of Lima. These factors also help explain the overall success of women in Peruvian subnational elections.

The effective quota can be defined as the minimum number of female candidates[14] required to satisfy the legal quota divided by the total number of candidates on the list. Quota laws typically produce different "effective quotas" for the same type of office because a fixed percentage is applied to electoral districts of varying magnitudes. Subnational elections in Peru are no exception. Thus, the application of a twenty-five percent quota in 1998 produced various effective quotas, ranging from 25.64 percent on the thirty-nine member Lima Provincial Council[15] to forty percent on five member councils.[16] However, over four-fifths of all municipal councils in Peru have only five members. Moreover, these five member councils, which have the highest effective quota, are overwhelmingly found in districts outside of Lima.

In 2002 a thirty percent quota was applied to municipal councils, as well as to the new regional councils of varying sizes. The change in the legal quota produced an effective quota of 42.86 percent for seven member councils, which accounted

Table 6.2: Relative Party Magnitude in Municipal and Regional Elections

DISTRICT MAGNITUDE	(1) SEATS WON UNDER "MAJORITY + 1" RULE	(2) RELATIVE MAGNITUDE OF LARGEST PARTY (%)	(3) CORRELATION WITH DISTRICT MAGNITUDE
In Municipal Elections:			-.796*
39 (Lima Provincial Council)	21	53.85	
15	9	60.00	
13	8	61.54	
11	7	63.64	
9	6	66.67	
7	5	71.43	
5	4	80.00	
In Regional Elections:			-.829**
2	12	60.00	
16	10	62.50	
13	8	61.54	
12	8	66.67	
11	7	63.64	
10	7	70.00	
9	6	66.67	
8	6	75.00	
7	5	71.43	

* Significant at the .05 level (2-tailed); **Significant at the .01 level (2-tailed).
Note: Column 2 is equal to Column 1 divided by district magnitude.
Based on Laws 26,864 and 27,683.

for thirteen of twenty-five regional governments before 2010 but are relatively few in number overall. The effective quota for five member councils remained at forty percent, which was still greater than those for councils of sizes other than seven. Thus, the impact of the effective quota continued to be greatest in the districts outside of Lima. However, the effective quota has exceeded the legal quota in almost all cases, benefitting women in subnational elections overall.

The relative magnitude of the largest party is simply its share of seats on the council. Under the "majority plus one" rule, this variable is high across subnational councils of varying sizes and highest in five member councils (four of five seats = eighty percent), as shown in Table 6.2. This table also shows significant negative correlations between the relative magnitude of the largest party and district magnitude, a factor long thought to enhance the election of women. Similarly, there are significant negative correlations between effective quotas and district magnitude (Schmidt and Saunders 2004, Table 4, 715).

The combination of high effective quotas and high relative party magnitudes produced guaranteed seats for women without placement mandates, primarily in five member districts. If all lists in a five member district are required to nominate at least two women and the winning list is awarded four seats, then at least one women will be elected on the winning list, even if both female candidates are placed in the last two positions. This guaranteed seat for a woman accounts for twenty-five percent of the party's delegation and for twenty percent of the council's total membership. This phenomenon largely explains why the female proportion of district councils outside Lima more than tripled from 6.96 percent in 1995, the last non-quota election, to 23.50 percent in 1998, when quotas were introduced.

The relationship between the effective quota and the relative magnitude of the largest party is not just a quirk of five member districts or Peruvian elections. In general, the proportion of seats that are guaranteed to quota candidates (G_Q) can be specified by the following formula:

$$G_Q = S_L/M - (1 - Q_E)^*K, \text{ if} \geq 0,$$

where S_L is the number of seats won by the largest party, M is district magnitude, Q_E is the effective quota, and K is the ratio of the number of candidates on each list to district magnitude. (Although G_Q may have a negative value, this result is the same as zero, or no guaranteed seats.) The above equation shows that the chances of guaranteeing seats for women can be enhanced not only by raising the effective quota—a rather obvious strategy—but also by increasing the relative magnitude of the largest party. Given that these two variables are both negatively correlated with district magnitude, it follows that G_Q is too.

In the case of five member districts, the largest party wins four out of five seats, so S_L/M = 4/5, or .80. The effective quota is .40 in a five member district and 1 - Q_E = .6. Moreover, in Peru, the number of candidates on each list is equal to district magnitude, so k = 1 and does not change the value of 1 - Q_E. Thus, G_Q = .8 - .6 = .2, or one out of five seats.

Although the phenomenon of guaranteed seats was most important in five member councils—which account for over eighty percent of all municipal councils in Peru and are concentrated in districts outside of Lima—once the legal quota was increased to thirty percent in 2002, it also occurred in seven member councils—which accounted for thirteen of the twenty-five regional governments before 2010. For seven member councils under a thirty percent quota, S_L/M = .7143 (see Table 6.2), Q_E = .4286 (see above), and 1 - Q_E = .5714. Thus, G_Q = .7143 - .5714 = .1429, or one out of seven seats.

Guaranteed seats produced by the effective quota and the relative magnitude of the largest party may also occur under closed-list proportional representation. Indeed, they have occurred in Peruvian municipal elections in the rare cases when a party wins a landslide victory and is awarded more than a majority plus one of the seats under the d'Hondt formula. However, guaranteed seats are far more likely under majoritarian list systems, such as those used in local and senate elections in some other Latin American countries. Elsewhere a colleague and I have shown that the formula outlined above is relevant to understanding cases outside of Peru (Schmidt and Saunders 2004, 727–730).

In 2010 the majority list system continued to be used in municipal elections, but regional elections were conducted under a new system mandated by Law 29,490. Voters cast separate ballots for executive and legislative positions. If no party ticket for regional president and vice-president won at least thirty percent of the vote in the first round, there was a runoff between the two top slates. Regional councilors were elected in provincial-level electoral districts—rather than by regional lists—with sixty-three percent chosen by plurality in provinces having only one representative and the remaining thirty-seven percent selected by closed list PR in provinces with multiple representatives (JNE 2010). Placement mandates were not used in the multimember electoral districts, whose average magnitude was less than three. The thirty percent gender quota applied to each party's lists of candidates in the region overall.[17]

Although this combination of plurality and closed list PR in low magnitude districts appeared prejudicial for women, the female proportion of regional councilors actually increased slightly in 2010, in contrast to slight decreases in women elected at the provincial and district levels (see Table 6.1). In 2010 women fared considerably better at the regional level than at the provincial level and slightly better at the regional level than at the district level outside of Lima. More research is needed to shed light on their unexpected success.

Quotas in Congressional Elections

Since 1992 Peru's national legislature has been unicameral. The Peruvian Congress is elected by the d'Hondt formula of proportional representation (PR) and a variant of open-list voting called the double optional preferential vote (DOPV). Voters first choose a list and then *may* cast preferential votes for up to two candidates on that list. Seats are allocated to parties or electoral alliances in accordance with the proportion of the vote for the respective list, but the number of preferential votes determines which candidates fill the seats won by each list. Under Fujimori congressional elections took place in a single national electoral district in 1992, 1995, and 2000, but the transitional government restored the system of regional electoral districts before the 2001 election.[18]

Table 6.3 displays the percentage of congressional seats filled by women, beginning with the Democratic Constituent Congress (CCD) in 1992.[19] It is important to note that female candidates had become politically competitive *before* the implementation of quotas. In 1992 women running on the pro-Fujimori list were more likely to be elected than men (Schmidt 2006, 154–155). In 1995, female candidates running on lists that won at least one seat enjoyed a higher rate of electoral success and received a higher average number of preferential votes than male candidates on the same lists (Schmidt 2003b, 128). Indeed, in the latter year Martha Chávez, a staunch supporter of Fujimori, won the highest number of preferential votes in the single national district. The chief obstacle to the election of women was a paucity of female candidates, who comprised only about a tenth of party lists in the early 1990s.

With the first application of a gender quota to congressional elections in 2000, the female percentage of candidates more than doubled. Women won 21.7 percent of congressional seats, doubling their share from the 1995 election. Although the quota was increased from twenty-five to thirty percent prior to the 2001 election, the proportion of women elected declined to 18.3 percent, due to the elimination of the single national district, discussed below, and the waning fortunes of Fujimori's

Table 6.3: Women Elected to Peru's Unicameral Congress, 1992–2011

	1992*	1995	2000	2001	2006	2011
(LEGAL QUOTA)	(None)	(None)	(25%)	(30%)	(30%)	(30%)
PERCENTAGE FEMALE	8.8	10.8	21.7	18.3	29.2	21.6

* Democratic Constituent Congress

Sources: JNE (2006a), Tuesta Soldevilla (2001:101–103, 107–110), and data provided by Zoila I. Cruz Molina of International IDEA.

electoral alliance. Nevertheless, Anel Townsend, running on the list of Alejandro Toledo—the eventual winner of the presidential race—won the most preferential votes in Lima, which has a third of Peru's electorate.

In 2006, the share of congressional seats held by women increased spectacularly to 29.2 percent, due to the better performance of female candidates in the provinces, especially on the lists of Ollanta Humala, who won the first round of the presidential race but lost the runoff. The presidential bid of Lourdes Flores Nano—who finished a close third —provided another incentive for parties to recruit competitive female candidates. Although men headed three-quarters of all lists, female candidates running on lists that won at least one seat achieved virtual parity, accounting for 38.3 percent of all candidates and 37.3 percent of the preferential votes (Gallo, Sample, and Schmidt 2008, 190). Keiko Fujimori, the daughter of the former president, received more than three times as many preferential votes as any other congressional candidate in the 2006 election.

After the 2006 election, a net loss of two congresswomen reduced the female percentage of legislators to 27.5 percent.[20] Nevertheless, in May 2011 the country ranked thirtieth out of 129 countries in the percentage of women in national parliaments (Inter-Parliamentary Union). Among Latin American democracies, it trailed only Costa Rica (38.6 percent), Argentina (38.5 percent), and Ecuador (32.3 percent). However, Costa Rica and Argentina both use placement mandates in their closed list systems, a combination that *guarantees* the election of a high percentage of women at the expense of voter choice.

Female candidates did not fare as well in the 2011 election, and women will fill only 21.6 percent of the seats in the new Congress that will take office in July of that year. This level of female representation is nevertheless twice that attained in 1995 before quotas and higher than the figure for 2001 (see Table 6.3). Moreover, Keiko Fujimori became the first woman to make the presidential runoff in Peru and may have been elected to the country's top office by the time that this book is published.

The prevailing view in the literature is that women are more likely to be elected on closed, rather than open, lists (Ballington 2005, 116; Farrell 2001, 167; Htun 2002, 31–33; Htun and Jones 2002; and Norris 2004, 197). In fact, the female percentages of legislators elected under these formats are very similar *on average* throughout the world, but there is a broad range of variation *within* each category (Schmidt 2005). Thus, we need to analyze specific features of the cases within each category. Indeed, several specific features of Peru's open list format have favored the election of women.

First, Peru's DOPV differs from the open list formats used in Brazil and Chile, in which most or all of the voters cast ballots for individual candidates. Many Peruvians do not cast one or both preferential votes. Survey data from the 2000 election show that poor voters are less likely to cast preferential votes and that those who do so are more likely to choose only one candidate. In addition, voters from lower socioeconomic strata are more likely to make errors in casting or counting preferential votes that often lead to the disqualification of individual ballots or entire precincts. In sum, the available evidence suggests that *within* each region valid preferential votes are more likely to be cast by better educated and more affluent citizens, who are likely to have more progressive attitudes towards the political participation of women than the overall regional electorate.[21]

A second characteristic of Peruvian open list voting—its duality—also appears to have facilitated the success of women. Rather than campaigning for women and against men, proponents of female representation can ask Peruvians to split their two preferential votes equitably between the genders. Many voters have adhered to the slogan of feminist NGOs, "Of your two preferential votes, cast one for a woman."

More broadly, multiple preferential votes may increase gender equity for reasons similar to the arguments for high district or party magnitude. Whereas the latter help parties to balance their tickets, the former might allow some voters to make a more "balanced choice." For example, a man with traditional values might be reluctant to cast his only preferential ballot for a woman, but willing to "risk" voting for a female candidate as one of his choices. According to this logic, Peru and other countries with multiple preferential votes should be, *ceteris paribus,* more likely to elect women than countries that have only one preferential vote, such as Brazil and Chile. Indeed, the female proportion of national legislators in Peru (27.5 percent at the time of this writing) is considerably higher than those for Brazil (8.6 percent) and Chile (14.2 percent) (Inter-Parliamentary Union).[22]

A third characteristic of Peruvian congressional elections—constraints on intralist competition—helps to ameliorate one of the chief concerns about gender parity under open lists. Htun and Jones (2002, 39) assert that women will be disadvantaged in open formats because they generally have fewer resources than men for individualized campaigns. Available evidence suggests that this assumption is true in Peru, where there is vigorous competition among candidates running on the same list. Indeed, in 1990 a deluge of tasteless television commercials by congressional candidates allied with Mario Vargas Llosa drowned out and sometimes contradicted the novelist's message, contributing to his defeat (Schmidt 1996, 337–340). Since this debacle, however, the leaders of Peruvian parties have usually placed limits on individual campaigns. Most importantly, congressional candidates seldom buy television commercials, which is the most effective way of reaching the electorate.

Fourth, the single national district that was used in the 1992, 1995, and 2000 elections for a unicameral legislature facilitated the initial electoral breakthrough of women. The single district allowed professional women—who are overwhelmingly based in Lima-Callao—to run for the entire universe of congressional seats. It also centralized nominations in the hands of national party leaders, who are generally more receptive to female political participation than regional bosses. Moreover, whereas congresswomen drew a majority of their preferential votes from Lima-Callao in 1995 and 2000, congressmen relied on the provinces for most of their support (see Schmidt 2003b, 127–128). The abolition of the single national district was followed by a decrease in the election of women in 2001 (see Table 6.3). Women won twelve of thirty-nine seats (thirty-one percent) in Lima and Callao but only ten of eighty-one seats (twelve percent) in the rest of Peru.

It should be noted that the single national district was not simply an artifact of high district magnitude. Whereas the latter variable has been linked to the success of women under closed list PR, it did not have a significant impact on the success of female candidates in either the 2001 or 2006 elections, which were conducted in multimember districts (Gallo, Sample, and Schmidt 2008, 193; Schmidt 2003b: 127).

Accounting for Gender Disparities in Re-Election

In a study undertaken for International IDEA, Patricia Zárate (2008) built an impressive data base that includes information on all Peruvian officeholders in 2006 and any offices for which they were candidates in the 2006 general and municipal elections. She found that only 29.9 percent of officeholders ran for re-election to the same office or were candidates for a different office in 2006. Moreover, the two genders had markedly different rates of incumbent candidacy. Whereas 34.3 percent of male incumbents were candidates, only 16.1 percent of female incumbents ran for office. In other words, male incumbents were more than twice as likely to pursue an office as were female incumbents. The data base also shows a smaller gap in rates of re-election: 35.1 percent of male incumbents who ran for office and 29.3 percent of female incumbents who did so were elected.

Schmidt (2010) shows that about half of the gap in rates of incumbent candidacy is explained by the concentration of women in offices that are less likely to generate bids for re-election or for another elective position. Most strikingly 80.8 percent of all female officeholders but only 64.8 percent of all male officeholders were members of district councils, which have the lowest rates of incumbent candidacy. Thus, the outstanding success of quotas at the district level is a double-edged sword. Moreover, executive positions, whose incumbents were more likely to run for re-election or pursue another office, accounted for 18.9 percent of all offices held by men, but only 2.64 percent of women officeholders.

Nevertheless, rates of incumbency candidacy are greater for men at all levels of government, and the gender gap is widest at the provincial and district levels. Somewhat surprisingly, Schmidt (2010) found that Peru's notoriously fragmented and volatile party system mitigates the gender disparity in incumbent candidacies. Women are about a third more likely to run on the lists of major national parties than those of minor parties, regional movements, or local organizations. Moreover, whereas incumbent female candidates were only about fourth-fifths as likely to win office as their male colleagues overall, there was virtual gender parity in the election of those running for re-election on the same party list. This difference suggests that women are better able to compete for list position within party structures—even those of minor, regional, and local parties—than as party-switchers or free agents. Women stand to gain if party competition becomes more regularized and actual nomination procedures are standardized and transparent (see Matland 2005, 95–96). Thus, stabilizing the party system and strengthening parties as institutions are important for gender equity as well as for the consolidation of Peruvian democracy. Moreover, the creation of clearer career paths through party structures might well reduce the tremendous disparity between men and women in executive offices.

Conclusion

The conventional wisdom posits that gender quotas are most likely to be successful under closed list PR in electoral districts of high magnitude and with placement mandates. The Peruvian experience, however, shows that gender quotas can facilitate the election of women in majoritarian list and open list PR systems. This case study has also shown that the logic of quotas can vary under distinct electoral systems. The conventional wisdom holds that high district magnitude reinforces quotas, and indeed this is usually the case under closed list PR. However, as discussed in this chapter, districts of high magnitude are actually a disadvantage under majority list systems and make little difference under open list PR. The effective magnitude of the highest party is critical to the success of quotas under majority list systems, as discussed in this chapter, but has no impact under open list PR (Gallo, Sample, and Schmidt 2008, 193). Finally, in Peru's 2010 regional election, women enjoyed electoral success under plurality and closed list PR without placement mandates in low magnitude districts—a phenomenon that merits additional study.

Chapter Seven

From Temporary Measures to the Parity Principle

The Case of Costa Rica

Ana Isabel García Quesada

Since 1821, when the country became an independent republic, four legislative milestones have helped to show how the political class gradually incorporated the principle of gender equality. In 1949, when the Constitution (still in effect) granted women the right to vote and be elected; in 1990, with the passage of the Law for the Promotion of Women's Social Equality (Law No. 7142) calling for political parties to incorporate women in their bodies and internal processes; in 1996 with the partial reform of the Electoral Code that introduced a forty percent legislative quota for women; and in 2009, when Law 8765 incorporated principles of equality, non-discrimination and parity in party structures, nomination lists for popular election, other mechanisms of alternation by sex in party lists and the use of financial resources for political training.[1] These legislative changes illustrate a social consensus about an ideal morality at given junctures.

Indeed, there is widespread agreement about the gap between legislation and social practice[2] in Costa Rica, as in the rest of Latin America, making it necessary for women to act as "watchdogs" after laws are adopted. What distinguishes Costa Rica's case, at least in the enforcement of laws promoting gender equity, is the ability and capacity of certain women and men to seek remedy for the actual violation of gender equality legislation. The evolution of Costa Rica's social policy and maturity of its democratic political system may have embedded the idea of gender equity in society, facilitating the passage and defense of legislation as well as respect for its correct application. In addition, 2010 will be remembered as a very special year in the nation's history. Not only was the parity clause implemented in elections for public positions, but Costa Rica elected its first female President. Finally, through the creation of the Institute of Formation and Studies in Democracy (Spanish acronym IFED), in the frame of the Supreme Tribunal of Elections (TSE), a mandate to consolidate the rights of the citizenship emerged.

The first sub-section of this chapter presents a highly condensed summary of the historical evolution and sociopolitical context of Costa Rican women, followed by a regulatory framework of laws on women's political participation and their participation in popularly elected positions. The final section looks at the challenges facing Costa Rican women that transcend just numbers and plurinominal popularly elected positions.

The Political and Social Underpinnings of Gender Equity in Costa Rica

Costa Rica is a small, Central American nation with a little over 4.5 million inhabitants (2010), and 49% of women. The trend toward urbanization has been moderate and relatively late compared to the rest of the Latin American countries, with 66% of the population now residing in cities. Population density is 141 people/km^2 and an estimated 7 percent are immigrants (mostly Nicaraguans). Relative to Latin America, Costa Rica is one of the only countries in an advanced phase of demographic transition. In other words, it has important features of population aging (average life expectancy at birth is 79) due to the relative accumulation of population at ages appropriate for the labor market and decline of the dependency ratio within households. The main differences by sex according to age groups occur in the more advanced years, where women are the majority due to higher male mortality.[3] At global levels, this country is considered one of the more consolidated democracies of the American continent, as noted in various studies.[4] This is depicted by the Democratic Development Index of the Konrad Adenauer Foundation and Poliat.com,[5] which places Costa Rica third in regional ranking.

Politically, Costa Rica is a representative democracy. The offices of president, two vice-presidents, 57 congressional deputies and 4910 municipal posts (including mayors, regents, *síndicos* (trustees), district council members, mayors and all of their respective alternates) are elected every four years by popular vote.[6] The pathway for accessing to these positions is through political parties which, according to the Constitution are "fundamental instruments of political participation" (art. 98). Notwithstanding, absenteeism has been rising as part of the political and party crisis in the region, reaching 31% and 72% respectively in the most recent national elections of February and December 2010 (as opposed to16% in 1970).[7]

Socioeconomically sound, Costa Rica along with Argentina, Uruguay and Chile, are characterized by reduced social gaps and high human development, according to the social welfare indicators of the Economic Commission for Latin America (ECLAC)[8] and the United Nations Development Programme's Human Development Index (HDI).[9] This situation is the result of a general tendency, albeit intermittent, of implementing welfare policies. This evolution is perhaps revealed more clearly in poverty and inequality indicators. In the mid-1950s, 50% to 60% of the entire population was in a situation of poverty, declining to 30% in 1980 and 20% at the end of the 1990s. For the last 20 years, the Gini coefficient shows income distribution with only minor variations until 1997, spiking noticeably until 2002 and remaining flat up to the present at 0.473. As indicated in a recent study on social spending in relation to the economic situation (Juan Diego Trejos, 2010), despite several economic contractions since 1981, real social expenditure shrank on only one occasion (1981–1984), in some way reflecting the degree of social sensitivity of its political class.

More specifically, concerning gender equality, Costa Rica's high Gender Inequality Index (GII) of 0.526 places it 62nd in the world (out of 171) and 6th in Latin America.[10] The GII is a composite index showing women's disadvantage in three spheres: reproductive health, empowerment and the labor market. A quick rundown of main indicators on the evolution of their socio-demographic profile[11] reveals that Costa Rican women have considerably reduced the average number of children, from seven in the 1950s to 2.1 in the first decade of this century, with the greatest differences appearing between high and low socioeconomic sectors (not place of residence). However, early pregnancy is quite high: 19% of births are to mothers aged 15 to 19. Percent of women heads of household has been on the rise, from 16% of all households in 1973 to 31% (32% in urban areas and 24% in rural zones) by the end of this decade. The illiteracy rate is low for both sexes though slightly higher for women (3.7 versus 3.9 in individuals over 15 years).

In Costa Rica women outnumber men at all levels of the educational system – an area where the gender gap shows men at a disadvantage. In the labor force, practically half of working-age women (over 15) in urban areas are inserted in some type of economic activity. Nationally, women have risen from 20% of the economically active population in 1970 to 40% in 2009, although surveys indicate unemployment is a greater problem for women (10% versus 7% of men) and they continue receiving lower pay (around 25% less) than men for similar work, especially in the informal sector.

Institutionalism and Public Policies for Gender Equity in Costa Rica

Public policies are processes of state action aimed at producing certain impacts on society; hence, gender equity policies refer to how a state decides to tackle the general problem of inequity between men and women. However, social policies are not the only ones responsible for the social welfare; economic growth is also essential. Thus, both types of policies must be adjusted and managed efficiently, and above all, promote a synergistic linkage between them. In addition, there are two types of social policies: those universal in nature—which seek the welfare of the population as a whole—and selective policies focused on reducing poverty, vulnerability and social exclusion. Gender equity policies come under the latter category. Finally, social selective policies must be articulated along with those of universal nature in order to maximize their effectiveness in the pursuit of overall social welfare.[12]

The incorporation of a gender perspective in Costa Rican has been slow and gradual, starting with at Executive Branch in the mid-1970s (in the frame of the First World Conference on Women), followed by the Judiciary (from the late 1980s and especially from the mid-1990s) and more recently within the Legislative. The executive began adopting gender equality mechanisms in the mid-1940s. Indeed, in Costa Rica, it is fairly simple to identify the periods of time when the Executive Power took the initiative to promote gender equality mechanisms, most obviously through bills sent to the Legislative Assembly. This is particularly the case when the executive power must abide to international commitments through organizations such as the United Nations or the Organization of American States. These commitments have implications for the other powers (as well as for other sectors), and certainly for the legislative in charge of ratifying international and regional agreements before they can be incorporated into national legislation.

On the regulatory plane, along with affirmative action, or measures to combat discrimination against women, other measures should be added, especially with respect to the workplace and health (maternity leave, breastfeeding, etc.). Since the 1990s, laws were proposed and passed to promote gender equity in other spheres of national social and political life. All of these laws have implications for public institutional activities, both in terms of the services they provide and their own internal operation. The broadest instrumental framework of these national laws is the United Nations Convention for the Elimination of All Forms of Discrimination Against Women (CEDAW), approved by Costa Rica in 1980 and ratified by its congress in 1984 (Law No. 6968). Two laws were later adopted to comply with this Convention: the Law on the Promotion of Women's Social Equality (No. 7142 of 1990) and the law creating the National Women's Institute (No. 7801 of 1998, INAMU). The latter covers the different spheres from which gender equity must be promoted in the country and based on public policy instruments, while Law 7142 is mostly declaratory.

In addition, the Law on INAMU establishes a mandate on state powers to institute gender equality policies, granting INAMU responsibility for promoting these policies (articles 3 and 4). It also calls on other forms of social organization and decision-making (unions, etc). Other laws regulate more particular aspects, such as those referring to domestic violence; sexual harassment in the workplace and educational settings; support for women heads of household in conditions of poverty or participation in positions of political decision. Regarding the evolution and type of public policies fostered in Costa Rica, between the mid-1970s and mid-1990s the executive branch created a number of agencies and initiatives to promote gender equity. These actions were isolated in character, lacked strategic responsibility and were aimed primarily at women's groups, with the organized non-governmental world and central Administration[13] acting separately. The so-called "National Mechanisms for the Promotion of Women" was created during this period, rising progressively in rank to that of an autonomous entity (INAMU).

Since the 1995 World Conference on Women (UN, in Beijing), gender-related public policies took on a strategic orientation, but were not consistent and were highly dependent on different governmental administrations, advancing toward more integrated and strategic action to promote gender equity at every level in the country and abandoning the emphasis on welfare to work exclusively with certain women's groups (in fundamental conditions of poverty). These changes reflected a new way of manifesting political will, shifting from declarations to commitments through national plans that identified specific actors, goals and responsibilities.

This strategic change began during the 1994–1998 period, when authorities approved two essential laws (the Law on INAMU and Law No. 7769 on Women in Conditions of Poverty) and initiated the "design and promotion of national plans and strategic programs aimed at complying with commitments under the Platform for Action"[14] approved in Beijing: the National Plan for Equal Opportunity between Women and Men (PIOMH), the National Plan for Attention and Prevention of Domestic Violence (PLANOVI), the Women's Focal Point of the National Plan for Combating Poverty (PNCP) and the Program for Promotion of Women's Active Citizenship (PROCAM).

During the next two administrations (1998–2002 and 2002–2006), INAMU had serious institutional difficulties and there was no continuity for comprehensive public policies that were originally designed, except those related to domestic violence and violence against women.[15] The monitoring and evaluation of public actions was weak during those eight years, and managerial difficulties were endemic.

During the 2006–2010 periods a strategic shift took place in INAMU, with the approval of the "National Policy on Gender Equality and Equity" (PIEG)

2007–2017 and its Action Plan for 2008–2012. A law passed (No. 8783) authorizing resources from the Social Development and Family Allowance Fund (FODESAF) to execute the "Inter-institutional Program Aimed at Women in Condition of Poverty". The PIEG and its action plan (85 Strategic Actions) are in the first years of execution, but had some organizations weaknesses particularly in its relation with other public entities responsible for accomplishing the agreed goals.[16]

This condensed summary of the evolution of public policies for gender equity in Costa Rica shows a country that has gradually included women's rights among its national priorities, putting emphasis on the institutionalization and the operationalization of those policies.[17] With respect to the focus of public policies, the strategic objectives of the current PIEG state that to achieve gender equity in the area of political participation and paid work, such equity must necessarily be obtained in the private spheres (concerning care of dependents), in access to and enjoyment of health and education, and in the protection of human rights, especially with respect to domestic violence.

Finally, as mentioned above, the other branches of power have also approved significant gender equity policies and mechanisms. This occurred particularly during the 2000s, through projects that created awareness in both the Judicial Power and Legislative Assembly and supported by various international agencies. For example, in 2000, the Judicial Power approved the creation of the Institutional Gender Commission in the Supreme Electoral Tribunal (TSE), and later the Gender Commission of the Judicial Power and the Technical Secretariat of the Judicial Power as well as the "Gender Equity Policy of the Judicial Power" in 2005 and the "Institutional Policy for Gender Equity and Equity of the TSE" in 2009.[18]

In the Legislative Power, the emphasis has been placed on the incorporation of affirmative action for women. The approach of institutionalization shifted in 1999 with the creation of the Permanent Special Commission on Women (12 special permanent commissions currently exist)[19] and in 2009, the Assembly Directorate approved the creation of the Gender Equality and Equity Technical Unit (UTIEG). Since then, and also in the frame of the PIEG, design and approval of the Assembly's institutional gender equity policy is also being promoted.

Thus, the executive branch in Costa Rica has been the main agent in the implementation of women-friendly mechanisms aimed at the general welfare of the population, while the other branches of government have also played their part and ensured that policies were applied. This overview reveals the level of institutionalization of gender perspective in Costa Rican public agencies as a whole. Despite differences in the approaches,[20] Costa Rica's political institutions demonstrate a general awareness that to construct a democratic society, gender equity is an intrinsic goal.

Evolution of the Legal Framework and Participation in Popularly Elected Positions According to Sex

Understanding the general framework of the political participation of women can be useful, as it reflects the evolution of political thinking—of those who have held congressional decision power, at least—in the discussion and approval of laws. There is general consensus that in Costa Rica the major aspects of discrimination have been eliminated through the judicial route by either passing specific legislation or reforming existing laws. Whereas such regulatory framework cannot be described here in-depth for reasons of brevity, within the context of the different international commitments, including the revision and promulgation of legislation, institutions in Costa Rica have improved the rights of women of all ages and conditions and their status in society.

The Constitution of the Republic (1949) establishes that no person may be subjected to discrimination contrary to human dignity (article 33, reformed in 1968) and that no one shall be subjected to cruel or degrading treatment (article 40). The Constitution establishes that it will procure the greatest welfare of all inhabitants in the country (article 50), particularly of women who are mothers and their sons and daughters (articles 51 and 55), especially with respect to work and education. Two articles (20 and 33) were modified at the end of the nineties to change the word "men" to "persons" (Constitutional Reform, 7880). Forty-five women-friendly laws were adopted within three periods of Costa Rica's history, the first between 1949 and the onset of the 1990s, the second during the 1994–1998 period, when the greatest number of laws and decrees were approved (60%, especially regarding public policy for women) and since the turn of the millennium, when fewer but nevertheless significant laws were approved. Moreover, 50% of those laws relate to family rights, including the situation of children and adolescents; 20% to situations of violence, sexual harassment and human trafficking; 15% to political rights and participation; 12% to laws that deal with gender equity, and an equal percent on the creation of institutions and gender policies. Of the remainder, three laws deal with labor rights, two with housing and one with health.[21]

Specifically regarding the rights of women as citizens,[22] their active participation dates back to the beginning of the 20th century "by a series of activities of political character—in which their presence becomes more visible—and emerged as fundamental precedents in the struggle for citizenship."[23] Thus, during the electoral process of 1923 the Feminist League, a social organization consisting mostly of teachers, was created to present a bill that would give women the right to vote. Between 1923 and 1943 a total of nine proposals were presented, yet women were not granted suffrage until 1949. In 1950 women voted for the first time during a plebiscite to determine the political and administrative pertinence of a territory

(La Tigra district) and at national level during the elections of 1953, when three women were elected as deputies.

Women's incursion in Congress expanded slowly but not continuously, and the initial count of three deputies would not occur again until the mid-eighties. After the passage of the Law on the Promotion of Women's Social Equality in 1990, the number of women deputies tripled (1994 elections) and practically quadrupled after the approval of the minimum 40% quota (1998 elections). The real quantitative leap took place when the Supreme Electoral Tribunal (TSE) began hearing cases of non-compliance with quota legislation. The proportion of women then rose to 35% (2002 elections) and almost 39% in the two most recent national elections.

Table 7. 1: Historical Evolution of Participation by Sex in the Legislative Assembly, According to the Initial Period of Each Legislature, 1953–2010

		MEN		WOMEN	
YEAR	TOTAL	ABS	%	ABS	%
1953	45	42	93.3	3	6.7
1958	57	55	96.5	2	3.5
1962	57	56	98.2	1	1.8
1966	57	54	94.7	3	5.3
1970	57	53	93.0	4	7.0
1974	57	53	93.0	4	7.0
1978	57	52	91.2	5	8.8
1982	57	53	93.0	4	7.0
1986	57	50	87.7	7	12.3
1990	57	50	87.7	7	12.3
1994	57	48	84.2	9	15.8
1998	57	46	80.7	11	19.3
2002	57	37	64.9	20	35.1
2006	57	35	61.4	22	38.6
2010	57	35	61.4	22	38.6
TOTALS	843	719	85.3	124	14.7

Source: Prepared by the author using the TSE computer database on votes and electoral pronouncements on elections held in those years.

As in other countries, in Costa Rica the explicit incorporation of women's suffrage and to be elected did not automatically turn into women accessing to popularly elected positions. Minimum quotas needed to be introduced to change this pattern. These mechanisms were first presented to the Legislative Assembly in the mid-eighties, but not approved on that occasion. In any case, the law for the Promotion of Women's Social Equality approved in 1990 contained a chapter on the promotion of women's political rights.

The debate generated around the passage of the 1990 Law changed the political mentality in Costa Rican society by linking ideas about rights, justice, participation and democracy. Several women's organizations and movements, as well as women in decision-making positions, seized this opening to delve more deeply into the analysis of these conceptual connections and generated new law proposals that would ensure a minimum floor for women's effective participation in popular elections. Another attempt to introduce a quota mechanism failed on a second opportunity when presented as part of a modification to the Electoral Code that was discussed between 1996 and 1997 without generating much debate. However, a quota proposal was once again included and this time, despite opposition from some men and women deputies, the legislative commission and subsequently the parliament voted in favor.

Article 60 of the Electoral Code states that "the delegations of district, cantonal and provincial assemblies must be formed by at least 40% women" along with a clause establishing that "when a party attains political participation of women in proportion to their number on the Voter Registration List, the measures cited in the last paragraph of article 60 of the Electoral Code may cease by resolution of that Tribunal". Difficulties were encountered in implementing the legislation during the following elections (of 1998) because it was imprecise as to how the quota should be implemented. After the election the proportion of women deputies rose from 16% to only 19%. Even though parties enforced the quota, women occupied the last places of the party lists with little real likelihood of being elected. The Supreme Electoral Tribunal's acceptance of the implementation of the quota, as well as the actual results of the elections,[24] triggered public and legal response from women who had been candidates or advocates of women's rights, such as the National Mechanism for the Promotion of Women (at that time the Women and Family Center, later INAMU).[25]

The resolutions issued by the TSE in response to these appeals specified several elements with respect to the minimum quota of women. First, concerning compliance (Resolution 1863), in the sense that parties should apply the quota in the portion of posts considered electable within the lists of candidates (with a real likelihood of being elected, or what is known as *mandato de posición*), as well as in the election of the delegates to territorial assemblies (district, canton, province).

This resolution also set out sanctions, including not registering lists failing to comply with the quotas in the manner decided by the TSE. In addition, TSE argued that "electable posts" should be calculated on the "average of the results obtained in the electoral races in which the political group has participated," which "would provide an approximation of positions with real possibilities of being elected." Finally, TSE also decided that in drawing up the list of candidates the quota should be applied alternating the sexes, as "a system allowing for proportional eligibility and with it the effectiveness of the gender quota." These resolutions were issued after the elections of 1998 and involved an intense process of adaptation for both party leadership and the TSE. The results of the next national elections demonstrated that the TSE's resolution had a significant impact, since the percentage of women deputies rose to 35% (and then to 38.8% in the two most recent elections).

Toward the end of 2001, the TSE promoted a sweeping new reform in the Electoral Code aimed at raising the standards of the Costa Rican electoral system, including the introduction of a parity clause. Public and political debate was not as polarized as it had been when the quota mechanism was proposed a decade before. Though not without pockets of resistance, the political class represented by members of political parties in the congress viewed democracy intertwined with gender equity. In 2009, the Legislative Assembly approved a new Electoral Code which explicitly recognized the principles of political participation by gender, parity and alternation;

> The political participation of men and women is a human right recognized in a democratic, representative, participatory and inclusive democracy, protected under the principles of equality and non-discrimination. Participation will be governed by the principle of parity, signifying that all even-numbered delegations, nomination lists and other bodies will be comprised of fifty percent (50%) women and fifty percent (50%) men, and in uneven-numbered delegations, nomination lists or bodies the difference between total men and women may not be greater than one. All nomination lists will use the mechanism of alternation by sex (woman-man or man-woman), such that the electoral ticket may not have two consecutive people of the same sex. (Article 2)

This is a qualitative leap for Costa Rica, since the quota mechanism is defined as a temporary measure to reduce women's under-representation in decision-making positions, while the parity principle is a definitive measure whose objective is that women and men share political power. The parity clause was first applied during the presidential and municipal elections of 2010 (February and December, respectively) and will be implemented for the first time during the 2014 national legislative elections.

The results of the 2010 elections reveal some limitations on the parity clause. For example, since parties can decide how to position their candidates on the lists—whether a male or female candidate should lead the list—parity may not be accomplished. This limitation may be particularly problematic for new or small parties. The other limitation is in uninominal elections, such as that of mayors. Since mayors were first popularly elected in 2002, only ten women out of a total 81 mayors (12.3%) were women and all of them were elected in 2010.

In sum, the reforms have resulted in a significant increase of women's participation in popularly elected posts. In more than 30 years of representing just 2% to 9% of the deputies, Costa Rican women broke through this ceiling in the elections that took place during discussion of the Law for the Promotion of Women's Social Equality, obtaining 12% and 16% of the total elected deputy posts in 1990 and 1994, respectively. That portion increased once again in the elections occurring a year after the 40% minimum quota was approved, although only to 19% (due to the aforementioned limitations.) The real quantitative leap took place in the 2002 elections when women accounted for 35.1% of the deputies elected, topping off at 38.8% during the last two elections.

At the municipal level, in the 1990 legislative elections women accounted for 14% of the total regents elected, a number that rose to 18% in the following elections and then doubled in 1990 (with the 40% quota already approved). Women and men shared equally these posts during the 2002 elections, but women dropped to 43% in the last two elections.[26] Finally, women' political participation in Costa Rica has always been among the highest in the region, even before the minimum quota was approved, and since 2010, it is one of the few countries in the world whose President is a woman.

Now that the Electoral Code Includes the Parity Principle; What is Missing?

Costa Rica has made important strides in the promotion and fulfillment of women' political and citizenship rights. Women in positions of power, national mechanisms for the promotion of women (CMF-INAMU), the TSE, the stability of the Costa Rican political system, a favorable position of major political parties and specialists, and organizations and women's movements have all supported the proposals and defended them against attempts to skirt the rules.

There is also a favorable public opinion about women's participation in politics in Costa Rica, seen as benefiting society from the complementary nature of the sexes. This favorable public opinion grew progressively in this country, from the late eighties, when the first proposal for a minimum quota was discussed, but especially after 1996, when the 40% quota was proposed and passed. This climate benefitted the 2009 approval of the parity and political participation law. Nonetheless, progress in the status of Costa Rican women, based above all on important improvements in education and health have been more difficult and reveal the need to focus in these areas of co-responsibility for family and dependent care, and family relations for those women involved in electoral-political life.

The existence of public policies promoting women and gender equity has been sustained since the end of the 1990s and a historical and investigative repository on women's gender situation and condition in the country have been promoted by different public and private entities at national and international levels. These have served to document and learn from experiences as well as strengthen the technical capacities of gender specialists. More recently, the creation by law (Electoral Code, article No. 309) of a new entity within the TSE, the Institute of Formation and Studies in Democracy (IFED),[27] with the purpose of strengthening democracy through assistance to parties, electoral training and knowledge management has been significant. TSE and IFED are working on the incorporation of gender equity criteria at both the institutional level and in the design of their areas, instruments and tools of work.

However, once the parity rule is implemented, Costa Rica will have to tackle some thorny issues in terms of the political participation of women and their exercise of citizenship.[28] First, there is the question on how to apply the parity principle in the election of uninominal positions (President of the Republic, mayors, municipal trustees (*síndicos*), and mayors and nominees heading the ballot for public posts. Current legislation establishes that for uninominal posts, parties must nominate three people in the case of presidential and mayoral tickets: the person aspiring to the main position and two alternates (first and second vice-presidents and first and second vice-mayors, respectively) and two people in candidacies for *síndico* and mayor; a principal and an alternate. The TSE explained (Resolution No. 3671-E8-2010) that the positions of President and Mayor are unique; with parties having the power to choose the person they will nominate for those positions. In other words, it is not possible to apply the parity principle and alternation mechanism in these cases. For all cases of uninominal ballots, TSE has indicated that the parity principle applies to the entire list of candidates, with a different form of regulating the way the alternation mechanism is applied.

TSE's understanding of the election positions is similar to its interpretation of the 40% quota, but there have been other alternative interpretations. According to some, the TSE could combine the two elements of the rule, taking as reference behavior over time, such as the number of ballots each party presents. This would mean, for example, that after a person of one sex headed a party's presidential nomination, the next time that party should have to nominate an individual of the opposite sex (alternation in time). In the case of ballots for mayors and *síndicos*, the regulation would become more complex; in addition to this time criteria one could add the quantity of ballots each party presents for each level of election (horizontal alternation as to who heads the ballot). However, the TSE has indicated that it cannot "define or validate a model" for regulating parity and alternation as this would affect the principles of autonomy of electoral circumscription (voting district) and democracy of the political parties.[29]

This has been an issue of debate in the Legislative Assembly since the Electoral reform bill was introduced, when representatives of INAMU and the Ombudsman of Human Rights proposed incorporating affirmative action mechanisms alongside those of alternation and the parity principle. The TSE's current interpretation also has consequences for the election of deputies, since there is a difference between the number of candidates of each sex that are nominated and the quantity of deputies that are actually elected according to sex. In other words, a party can present lists of deputy candidates with an equal number of men and women, also in electable positions, but given that they may choose the leader of the list, this may result in more people of that sex being elected. For example, during the last national legislative elections, when the 40% gender quota mechanism was applied, women did not obtain the minimum 40% of the seats, and in recent municipal legislative elections when the parity principle was applied, women accounted for only 42.8% of the total regents actually winning seats (38.6% holding this position as principle and 47.1% as alternates).

There are also questions about the current interpretation of parity, in the sense that it should not be understood as a maximum of 50% women (and men), but as a floor. This is an interesting debate, as it reverts to the alternative of minimum quotas. For some people (including the author of this chapter), the idea of a minimum quota is more attractive in fostering democracy with gender equity criteria, as it defines a floor or minimum percentage below which no sex must ever again be represented, but leaves a margin allowing voters to decide among candidates, regardless of their sex. It should be pointed out that thus far, it appears that parity has in general been interpreted as an aspiration to be attained, although it is still too soon to arrive at these conclusions.

Others question whether parity and alternation might actually be limiting women's chances to participate, inasmuch as there can be no party that nominates or is formed only by people of a same sex (precluding a feminist party). The parity principle is also questioned because it does not resolve representativeness of the diversity of women in terms of ethnicity, race, age group, and area of residence, socioeconomic conditions and other issues. Finally, there is the challenge of applying the principles of parity and non-discrimination for reasons of gender to specific public posts or posts in collegial bodies, including the government cabinet and boards of directors (of banks, autonomous entities, etc.), where women have been excluded. It is possible that monitoring the law enforcement to apply the criterion of equity in the formation of the boards of associations and trade unions may be also applied at the state level.

Another problem is that of financing candidates. TSE has demonstrated abundant capacity and rigor regarding the enforcement of parity in the area of financing. The application of the parity principle in financing has been interpreted as the quantity of people of both sexes who access the resources parties they receive. According to Costa Rican legislation (art. 96 of the Constitution and articles 89 to119 of the Electoral Code), the State contributes significantly to financing for electoral campaigns and since the recent reform, those resources can also be allocated for organizational aspects of the political parties and continuous training. The Electoral Code also establishes (art.52, item p) that: "What the political party makes available for training must be permanent and responsive to parity for both men and women (...)," something TSE will corroborate through accounting reports showing training expenditures, including "amounts and activities, [allocated] for the formation and promotion of both genders in conditions of due equality" (article N. 103). Since this regulation is not yet being applied because the reform is so recent, different sectors are encouraging TSE to define more precisely its interpretation of what such parity involves, incorporating elements of training, content, as well as the training men on gender equity.

Article 52 establishes that the parties' objectives to "train, form, and promote knowledge of human rights, ideology, and gender equality; [and] to encourage leadership, political participation, empowerment, postulation and the exercise of decision-making posts, among others". It would be useful, for example, to include a gender criteria as well as a socioeconomic analysis with gender perspective. It should be also recommended to create a follow-up, monitoring and verification system. This would facilitate TSE's efforts to identify possible evasive ploys or gaps in the rules, so that, like the quota mechanism, measures can be established to prevent such possibilities.

Finally, with regard to follow-up mechanisms, it should be noted that a few months after the recent reform, an appeal of unconstitutionality was lodged against the alternating mechanism, arguing that it undermines the electorate and restricts the election of the most ideal individuals and violates their rights to access public posts in conditions of equality. The TSE responded immediately, providing the Constitutional Chamber extensive explanations of the underpinnings of this mechanism (TSE Document -2138-2010). Different sectors and entities have expressed their concern about the appeal. For example, in an event organized by TSE/IFED-UNDP (2010) it was stated that "there can be no law without a mechanism; if the alternation mechanism fails, parity fails; it would have no validity". As of January 2011, the Constitutional Chamber has yet to make a decision on the appeal.

At the technical level, the challenges here relate to the power, capacity and function of the TSE and the recently created IFED in strengthening political parties and citizenship in general, so that the principle of gender parity materializes in the political and electoral arena. As it occurred with the minimum quota, the interpretative phase of the parity rule is significant. The challenge lies in tying the international framework of women's human rights and the Electoral Code's main guiding principles, with its competencies concerning the activity of the political parties. IFED may contribute in this sense, since its objectives and areas of work must be directed toward citizenship-building and its authorities have already expressed interest in incorporating the gender dimension in its regular activities. For this, it will be necessary that both IFED and the TSE develop an internal process for strategic institutionalization of the gender dimension. Even though the authorities have so far welcome the changes taking place over the last thirteen years, the institutional culture can still permeate with stereotypes and officials may not have enough tools and knowledge to apply that perspective adequately and comprehensively. It would be a mistake to assume that just having the rule is sufficient to alter cultural and institutional patterns within the entity. In addition, if the TSE and IFED are to institutionalize the gender perspective adequately, its incorporation must be consolidated at the organic and programmatic levels; for this it is highly advisable that the Gender Unit and the work of the TSE's Gender Commission be strengthened, along with intervention of the two entities at the level of institutional planning.

Finally, with respect to IFED's work with political parties, an important task will be to give more meaning to the concept of training and support so that the parties interpret and incorporate the Electoral Code's parity and non-discrimination principles adequately. In relation to strengthening leadership programs, efforts must be intensified so that these are exercised effectively by both men and women including statistical analyses. In order for women to advance in the political and electoral arena it is highly important that the State promote, consistently and continuously, public policies benefitting women and gender equity, and that these be conceived with a comprehensive and strategic vision. Likewise, real progress will occur only when these measures are operationalized through action plans and programs and through follow-up mechanisms. The challenge for Costa Rica is whether public agencies will be capable of incorporating policies for gender equity. In this sense, INAMU is called to play a central role as the technical governing entity concerning the gender theme in the Executive Power, but also the Ministry of Planning (MIDEPLAN) and governing entities of the social sector, which must oversee full compliance with public policies.

At the socio-cultural and organizational level, efforts need to be intensified in several areas: a) promotion and strengthening of leadership programs; b) internal empowerment of women, so they can exercise quality leadership with a vision of gender equity; c) a common objective for both men and women in understanding gender equity as part of the collective welfare of society, rather than an issue only for women's benefit; d) promotion of women and men's active citizenship; e) promotion of co-responsibility in the care of dependents and family; f) promotion of harmonious family relations, especially in the case of women politicians; g) improve communication to adequately and effectively transmit the concept of parity and the strategic importance of constructing more equitable societies; h) and finally, an understanding from the part of social organizations that parties are not the only vehicle for participating in politics and that they can also help achieve gender equity in their organizations, including the implementation of parity principles.

For political parties, the main challenge consists of turning the principles of parity and non-discrimination into assets for the modernization of parties, making them inclusive and participatory structures. The democratic climate leading to greater female participation within political parties and in public decision-making positions can help improve the political system in general. Further, it is necessary for parties to understand that the parity principle is not in conflict with affirmative action measures that can be used as a medium to promote women's participation in their structures and in party politics in general. In this sense, entities like the TSE and others interested in achieving gender equity may help reinforce the promotion of women's participation—something requiring greater alacrity in the case of parties that nominate cantons and provincial candidates.

Within the next two electoral cycles a more rigorous analysis of the parity clause is likely. What needs to occur quickly is to expand the arena in which these rules have been circumscribed, since this issue not only refers to the electoral sphere. It also requires comprehensive public policies to promote gender equity that are sustained over time, as well as a socio-political platform solid enough to provide fertile ground for the idea of women's and men's complementary qualities in order to build equal citizenship, promote general well-being and consolidate democracy.

Chapter Eight

Women's Quotas in the Dominican Republic

Advances and Detractions

Jacqueline Jiménez Polanco[1]

During the last two decades, following the recommendations of the Fourth United Nations World Conference on Women (UNWCW) held in Beijing in 1995, Latin American women serving in political parties and Non-Governmental Organizations (NGO's) spearheaded mobilization efforts to increase their access to policy-making through the implementation of gender-based quotas.

In compliance with the Latin American regional pattern, the Dominican Republic became the first Caribbean nation to implement a quota law for women in electable positions in 1997.

Akin to other nations in the region, the application of quotas in the Dominican Republic has been constantly challenged by both cultural and institutional obstacles. Consequently, the quota laws have had unassertive effects in steadily increasing the number of women in electoral posts. Gender quotas have propelled, however, enduring social and political actions that have raised awareness in society about the importance of women's political representation as a means to reinforce the democratic culture and its equitable institutional practices. (Jiménez Polanco 1999, 2001).

This chapter analyzes the effects of quotas in the Dominican Republic in a comparative regional perspective. It examines the effects of quotas in gradually increasing Dominican women's political representation and the cultural and institutional barriers to their effective application in congressional seats and municipal posts. The main cultural and institutional challenges to the effective application of quotas are posed by the male-dominated political culture epitomized in the post-authoritarian patrimonial party organization and centralized leadership of the three major parties PRD (Dominican Revolutionary Party), PRSC (Christian Socialist Reformist Party) and PLD (Dominican Liberation Party), and the proliferating neoliberal anti-party movements and birthright candidacies. An overview of the historical and contemporary political processes shows that the Dominican women politicians have counterbalanced important obstacles to their participation in decision-making by developing a nonconformist blend-model of cooperation with the male-dominated party leadership and integration into the international and local mobilization efforts to increase women's political representation. Women accommodate to the traditional political standards whilst build contingent intra- and inter-party/NGOs agreements. This strategy allows them to seize some levels of power while putting into effect equitable public policies for the benefit of the historically marginalized groups in society.

This chapter argues that the success of quotas in gradually increasing the number of women in top political positions in the Dominican Republic depends on its effective application in closed party-lists proportional representation (PR) systems and large districts. This constitutes a huge political barrier due to four major factors: (1) the prevailing open-party lists PR system in the Chamber of Deputies and open-party lists single-majority system in the Senate and Mayoral posts; (2) the distribution of votes in districts of small and medium magnitude; (3) the rampant atomization of major party organizations and their weak leadership; (4) the replacement of the patrimonial party organization and centralist leadership model by clientelist anti-party movements and birthright candidacies. During this thirteen year-long journey with quotas the male leaders have acknowledged the obstacles to the effective application of this affirmative action mechanism and the best means to overcome them. They have become aware of the benefits of applying a closed-party list PR system in districts of large and medium magnitude in the election of municipal councils, which have allowed women to achieve the minimum thirty-three percent of the quota. This author asserts that this is the beginning of a real change in the political culture and citizenship model. The effective implementation of a gender-balanced political representation is gradually debunking the patriarchal political practice and discourse and, therefore, transforming the post-authoritarian pattern into a more pluralistic one.

Do Numbers Matter? The Quota Boom in Latin American Parliaments and Its Effects in the Dominican Republic

When national quotas broke the Latin American political surface in Argentina in 1991, Center-Left parties in Mexico (PRD) and the Dominican Republic (PRD) implemented statutory quotas. In the 2000s national quota laws were applied in Argentina, Bolivia, Brazil, Costa Rica, Dominican Republic, Ecuador, Mexico, Panama, Honduras, Paraguay, and Peru. Colombia and Venezuela had quota laws for a brief period.

In the Dominican Republic, the ongoing debate about quotas has incited a pluralistic discourse challenging pervasive anti-democratic norms and patriarchal practices. The slow but steady growing presence of women in the Dominican Congress has allowed the approval of policies benefiting the disadvantaged sectors. This, in turn, has increased society's confidence in the capacity of women to efficiently perform traditionally male-dominated positions, like serving in electoral office, and challenge anti-democratic behaviors. The numerical increase of women deputies has also propelled a tendency towards a gradual gender-balanced representation in the municipalities, the judiciary, and the executive.

At the regional level over time, quotas slightly increased women's parliamentary representation moving from three percent to 12.7 percent in the Lower/Single

Table 8.1: Women's Seats in Lower & Single Houses with Quotas, 2000–2010

COUNTRIES WITH QUOTAS	2000	2001	2002	2003	2004	2005	2006	2007	2008	2009	2010
Argentina	26.5	30.7	30.7	30.7	33.7	36.2	35.0	40.0	40.0	38.5	38.5
Bolivia	11.5	11.5	18.5	18.5	19.2	16.9	16.9	16.9	16.9	22.3	25.4
Brazil	5.7	5.7	8.6	8.6	8.6	8.6	8.8	9.0	9.0	8.8	8.8
Colombia	11.8	11.8	12.0	12.0	12.0	12.0	8.4	8.4	8.4	8.4	8.4
Costa Rica	19.3	19.3	35.1	35.1	35.1	35.1	38.6	38.6	38.6	38.6	38.6
Ecuador	14.6	14.6	16.0	16.0	16.0	16.0	25.0	25.0	25.0	32.3	32.3
Honduras	9.4	5.5	5.5	5.5	5.5	23.4	23.4	23.4	23.4	18.0	18.0
Mexico	16	16	16	22.6	22.6	24.2	22.6	23.2	23.2	27.6	26.2
Panamá	9.9	9.9	9.9	9.9	16.7	16.7	16.7	16.7	16.7	8.5	8.5
Paraguay	2.5	2.5	2.5	8.8	10.0	10.0	10.0	10.0	12.5	12.5	12.5
Peru	17.5	17.5	17.5	17.5	18.3	18.3	29.2	29.2	29.2	27.5	27.5
Dominican Republic	16.1	16.1	17.3	17.3	17.3	17.3	19.7	19.7	19.7	19.6	20.2
Venezuela	9.7	9.7	9.7	9.7	9.7	17.4	18.0	18.6	18.6	17.5	17.5

Source: Inter-Parliamentary Union—Women in National Parliaments, 2000-2010; http://www.ipu.org/english/home.htm.

Houses and from ten percent to 11.7 percent in the Upper Houses between the 1980s and the 1990s. (IPU 1995). This moderate trend persisted in the second half of the 1990s and congresswomen reached an average of 15.4 percent of the seats in the Lower and Single Houses and 13.9 percent in the Upper Houses. (IPU 1999). Following the regional trend, Dominican women deputies reached 11.7 percent in 1994 and 16.1 percent in 1998, but their representation in the Senate barely increased from 3.3 percent in 1994 to 6.7 percent in 1998. (Jiménez Polanco 2008, 172). In contrast, women's seats flourished in other national Lower and Single Houses to proportions as high as 27.6 percent in Argentina in 1997 and 19.3 percent in Costa Rica in 1998. (Jiménez Polanco 1999).

The first decade of the 2000s saw a small increase in the average percentage of women in the American parliaments (including the United States, Central/South America and the Caribbean) ranging between fifteen percent and twenty-three percent in the Lower and Single Houses and between seventeen percent and twenty-three percent in the Upper Houses. The regional average for the Americas was slightly higher than the worldwide average that ranged between fourteen percent and 19.3 percent in the Lower and Single Houses and between thirteen percent and twenty-two percent in the Upper Houses.(IPU 2000–2010). This was an effect of the flow in the percentages of women's seats in the Latin American national legislatures with quotas that ranged from 2.5 percent to forty percent in the Single and Lower Houses (Table 8.1) and from 3.1 percent to 47.2 percent in the Upper Houses (Table 8.2).

In the Dominican Republic, the slight increase of sixteen to twenty percent in the Chamber of Deputies has kept it far from Argentina, Bolivia, Costa Rica, Ecuador,

Table 8.2: Women's Seats in Upper Houses with Quotas, 2000–2010

COUNTRIES WITH QUOTAS	2000	2001	2002	2003	2004	2005	2006	2007	2008	2009	2010
Argentina	2.8	33.3	33.3	33.3	33.3	41.7	43.1	38.9	38.9	35.2	35.2
Bolivia	3.7	3.7	14.8	14.8	11.1	3.7	3.7	3.7	3.7	41.7	47.2
Brazil	7.4	7.4	12.3	12.3	12.3	12.3	12.3	12.3	12.3	12.3	12.3
Colombia	12.7	12.7	8.8	8.8	8.8	8.8	11.8	11.8	11.8	11.8	11.8
Mexico	15.6	15.6	15.6	15.6	15.6	21.9	17.2	18.0	18.0	19.5	19.5
Paraguay	17.8	17.8	17.8	8.9	8.9	8.9	8.9	13.3	15.6	15.6	15.6
Dominican Republic	6.7	6.7	6.3	6.3	6.3	6.3	3.1	3.1	3.1	3.1	9.4

Source: Inter-Parliamentary Union—Women in National Parliaments, 2000–2010; http://www.ipu.org/english/home.htm.

Mexico and Peru that reached between twenty-five and forty percent. The Caribbean nation has also upheld the smallest percentages in the Senate ranging between 6.7 and 6.3 percent from 2000 to 2005, 3.1 percent from 2006 to 2009, and 9.4 percent in 2010, which represents the lowest percentage in the latest legislature region-wide.

United Nations' Expectations and Regional Quota Performance

The common pattern in Latin American parliaments is the deviation from the implementation of a quota of thirty percent as endorsed by the United Nations' Economic and Social Council (ECOSOC) and implemented worldwide as it was examined in the world review on the implementation of the Beijing Platform for Action (PFA) in 2000.[2] The reports indicate that although some progress has been made within societies to recognize the significant role of women in decision-making posts at all levels (intergovernmental, governmental, and non-governmental) and a greater number of countries applied affirmative action policies (including quotas), there has been a persisting gap between *de jure* and *de facto* equality. The review found that "the actual participation of women at the highest levels of national and international decision-making has not significantly changed since the time of the Fourth World Conference on Women in 1995."[3]

The PFA states that "although women make up at least half of the electorate in almost all countries and have attained the right to vote and hold office in almost all States Members of the United Nations, women continue to be seriously underrepresented as candidates for public office". It also stressed that "despite the widespread movement towards democratization in most countries, women are largely underrepresented at most levels of government, especially in ministerial and other executive bodies, and have made little progress in attaining political power in legislative bodies or in achieving the target endorsed by the Economic and Social Council [ECOSOC] of having thirty percent of women in positions at decision-making levels by 1995." The PFA declared that the goals of equality, development, and peace could be only achieved with the active participation of women and the incorporation of women's perspective at all levels of decision-making.[4]

Doing So Much with So Little: Dominican Women's Political Mobilization and Performance with Quotas

During the mobilization efforts for the approval of a gender-based quota, women politicians of the Center-Left PRD and Center-Right PRSC and PLD allied with institutional feminists affiliated with the Research Center for Feminine Action (CIPAF) to make a contingent agreement that led to the creation of the Women's Equal Opportunity Plan (PIOM). Accordingly, under PRD control (1996–2000) Congress passed the Electoral Law 275-97 establishing a women's quota of twenty-five percent of the seats in the Upper and Lower House. The Law was reformed in 2000 to increase the quota to thirty-three percent of women in the Lower House and the municipal councils (*regidurías),* and fifty percent in mayoral posts or *sindicaturas* (today *alcaldías).*

The approval of the national quota law in the Dominican Republic was the result of a long-standing mobilization process initiated in the early 1980s that, following CEDAW's recommendations, led to the foundation of several gender-based governmental and non-governmental institutions, such as the National Directorate for the Advocacy of Women (DGPM) founded in 1982 during the PRD administration. Following the recommendations of the Nairobi Declaration, the DGPM co-sponsored the creation of the Coordinating Committee of Women's NGOs (COGAM) in 1986. In compliance with the Beijing PFA, the DGPM launched in 1997 the National Plan for Gender Equity (PLANEG) with Gladys Gutiérrez's leadership in the PLD. In 1999, the Law 86-99 transformed the DGPM into the ministerial body Women's State Secretariat (SEM).

Additionally, in the 1994–1998 legislatures the Honorary Women's Advisory Committee for the Senate (CHMAS) was created. Led by the PRD Senator Milagros Ortiz Bosch and integrated by both women politicians and institutional feminists, the CHMAS submitted a bill for the approval of the 1994 Belem do Para's Convention on the Prevention, Punishment and Eradication of Violence against Women. This prompted the enactment of several bills addressed at protecting the rights of women, children, and immigrants, such as the Law 24-97 on Domestic Violence, the Law 137-03 on Migrants and Human Trafficking (*Tráfico Ilícito de Migrantes y Trata de Personas*) and the Law 88-03 on Shelter Centers (*Casas de Acogida o Refugios*).

Women's mobilization efforts also breached the long-standing tradition of women's exclusion from party executive positions through the implementation in 1994 of a statutory quota of twenty-five percent in the PRD (Jiménez Polanco 1999, 88–89). The approval of a quota in the oldest Dominican party prompted a gradual increase in the number of seats achieved by PRD's women in the Chamber of Deputies. It also facilitated the election of Milagros Ortiz as a Senate candidate in the party primaries. She was the only woman senator in the 1994–1998 legislatures and the candidate who won the largest amount of the overall votes cast in the 1994 congressional elections. Although the PRD statutory quota did not prompt a significant increase of woman senators, it helped to strengthen Ortiz's long-standing leadership.

Dr. Ortiz Bosch was reelected for a second senatorial term in 1998. During her tenure in the Senate she pushed forward the approval of important bills related to the recognition and protection of the civil and economic rights of women and children in domestic partnerships. These bills included the recognition of equal rights for both "natural" and "legitimate" children (children born outside and inside the marriage), two imperative bills in a nation where concubinage has always been the most popular nuclear family pattern. She also worked in the reform of the agrarian law to adopt a gender-balanced policy for the equal distribution of lands between women and men farmers. In addition, Senator Ortiz Bosch participated in the organizational judicial committee that led to the foundation of a national school for judges (*Escuela National de la Magistratura*). Ortiz Bosch became the most prominent woman politician nationwide, which allowed her to resign from the Senate, run for the PRD vice-presidential candidacy and after winning the elections, she became the first woman Vice President in the country's history.

Good Wills and Real Obstacles: The Minimalist Effects of Quotas in the Dominican Parliament

Party leadership acknowledges the fact that adopting gender-balanced policies will help consolidate the country's democratic system, yet, it has been reticent to follow suit. This demonstrates a double standard driven by traditional cultural beliefs. The Dominican Republic has a frail democratic citizenship model, whose leadership discourse navigates in the edge of the ideal pluralistic values and the real authoritarian practices. Therefore, it is not fortuitous that despite the legal increase in the percentage of quotas, Dominican congresswomen have not achieved the minimum rate established by the law in the last thirteen years since the law has been in place.

The Electoral Law No. 275-97 established a quota of twenty-five percent in a time when the Lower House had a closed-party lists PR system and the districts were binomial, trinomial, and of small (4–6 seats), medium (7–11 seats) and large (12–44 seats) magnitudes. The Electoral Law No. 12-2000 increased the quota to thirty-three percent and this percentage was maintained by the Electoral Law No. 06–2006. The thirty-three percent quota has been applied in the legislatures of 2002, 2006, and 2010 during which electoral reforms established an unblocked close-party lists PR or preferential system with votes allotted in binomial, small and medium magnitude districts.

Figure 8.1 shows the minimalist effect of the twenty-five percent quota in the 1998 legislative elections. Although the elections were held under a closed-party lists PR system, the Law did not mandate parties to allot women in electable positions. Women candidates were allocated in the last places of the party lists. There-

Figure 8.1: Dominican Women's Seats in the Lower and Upper House, 1998–2010

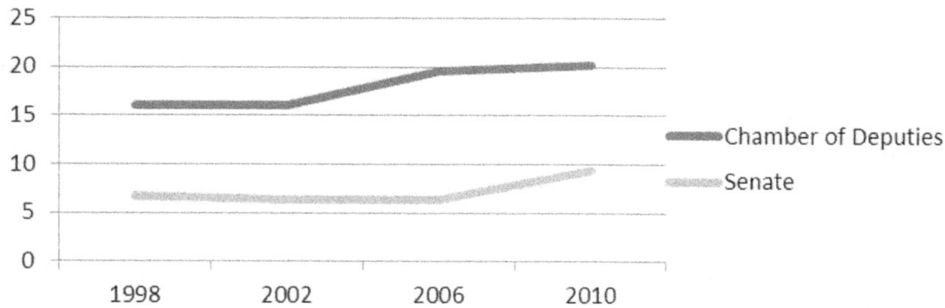

Source: Official bulletins of the Central Electoral Board (Junta Central Electoral), 1998-2010.

fore, they achieved 16.1 percent of the seats compared to the 11.7 percent they achieved in 1994 before the application of the quota.

Table 8.3 shows that the application of the thirty-three percent quota in districts of small and medium magnitudes and in unblocked close-party lists PR or preferential voting system left the women deputies seats inalterable in 2002 (six-

Table 8-3: Women Deputies Elected in 1998, 2002, 2006, 2010

YEAR	DISTRICTS SIZE	SEATS #	WOMEN #	WOMEN %
1998	Small	70	10	14.3
	Medium	21	2	9.5
	Large	58	12	20.7
	TOTAL	149	24	16.1
2002	Small	130	20	15.4
	Medium	20	4	20
	TOTAL	150	24	16
2006	Small	118	22	18.6%
	Medium	60	13	21.7%
	TOTAL	178	35	19.7%
2010	Small	118	23	19.5%
	Medium	60	14	23.3%
	TOTAL	178	37	20.8

Source: Official bulletins of the Central Electoral Board

teen percent) and allowed a slight increase in 2006 (19.6 percent) and in 2010 (20.2 percent). Ironically, the 0.6percent increase in the women's deputy seats in 2010 was not as a result of the quota, but of the creation of five new congressional seats (from 173 seats to 178) for the so-called "national deputies" in which one of the elected candidates happened to be a woman. National deputies are not, however, elected representatives to the Dominican national congress but members of the Central American Parliament. The manipulation of the electoral system to create these confusing and overlapping parliamentary seats constitutes a typical expression of the major parties undemocratic tradition of tricking the legal system to satisfy the selective incentives of their male members and allies while giving the appearance of an increasing pluralistic and gender-balanced representation.

A previous illustration of this devious institutional barrier happened when the Law No. 275-97 extended the application of the twenty-five percent gender quota to the senate but its application in the 1998 elections was inconsequential due to the Senate's single-majority system. Figure 8.1 shows an insignificant increase of women senators, from 3.3 percent in 1994 to 6.7 percent in 2008. Since then, the percentage of women senators remained stagnant until 2010 when women attained a greater but still low 9.4 percent of the seats. The Senate single-majority electoral system has not been altered to facilitate the application of quotas. After the 1998 quota fiasco in the Senate, women politicians and scholars discourse and mobilization efforts led legislators to tacitly recognize the technical impossibility of applying quotas in a single-majority voting system. Therefore, the Electoral Laws No. 12-2000 and No. 06-2006 do not contemplate the application of the quota in the Senate, but instead of mentioning the alteration of the previous law through the elimination of quotas in the Senate, the law is mute as if the legal application of the quota in the Senate had never been established (Jiménez Polanco, 2002).

The thirty-three percent quota at municipal levels has been applied indistinctively to either the mayor or deputy mayor posts through a single-majority vote, but parties nominated more women to deputy positions rather than to mayoral posts, which has produced an unsteady increase of women mayors with 7.2 percent in 2002, 11.3 percent in 2006, and 5.8 percent in 2010. This also generated a steady growth of women deputy mayors with 92.8 percent, in 2002, 88.7 percent in 2006, and 99.3 percent in 2010. The percentage of Dominican women mayors is similar to the regional average (5.5 percent). Women who have been elected to the mayoral offices have developed successful policies through the implementation of a decentralized administration model based on a participatory assembly system in which the presence of representatives of civil society in decision-making, including the budget approval, has guaranteed transparency and accountability (Quehaceres 2006, 6).

Table 8.4: Women Elected in Municipal Councils, 2010

DISTRICTS SIZE		DISTRICTS #	SEATS #	WOMEN #	WOMEN %
Small	5 seats	87	435	141	32.4%
Medium	7 seats	34	238	84	35.3%
	9 seats	14	126	41	32.5%
Large	10 seats	1	10	2	20.0%
	11 seats	5	55	17	30.9%
	12 seats	2	24	8	33.0%
	13 seats	10	130	49	37.7%
	14 seats	1	14	4	28.6%
	15 seats	2	30	9	30.0%
	17 seats	4	68	21	30.9%
	19 seats	1	19	7	36.8.%
TOTAL		161	1149	383	33.3%

Source: Official bulletins of the Central Electoral Board, 2010

Table 8.4 shows that the application of the thirty-three percent quota in the city councils' closed-party lists PR in districts of large, medium and small magnitudes has proved to be successful, allowing a steady growing representation of municipal councils by women (*regidoras*) in districts of large magnitude with 28.5 percent in 2002, 29.1 percent in 2006, and 33.3 percent in 2010. It has also let a steady increase of women deputy councils with 31.1 percent in 2002, 29.9 percent in 2006, and 35.2 percent in 2010. The percentage of Dominican women councils is higher than the regional average (twenty-one percent). The idea of increasing the political representation of women at municipal levels forms part of a strategy launched by the UN in the late 1990s, which attempts to encourage the access of women in decision-making posts at national levels through gradually strengthening their leadership in local communities.

Cultural and Institutional Obstacles to the Efficacy of Quotas

Gender quotas have gradually changed institutional rules, but as legal instruments they do not have the power to remove pervasive cultural, political and social obstacles that have hindered their effective application. The mounting obstacles to the efficacy of quotas show that rigid cultural traditions resulting from the social hierarchies of class, race, sex, and gender may be overcome only in the long term.

Latin American cultural and social traditions are intricately intertwined with the models of citizenship and political systems operating within particular countries. Consequently, they have brought about institutional and technical barriers that male leaders have enforced to mismanage the quota laws. In addition, the socioeconomic effects of globalization through corporate capitalism hamper the efficacy of quotas through the increasing high cost of electoral campaigns, the commercialization of votes, and the spoiling party system that results in the control of political machineries by wealthy male groups that highly restrict the competition of women and other candidates with poor financial resources. Therefore, the insufficient allocation of public campaign funds and technical support has hindered the possibilities of women to be elected despite their sky-scraping popularity during the electoral campaigns.

The main cultural obstacles draw from prevailing patriarchal values and practices, in which men traditionally dominate the public domain. The *machismo* tradition, ingrained in the predominant Roman-Catholic religious beliefs, saturates parties and electoral institutions, barring women from the political prerogatives expected from quota laws. Male leaders have deterred the effective application of quotas by tricking the electoral and party systems as a means to marginalize women from decision-making positions. Also, the patrimonial, classist and racist birthright-candidate tradition (*candidato nato*) has hampered the effective application of quotas and the election of women and other subordinate sectors (racial, class-based, and sexual minorities). The birthright tradition has been sustained through the *preferential* vote in party-list systems that include either the open lists (i.e. Brazil) or the so-called unblocked-closed party lists (*listas abiertas* and *listas cerradas desbloqueadas*) (i.e. Dominican Republic).

Besides the open party-lists, the major institutional obstacles to the application of quotas include the weak distribution of seats in districts of small and middle magnitude; the lack of mechanisms ruling the percentage of women to be elected per district; the absence of rules to allocate women candidates to electable positions in closed party-list proportional representation (PR) systems; the inefficacy of quotas in candidate-centered voting systems (i.e. open party-list PR and party-list majority—single or binomial systems). Furthermore, since quotas have not influenced legislating within parliaments, most congresswomen have been relegated to the traditional "female domain" on standing legislative committees such as education, family, female affairs, housing, and senior and youth issues. Consequently, despite the quota laws, congresswomen have continued to wield little influence in traditionally male-dominated areas, such as constitutional affairs, energy, internal security, justice, mining and industry, municipal affairs, national defense, national and international economy, political judgment, technology, and transportation. (Jiménez Polanco 1999, 2001, 2002, 2004, 2005, 2008).

What Weighs More in the Efficacy of Dominican Quotas: Cultural, Institutional Challenges, or Both?

The establishment of a quota-law represented a great challenge to the Dominican Republic's patriarchal cultural tradition, the patrimonial style of its political system and its charismatic party model depicted in the control of public offices by the male leaders of dominant parties. Following Trujillo and Balaguer's unthreatening autocratic notion of "equilibrium at home and state", male leaders have traditionally barred women from meaningful participation in top political posts as a mean to build a masquerade gender-balanced profile that would help them sustain their local, national, and international legitimacy.

Dominican men have typically gotten women on the political board through a traditional discourse in which they would recognize women's salient contributions to the development of the nation's values as mothers, wives, daughters, sisters, and teachers. They have not really appraised women's access to political positions as a means to promote gender equality, but as a means to strengthening their own leadership. Therefore, the dominant parties agreed to enact a quota-law to benefit from a national and international image that would eventually depict them as modern and democratic, but in fact they fear that a real increase in the number of women occupying political posts might threaten their power. This pattern is epitomized in the male politicians' discourse in inter-party and civil organizations forums in which they would tend to argue that quotas contradict the principle of equality as women are given preferential treatment over men, or that quotas are undemocratic as the final decision is not left entirely to the voters, and that women should compete with men for political positions on the basis of their qualifications and not on the benefits of the quotas. In compliance with their camouflaged political discourse, the male leaders have been constantly overruling the electoral laws and enforcing technical obstacles to the efficacy of quotas.

As a result, the quota law has not resulted in a large numerical increase of Dominican women in legislative and municipal positions. However, women's access to participation in decision-making and power and their prolific performance have effected a salient change in the citizenship model and the political discourse and praxis, all of which have helped build a more pluralistic society. An understanding of the importance of this phenomenon may be achieved through contextualizing the political environment in the Caribbean nation during the application of the quota law and the women's political participation historical background under authoritarian and democratic regimes.

Dominican Women in Politics since the 1960s: Authoritarianism and Democracy

In 1997 when the first quota law was approved, the Dominican Republic was commemorating almost two decades of its second wave of democratization launched with the 1978 presidential and congressional elections; a long and intricate process during which the male leaders controlled politics through disputed elections, clienteles, and corrupted quasi-polyarchies. (Jiménez Polanco 1994, 1999b).

The Dominican Republic first experienced a momentary spurt of democracy back in 1963 during Juan Bosch's brief presidency with the PRD following the breakdown of General Rafael Trujillo's bloody and long-standing dictatorship (1930–1961).[5] Bosch's democratic regime was crushed by a coup d'état after seven short months with the assistance of the Catholic Church and the military combined with John F. Kennedy's evident fear of the potential appearance of another Castro in the Caribbean during the Cold War era. The Church and military launched an anti-communist campaign against Bosch's democratic profile that ignited Kennedy's desire to avoid the further spread of communism in the Americas. These factors prompted the breakdown of Bosch's constitutional regime and a subsequent turbulent period of political instability and social mobilization. The military coup, in turn, led to a civil war (*Revolución de Abril*) and a second U.S. military occupation in 1965, and Joaquín Balaguer's twelve-year long (1966–1978) authoritarian regime. (Jiménez Polanco 1999b).

During his brief presidential term, Bosch launched a process of secularization that for the first time in the nation's republican history allowed the congressional passage of a new constitution that established equal rights for women and men in labor, salary, education, and marriage; women's protection during pregnancy; and equal rights for children born both inside and outside marriage. The Congress also passed a civil divorce law and launched a process of secularization through the elimination of the historical economic and political privileges of the Catholic Church through the Concordat.

It was during the 1960s convulsive political period that Milagros Ortiz Bosch started her political career with her uncle Juan Bosch. When Bosch left the Center-Left PRD in 1973 to found the Marxist-Leninist PLD, Ortiz Bosch did not follow him but instead stayed in the PRD. During her tenure in the Senate (1994–1998/1998–2000) and the Vice-Presidency (2000–2006), Ortiz Bosch remained firmly attached to the PRD's Center-Left original ideology and social policies originally epitomized in the 1962 social-democratic Constitution.

The recognition of women's citizenship rights during Bosch's short presidency and the subsequently active participation of students and middle-class women in the civil war set the scene for the development of the organized feminist movement in the leftist Dominican Women's Federation (*Federación Dominicana de Mujeres*) in the 1960s, the Women's Promotion Group (*Grupo Promoción de la Mujer*) in the 1970s, and CIPAF in the 1980s. Founded by the institutional feminist Magaly Pineda, CIPAF became the first women's NGO in the Dominican Republic.

Women's political mobilization was halted during Balaguer's autocratic regime (1966–1978).[6] A former fervent Trujillo's acolyte and president-puppet in 1959, Balaguer established a gory dictatorship with modernizing features. He adopted a Trujilloist gender parallel politics based on the patriarchal style of co-opting women to play traditional female roles in governmental posts (i.e. Altagracia Bautista de Suárez as State Secretary of Education) and lead charity activities under the umbrella of his sisters' Love Crusade (*Cruzada del Amor*). Meanwhile, he destroyed any sort of opposition by the use of state violence through the assassination, disappearance, and expatriation of many Dominican women and men.

Many women and men lost their lives in the brutal hands of Balaguer's militia (*Banda Colorá*) during the toughest period of his autocratic regime between 1970 and 1974. Some of the women were martyrs who represent until the present day a symbol of the Dominican women's long-standing struggle for social justice, equity and equality. One of them was the vibrant illiterate black rural leader Florinda Muñóz Serrano, better known as Mamá Tingó, who was assassinated by a landowner's foreman on November 1, 1974 after advocating in court the rights of 350 farmer families from the Christian Agrarian League to hold and cultivate their lands. Mamá Tingó's death took place during Balaguer's infamous agrarian reform, through which the government dispossessed land workers (*campesinos*) from their small plots and conferred them to civil and military landowners (*terratenientes)* in exchange for their political allegiance and electoral support.[7] Balaguer's infamous social policies were also rejected by different urban sectors including students from public high schools and universities who held recurrent antigovernment mobilizations such as those in the campus of the Autonomous University of Santo Domingo, (*Universidad Autónoma de Santo Domingo,* UASD), in one of which the student Sagrario Díaz was assassinated by a military shoot on April 4th 1972.

After a twelve-year long reign of injustices and terror, U.S. President "Jimmy" Carter pressured Balaguer to embrace the institutional changes brought about by the Latin American third democratic wave and accept the results of the 1978 competitive elections that ended his time in office. The mobilization efforts of women politicians and institutional feminists expedited the democratic transition and their participation in the United Nations Women's Decade (1975–1985) fueled their incorporation into political parties and official institutions.

Women's Role in the PRD Democratic Governments 1978–1982, 1982–1986

During the PRD's democratic presidencies the Dominican people saw an increase in women's political mobilization at the grass-root level and the creation of several governmental and non-governmental organizations, such as the DGPM and COGAM.

Antonio Guzman's triumph in the 1978 elections allowed him to seize the first fully-accomplished democratic presidential term in Dominican history. His government opened the door to a new era in which the Dominican people would participate in pluralistic electoral process and would see themselves represented by both male and female figures with the president and the First Lady. In her role as First Lady, René Clan de Guzmán led the humanitarian governmental organization National Council for Children (*Consejo Nacional de la Niñez*, CONANI) that provided education programs and social services to poor children and single mothers. Unfortunately, Antonio Guzmán committed suicide in the presidential palace two months after the 1982 elections, presumably due to the shame caused by his daughter Sonia's highly corrupt activities and the president's fear that his family's deeds would be revealed during the PRD new presidential period. (Jiménez Polanco 1999b, 517).

Despite the Guzmán's family economic scandals, the PRD seized control of the presidency for a second period (1982–1986) following the success of Salvador Jorge Blanco in the 1982 competitive elections. Following the previous presidential administration, the First Lady Acela Mera de Jorge Blanco assumed CONANI's leadership. During Jorge Blanco's tenure the social effects of his austerity neoliberal program prompted the elimination of state subsidies for basic foods and budgetary cuts in social services such as health and education, leading to insurgent collective actions, particularly among poor urban women who organized themselves in neighborhood groups through the 1984 "*Pobladas*", the biggest social revolts to ever occur in the country since the 1960s. Popular mobilizations questioned the democratic legitimacy within the nation-state structures and propagated anti-party sentiments within society. The rampant corruption and the social effects of the PRD's neoliberal policies led to its electoral decline and the subsequent return of Balaguer to the presidential office after succeeding Jacobo Majluta (PRD) in the 1986 disputed elections.

Women's Role in the PRSC Governments 1986–1990, 1990–1994, 1994–1996

Balaguer won the disputed 1986 elections to Jacobo Majluta (PRD) and returned to the presidential palace with the PRSC.[8] He combined his traditional women's charity program with Love Crusade with the appointment of upper-class young women (i.e. Maribel Gassó) to sub-secretariat and secretariat positions, which allowed him to attract the support of members of the 1970s generations who were not familiar with his long-standing authoritarian style. The then octogenarian leader occupied the presidency for a ten-year long period, during which he also won the 1990 disputed elections to his historical and also octogenarian adversary Juan Bosch (PLD).[9]

During Balaguer's presidential terms in the 1990s the PRD and PLD parties factionalized and their bases weakened. Since the major worker unions were affiliated with the Center-Left dominant parties, the party leadership division and the atomization of their popular bases also affected them. Therefore, neither the parties nor the unions represented a challenge to Balaguer's undemocratic politics, which allowed him to govern with a camouflaged anti-party and anti-parliamentary movementist and delegative style in which the president apparently respected the political debate while simultaneously weakened the parliamentary work through the frequent imposition of decrees. Balaguer's anti-democratic style limited the counterbalance of the legislative to the executive in a winner-take-all presidential regime, which allowed him to impose the IMF neoliberal policies ease. (Jiménez Polanco, 1999b, 2006).

Balaguer's lack of formal opposition and his economic policies stirred up the formation of a coalition of popular organizations united under the umbrella of the Popular Struggle Committees (*Comités de Lucha Popular*, CLP) led by Virtudes Alvarez, an energetic woman from the impoverished and populous neighborhoods of urban Santo Domingo. Virtudes constituted Balaguer's primary opposition through the important role she played in the social uprisings against the perverse and pervasive repercussions of the IMF structural adjustment's program. To counteract the social effects of his economic policies, Balaguer demobilized the CLP through an effective disguise adaptation of his traditional authoritarian style into a formal pluralistic regime. In a condescending and patronizing speech Balaguer publicly recognized his "admiration" for Virtudes' "frail figure" and "persuasive" discourse, while his acolytes built a media profile accusing her of accepting bribes from the government and his mercenaries threatened to attempt against her physical integrity. But this shivering challenge did not stop Virtudes' political work and she has continued to nurture her rock hard leadership in the Leftist party MIUCA-Movement Unity and Change (*Movimiento Unidad y Cambio*), which develops important social programs for poor local communities, is the most popular minor party nation-wide, and holds international support from Leftist unions and party organizations in Spain.

In the early 1990s women's mobilization was at its highest peak and institutional feminists discussed their demands with party leadership. During the 1994 electoral campaign, inspired by the need of socioeconomic reforms and the weak programmatic platforms of dominant parties, institutional feminists affiliated with CIPAF launched the Feminist Minimum Program (*Programa Mínimo Feminista*) through which they advocated women's equal voting opportunities and the incorporation of the Women's Equal Opportunity Plan (PIOM) into the party platforms. The Program included fully incorporation of women into the national development policies, reform of discriminatory laws against women, non-sexist education, no violence against women, punishment to rapists, protection to mistreated women, better quality of public education, electricity, health and drinking water services, free and voluntary maternity, shared domestic work, responsible paternity, children day care centers, proportional participation of women in Congress and Government, creation of the Women's State Secretariat, equal salary for equal work, women farmers' rights to land, and new women's image in the mass media. PIOM advocated political participation, development policies legislation, labor participation, education and culture, health and reproductive rights, and fight against domestic violence. (Quehaceres 2006).

Women's Role in the First PLD Government 1996–2000

The 1996 elections allowed the presidential victory of Leonel Fernández, whose government centered around a free-market economic policy and a paternalistic and patriarchal incorporation of women into politics through the establishment of the Social Plan (*Plan Social*), an official charitable organization led by female relatives that would help him gain some popular support to counteract the hostility of a Congress fully controlled by the opposition (PRD-PRSC in 1994–1998 and PRD in 1998–2002).[10] In addition, like other Latin American Centrist leaders, Fernández put into practice the habitual co-optation of women to occupy executive positions in resource-poor secretariats, such as the newly-founded Women's Secretariat. During his presidential term (1996–2000) the National Plan for Gender Equity (PLANEG) was created, and the National Directorate for the Advocacy of Women (DGPM) acquired the ministerial range of Women's State Secretariat (SEM). The creation of the SEM sparked a slight increase in the number of women in executive positions of state secretariats that rose from 11.8 percent in 1994 to 19.0 percent in 1997 (Jiménez Polanco 1999, 89).

The first quota law was approved during Fernández's second year in the presidency by the major opposition parties in Congress, the Center-Left PRD and Center-Right PRSC. Congresswomen Dolores González, María Rosa Belliard, Milagros Díaz and Bienvenida Peña of PRSC and PRD played an important role in the inter-party advocacy for the Electoral Board's efficient application of the quota during the 1998 legislative elections. At the time, the official Center-Right PLD held a minimal representation in Congress (10.8 percent and 11.4 percent in the Lower House and 3.3 percent and 6.7 percent in the Upper House in the 1994–1996 and 1998–2002 legislative terms respectively) and women politicians occupied the lowest party executive positions in the PLD (10.3 percent) compared to the PRSC (11percent) and the PRD (12.6 percent). (Jiménez Polanco 1999, 88–89, 278–282). Historically identified as a Marxist-Leninist party from its foundation in 1973 until the end of Bosch's charismatic leadership and the party twist to the Center-Right in the early 1990's, the PLD's gender politics paralleled other Latin America Leftist organizations in which women did not occupy top party positions despite their imperative work in the base. Since the 1990s until the present day, women in the PLD have continued to play a small role in the party politics. Therefore, the congressional passage of several gender-based laws (i.e. quotas, domestic violence, and agrarian reform) was not an accomplishment of the PLD but of the PRD and PRSC.

Women's Role in the Alternate PRD and PLD Governments, 2000–2004, 2004–2008, 2008–2012

In 2000 the PRD won the presidential elections for a third term with Hipólito Mejía as president and Milagros Ortiz Bosch as vice-president. During her tenure as vice-president Milagros Ortiz also served as Minister of Education and as a minister she moved forward important social policies addressed at increasing the state funds for education, implementing racial/ethnic, sex/gender-balanced comprehensive methods in the textbooks, and protecting the educational rights of Dominican children of Haitian descent.[11]

But despite her long-standing popularity, *Doña* Milagros' access to the vice-presidential post was not an easy journey. First, she faced the challenges posed by the male-dominated party machinery led by Mejía and his conservative faction Hipólito's Presidential Project-PPH (*Proyecto Presidencial Hipólito)* that moved the party from the Center-Left to the Center-Right and forced Ortiz to renounce to her legitimate aspirations to the presidential post. Second, she was the spot of misogynistic sexist attacks from the opponent PLD during the campaign through accusations of being an alcoholic and rumors of being a lesbian, which in the pervasive authoritarian double moral standard rooted in the Dominican Catholic and Protestant traditions could be considered worse than being accused of committing acts of corruption. In addition, she had to stand up for the PRD's gender and racial inclusive practices recurrently turned down by the rhetorical gaffes of her patriarchal counterpart President Mejía, including his use of homophobic expressions against his PLD opponents and racist and sexist expressions towards women and men during media interviews at the local and international levels.

Mejía's presidential office implemented important social programs addressed at reducing poverty, such as breakfast in public schools, subsidy cards for single-mothers, and reconstruction of shanty-towns through replacing mud-floors for cemented-floors in homes. Additionally, the political stability of his first three years in power fostered the trust of international financial institutions towards the nation's macroeconomic growth, which led to an increase in the amounts of loans approved to develop social programs. By the end of his presidential term, however, Mejía had become the most unpopular political figure of Dominican modern history due to several factors that included the socioeconomic effects of his neoliberal policies among the middle and lower sectors, his anti-democratic measures against the mass media critics, his leading role in both the injudicious constitutional reform to pursue an immediate presidential reelection and the fake party primaries that were opposed by Vice-President Milagros Ortiz and generated an internal division of the PRD between the PPH and the orthodox anti-reelection faction led by Hatuey De Camps who left the PRD to found the Revolutionary Social Democrat Party (*Partido Revolucionario Social Demócrata*, PRSD).[12]

The PLD returned to the presidential office for a second term in 2004 following the electoral triumph of Leonel Fernández over Mejía in the first round in a violent electoral process that left several people dead and wounded. Two years after the elections, a group of PLD women from the SEM organized a National Conference on Gender Equity. With the support of the State Secretary and long-standing PLD leader Gladys Gutiérrez, her assistant and former congresswoman Ramonita García moved forward the preparation of a working paper that would be the foundation of the conference and in which for the first time in the PLD history women politicians disclosed data about their underrepresentation in party executive positions (twelve percent), government (four to twelve percent), parliament (zero to fifteen percent), and mayor offices (twelve to twenty-four percent). They also raised awareness about the importance of quotas and their effects in increasing women's political representation. Some PLD women candidates were frustrated with the administration of the 2004 electoral process and the distribution of posts by the party machinery that resulted in their deprivation from legitimately won positions.[13]

In 2006, institutional feminists of CIPAF launched a training program for women candidates to the legislative and municipal elections to counteract the negative effects of the preferential vote on the gender quota through benefitting individual birthright candidates (Quehaceres 2006).

In 2008, Leonel Fernández renewed his presidential post for a third period after his electoral victory over Miguel Vargas (PRD). During the first two years of his incumbency, the country experienced a macroeconomic growth that did not result in developing public policies to reduce poverty and social inequity. In addition, there was a general perception of an increment in the levels of corruption in public institutions. This, in turn, increased the levels of social dissatisfaction and political disaffection through recurrent civil mobilizations in which popular and middle sectors expressed their rejection against the reigning post-authoritarian political model embedded in the constitutional reform, presidency, major political parties, low enforcement institutions, Congress, and Catholic and Protestant churches.

The main concern was Fernández's 2009 constitutional reform that generated civil mobilizations and negative responses to its approval from several social sectors that with the slogan "That is not my Constitution" (*Esa no es mi Constitución*) rejected the procedure and several elements of the substantive law. Feminist organizations opposed the confessional feature of the Dominican state and its penalization of abortion in Article 37 since it operates against the will of eighty percent of the population who favored it for therapeutic reasons when the woman's life were at risk.[14]

2008–2010 also saw an increasing mobilization of women and youths against state violence, police brutality, and environmental pollution by gold mining corporations, such as Barrick Gold. Also women journalists, such as TV producer Nuria Piera developed a non-compromising mass media model that was constantly informing on the responsibility of public and private institutions and individuals in corruptive activities and violations of the human and citizenship rights.

Conclusions

After thirteen years since the implementation of the gender quota law in the Dominican Republic women politicians are still far away from the minimum thirty percent endorsed by the UN ECOSOC in 1995. However, the percentage of women in the Chamber of Deputies has steadily grown reaching twenty percent in the 2010 legislative elections and nine percent in the Senate. At the municipal level there has been an increase of women councils to 33.3 percent and a decrease of women mayors to 5.8 percent. The positive effect of quotas in increasing the percentage of women in electoral seats, although at a slow pace, has allowed them to advance legal reforms that have contributed to the development of a more equitable and participative society. In addition, it has created a social awareness of the importance of incorporating women in decision-making posts as a means to achieve equality and development. Women politicians are building a more inclusive democratic political discourse and citizenship model that is persistently challenging the post-authoritarian patriarchal culture in Latin America. There is still a long way to go to remove traditional cultural patterns and institutional practices that challenge the citizenship's rights of women and other marginalized groups to equitable political representation.

CHAPTER NINE

From Vanguard to Straggler

Women's Political Representation and Gender Quotas in Uruguay

NIKI JOHNSON AND VERÓNICA PÉREZ

This chapter examines the process that led to the passage of a quota law in Uruguay in April 2009 and its first implementation in internal elections just two months later. As well as exploring the factors at national-level that influenced both the timing and content of the new legislation, we reflect upon how the process and result compare with quota laws in force in other countries in the region.

The chapter is organized as follows. In the first section we place the quota law within the historical panorama of women's political representation in Uruguay, and trace in the post-dictatorship period the series of failed attempts made by women from all political parties to get affirmative action legislation passed. The second section provides a reconstruction of the process that finally led to the passing of gender quota legislation in 2009 and an analysis of the contents and implications of the new law. In the third section we undertake a quantitative analysis of the first implementation of the law in the internal elections to party national conventions in June 2009, exploring the extent to which parties only made the minimum effort required to comply with the law or whether there is any evidence that parties positively promoted a greater participation of women candidates. The fourth section evaluates the impact of the quota in the composition of the party national conventions elected in June 2009 and of its non-application in the parliamentary elections in October of the same year. The chapter ends with a series of reflections on the future application of the quota law in the 2014/2015 electoral cycle and its long-term implications for women's political representation in Uruguay.

From Early Promise to Late Developer

On paper, Uruguay appeared to be a prime candidate for early adoption of gender quota legislation. Historically, the country was at the vanguard in its defense of women's political equality, not only within the region, but in the world. In December 1932 it became the first Latin American country to give women equal and unrestricted rights to elect and be elected,[1] following a sustained campaign by the women's movement, and more importantly backed by the conviction of the dominant *batllista* faction of the hegemonic Colorado Party (*Partido Colorado*, PC). The *batllistas* were the first to present a suffrage bill in 1907 and their historic leader, José Batlle y Ordóñez, architect of the modern Uruguayan state, defended women's suffrage in editorials written under the pseudonym "Laura" in the daily newspaper *El Día*.[2] Another staunch supporter of votes for women was Emilio Frugoni, founder of the Uruguayan Socialist Party (*Partido Socialista*, PS), which held few seats in parliament but wielded considerable influence through the press, the principal medium of communication at the time.

Women first voted in 1938, but it was in the following elections that the expansion of women's political rights was felt. In 1942, there was a 60.9 percent in-

Figure 9.1: Female Parliamentary Representation Rates: Uruguay Pre- and Post-Dictatorship Periods (1942–1971, 1984–2009)

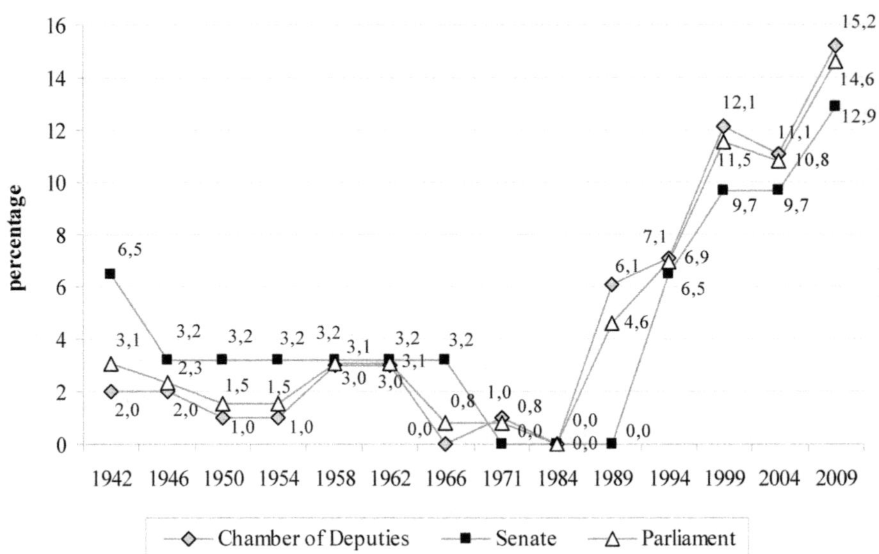

Source: Data from the Electoral Court (Corte Electoral) and the Uruguayan parliament website (www.parlamento.gub.uy).

crease in the number of votes cast, reflecting the increased registration and participation of female voters.[3] In these elections the *batllista* faction's list included twenty-one women candidates,[4] and the first women legislators entered parliament: two deputies and two senators.[5] Over the next three decades, until the military coup in 1973, women legislators continued to enter parliament at every election, although the 3.1 percent female representation rate reached in 1942 was never surpassed (see Figure 9.1).

Following the eleven-year interlude of authoritarian rule, not a single woman legislator was elected to the first parliament of the post-dictatorship era. After this inauspicious return to democratic rule for Uruguayan women, the percentage of female legislators rose slowly but steadily until 2004, when it appeared to hit a glass ceiling: the elections that year returned the same number of female senators (three) and eleven, or one fewer, women deputies than in 1999. In the 2009 elections the number of successful female candidates rose once again, albeit by less than four percentage points.

In short, Uruguay is characterized by its early recognition of equal political rights for women, which did not then translate in practice into significant levels of female access to elective posts. Three-quarters of a century after Uruguayan women were granted the right to elect and be elected, the female parliamentary representation rate remains below fifteen percent. As in all countries in the region, formal political equality did not bring about substantive equality in the exercise of political power. As we shall see later in this chapter, while male Uruguayan political leaders have become aware—in particular over the past decade and a half, during which time the percentage of women in parliament has been adopted as an indicator of gender equality and human development in several international indexes—of how badly these data reflect on what is considered one of the region's most democratic countries, they have remained reluctant to embrace affirmative action measures, such as quotas, that could redress this inequity.

It is also worth noting that from a technical point of view Uruguay's electoral system has two central characteristics that, according to the comparative literature, would facilitate an effective application of gender quotas—proportional representation and a voting system that uses closed and blocked electoral lists.[6] However, as we shall see below, certain peculiarities of the electoral and party systems tend to circumscribe the impact of gender candidate quotas in the Uruguayan case.

In spite of the apparently favorable precedents and conditions for an early passage of gender quota legislation in Uruguay, it is one of the last Latin American countries to pass such a law: following the ground-breaking legislation adopted in Argentina in 1991, between 1996 and 2000 another eleven countries in the region passed quota laws.[7] However, Uruguay's late reaction was not due to an absence of quota bills on the legislative agenda, nor to a lack of early mobilizing on this issue by the women's movement. In fact, the 2009 law has behind it a lengthy record of activism on this issue by women from different arenas—political parties, the women's movement and the academia.

These women have been united in their conviction that if affirmative action mechanisms were not adopted, Uruguayan democracy would remain "incomplete". They have argued that the underrepresentation of women is not only unjust, in that it disregards the equal rights of women to participate in the government of the nation, but also has negative implications for public policy making, which, if it does not include women's perspective, will be neither effective nor efficient.[8]

The campaign that eventually led to the passage of the quota law began with the incredulity felt by women politicians and members of the recently formed social women's movement when, in spite of the formal recognition of women's right to participate in the political life of the nation and the important role played by them in the opposition to the dictatorship, the dawning of the new democratic era did not bring increased access for women to traditional political arenas: in the 1984 elections not a single woman was elected to parliament, prompting the women's movement to emphasize the need to construct a true democracy under which the rights of all citizens would be fully respected.

The absence of women *titulares* in the Chamber of Deputies between 1985 and 1990, and in the Senate until 1995, did not mean, however, that women were entirely absent from parliament since, under the Constitution (article 116), candidate lists must include *suplentes* (alternates), who replace the *titular* (titleholder) on a temporary or permanent basis when s/he is absent or vacates the seat. These brief *suplencias* were regarded as an opportunity by women activists to present initiatives that would introduce new issues on to the legislative agenda, such as childcare provision, equal rights and treatment at work, as well as affirmative actions to promote women's access to elective posts.[9] So it was that the first quota bill was presented in 1988 by Alba Cassina de Nogara, a *suplente* deputy from the PC and a member of the Uruguayan National Council of Women (*Consejo Nacional de Mujeres del Uruguay*, CONAMU), one of the earliest Uruguayan women's suffrage organizations, whose members had drawn up the bill, foreseeing the possibility that Cassina de Nogara would at some point occupy a seat in the Lower House.

Over the next twenty years, another seven legislative initiatives proposing affirmative actions to guarantee women's access to elective posts were presented in parliament, of which just one reached the plenary discussion stage in at least one of the Houses, apart from the 2006 bill that finally became law in 2009 (see Table 9.1).

As shown in Table 9.1, all of the bills included some kind of placement mandate and sanctions, two of the conditions identified by Archenti and Tula as imperative for quota laws to be effective.[10] While the last initiative proposed the creation of an incentive structure to encourage parties to apply the quota, all but

Table 9.1. Bills Proposing Affirmative Action Mechanisms: Post-Dictatorship Period

BILL NUMBER	DATE	NUMBER, SEX AND PARTY OF SIGNATORIES	OUTCOME	CONTENTS		
				PERCENTAGE & APPLICABILITY QUOTA	PLACEMENT MANDATE	SANCTION
C.RR. 3093/1988	11/15/1988	1 woman (PC)	Shelved without treatment.	Maximum of 75% of candidates of either sex in electoral lists.	Applicable every four places up till no. 12.	Non-acceptance of lists by political parties, electoral boards and national Electoral Court.
				Alternating male/female candidates.	From position no. 13 till end of list.	
C.RR. 2235/1992	09/10/1992	2 men (FA; NE)	Annexed to bill C.RR. 1369/1991. Shelved.	Maximum of 75% of candidates of either sex in lists of titulares and suplentes.	Applicable to the first 8 places on lists.	None
C.RR. 2280/2002 C.SS. 1181/2003	07/09/2002	5 women (1 PN; 3 FA; 1 PI)	Modified in Committee; discussed and voted on in Chamber of Deputies, but quota not approved; shelved in Senate.	Maximum 2/3 candidates of same sex, in all national, departmental and internal party electoral lists; mirror representation for party executives (eliminated at Committee stage).	Applicable every three places throughout lists; should not necessarily apply to third place.	Non-registration of lists by electoral authorities.
C.RR. 3343/2003	09/09/2003	1 woman (PN)	Shelved without treatment.	No more than 3 candidates of the same sex.	First 4 places on the list.	Reduction of 25% in State electoral subsidy.
C.SS. 1235/2003	10/23/2003	2 women, 7 men (FA)	Shelved without treatment.	Identical to modified version of C.RR. 2280/2002 approved at Committee stage.		

Table 9.1 cont.

BILL NUMBER	DATE	NUMBER, SEX AND PARTY OF SIGNATORIES	OUTCOME	CONTENTS		
				PERCENTAGE & APPLICABILITY QUOTA	PLACEMENT MANDATE	SANCTION
C.SS. 455/2006 C.RR. 2589/2008	03/08/2006	2 women, 10 men (FA)	Modified in Committee; discussed and modified version passed by Senate; passed by Chamber of Deputies.	Maximum 2/3 candidates of same sex in lists of titulares and suplentes.	Every 3 places. Lists with only 2 titulares must be of different sex.	Non-registration of lists by electoral authorities
C.RR. 816/2006	03/08/2006	7 women (1 PN; 6 FA); 4 men (FA)	Shelved without treatment.	Identical to original version of C.SS. 455/2006.		
C.SS. 625/2006	09/06/2006	1 man (FA) introduced quota article	Discussion at Committee stage did not cover the article on the proposed incentive to the quota; discussion was abandoned in favor of another bill under treatment in Committee at the same time.	Original bill on financing and functioning of political parties included no reference to quota; modification introduced at Committee stage proposed inclusion of candidates of both sexes in lists of titulares and suplentes.	Applicable every 3 places at least till number 30; lists with only 2 titulares must be of different sex; candidacies to intendente (1 titular and 4 suplentes) must include at least 2 women.	Instead of a sanction, those lists that comply with the quota to receive an incentive of an additional 15% to their State electoral subsidy.

Source: Information from the Uruguayan parliament website.

two of the other bills, which proposed a compulsory quota, specified as sanctions the non-registration of lists by the electoral authorities, a secure method of compliance control, given the highly stable and institutionalized nature of the Uruguayan electoral system.

Promoters of these initiatives made reference to the various international-level agreements which Uruguay was party. In fact, the early presentation of the first bill was in part prompted by the fact that in November 1986 Montevideo hosted the UN Conference on Women, Population and Development in Latin America; Recommendation 7 of the Declaration that closed the conference referred to the need to "implement adequate mechanisms [...] to guarantee women's right to occupy seats in parliaments and other state bodies where development policies are formulated, evaluated and implemented". Not surprisingly, a requisite reference was the Convention on the Elimination of all forms of Discrimination Against Women (CEDAW, in particular, article 7, paragraphs a and b), and, following the Fourth United Nations' World Conference on Women (Beijing, 1995), the Beijing Platform for Action (especially paragraphs 186, 190, 192).

In addition to the legislative initiatives, the cause of promoting greater access by women to political office was championed by women's movement organizations and by female political activists working in cross-party coordinating bodies. They developed strategies to lobby male activists and political leaders to promote public debate. Three main debates on the quota were organized between 1989 and 2003, the first by CONAMU in 1989, at which presidential candidates were asked to give their opinion of the quota, on the eve of the national elections. The second was organized in May 1997 by the Network of Political Women (*Red de Mujeres Políticas*, RMP)[11] and the third, three months later by National Follow-up Committee on Beijing (*Comisión Nacional de Seguimiento de los Acuerdos de Beijing*, CNS), both seeking to inform politicians of the Beijing Agreements and pressure political parties to take action.[12] Finally, the two times that bills reached plenary discussion – in 2003 and 2008, the Bicameral Women's Bench (*Bancada Bicameral Femenina*, BBF).[13] invited researchers from the Gender Politics Area of the State University's Political Science Institute to present the findings of their research, as backing for their arguments in support of the quota.[14]

As can be observed in the third column of Table 9.1, women were the principal promoters of the quota in the legislative arena. It also shows that in terms of promoting the quota bills, the left-wing Broad Front (*Frente Amplio*, FA) appears the most actively supportive. While various male legislators from the FA signed quota bills over the years, as did one from the center-left New Space (*Nuevo Espacio*, NE), none from either the PC or the National (*Partido Nacional*, PN) or Independent (*Partido Independiente*, PI) parties did. This is coherent with the fact that the only two factions to adopt voluntary quotas prior to the passing of the law were both from within the FA: the PS in 1991 and the Artiguista Sector (*Vertiente Artiguista*, VA) in 2006.[15]

The legislative Process: One Step Forward, Two Steps Back

By reviewing the legislative process that led to the passage of the quota law, as well as the specific electoral rules that it introduced, it becomes clear that its sanction did not represent a turn-around in the dominant position of Uruguayan parties with respect to affirmative action measures.

Table 9.2 provides a step-by-step summary of the process through which the quota bill was presented, discussed and eventually approved. As one can see, more than two years passed between the presentation of the original bill on International Women's Day in 2006 and initiation of its treatment in the Senate Constitution and Legislation Committee (Constitution Committee). After its adoption in the Senate, another ten months passed before the bill was debated in the Lower House. Given the history of the treatment of quota bills in parliament, it is difficult not to see this as evidence of deliberate delaying tactics, especially as PN senators then argued during the debate on the bill that it was not advisable to pass a quota law so close to the elections because it did not give parties time to study the new rules and it might be interpreted as a move to benefit specific individuals.[16]

Furthermore, the bill only entered the Lower Chamber for debate once pressure had been exerted from both within and outside parliament. An important lobbying tool was the official rebuke that Uruguay received from the CEDAW Committee of Experts in its Observations on the implementation reports presented by Uruguay in October 2008. The CEDAW Committee stated its concern that "women are still insufficiently represented in political and public life" in Uruguay, and explicitly exhorted the member state to "speed up the passing of the quota bill."[17] On December 3, 2008 these observations were presented to the Chamber of Deputies' Constitution, Codes, General Legislation and Administration Committee (Constitution Committee), which was due to study the bill, by the PN deputy Beatriz Argimón, a founding member of the BBF.[18] The CEDAW Committee's critique was also referred to in the press statement released by the RMP a week later, on International Human Rights' Day. However, it was not until Argimón again urged the Committee to begin treatment of the bill on March 11, 2009,[19] that its members decided unanimously to remit the bill directly for debate in the Chamber without prior discussion in the Committee. By then, the internal elections were just over three months away.

The passage of the bill without modifications by the Chamber of Deputies on March 24 appeared to signal the end of the two-decade-long struggle to win

Table 9.2: The Legislative Process: from the Presentation of the Quota Bill, to its Application as Law in the June 2009 Internal Elections

DATE	PROCESS
03/08/2006	Bills C.SS. 455/2006 and C.RR. 816/2006 presented simultaneously in the Senate and Chamber of Deputies.
05/22/2007	Senate Constitution Committee begins treatment of the bill (1 session).
04/08/2008	Senate Constitution Committee resumes treatment of the bill (3 sessions).
04/22/2008	Modified version of the bill approved by Senate Constitution Committee.
05/05/2008	Discussion of bill begins in Senate Chamber, with interventions by 5 senators. Discussion is postponed till 21 May.
05/21/2008	Discussion of bill continues in Senate Chamber, with interventions by 14 senators. PN senators present proposal to modify bill.
05/28/2008	PN senators' bill voted affirmatively.
11/14/2008	CEDAW Observations on Uruguay's periodic report recommend that quota law be passed urgently.
12/03/2008	Deputy Argimón (PN) presents CEDAW Observations in Chamber of Deputies' Constitution Committee.
12/10/2008	Network of Political Women issue press statement exhorting parliament to discuss the bill.
03/11/2009	Argimón urges Chamber of Deputies' Constitution Committee to begin treatment of the bill.
03/24/2009	Bill debated and passed without modifications in Chamber of Deputies.
03/26/2009	Law regulated by Electoral Court for application in internal party national convention elections, June 28, 2009.
03/31/2009	Bicameral Women's Bench press statement expressing rejection of Electoral Court's interpretation of the law.
04/16/2009	Quota Law No. 18476 enacted by Executive.
04/21/2009	Bill C.RR. 3201/2009 to interpret certain provisions of Law 18476 presented in Chamber of Deputies by 9 women (2 PN; 7 FA) and 12 men (1 PC; 2 PN; 9 FA). Bicameral Women's Bench hold press conference.
04/22/2009	Bill C.SS. 1494/2009, identical in content to bill C.RR. 3209/2009 presented in Senate by the whole FA bench (4 women, 11 men). Senate convenes extraordinary session to discuss bill, which wins the unanimous support of the 24 senators present (PC senators absent).
04/22/2009	Chamber of Deputies' Constitution Committee approves bill C.RR. 3201/2009

Table 9.2 cont.

DATE	PROCESS
04/28/2009	Bill passed in Senate enters Chamber of Deputies.
04/30/2009	Chamber of Deputies' Constitution Committee approves bill C.SS. 1494/2009, passed by Senate.
05/05/2009	Chamber of Deputies passes bill to interpret Law No. 18476.
05/15/2009	Interpretative Law No. 18487 enacted by Executive.
05/29/2009	Closing date for registering electoral lists for internal elections.
06/28/2009	Primaries and internal elections to party national and departmental conventions.

Source: Information from the Uruguayan parliament website.

recognition of the need for affirmative action measures to ensure greater gender parity in political representation. However, there proved to be one more challenge to overcome. Political parties were required to include the quota in their electoral lists before May 29, for the internal elections in June. For these elections parties were allowed to present ballot papers with separate lists of *titulares* and *suplentes* (*sistema ordinal*) or with a single list, where the list of *suplentes* starts with the first candidate not elected (*sistema preferencial*), or with a list of *titulares* each of whom has their respective *suplente* (*sistema respectivo*). While the law states in its article 2 that the quota provisions should be applied to both lists, *titulares* and *suplentes*, the Electoral Court decided that, in the case of the *sistema respectivo*, the quota should be applied integrating the two lists in one, with *titulares* and *suplentes* alternating. What this meant in practice was that, by using this system of *suplencias*, parties could place their female candidates only in *suplencias* and still comply with the quota.

The Bicameral Women's Bench immediately held a press conference during which women politicians from all parties rejected this "unjust and perverse" interpretation of the law, which reflected the "patriarchal and machista" mindset that continued to present an obstacle to women's full and effective participation in the country's political life. In the face of this threat, the female legislators submitted, with the support of male members from the three parties, urgent bills in both the Senate and Lower House to "interpret" the quota law, clarifying that the quota should always be applied separately to the lists of *titulares* and *suplentes*. This bill was given priority treatment, passed quickly by both Chambers and enacted just two weeks before the list registration period closed.

The version of the bill that finally became Law 18476 in April 2009 established as mandatory for political parties to include candidates of both sexes in the lists presented at any of the three elections—party conventions, parliamentary and departmental—that comprise the five-yearly electoral cycle in Uruguay,[20] and also in all internal elections to elect party officials. However, under pressure from PN senators, the original formulation, which proposed the quota as a permanent measure, was progressively restricted, first at committee stage and later during the debate in the Chamber. While it was necessary to forge an agreement with the PN to ensure the special majority needed to pass the law,[21] the reach of the original bill was thus severely limited, curtailing its potential impact: in the case of the party convention and internal elections it would be applied from 2009 and remain as a permanent electoral norm; on the other hand, for national and departmental elections—in other words, the positions of greatest power and status in the Uruguayan political system—the law would not come into force until 2014–2015 and would only apply to that single electoral cycle.

The law, therefore, can be seen as a timid and untimely step forward in comparison with international trends. In this sense it should be noted that Uruguay passed a law on quotas at a time when not quotas, but gender parity in political representation is being advocated in theory and implemented in practice. Indeed, less than two years before, Uruguay was a signatory of the Quito Consensus[22] which "[r]ecognizing that parity is one of the key driving forces of democracy", had agreed "[t]o adopt all necessary affirmative action measures and mechanisms, including the necessary legislative reforms and budgetary allocations, to ensure the full participation of women in public office and in political representative positions with a view to achieving parity in the institutional structure of the State."[23] There are also examples of practical application of parity measures in the region, such as Ecuador's modification to its quota law in 2000, which established that the baseline thirty percent gender candidate quota would increase progressively by five percent every election until reaching fifty percent parity, and Michelle Bachelet's designation of a gender parity ministerial cabinet when she first came to power in 2006.

But even in comparison to the majority of the quota laws passed in the rest of Latin America a decade earlier, the Uruguayan legislation leaves much to be desired. Its most problematic aspect is the temporal restrictions that the law establishes in the case of the national and departmental elections, which make it inconsistent with the concept of affirmative action on which it is supposedly rooted. First, because, although the law implicitly—and the parliamentary debate explicitly—acknowledges that problems exist with the translation of formal rights into practice, at the same time it postpones and limits the effective realization of those rights. Women's political rights thus appear to be low-priority and their status as equal citizens is compromised. Second, the Uruguayan quota law disregards the definition of the "temporary" nature of quota measures as defined in article 4 of the CEDAW ("these measures shall be discontinued when the objectives of equality of opportunity and treatment have been achieved") and further clarified in 2004 by the CEDAW Committee's General Recommendation Number 25.

Some of the apparent reasons for the practical limitations of Uruguay's quota law can be found in the parliamentary discussions of the bill. The Senate debate in particular was marked by the peculiarity that, although the bill eventually received just two negative votes (both from PC senators) various members of the FA and PN benches argued against the initiative before voting affirmatively. In general, those who argued against the quota acknowledged neither the role nor the responsibility of political parties and their leadership on women's marginalization in posts of political power, and more than one resorted to univocal explanations and essentialist visions of women's identity. Thus women's limited presence in political posts is construed as a women's problem, linked to a lack of vocation or will, or to self-exclusion, resulting from the "different interests" that women have "from a biological point of view,"[24] relating to "*every* woman's role as a mother."[25] Other opponents of the bill accused Uruguayan society as a whole of being the culprit, actively resisting women's greater integration into political life and simply regarding it irrelevant.[26] Nonetheless, these legislators at the same time expressed their conviction that "no one would refute the claim that women are owed a greater share of representation in the Uruguayan national parliament."[27] It would appear, then, that while not subscribing to what is gradually emerging as the dominant discourse and practice on gender equality in political representation at international level, and the male Uruguayan political elite deemed it necessary to take the politically correct path.

Implementation of the Quota Law: Electoral Lists of the 2009 Party National Conventions

In this section we propose to assess the first-time application of the quota law in Uruguay in two aspects. Firstly, insofar as article 3 of the law states that "the Electoral Boards will control the application of the quota and disqualify any electoral lists that do not comply with the minimum required", it is not a question of observing whether or not parties complied with the quota, but rather to examine *how they applied* it. As the comparative literature shows, the existence of a quota law does not necessarily mean an end to party opposition to quotas, and there are countless examples from Latin American countries of parties seeking loopholes in the law to evade their obligations.[28] Did parties only meet the minimum requirements set out in the law, or did they go beyond these? What inter-party differences can be observed with respect to the application of the quota? Secondly, since the 2009/2010 electoral cycle is the third to include elections to party conventions, it is possible to evaluate the effect of the quota by comparing the presence of female candidates with data from the previous elections (1999 and 2004).

Due to the huge volume of data that derives from the entire set of electoral lists presented in 2009 to party conventions,[29] we restricted the universe of analysis according to the basic criterion that our interest lays in exploring women's real access to positions of power. We therefore focused, in the first place, solely on the national—not departmental—party conventions of the four parties that subsequently gained parliamentary representation: the FA, PC, PN and PI.[30] In addition, we considered only successful lists, that is, those that actually won seats in the conventions. This totaled 383 ballot papers distributed as follows: PN 139, PC 119, FA 102 and PI 23. Since the national party conventions have a total of 500 seats, each ballot paper could include up to a maximum of 1000 candidates: 500 *titulares* and 500 *suplentes*. We therefore also restricted our universe, on the one hand, to the lists of *titulares*, in the understanding that in principle these are the candidates who will actually go on to occupy the seat.[31]

On the other hand, considering that the electoral lists are closed and blocked, only a certain number of places can be regarded as "safe". This depends on the number of seats in dispute, the total number of lists competing for those seats, and the vote-winning capacity of each list. Due to the fact that, as we have seen above, the three main parties have a high rate of fractionalization (that is, a large number of lists won seats in the national conventions), the vast majority of their lists (close to ninety percent) won fewer than ten seats (see Figure 9.2).

Figure 9.2: Distribution Among lists of Seats in Party National Conventions (by Party)

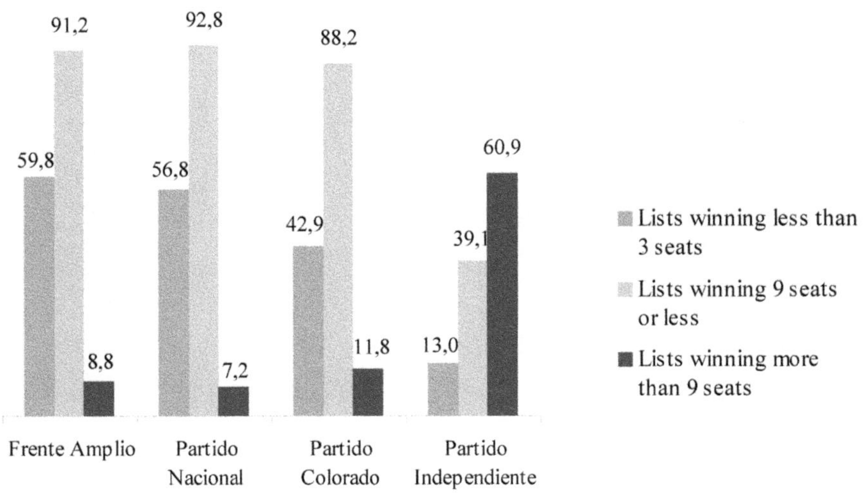

Source: Electoral lists to party national conventions.

For this reason, we centered our analysis of the application of the quota mainly on the first nine places on the lists, which even in the case of those lists that won more seats are clearly the safest and most important positions.

As we have observed in previous studies,[32] traditionally the presence of female candidates on electoral lists increases as their chances of electoral success decrease: thus, more women are to be found on lists that do not win seats and in places further down those lists that do. Institutionalist theory provides a simple explanation for this phenomenon: parties (and their leaders) are rational actors who seek to maximize their benefits in the context (electoral rules) within which they operate,[33] which means, in concrete terms, seeking to win the greatest possible number of votes. When it comes to nominating candidates, therefore, the most rational way of maximizing their chances and minimizing their risks is to reselect incumbents or to select new candidates with characteristics similar to incumbents. Following this logic, and since political elites are generally dominated by professional males from the dominant ethnic group?, the chances that members of other social groups—including women—may be selected as candidates are greatly reduced in comparison with the chances of current office-holders. In view of this, our working hypothesis was that parties would tend to comply with the minimum required by law.

The first dimension of our analysis sought to test the hypothesis that even under the quota, female candidates tend not to be distributed evenly throughout the list, but rather appear concentrated in lower positions. Figure 9.3 shows that this proved

Figure 9.3: Placement of Women Candidates on Successful Electoral Lists: Party National Convention Elections 2009

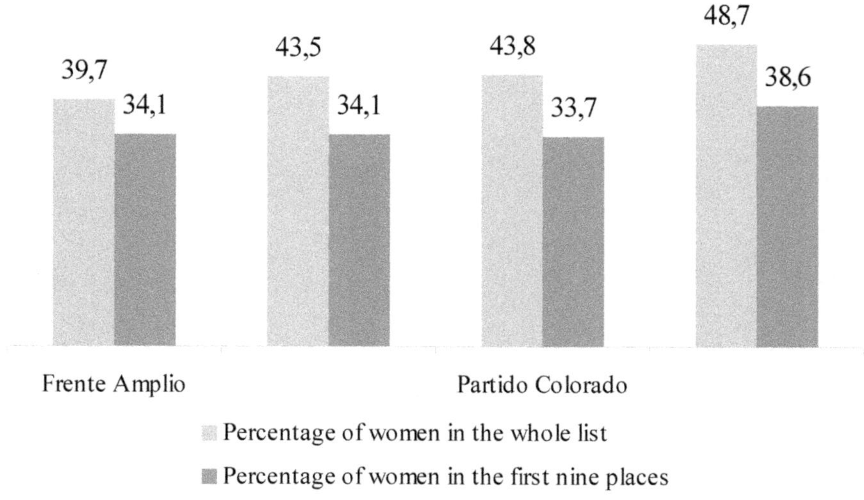

Source: Electoral lists to party national conventions.

Table 9.3: Possible Combinations of Candidates for Each Triad of Places on the List, According to the Quota Law

COMBINATION	ORDER AND SEX OF CANDIDATES
1	man-man-woman
2	woman-man-man
3	man-woman-man
4	woman-man-woman
5	man-woman-woman
6	woman-woman-man

Source: Based on provisions of quota law.

true in the case of the 2009 elections to national party conventions: all parties include a smaller proportion of women candidates among the first nine places on their lists than overall.

While these figures are still far from a parity distribution of female and male candidates on party lists, the application of the quota considerably reduced the gap between the percentage of women in the list as a whole and the percentage of women in "winnable" positions. If we compare the proportion of female candidates in the first three places, taking all party lists together, with data from the 2004 internal elections, we see that the percentage of female candidates in winnable positions increased significantly: while in 2004 there were no more than fourteen percent of women in these positions, in 2009 women occupied over thirty percent of these candidacies.

In order to assess how the parties applied the quota, we drew up a typology of possible placement patterns. Since the law establishes that the quota must be applied every three places, there are six possible combinations (see Table 9.3).

Given that historically it is women candidates who have been excluded or marginalized on electoral lists and that this is the disparity that the law seeks to compensate for, we defined the following four indicators to measure how parties applied the quota.

1. Lists that include the *minimum number of women* candidates allowed by law—one every three places, which in the above table corresponds to any of the first three possible types of combination.
2. Lists that show a *minimalist application* of the quota—that is, they not only include just one female candidate in each triad of places, but also place her in the lowest position (third, sixth, ninth); option 1 in the above table.

3. Lists that include *more than the minimum number of women* candidates required by law—in other words at least one of the first three triads must include at least two women; options 4, 5 or 6 in the table.
4. Lists *headed by women* candidates; options 2, 4 or 6 in the table.

As Figure 9.4 shows, the vast majority of lists studied included no more than the minimum number of women needed to meet the legal requirement, that is, just three female candidates among the first nine positions: over ninety percent of FA and PN lists, and over eighty percent of PC lists follow this pattern. Even in the case of the PI, more than half its lists share this pattern, albeit to a much smaller extent than in the other parties.

In addition, over sixty percent of both PN and PC lists show a minimalist application of the quota in their first nine places; in other words, in almost two-thirds of their successful electoral lists only one out of every three candidates in the top nine positions was a woman, and she always appeared in the third place of each triad. In contrast, a much smaller proportion of PI lists—just over a quarter—applies the quota in a minimalist fashion and over forty percent include more than three women among the first nine candidacies, although none of its lists was headed by a female candidate.

On the other hand, it is in the FA that we find the greatest number of lists that include only three women among the first nine places, and conversely the smallest

Figure 9.4: Application of the quota in successful electoral lists, party national convention elections 2009

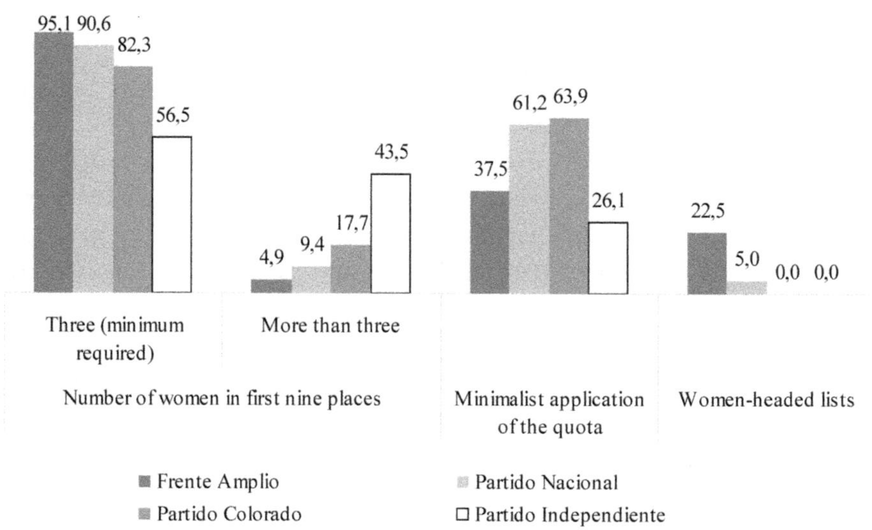

Source: Data from electoral lists.

proportion of lists with more than the minimum required number of female candidates. However, less than forty percent of FA lists show a minimalist application of the quota –far fewer than in the case of the PN or PC. One of the main factors influencing this indicator is the far greater presence of FA lists headed by female candidates. Nonetheless, it should be noted that the FA's performance in this last indicator is not strictly comparable to the PN's performance, since in the former case it reflects the repeated presence of the same female candidate on nineteen lists, while in the case of the PN the five lists were headed by five different women.[34]

In general, then, the major Uruguayan political parties basically applied the quota in a mechanical fashion in the June 2009 elections to party national conventions. This can be seen as coherent with the reluctance of a good part of the male political elite to promote actively female candidacies as was evident in the parliamentary discussion of the quota bill.

The Impact of the Quota

In spite of the fact that the quota was applied in minimalist fashion, it generated an important increase in the number of women national convention members, in comparison with the previous two elections (see Figure 9.5).

Figure 9.5: Evolution of the Rate of Female Representation in Party National Conventions, 1999-2009

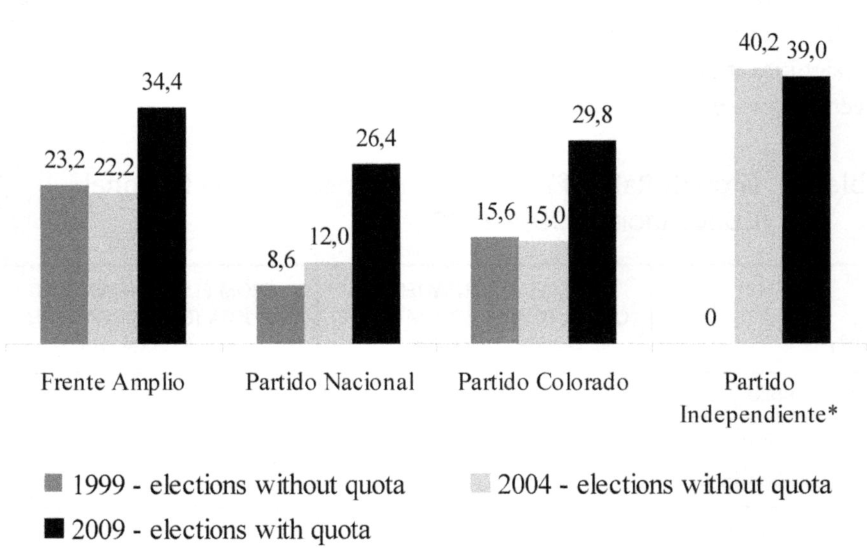

Source: Electoral results from the Electoral Court.

As a result of the 2009 elections the PI showed the highest rate of female representation in its national convention, with almost forty percent women members elected; the PN, on the other hand, had the worst showing, with just over a quarter of female convention members. The PC, for its part, elected almost thirty percent women convention members, while the FA elected close to thirty-five percent female members.

It should be noted that these inter-party differences reflect not only differences in how each party applied the quota to their electoral lists, but also the different levels of fractionalization in the final composition of their national conventions. Thus, the PN, which has the lowest rate of female representation, is also the convention with the highest number of successful lists (139); at the other end of the scale, the PI shows the highest percentage of women members, as well as the lowest number of lists winning seats (23). In short, when the seats are distributed among a greater number of lists, this tends to limit the impact of the quota.

When we compare these results with those from the previous two party national convention elections (see above Figure 9.5), we see that all parties except for the PI register a significant increase in their percentage of female convention members. Table 9.4 shows the growth rate in women's presence in national conventions from one election to the next.

The quota had the greatest impact on the PN's convention, with a female member growth rate of 120 percent. The PC shows a similar tendency, increasing its female cohort by almost 100 percent, in stark contrast to the negative growth rate it registered between the two elections in which no quota was applied. In the case of the FA, although the quota had a less marked impact, which can be explained by its higher initial female representation rate, the growth rate of fifty-five percent is still significant and once again contrasts with the negative growth registered between the two previous elections.

Table 9.4: Growth Rate of Women's Presence in Party National Conventions, 1999–2009

PARTY	FROM ELECTION WITHOUT QUOTA TO ELECTION WITHOUT QUOTA (1999–2004)	FROM ELECTION WITHOUT QUOTA TO ELECTION WITH QUOTA (2004–2009)
Frente Amplio	-4,3	55,0
Partido Nacional	39,5	120,0
Partido Colorado	-3,8	98,7
Partido Independiente	n. a.	-3,0

Source: Electoral results from the Electoral Court.

To sum up, if we consider the performance of these three parties over the three electoral periods, it is clear that the application of the quota marks a turning point in the trend in female representation in their national conventions. In the case of both the FA and the PC, the quota broke through the apparent ceiling that had maintained women's representation rates at the same level in the two previous ballots. In the case of the PN, which in all three instances has registered the lowest proportion of female convention members, the application of the quota in 2009 increased threefold the growth rate registered between the two elections without quotas.

The PI is a case apart. Instead of increasing its female representation rate between 2004 and 2009, as do the other three parties, it registered a slight drop in the presence of women convention members. The reason for this apparent anomaly is that in 2004 the party had already voluntarily adopted the same minimum candidate gender quota that was later established by law. As a result, with the application of the now legal quota in 2009, the PI maintains approximately the same level of female representation in its national convention as before. Finally, although the PI registers a slight decrease in its percentage of female convention members, its low rate of fractionalization means that not only does it perform better than the other parties, but also exceeds in its results, as well as in its lists, the minimum established by the quota law.

Given the favorable rhetoric of the party leaders, and the evidently positive impact of the application of quota in the elections to party conventions, it seemed relevant to explore whether the application of the quota in the internal elections had a knock-on effect on the gender composition of the electoral supply in the parliamentary elections, held four months later. In theory, although the quota did not come into force for the national elections in 2009, the significant increase in the levels of female representation in party conventions could have had a positive effect on the nomination of parliamentary candidates, whether as a result of a "trickle-up" effect or of pressure exerted by the critical mass of newly elected female convention members. In fact, this was one of the arguments used by PN legislators to justify their proposal to establish the quota as a permanent mechanism for internal elections, but not for national and departmental elections. However, in practice it proved not to have any such knock-on effect on female candidacies to parliament: in contrast to the quantitative leap in female representation in the party conventions, the percentage of women elected as *titulares* to the Uruguayan parliament increased only slightly, from 10.8 percent to 14.6 percent.[35] This gives a positive growth rate of 35.2 percent, twenty points lower than the smallest positive rate, registered by the FA, between the 2004 and 2009 internal elections (see above, Table 9.4). How different would the scenario have been if the quota had come into force for national elections at the same time as for the elections to party conventions?

Figure 9.6 shows a simulated impact of the quota for female candidates, if implemented during the parliamentary elections of October 2009. The simulation was conducted taking into consideration two basic premises: firstly, that parties would apply the quota in a minimalist fashion, that is they would place their female candidates in the lowest possible positions throughout the list; but secondly, that women candidates who occupied positions higher than the minimum required by the quota would retain their places on the lists. In other words, if a list were headed by a woman, but included no other female candidates, the quota was considered to be covered for the first triad, while the next female candidate should appear in the sixth position (the lowest possible place in the second triad).

As Figure 9.6 shows, if the quota had come into force for the parliamentary elections, overall another seven female legislators would have been elected. Instead of 19 women members of parliament, there would have been 26, increasing the female representation rate to 20%. Although the application of the quota would not have translated into a third of seats held by women, the increase is by no means insignificant.

As has been signaled previously both for Uruguay and in the comparative literature, certain characteristics of electoral systems may affect the effectiveness of the quota.[36] As is clear from Figure 9.6, in the Uruguayan case one important factor is

Figure 9.6: Quota Simulation for the 2009 Parliamentary Elections: Number of Elected Women Legislators

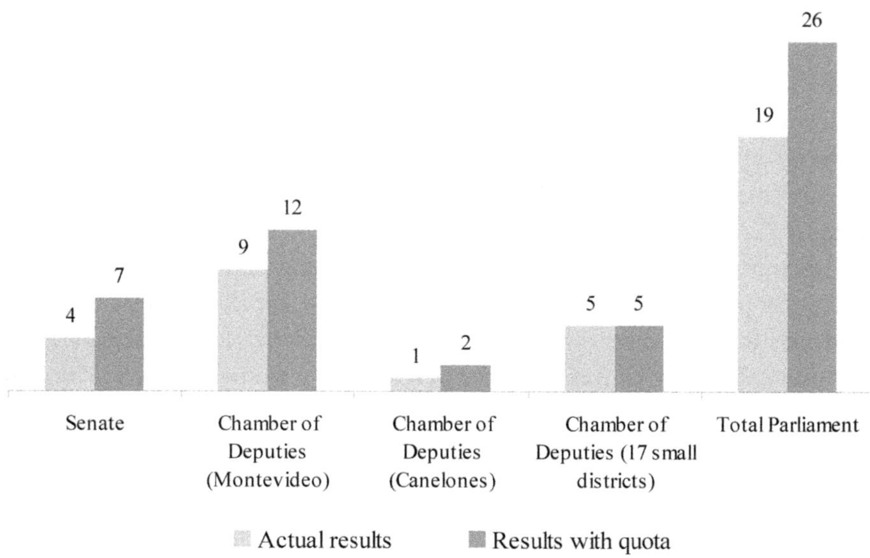

Source: Data from electoral lists and electoral results from the Electoral Court.

the district magnitude.[37] The impact of the quota is most greatly felt in the large electoral districts—the Senate (national constituency of 30 seats) and the district of Montevideo in the Chamber of Deputies (41 seats). In contrast, the quota would have only a limited impact in the medium-sized district of Canelones and no effect whatsoever in any of the other seventeen small electoral districts of the Lower House.

Another factor that is often cited as influencing the impact of the quota, even in electoral systems with large district magnitude, is the number of parties with parliamentary representation: the greater the number of parties that gain access to parliament, the more limited the effect of quotas, since the distribution of seats is more fragmented. In Uruguay, however, the problem is not the number of parties that win seats, but rather the fact that the electoral rules allow individual factions within parties to present lists of candidates which compete with each other under the same party banner, resulting in the fractionalization of party benches in parliament. In other words, the greater the number of lists that win parliamentary representation in each district, the less effective is the quota, since the seats won by each party are distributed between a greater number of factions. Thus, while just three parties won representation in the Senate, its thirty seats were divided between ten successful lists. Similarly, just four parties, but fourteen lists won seats in the Chamber of Deputies.[38]

To sum up, what this simulation shows is that if parties had voluntarily applied the quota in the 2009 national elections, there would have been a noticeable increase in the rate of women's parliamentary representation, despite the fact that the Uruguayan electoral system has certain particularities that may reduce the impact of the quota.

Conclusions

The 2009 electoral cycle allows us to draw some preliminary conclusions about the application of the quota in Uruguay, several of which coincide with observations already made in the comparative literature on this subject. First, it is clear that, in spite of the limitations of the law, its enactment represented a turning-point in the history of women's political participation in Uruguay. When female candidates' electoral success rates in the two prior internal elections (without quotas) are compared with their success rates in the 2009 elections (with quotas) it becomes clear that the quota is an extremely effective measure to help increase in the short term women's access to elective posts.

The Uruguayan case also shows that parties tend to apply quotas in a minimalist manner to their electoral lists, which reveals their continued resistance to regarding as a priority in practice, and not only in rhetoric, the goal that quotas seek to meet—a balanced representation of women and men in political decision-making arenas. In short, without the law it is highly unlikely that the results that were registered in the internal elections would have been reached.

This is further confirmed by examining whether the application of the quota in the elections to party conventions had a knock-on effect on the composition of electoral lists presented in the subsequent parliamentary elections: the small increase in the percentage of women members of parliament can be regarded as little more than vegetative growth. The candidate selection processes and procedures to draw up electoral lists used by Uruguayan political parties are complex and marked by informal practices and power dynamics that transcend the formal internal party organs of representation.[39] Without the legal obligation of the quota, women's chances of influencing the legislative recruitment process are greatly reduced, which inevitably then results in a weak presence of women in elected organs of political representation.

If the Uruguayan quota law is not to become a dead letter following its single application in national and departmental elections scheduled for 2014/2015, women politicians will need to ensure that the evaluation of its application envisaged in article 5 of the law goes beyond the self-congratulatory rhetoric that characterized the parliamentary speeches of male political leaders anxious to be regarded as politically correct, but reluctant to lose their monopoly on political posts.

CHAPTER TEN

Gender Quotas in Former Communist and Post-Conflict Countries

The Cases of Armenia, Bosnia-Herzegovina, and Serbia

LAMAN TASCH

In most countries of the world women are widely underrepresented at every level of political decision-making.[1] This is arguably one of the most significant impediments for the proper functioning of both established democracies and newly democratized countries, as well as for peace-building efforts in post-conflict societies.[2] Although it is often debated that gender quotas are efficient gender-mainstreaming mechanisms in the absence of more comprehensive reforms that would benefit women more generally,[3] women's participation in politics is often considered a pre-condition for the consolidation of democratic systems.[4] This is especially the case for countries that have experienced armed conflicts, where international organizations are actively involved in their post-conflict recovery and state-building processes. For many of these international organizations, increasing the participation of women in politics and using various affirmative action measures like gender quotas, are important for ensuring sustainability during the peace-making processes of the countries they support.[5]

It is often argued that the Beijing Declaration and Platform of Action, which were adopted at the Fourth World Conference on Women (15 September 1995),[6] transformed gender quotas into an international trend and served as a means for their diffusion. Although the Beijing Declaration and Platform of Action do not discuss gender quotas directly, they view affirmative action as necessary to promote gender balance in politics. That is why gender quotas are sometimes considered "fast track" mechanisms and viewed as a new interpretation of gender equality.[7]

Women's rights, including empowerment of women through the encouragement of their political participation, are increasingly considered by the United Nations (UN) as an indispensable aspect of human development in the developing world. The United Nations Development Program elaborated numerous empirical tools to account for various aspects of development include social and political rights, such as the *Gender-Related Development Index* and *Gender Empowerment Index.*[8]

The role of political women in post-conflict societies has been given special attention at the UN and at the Organization for Security and Cooperation in Europe (OSCE), in particular, for the cases studied in this chapter. As it is stated in the United Nations' *Guide to Promoting the Participation of Women in Elections,* the participation of women is an indispensable aspect of the democratization process in post-conflict societies and it is viewed as a central element for peace-building efforts.[9] The United Nations Security Council's Resolution (UNSC) 1325 of October 2000, also considers political participation of women in post-conflict societies as a means for long-term peace.[10] UNSC 1325 recognizes that any conflict-preventing and peace-building efforts require an increasing participation of women.[11] In October 2005, the UN Security Council issued an action plan for the implementation of UNSC 1325 and recommended specific actions to ensure the representation of women at all levels in decision-making posts, including the adoption of gender quotas.[12] As of 2010, sixteen countries adopted national plans integrating the provisions of UNSC 1325,[13] Such provisions helped reinforce an international model in which women are located at the heart of any peace-building and conflict-preventive measures.[14]

This is not surprising. There has been a rise in inter-communal violence worldwide since the end of the Cold War and the situation still remains unstable. These types of conflicts had numerous repercussions: first, they interfere with the consolidation of democratic regimes and the strengthening of political institutions. Second, they allow politics to be controlled by nationalist, often anti-democratic and heavily male-dominated political actors. Third, although women do sometimes participate in these conflicts as soldiers and commanders, a majority of the combatants and decision-makers are men, whereas a majority of the victims are women. In addition, the emergence of conflicts reinforce traditional gendered values, thus confine women to the role of mothers and caregivers and create cultural obstacles for their activism in the public sphere.[15] At the same time, conflicts weaken the state in terms of its capacity to govern and perform basic functions, and rendered it vulnerable to the influences of international organizations, which provide resources vital for its survival.[16] Under these conditions, an increasing participation of women in politics is viewed as contributing not only to the democratization of post-conflict societies by increasing the sheer number of women actively involved in politics, but also to the long-term peace and stability by challenging the power of nationalist male politicians.

When civil society is weak and power is in the hands of nationalist leaders, as it is often the case in post-conflict societies, international organizations serve as a vehicle in which the spread of international norms and innovations, including gender quotas, may play a significant role. The question is whether these reforms are able to create real change for women. In order to answer this question, this chapter will analyze three former communist, post-conflict countries currently with legislative quotas: Armenia, Bosnia-Herzegovina and Serbia, and will compare the processes leading to the adoption of quotas, its implementation and its effects on society in general.

Gender Quotas in Armenia

The Republic of Armenia became independent from the Soviet Union in 1991. Its National Assembly (legislative branch) is elected through a mixed electoral system, in which forty-one of 131 total seats are allotted by a simple majority vote in the forty-one single-member constituencies, while the remaining ninety seats are elected though proportional representation by party lists (with five percent threshold). The number of seats elected by a majority vote used to be fifty-six prior to the 2005 changes in its electoral law. The reforms had benefitted women by extending the number of PR seats and thus, the chance of women to be elected.[17]

Armenia was familiar with gender quotas from its pre-1991 Soviet past, when gender quotas were enforced to demonstrate a commitment of the ruling Communist Party to the principles of gender equality, although they were never codified in the form of law. Thus, up to 1991 a third of all deputies of the Armenian Supreme Soviet (legislative body under Soviet Union) were women. However, this representation remained highly symbolic. Not only men and women deputies of the Supreme Soviet had little real power, but also women were severely underrepresented in the high echelons of the Communist Party.[18] The transitional democratic period started with the collapse of the Soviet Union in 1991 and legal mechanisms to include political women in the new transitional government that came thereafter. However, in Armenia gender quotas were strongly associated with the communist past. Yet, the Soviet implementation of gender quotas did not bring political empowerment to women. This factor often explains the aversion towards gender quotas by many ordinary citizens in former communist countries. Although there were numerous women's NGOs, they did not have, or rather they were not allowed to have any influence in decision-making at high levels of power in Armenia. In addition, there was not a strong women's movement that explicitly supported gender-based legislative quotas in the 1990s. Gender quotas were then and still are today a controversial issue in Armenia, even among women.[19]

International bodies played a significant role in the adoption of legislative quotas in Armenia since quotas were viewed by international organizations as valid measures to attract all members of society into politics and improve Armenia's human rights record.[20] Armenia signed the Convention on the Elimination of all Forms of Discrimination Against Women (CEDAW) in 1993.[21] CEDAW does not require the adoption of the gender quotas *per se*, but does require that the signing parties adopt all the necessary measures to eliminate any obstacles that may threaten the participation of women in politics.[22] CEDAW reports on Armenia claimed that although the country did not have any legal obstacles to women's participation in politics, its significant dropout was due to informal impediments including cultural obstacles, such as stereotypes about the nature of politics and the role of women, a weak civil society including women's organizations, and weak public support for gender quotas due to traditional gender-based family roles that created a double burden for women and left them without resources for political activism.[23]

A brief discussion of Armenia's transition from communism to an electoral democracy helps to shed light on the situation of political women in the country during this period and beyond. Since the late 1980s, Armenia was involved in an ethnic conflict with neighboring Azerbaijan over the Nagorno-Karabakh Autonomous region of Azerbaijan that was heavily populated by Armenians. It escalated into violent clashes between Azerbaijanis and Armenians in both countries, leading to thousands of people killed and displaced on both sides. Evolution of this conflict was accompanied by the rise of nationalist political forces in both countries and mass mobilization along national pride and ethnic hatred.[24] Numerous nationalist political organizations and parties emerged and became influential in Armenian politics during the 1990s. In addition, bitter rivalry among these parties and organizations destabilized the country politically, leaving little room for the discussion of gender issues. The problem with the increased role of nationalism and ongoing violent conflict is not only that it militarizes politics and leaves no room for female activism, but also that it emphasizes the primordial characteristics of nations, which views women as mothers and caregivers rather than leaders.[25] This influences the social perception and attitudes towards women in politics. Recent CEDAW reports discuss the negative impact of gender stereotypes for women in politics.[26] Besides, women constitute more than half of the refugees, whose political rights are often hindered by the ambiguities related to their citizenship status.[27] It was not until the late 1990s that there was a normalization of Armenian politics and a decreasing influence of nationalist forces.[28]

In 1999, legislative quotas for women were introduced in Armenia through its new *Electoral Law*. The law required that women should comprise at least fifteen percent of the candidates in the proportional representation (PR) party lists, and required that for every tenth candidate, one should be a woman (Article 100).[29] The first elections under the new law were held the same year, but only four women (four percent) were elected to the National Assembly due to reported irregularities.[30] The gender quota provision was ignored by most political parties and this blatant violation was not penalized by electoral authorities.[31] During the 2003 parliamentary elections, political parties included the fifteen percent of women required by law in their party lists. Yet, only seven women (5.3 percent) won seats in the national Assembly. International observers noticed that political parties showed no interest in encouraging the political participation of women, supporting women candidates, or addressing women's issues. Besides, many women had negative attitudes towards gender quotas because they viewed them as remnants of the communist era.[32] The last 2007 parliamentary elections were conducted fairly, according to international observers. This time a number of political parties exceeded the minimum fifteen percent required by Armenia's gender quota law.[33] As a result, the number of elected female deputies rose to twelve (9.16 percent).[34] Women's organizations were also more active in advocating the need to increase women's political representation. For example, the Women's Forum was established by the National Democratic Institute in 2006 with a wide range of purposes, including the participation of women in politics, although without specific reference to gender quotas.[35] Despite this relative improvement, the number of women parliamentarians in Armenia is less than in the neighboring countries of South Caucasus, Georgia and Azerbaijan, where gender quotas do not exist.[36] A recent study reveals that although most of the respondents were in favor of women representation in decision-making posts, many of them were still against gender quotas as a means to achieve this end. The same study points out that the efforts of international organizations operating in Armenia also remained insufficient in terms of wielding a strong mobilization of women in support of gender quotas.

Most political parties are not enthusiastic about promoting and nurturing their women candidates. Their gender-related programs are usually centered on women's role as mothers and caregivers and thus, reinforce traditional gender roles and may hinder women's participation in politics. In addition, women lack the financial support and connections to survive in the male-dominated political environment and they often have to compete with businessmen and oligarchs. At the same time, those who favor gender quotas as a means to encourage women in politics and actively seek higher positions in the decision-making bodies argue in favor of increasing the percentage of women required by the current gender quota law.[37] It seems that the effectiveness of gender quotas in Armenia will depend on whether political parties are willing to nurture and support their female candidates, and on the social acceptance of females as reliable and competent leaders.

Gender Quotas in Bosnia-Herzegovina

The issue of women's rights in Bosnia-Herzegovina is more complicated; women suffered as primary victims of the ethnic cleansing of 1992–1995; they were a majority of the refugees and the subjects of mass rapes.[38] The rise of nationalism in the former Yugoslavia along with deteriorating economic conditions during the late 1980s and early 1990s led to a dramatic decline in the political participation of women. This was in contrast to the earlier socialist period when women, although facing informal social and political discrimination, had formal equal rights recognized by the Yugoslav constitution and verbally supported by communist leaders. Like in Armenia, in the Socialist Federal Republic of Yugoslavia (SFRY) around thirty percent of the seats in the country's major governing institutions were allocated to women, but, similarly to other socialist countries, these women had little real power. Besides, women preserved most of the traditional roles as mothers, wives, and care-givers.[39]

Spread of nationalism, mass nationalist mobilization and escalation of intercommunal ethnic war was also an issue in Yugoslavia during the Post-Cold War era. Nationalism in its primordial form, advocates birth-given identity and ethnic nations as perennial communities with centuries-long traditions. When this is combined with the militarization of society, little room is left for women to have any influence in politics. Unlike Armenia where violent conflict took place outside its borders, Bosnia-Herzegovina witnessed the bloodiest clashes in its territory. Although Bosnian women did not develop a strong anti-war movement, they turned to be this war's primary victims.[40] The impact of the brutality used against women in Bosnia-Herzegovina is still felt today. This was one of the reasons why local and international policy-makers were involved in the process of post-war reconstruction and came to believe that including women in political posts was vital for building sustainable peace in the country.[41] War in Bosnia-Herzegovina ended with the Dayton Accords of 1995. The Accords also known as the "General Framework Agreement for Peace in Bosnia-Herzegovina"[42] re-designed Bosnia-Herzegovina and included a massive involvement of international organizations and several NGOs (43). The Dayton Accords resulted in the writing of a new constitution and the creation of the office of the UN High Representative which, rather than the country's parliament, made the most important political decisions.[43] At the same time, the Dayton Accords did not contain any provisions regarding the political participation of women or of gender quotas in particular.

In 1996, Bosnia and Herzegovina was declared a federation composed of Bosnia and Herzegovina and Republika Sprska, each with its own parliaments and a federal-level bicameral Parliamentary Assembly. The Parliamentary Assembly is composed of the House of People with fifteen seats indirectly elected by the parliament, and the House of Representatives with forty-two seats directly elected through a PR system. The Parliament of the Federation of Bosnia and Herzegovina has twenty-eight seats, twenty-one are elected from multi-member constituencies and seven from compensatory lists; while the parliament of Srpska has fourteen seats, nine are elected from constituent districts, and five are selected from compensatory lists.[44] After the 1996 elections, only one woman (2.4 percent) was elected to the House of Representatives; seven women (five percent) were elected to the parliament of the Federation of Bosnia and Herzegovina and two women (1.9 percent) were elected to the parliament of Srpska.[45] Unhappy with these results, international organizations, especially OSCE, pressed for a thirty percent legislative gender quota.[46] New electoral rules were implemented during the 1998 elections and resulted in a significant increase of elected women: twenty-six percent of women were elected to the House of Representatives; fifteen percent of women were elected to the parliament of the Federation of Bosnia and Herzegovina and 22.8 percent were elected to the parliament of the Republic of Srpska.[47] Open-party lists, instead of closed-party lists were introduced during the 2000 elections.[48]. Under closed-party lists, the order of the candidates in the party lists was determined by political parties. This can be problematic in an ethnically divided society like Bosnia where political parties are often associated with certain ethnic groups, and its closed-list system allowed reinstating old nationalist leaders into power. Under open party list system, voters were allowed to decide on the candidate to be elected. This creates intra-party competition and new party members have a better opportunity to be elected.[49] Yet, this system did not benefit women. As a result of the 2000 elections, women representation in all three parliaments dropped dramatically.[50]

In 2003 the parliament of Bosnia-Herzegovina adopted a *Law on Gender Equality*. A National Gender Action Plan was implemented two weeks before the 2006 elections. Gender Equality Agencies were created at all state levels.[51] The elections to the House of Representatives of Bosnia-Herzegovina took place in October 2006.[52] The parties complied with the minimum thirty percent of women candidates.[53] However, the elections did not bring any improvement on women's representation. As in the previous elections, only six women (14.29 percent) were elected to the House of Representatives.[54]

It seems that despite legal provisions and state efforts to encourage women participation in politics and enhance women representation in legislative bodies, women remain politically inactive and underrepresented in Bosnia and Herzegovina. Scholars claim that this not only due to its open-list electoral system, but also to the fact that legal measures do not match real changes in society: mass media continues to discriminate women and political parties do not support their female candidates or their concerns for gender issues.[55]

Similarly to Bosnia-Herzegovina and Armenia the impact of gender quotas in Serbia has been affected by its socialist past, recent involvement in bloody ethnic conflicts and involvement of international organizations. However, different electoral rules and a strong women's movement have made the implementation of gender quotas in Serbia relatively more successful, though women are still underrepresented at all levels of political power. This is explored in the next section.

Gender Quotas in Serbia

Like Bosnia-Herzegovina, when Serbia was a part of the Socialist Federal Republic of Yugoslavia until 1992, women were given opportunity to take approximately one-third of seats in all political bodies.[56] After the fall of Communist Yugoslavia in 1992, the first multiparty elections were held in the Serbian parliament. These elections resulted in the victory of the Socialist Party of Serbia led by Slobodan Milosevic. His party and other leading parties used strong nationalist rhetoric during their electoral campaigns. Although former socialist leaders continued to dominate the new political landscape of Serbia, representation of women fell to five percent during the 1992 elections.[57] Following constitutional changes new elections were held in less than a year. Milosevic's party and other radical nationalists continued to dominate a Serbian parliament, while representation of women fell to 2.8 percent.[58] Serbian nationalists remained at the center of Serbian politics throughout the 1990s. This period was characterized not only by the continuation of a repressive regime that limited political rights and freedoms for men and women, but also by ongoing ethnic conflicts between Serbia and Bosnia-Herzegovina, Croatia, and the Kosovo region of Serbia.[59] Like Bosnia-Herzegovina, Serbia signed the Dayton Accords in 1995 and had to abide by them; however, this did not lead to any changes in Serbian politics, because Milosevic used them to market himself as a peace-maker.[60]

Like in Armenia and Bosnia and Herzegovina, women experienced a double burden in the ongoing political situation. One the one hand, domination of nationalist political forces and militarization of Serbian politics marginalized women and discouraged them from participation in public life. Women were praised as mothers and caregivers of the Serbian nation, not as active players in Serbian governance.[61] On the other hand, women constituted a majority of the refugees and displaced persons, and carried a major burden of hardening economic conditions.[62] Not surprisingly, women became active in the anti-war and anti-Milosevic political forces through civil society organizations in the 1990s.[63] Activism of women was crucial during the campaigns for Serbia's legislative elections of 2000, which led to the victory of opposition forces and an end of the Milosevic era in Serbia.[64] This activism was encouraged by the Gender Task Force (GTF) of the Stability Pact for

South Eastern Europe.[65] The GTF became a vigorous force for Serbian women in early 2000. In February 2000 it held a conference in Serbia that brought together women from various opposition (to Milosevic) political parties. It also created three women's networks composed of NGOs, political women, and women in the media.[66] These efforts resulted in a significant increase of women political candidates during the 2000 elections and in the highest voter turnout of the decade.[67]

According to the 2000 *Law on the Election of Representatives*, Serbian citizens had to elect 250 deputies to the unicameral National Assembly of the Republic of Serbia using closed party list proportional representation system with no special provisions regarding women.[68] This did not improve women's political representation; only 7.25 percent of the elected deputies were women.[69] Observers from OSCE asserted that "party leadership and election officials remain generally unaware of the issue of women's representation and of the drastic effects of the transitional government on women's economic and social status."[70] The situation changed after the 2003 parliamentary elections (which took place after the formal establishment of the State Union of Serbia and Montenegro), when over twelve percent of the elected deputies were women. During the election campaign, women's organizations ensured that most of political parties had around twenty percent of women in their candidate lists. However, women remained heavily underrepresented in major decision-making structures of the Serbian government.[71]

Women's organizations increased their efforts to incorporate women in politics with some success. Indeed, two women-friendly policies were adopted; the *Local Elections Law* in 2002, and a T*he Election of Deputies in the National Assembly Law* in 2004.[72] According to the 2002 *Law on Local Elections*, "one of every four candidates in the list shall be of the sex that is less represented in the list, and the total number of the less represented sex in the list may not be smaller than thirty percent."[73] Article 40a of the 2004 *Law on the Election of Deputies in the National Assembly*[74] also provided a similar quota provision based on sex and both laws penalized political parties for violating the quota provision. The problem with the gender quota was that a requirement to have every fourth candidate to be a woman implied that twenty-five percent of the candidates had to be women, not thirty, as stated by law. Besides, these laws regulated a distribution of the candidates in party lists and as it is the case with legislative quotas in many other instances, they do not necessarily result in an equivalent percentage of seats in parliament. They also contained other provisions (Article 84) that allowed political parties to replace even wining female candidates with other, often male members.[75] How did these rather loose and equivocal gender quota provisions affect women representation? Could their effect be mediated by the efforts to introduce new gender equality mechanisms, such as a Gender Equality Committee (2003) within Serbia's parliament (Under Article 68 G of the Rules of Procedure of the Serbian National Assembly, Official Gazette of the Republic of Serbia, No. 57/2003), a Gender Equality Council (2003), as a governmental working body and numerous bodies at provincial levels?[76]

Following Montenegro's declaration of independence in 2006 and the end of the State Union of Serbia and Montenegro,[77] Serbia adopted a new constitution,[78] which had numerous provisions regarding gender equality.[79] In January 2007 Serbia held elections to its National Assembly. Women's organizations were active again, campaigning in favor of women's issues and female candidates in the political parties.[80] Despite the fact that radical nationalists won 32.4 percent of the seats in the National Assembly and that women candidates did not receive the same media attention as male candidates during the campaign,[81] 20.4 percent of all elected deputies in 2007 were women. Most of female candidates emerged from non-nationalist political parties.[82] Moreover, most of the parties complied with the thirty percent gender quota in their candidate lists.[83] Radical nationalists, who held power after the 2007 elections, were unable to form a government. Besides, in February 2008, Kosovo declared its independence from Serbia.[84] That was why in March 2008, the president of Serbia dissolved the National Assembly and announced new elections. These elections resulted in the victory of the non-nationalist political party ruling the country today, although nationalists remained strong. Moreover, despite the fact that a majority of the political parties did not fulfill the required thirty percent quota, 21.60 percent of the elected deputies were women.[85]

It seems that despite a continuing negative influence of nationalist political forces for Serbian women and the fact that political parties functioned around male-dominated oligarchies,[87] gender quotas, combined with women's activism, the influence of European institutions, and closed-list PR had a positive impact on an increasing political participation and representation of women in Serbia. Today Serbian women enjoy one of the highest percentages of female parliamentary deputies in Eastern and Central Europe.

Comparative Achievements of Legislative Quotas in Armenia, Bosnia-Herzegovina and Serbia

Women in Armenia, Bosnia-Herzegovina and Serbia enjoyed relative (at least formal) support from the ruling political forces before the advent of the bloody ethnic wars in the 1990s. Armenia was involved in the war with neighboring Azerbaijan. Although there was no fighting on Armenian territory, Armenia suffered economically and received a large inflow of refugees, most of whom were women. Bosnia-Herzegovina not only had a brutal ethnic war, but also experienced genocide and what some scholars call *gendercide* in its territory. Serbia suffered from its involvement in an ethnic conflict with Bosnia and Herzegovina and Croatia, as well as with

Table 10.1: A Comparative Analysis of Gender Quotas Armenia, Bosnia-Herzegovina, and Serbia

	TYPE OF PARLIAMENT	ELECTORAL SYSTEM	TYPE OF GENDER QUOTA**; %; YEAR	PERCENTAGE CHANGE SINCE INTRODUCTION OF QUOTA***
Armenia	Unicameral	Closed party list PR* system	Legislated candidate quota; 15%; 1999	129% increase (from 4% in 1999 to 9.16% in 2007
Bosnia and Herzegovina	Bicameral	Closed party list PR* system in 1999 Open party list PR* system since 2000	Legislated candidate quota; 30%; 1998	45% decrease (from 26% in 1998 under open-list PR* system to 14.29% in 2006 under open-list PR system)
Serbia	Unicameral	Closed party list PR* system	Legislated candidate quota; 30%; 2004	5.8% increase (from 20.4% in 2007 to 21.6% in 2008

*PR = Proportional Representation
** For national parliaments only
*** Percentage difference in the percentage of the elected women deputies from the first post-quota elections to the last elections

Kosovar Albanians. Ethnic conflict meant not only economic hardship and destruction, but also the primordialization and militarization of domestic politics leading to the alienation of women from public life. In all three cases, ethnic wars ended with an active involvement of international organizations, which played an important role in the domestic policies of these countries and encouraged the participation of women in politics. They encourage women to participate for the sake of democratization and to neutralize the influence of nationalist politicians. Impact of gender quotas in the three post-conflict post-socialist countries Armenia, Bosnia-Herzegovina and Serbia can be summarized in the table below.

As it is clear from the table above, both a willingness of major political actors to be more inclusive of women and the type of electoral systems mattered on whether gender quotas were implemented successfully in these three post-conflict societies. Closed party list PR systems (like in Armenia and Serbia) allow political parties to promote their female candidates to their representative bodies, while open party list PR systems limit the chances of women to be elected in more traditional political cultures. In all cases, the wording of the laws allowed for possible (and real) manipulations. Another important finding is that when international organizations are actively involved in the democratization process, collaboration of members of civil society organizations becomes crucial for the success or failure of the democratization process. For example, while Armenian women activists remain skeptical about the benefits of gender quotas, Serbian women were more active in pressing for gender quotas and hence more successful in their implementation.

In conclusion, an examination of gender quotas in Armenia, Bosnia-Herzegovina and Serbia shows that gender quotas do lead to an increase political participation and representation of women in post-conflict countries. But it also depends on the electoral system, design of the electoral laws, support of the civil society, political will to implement quotas, and also changes in the patriarchal values of a given society and the strength of political forces willing to take gender issues seriously. Taking into consideration that many post-conflict societies need to address issues concerning women, it is noteworthy that with well-designed electoral laws and benign politicians, it is possible to achieve positive results that will benefit both women and democratic governance in these countries.

CHAPTER ELEVEN

Diffusion of Gender Quotas in Latin America and Beyond

Advances and Setbacks in the Last Two Decades

ADRIANA PIATTI-CROCKER

Policy diffusion typically refers to the "process of policy learning or emulation in which policymakers view the experiences of others as models either to follow or avoid" (Guenther 2008). As discussed on Chapter One, most of the diffusion scholarship has focused on analyzing the factors leading to the diffusion of policy, starting with the innovator and then examining the bandwagon effect of policy adoption in other countries or social environments. In addition, more recent works employ an integrative methodology, utilizing internal determinants (organizational resources, institutions, political actors) and external factors (regional trends or demands) to explain the dynamic process of diffusion (Berry and Berry 1990, Crocker 2005, 2007, and 2010, Daley 2007, Dolowitz and Marsh 1996, Guenther 2006). This scholarship focuses on uncovering the factors that lead to policy adoption in a given unit of analysis and thus, it utilizes policy enactment as dependent variable. Chapter One, analyzed the diffusion of legislative quotas by employing both external and internal determinants. Chapters Two through Ten examined country-cases and interpreted internal processes of policy innovation in these countries, institutional and socio-economic obstacles in their implementation, the role of external factors, such as international and regional conferences and organizations, and the diffusion of policy at sub-national levels in some cases.

In addition, scholarship on diffusion analyzes the emulation trends (Bernard and Killworth, 1973, Mintrom and Vergari 1998, Rogers 1981 and 2003, Simmons, Dobbin and Garrett 2006, Crocker 2005 and 2007) and examines the influential role of time in the diffusion of innovations. For example, Rogers (2003) claims that a given social network may follow a series of phases of development shaped by the passage of time; whereas, during the early stages following an innovation the likelihood of diffusion increases with the passage of time, as the social network driving the process matures, the likelihood of diffusion decreases. This seems to have been the case in Latin America when taking into consideration countries as units of analysis; whereas a rapid diffusion of policy occurred during the period of 1996–1998 in the region, since the turn of the millennium, only Uruguay has adopted legislative quotas and two of the original adopters (Venezuela and Colombia) have revoked their legislation. This chapter will shed light on this regional trend since the turn of the millennium and will incorporate external and internal developments to explain the stalled diffusion of legislative quotas in Latin America. A second section of this chapter will include a short summary of the findings discussed in this book, will examine cases of policy expansion in the region and beyond, and will analyze institutional and cultural factors that have discouraged the inclusion of women in legislatures, even after the implementation of legislative quotas.

Time is of Essence: From Diffusion to the End of a Wave?

The process of diffusion is concerned with both the spread of phenomena through a population over space and through time. In fact, when defining diffusion, Rogers (1981, 2003) claims that it is "the process by which innovation is communicated through certain channels *over time* among the members of a social system."[1] Accordingly, when explaining diffusion much of the literature review deals not only with internal and external variables, but also with cross-temporal analyses to explain why similar phenomena occurs in one or more regions in several different time periods and derive from this some knowledge of change in the areas of study.[2]

Literature on diffusion (Bernard and Killworth, 1978, Mintrom and Vergari 1997, Crocker 2007, and Rogers 1981 and 2003) suggests that there are broadly defined stages in the diffusion process shaped by the passage of time. First, there is a relatively low level of interpersonal communication (socialization), as individuals or groups of individuals do not know whom to talk to. Networks links are mainly with others in a similar role and generally consist of *homophilous* individuals or groups.[3] During a second stage, there is a high rate of interaction as individuals begin to get acquainted with others, understand policies and how they could work in their own internal structures. Here cliques grow together to form a connected network increasing the chances of diffusion of an innovation. Thereafter, at a third stage, a high degree of stability occurs in the communication structure, and the rate of interaction levels off or decreases. Thus, as the network matures there is gradually a decrease or change in the system's communication structure.[4]

This seems to have been the case of gender quotas in Latin America and even beyond the region. Following the adoption of the 1991 legislative quota in Argentina, several regional organizations served as networks among political women in Latin America. Organizations such as Friedrich Ebert Foundation of Argentina, ECLAC and PARLATINO, contributed to an increasing rate of interactions and discussion of policies within the regional environment. More particularly, the 1995 Fourth World Women's Conference in Beijing was crucial in the diffusion process of legislative gender quotas in Latin America because it provided momentum for the diffusion of gender quotas both across the region (Camacho Granados, 1997; Htun and Jones 2002; Krook 2006) and beyond the region, as explained by Tasch in Chapter Ten. As a result of this external environment and other internal developments discussed in previous chapters, the adoption of legislative quotas peaked in Latin America during the 1996–1998 period when ten Latin American countries adopted the legislation. Moreover, UN Security Council Resolution 1325 and regional organizations, such as OSCE, promoted the adoption of gender quotas as a means for long-term peace in post-conflict societies. Tasch claims that "as of 2010, sixteen countries adopted national plans integrating the provisions of UNSC 1325" (179).

Yet, whereas legislative quotas became more of a trend in Eurasia and Eastern Europe since the turn of the millennium, the diffusion of legislative quotas has practically stalled in Latin America during the same time-period and even reversed in two of the original thirteen countries. Venezuela revoked its gender quota in 2000 and Colombia's law was declared unconstitutional in 2002.

This *stalled diffusion* in Latin America may be due to a decline of women activism after the *Beijing quota movement* of the mid-1990s. For those countries with the legislation "after the adoption of quota laws, women's coalitions disbanded as their members returned to their prior commitments and became reabsorbed into their

Figure 11.1: Adoption of Gender Quotas in Latin America 1991–2010

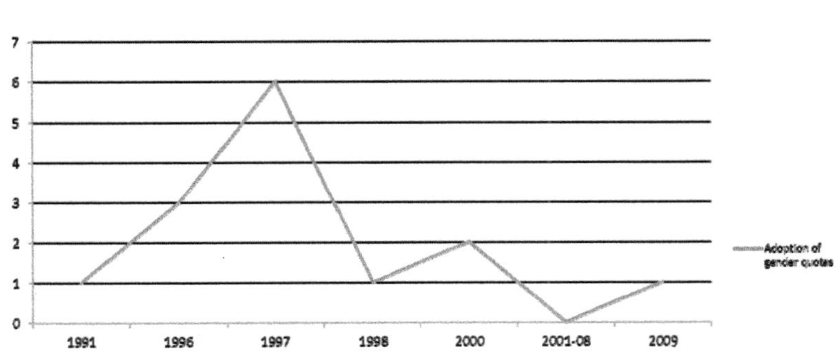

parties" (Htun 2000, 14). Yet, momentum has shifted also at regional conferences and within regional organizations. In fact, organizations that were very active during the 1990s *quota movement* in Latin America, since the turn of the twenty-first century, have been less active in some cases and more inclined to support resolutions that deal with the social protection of women. For example, during the six-year period of 2004–2010, a large proportion of PARLATINO's resolutions focused on the "sexual exploitation of young women and the promotion of a "continent" without violence against women rather than on gender quotas (PARLATINO, 2010).

In 2003 the former PARLATINO's *Commission of Gender and Equity*, merged with the *Commission on Childhood and Youth*, now the *Commission of gender, and Equity, Childhood, and Youth*. Changing the commission's name should not have further implications if its resolutions still focused on the promotion of gender quotas, but as discussed above, this has not been the case. Indeed, during the period between 1993–1994 several of the commission's resolutions called for an increase in the proportion of women in politics, including a petition to the Inter-Parliamentary Union that called to "correct the current disequilibrium in the participation of men and women in political life" (*Proyecto de Plan de Acción de la U.I.P para Corregir los Actuales Desequilibrios en la Participación de los Hombres y de las Mujeres en la Vida Política*). Yet, later resolutions and recommendations were fewer and emphasized the more general theme of improving the socio-economic status of women in Latin America. For example, during the 2004 meetings, PARLATINO's resolutions focused on the need to increase educational and labor opportunities, and equal pay for equal work intended to improve the status of women. Further, in 2009 there was only one recommendation that dealt with gender parity in decision-making, whereas a preponderant majority of recommendations dealt with other issues such as violence against women, reproductive health and the eradication of child labor among other issues (Parlatino, 2009). This broader focus may be due to the fact that after the adoption of quotas in twelve Latin American countries during the 1990s and one in 2000 the system's communication structure changed or matured.

As briefly discussed in Chapter One, ECLAC was also a significant source of *socialization* in the diffusion of gender quotas in Latin America. Similarly to PARLATINO, ECLAC has endorsed broader socio-economic policies than further advancing affirmative action for women. For example, during its 2006 regional conference, affirmative action was not even included in ECLAC's agenda. Instead, and given the poor economic performance of some Latin American countries, its resolutions advocated the adoption of institutional mechanisms to secure the *social protection* of women, implement strategies to coordinate the dual role of family and salaried work for women, and to promote the ratification of the convention de *Belem do Para* for the prevention, punishment and eradication of violence against women in those countries that are still not party to the treaty (ECLAC, 2006).[6]

Figure 11.2: Resolutions Dealing with Political Participation of Women (2004–2010) Compared to (1993–1994) in Percentages

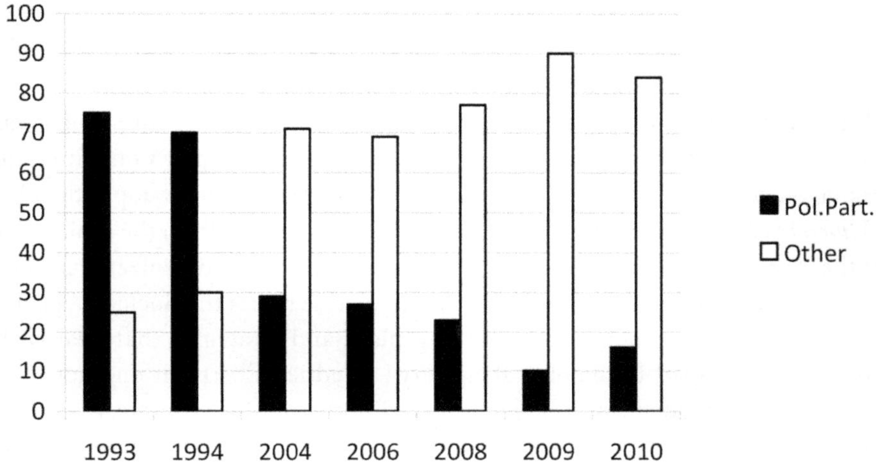

Source: PARLATINO

Two years earlier, the Mexico Consensus (2004) called for the inclusion of affirmative action for women, but it did so within the much broader context of general labor standards when it urged Latin American countries to "adopt proactive policies to promote job creation, including affirmative action for ensuring that men and women enjoy equal conditions in the labor market." It is noteworthy that during the regional conference of August 2007, one of the two major themes in the conference's agenda dealt with *the Role of Latin American and Caribbean Women in Gender Equality* and discussed the adoption of gender quotas. Yet, the arguments in favor of gender quotas were heavily rooted on the more general concept of human rights, rather than the narrower discourse of political equality.

More recently, the Division for Gender Affairs Institute at ECLAC has made significant efforts in attempting to monitor the status of women throughout Latin America and the Caribbean by creating a "Gender Equality Observatory." According to the Institute's website, three aspects of gender equality are taken into consideration by the *Observatory*: the economic aspect, which entails the ability to generate income and to control assets and resources; the biological aspect, which involves the rights of women to have control over their own bodies; and a political area, which requires the " full participation" of women in decision-making (Division for Gender Affairs-ECLAC, 2010). In the latter case, gender quotas are mentioned specifically as positive and effective measures to increase the proportion of women in governmental posts. In addition, the Beijing + 15 campaign, also sponsored by the

Institute, sent out a questionnaire requiring all Latin American countries and parties to the Beijing Platform For Action to report new institutional and legal mechanisms introduced by these countries on behalf of women. In sum, whereas PARLATINO has been more inclined to emphasize the social and economic protection of women in Latin America, in recent years ECLAC, has been more evenly divided in pursuing the different aspects of gender equality in the region.

Finally, the Argentine chapter of the Friedrich Ebert Foundation, which was quite involved in the early process of quota diffusion (see Chapter One); it is still working on political equality but primarily within Argentina. For example, the *Foro de Mujeres Políticas* gathers annually, but only includes women from the capital city and the Argentine Provinces. In addition, and similarly to the organizations mentioned above, Ebert has been dealing with very diverse topics that include equality between men and women in the working place and strategies that deal with women's poverty, apart from political equality (Friedrich Ebert Stitfung, 2009).

Endorsing a broader aspect of gender equality through social protective legislation instead of the narrower theme of gender quotas may be due to an increasing gap between the rich and the poor in the last decade, particularly among women. In its overview of the state of the world population the UNFPA in 2002 claimed that:

> It is seven years since the Fourth World Conference on Women noted the feminization of poverty and the world's nations pledged themselves to work for gender equality and social development as a means of reversing the trend. ....since the Millennium Summit in 2000, concern with ending poverty has intensified in the international community and the United Nations system, but there is less systematic effort towards ending poverty among women. Moreover, more women than men live in poverty, and the disparity has increased over the past decade, particularly in developing countries ... Gender disparities persist because social and legal institutions still do not guarantee women equality in basic legal and human rights, in access to or control of land or other resources, in employment and earnings, and social and political participation. These disparities have serious consequences, not only for women themselves, but also for their families and for society at large. (United Nations Population Fund Report, 2002, 3)

In summary, it is apparent that since the turn of the century, regional organizations that were critical in the diffusion of gender quotas in Latin America have been more inclined to promote a broader interpretation of women's rights. In other words, as the network links *matured* a change in the system's communication structure followed for Latin American women. Yet, it is also possible that regional socialization on behalf of gender quotas may be re-energized given the most recent focus on gender equality in politics sponsored by the Division of Gender Equality at ECLAC or through other UN bodies, as has been the case of the former communist and post-conflict countries studied in this volume (see Chapter Ten).

Internal Developments

Apart from the regional network, efforts to adopt gender quotas in countries beyond the current twelve Latin American countries with legislation have been numerous but often futile. For example, in 1997 the Guatemalan Women's Civic and Political Alliance and the National Office on Women proposed a gender quota bill that would have required that no more than forty-four percent of its candidates be of the same gender on all party lists at both the municipal and national levels. The original proposal was rejected, but the bill was amended to include a thirty percent quota. Although the bill collected more support than expected, its passage required a two-thirds majority, which was not achieved (Quota Project, 2010).

In Venezuela, where legislative quotas were adopted in 1998 but revoked in 2000, policy-makers shifted their efforts from issues concerning gender parity to the social protection of women. Among those efforts, Doris Acevedo, the Venezuelan representative at the Commission of the Status of Women (UN), identified the creation of the Women's Development Bank in 2001, which aimed to advance the situation of women with low incomes and those living in extreme poverty, and created programs to provide micro-credit for women entrepreneurs. The Women's Institute also provided job training in non-traditional areas in order to overcome employment segmentation and illiteracy. However, according to Acevedo, there was only limited progress in the promotion of the political participation of women. In 1999 and 2000, some fourteen percent of women were elected to positions in local municipalities, state assemblies and the National Assembly. Acevedo claimed that "the government was committed to overcoming the social divide," but "the programs (have) fall(en) short of develop(ing) a political culture that would integrate gender equality into the political and governmental agenda" (Commission on the Status of Women, 2004). A shift, albeit modest occurred in April 2004, when the *Consejo Nacional Electoral* (CNE) adopted an administrative resolution that recommended the participation of women in politics. In 2005, Venezuela's electoral gazette published by the Council demanded political parties to ensure female representation in its electoral lists. Furthermore, the CNE may mandate parties to implement such recommendation and publish the list of parties not abiding by the regulations. Consequently and even without a quota law, the proportion of women in Venezuela's legislative elections jumped from 9.7 percent in 2004 to 17.4 percent in 2005. However, these changes may be quite volatile since they were enforced by the executive branch and there is no legislation or constitutional reform to support them.

In Chile, gender quotas have been long established at party levels. For example, the Party for Democracy (PPD) has had a twenty percent quota for women since 1988. Chile's Socialist Party (PS) later introduced a twenty percent quota that was raised to thirty percent for the 1997 and 1998 elections. It then changed to a neutral quota whereby, neither sex may occupy more than seventy percent of the seats in parliament (Party statutes, Article 40). In addition, the Christian Democratic Party (PDC) has a twenty percent quota for women. Yet, quotas at party levels have been weakly enforced and thus, have not been translated into gains for women. In 2010, there were only 14.7 percent of women legislators in the Lower House and 13.1 percent in the Senate. Indeed, even when governed by a woman president until early 2010, efforts to adopt quotas in Chile have encountered opposition. According to Daniela Estrada (2006) "criticisms of a proposal (to introduce gender quota legislation) have led the executive to consider alternatives, such as promoting a protocol by which political parties would commit themselves to include more female candidates." Rogers (1981, 193) claims that network links will increase the likelihood of innovation as long as " the innovation is compatible with the norms of the system." In the case of Chile, legislative quotas may not be compatible with its current binomial electoral system.[6]

As discussed in Chapter Nine, Uruguay adopted a legislative quota in 2009, after two decades of women's struggle. The law establishes a minimum of thirty percent quota for candidate lists and it is a gender neutral quota, requiring party candidates of both sexes to be represented in every three places of their electoral lists. However, the law did not exclude substitutes in the quota count, a loophole that was later regulated by Uruguay's Electoral Court, but not after a strong mobilization of women legislators (*Bancada Bicameral Femenina*). More importantly, as explained by Johnson and Pérez in Chapter Nine, Uruguay's quotas are still temporary remedies and will be implemented at the national level for the first time during the 2014 elections (Instituto Nacional de las Mujeres, 2010). Other Latin American countries, including Colombia, El Salvador, Haiti, and Nicaragua, have yet to adopt legislative quotas.However, with the exception of Haiti and Colombia, party-level quotas have been enforced in most Latin American countries (Quota Project, 2010).

Women and Politics: Two Decades of Advances and Obstacles

Despite stalling legislative quotas since the turn of the millennium, political women have gained increasing access to positions of power in Latin America.

Within the last decade, there have been an unprecedented number of female presidents (Argentina, Brazil, Chile—until 2010—and Costa Rica) and a greater percentage of female candidates for the highest positions in government. For example, in 2003, an average of eighteen percent of governmental ministries were held by women in Latin America (five percentage points above the world average), and according to Escobar-Lemon and Taylor-Robinson (2005) between 2000 and 2003, women headed traditionally male cabinets such as the Ministries of Defense (Chile and Colombia, and later also in Argentina and El Salvador), Finances (Costa Rica, Ecuador, Guatemala, Honduras, and Venezuela), and Foreign Relations (Chile, Colombia, El Salvador, and Mexico). In addition, there are two female members in Argentina's National Supreme Court for the first time in the country's history. Finally, as discussed in García Quesada's Chapter Eight, one of the most auspicious trends in Latin America has been the adoption of a parity law in Costa Rica. Even with some possible future constraints, this law is the first of its kind at national level in Latin America and it is enforceable beyond legislative seats. Thus, it seems that the region as a whole has made substantive advancements in favor of women.

Regarding women legislators and besides the cases discussed in this volume, both Bolivia and Ecuador have made major strides following the adoption of legislative quotas in 1997. Whereas Bolivia has forty-seven percent of female national senators—the largest proportion in the region—due to its recent constitutional reforms (see Chapter One of this volume), article three of Ecuador's reformed constitution advocates "the equal participation of men and women as candidates in popular elections," a clause that led to the regulation of the 1997 law that established only a twenty percent quota for women. The administrative regulations of 2000, mandated a five percentage point increase of the quota on each election (presidential, legislative and local) until the quota reaches forty-five percent. In 2002, the country's Highest Court ruled that the only alternating formula allowed by the regulations required "men to come after women and vice versa for the top of the list until the quota is met" (Quota Observatory, 2010). Ecuador has today thirty-two percent of women in the House.

Beyond Latin America and due to a combination of international conferences and norms such as the Beijing Declaration and Platform of Action, gender quotas became an international trend that served as a means for cross-regional diffusion. These documents view affirmative action as necessary to promote gender balance in political posts of high-ranking. Moreover, the United Nations Security Council's Resolution (UNSC) 1325 of October, 2000 advocates the political participation of women in post-conflict societies as a means for long-term peace. These international norms combined with national women organizations and policy-makers led the former communist, post-conflict countries of Armenia, Bosnia-Herzegovina and Serbia to adopt legislative quotas for women and to an increase political participation and representation of women, in some cases more successfully than in others.

However, even those countries with legislative quotas discussed in this volume have experienced significant limitations for women politicians, due to several institutional, socio-economic, and cultural obstacles. For example, according to Archenti and Tula (Chapter Two) despite the impressive increase of women legislators in post-quota Argentina, in recent years, this increase "has stalled." The authors argue that in the configuration of party lists, "political parties tend to observe the strict minimum quota required by the law. Thus, there seems to be a glass ceiling for women, where the minimum percentage of women that quota laws impose has been taken as a maximum percentage by political parties." Araujo and Alves (Chapter Five) claim that in Brazil "the number of women candidacies grew in 2010, in comparison to previous years, but the figure did not reach the minimum of thirty percent" required by law. Yet, apart from the legal loopholes, women faced several other obstacles in Brazil including the fact that "political capital, in its diverse forms" seems to be a decisive factor for the election of women and "is more easily reproduced if the individual is already a member of parliament" (74). As suggested by the authors, despite the advances of women in the labor market and as politicians, "there is still a significant conservative streak with regard to the values of the Brazilian people. This dual perception, defined by the traditional role of men—the public person and the provider—and women—private and the caregiver—are still prevailing values in Brazil" (71).

Disregarding the significance of quota design has been a trend in the region and beyond. Yet, whereas in Peru, neglecting "how quotas would actually work in conjunction with the very different rules used in the country's congressional and regional/municipal elections" may have been "a blessing in disguise" (Schmidt, 103), in many other countries this oversight has obstructed the effective implementation of quotas. As stated by Piscopo initial quota laws in Latin America have tended to be "weak and non-binding" (40) and have led to numerous amendments and reforms throughout the region that have been enforced in some cases more effectively than in others. This trend is seen in Mexico for example, where repeated reforms to remedy legal loopholes "reveal a problem with Mexican quota policies, that political parties are unwilling to comply unless they are compelled to do so." Zetterberg suggests that in Mexico the adoption of quotas may have increased the chances of women being elected to public office, "but the quota policies have not eradicated the patriarchal structures within political parties, nor have they made the selection of female candidates a natural part of their work" (68). A Panista female politician cited in Piscopo's Chapter Three claimed that "If the quota were not in place, it would not be followed" in Mexico (52). Similar problems were experienced in Argentina and Brazil (as stated above) and in the Dominican Republic, where quotas "have had unassertive effects in steadily increasing the number of women in electoral posts," (xxx) due to both institutional and cultural factors. These seem to be also a problem for women politicians beyond the region, as seen in Chapter 10.

Thus, despite auspicious trends for women in the post-quota countries studied in this volume, there are cultural, socio-economic, and institutional obstacles that women politicians still face today. As discussed in Polanco's Chapter Eight, the Beijing's Platform for Action Report (PFA, 2000) claims that "although women make up at least half of the electorate in almost all countries and have attained the right to vote and hold office in almost all States Members of the United Nations, women continue to be seriously underrepresented as candidates for public office" even in countries with legislative quotas, as seen in this volume. This is a significant problem in current world affairs, since as stated by the PFA, "the goals of equality, development, and peace" may " only be achieved with the active participation of women and the incorporation of women's perspective at all levels of decision-making" (134).

Final Considerations

Diffusion may be seen logically as an external or an internal process. In the first case, external factors influence the domestic affairs of a state. In the second it is a subfield of linkage politics, where both internal and external events interact within a state (Starr 1991, Berry and Berry 1990, True and Mintrom 2001). Thus, an appropriate explanation of diffusion should be given in terms both of the unit of analysis (e.g. states, individuals, or groups of individuals) and the social structures in which these units are embedded (e.g. world or regional systems). This book dealt with both dimensions by emphasizing processes of international diffusion through global and regional socialization, and describing the internal factors in twelve case-studies that led to a gender quota wave in the region and beyond.

Chapter One, claimed that the adoption of legislation in Argentina in 1991 initiated a trend at cross-national levels. Although political parties in many European countries and the PJ in Argentina had implemented gender quotas earlier, and some regional debate was evident at the time, the mandatory countrywide legislation adopted in 1991 by Argentina was the first of its kind. The Argentine gender quota legislation was precisely the "take-off point" for the sort of "bandwagon effect" (John Kingdon 1995). It gave rise to a gender quota movement in the region that was successful in passing similar legislation in twelve other Latin American countries. As explained in this book, this process was instigated by transnational organizations and conferences, a process referred in this volume as *socialization*, where women discussed the need to implement gender quota laws in their countries and Argentine politicians were invited to explain the country's experiences with the innovative legislation. In addition, various domestic factors, including the demands of feminist organizations, women legislators, heads of state, and women's governmental organizations were critical in shaping the internal process. Finally, legislative quotas have been enforced beyond the region with the purpose of promoting long-term peace. Encouraged by international and regional organizations, such as the UN Platform for Action, UNSC Resolution 1325 and the OECD, quotas have been also implemented in a number of post-conflict countries.

Overall, female legislative representation has increased since the adoption of legislative quotas in all the cases examined in this volume. Yet, quotas were enforced more successfully in some cases than in others, due to several institutional, cultural, and socio-economic factors. More impressively, many of the countries discussed in this volume have expanded their legislative quotas in quantitative terms-the minimum percentage required by the quota—territorially—extended to other regions or provinces sub-nationally- and beyond the legislatures to other governmental posts of high-ranking. Yet, in all the countries studied in this book, women legislators still face significant institutional and socio-economic obstacles, leading to "glass-ceiling" effects.

Finally, efforts to diffuse gender quota legislation beyond the original adopting countries have been numerous but modest. However, with an increase of women in positions of power, more serious attempts are expected. Yet, it is very probable that future adoption of legislative gender quotas will not spread in the form of a wave as it happened in Latin America of the 1990s but as it occurred in Uruguay, in more isolated forms and only after internal structures are modified or *re-invented* to absorb such innovations. Overall, the integrative approach employed in this book helped to overcome significantly the methodological divide between what occurs within a state (the domestic realm) and what occurs outside of it (the international realm). Certainly, such integrative perspective has helped interpret more adequately the factors that led to the adoption and diffusion of legislative quotas in Latin America and beyond.

Notes

Introduction

1. There are several other categorizations of gender quotas (see for example, Dahlerup, 2007, Matland, 2006) but the author retained the three categories of reserved seats, party-level, and legislative quotas for this book (See also Krook 2009, who uses this classification as well). Some scholars have suggested that reserved seats are not gender quotas per se, because these mechanisms do not influence candidate nomination processes but instead, make specific provisions as who may gain a seat in parliament (Dahlerup, 2006a).
2. In fact, a survey of around 2000 Latin American citizens, in six major cities—Buenos Aires, Sao Paolo, Rio de Janeiro, Bogota, Colombia, Mexico city, San Salvador—conducted by Gallop on behalf of the Inter American Bank of Development (IBD) demonstrated that a majority believed that women can make better leaders and produce better governments than men. For a full report on the Gallup poll, please see the Inter-American Dialogue website available at: www.thedialogue.org.
3. Critical mass theories are quite controversial. Some scholars argue that critical mass puts a burden on female legislators, who feel the pressure to legislate on behalf of women (Trimble, 2006). Others argue that critical mass alone does not guarantee legislation in favor of women, since other intervening factors play a major role (Childs and Krook 2006, Dahlerup 2006).

Chapter One: Jumping on the Bandwagon

1. Ann Florini, "The Evolution of International Norms." *International Studies Quarterly.* 40 (1996), 371. Ann Florini refers to the innovation-diffusion of policy as an "evolutionary

model," and explains that within the constructivist approach this model attempts to explain how norms are transmitted from one individual to another. According to Florini, the evolutionary model is rooted on constructivism and claims that accepted norms do not merely reflect the interests of big states but rather they are the result of an evolution of values and beliefs. Indeed, existing institutional arrangements themselves may contribute to a learning process that enhances convergent state policies.

2. As women's movements under the law expanded advocating global standards, CEDAW served the important function of increasing the legitimization of women's demands. By accepting the convention, states commit themselves to undertake a series of measures to end discrimination against women, including legislation and temporary special measures, so that women can enjoy all their human rights and fundamental freedoms. Furthermore, countries that have ratified or acceded to the convention are legally bound to put its provisions into practice and the country is committed to submit national reports, at least every four years, by which it must present the measures taken by the government in compliance with treaty obligations. In addition, in the latter period of global democratization trends, the convention was to serve as the basis of constitutional development for all signatory states (Ellen Dorsey. "The Global Women's Movement." In *the Politics of Global Governance: International Organizations in an Interdependent World,* ed. Paul Diehl: 335–360. Boulder, Co: Lynne Rienner, 1997). Apart from becoming a party to the Convention in the mid-1980s, Argentina mentioned in various reports following regional women conferences that CEDAW was one of the country's primary legal sources for the adoption of legislative quotas in the country. For more information on this topic see Adriana Piatti-Crocker (2010) "Constructing Policy Innovation in Argentina: From Gender Quotas to Same-Sex Marriage." In *Same-Sex Marriage in the Americas: Policy Innovation for Same-Sex Relationships,* eds. Jason Pierce son, Adriana Piatti-Crocker and Shawn Schulenberg. Boulder, Co: Lexington Books.
3. Even though there is not a clear number of "norm entrepreneurs" participating in the debate and pressing for policy change, those interviewed for this project revealed to the author that the women initially involved in the process "were the few and always the same ones." (Interviews with Maria Jose Lubertino May 13, 2003; Virginia Franganillo, May 30, 2003; Monique Aschtul and Maria Luisa Storani May 21, 2003; Cecilia Lipsicz May 27, 2003; Maria Rigat May 23 , 2003; and Marcela Rodriguez June 4, 2003). Yet, the proportion of women actively participating in political parties at lower levels was almost half of all members in Argentina at the time when gender quotas were debated in the country's legislature (Lubertino 2003).
4. One of such meetings in Paraguay was attended by political women of the Partido Febrerista (Paraguay), Frente Amplio (Uruguay), Worker's Party (PT) Brazil, the UCR and Popular Socialist Party (PSP) from Argentina, and representatives of the left from Chile, among others.
5. On November 16, deputies Allegrone de Fonte, Gómez Miranda, Botella, Fernández de Quarrancino, Macedo de Gómez, and Mojardín introduced an alternative bill that included gender-neutral quotas. Under the terms of the second bill no list of candidates for the chamber could include more than seventy percent candidates of the same gender. It also incorporated a placement mandate (Gallo & Giacobone 2001: 7). This bill was defeated in favor of Malharro's "less radical" legislation.
6. Interestingly, representatives of both the Conservative (UCEDE) and Socialist (MAS) parties, who may be placed ideologically in opposite extremes, argued against the bill along sim-

ilar philosophical lines: that affirmative action would promote reverse discrimination and violate the Argentine Constitution (Chamber of Deputies, National Debate, in Gallo and Giacobone 2001).

7. Under the 1993 executive decree, Menem created the Cabinet of Women's Councils. The Cabinet was composed of eight women with liaisons to the CNM and was primarily in charge of enforcing the gender quota legislation. Political opposition claimed that the cabinet was biased because its eight members were all PJ women (Amad o1993).
8. Another method used to demonstrate diffusion is through statistical analysis. My Ph.D. Dissertation (2005) employs an Event History Analysis (EHA) to demonstrate cross-national and sub-national diffusion. My findings indicated that those Latin American countries where civil liberties were protected to a greater degree, with a larger number of national mechanisms for women, with a larger proportion of women legislators, and a greater number of NGOs and IGOs were more inclined to adopt gender quotas or adopt them sooner. For more information on this analysis please see .http://www.iadb.org/sds/prolead/site_15_e.htm.
9. In order to assess the relative significance of the various conferences and organizations during the "socialization" process, forty-four Argentine women were interviewed, including legislators, women holding high-ranking positions in governmental organizations at the provincial and national levels, national and provincial legislators, and the largest non-governmental organizations in the country. This project used key informants who guided the researcher towards people and organizations for interviews. The research also used archival documentation, papers, and e-mail communications to contact Latin American women outside of Argentina to determine whether the Argentine experience did in fact play a role in the adoption of gender quotas across the region.
10. For example, the organization's 1996 report advocated the use of affirmative action for women to secure "equality of results " between genders in Latin American and Caribbean countries (ECLAC, Women and Development Unit, 1996).
11. In an interview with the author, Maria José Lubertino claimed that she was invited to New York and the Philippines to talk about the Argentine experience. Moreover, PROLEAD organized a conference in Mexico and one of the main topics of debate at the conference was the Argentine experience with gender quotas (Interview with Lubertino: May 13, 2003). In an interview with the author, Marcela Durrieu revealed that she was invited by the Inter-American Bank of Development (IBD) in early 1992 at a conference in Guadalajara, Mexico to explain the innovative Argentine gender policy. In addition, Durrieu asserted that Liliana Gurdulich, the Argentine representative to the Division of the Advancement of Women (DAW) spoke frequently at DAW meetings about the Argentine experience with its gender quota (interview: June 6, 2003).
12. Mona Krook (2006) argues that while "international documents and meetings serve as catalysts by introducing or popularizing new ideas…most of the "work" in these campaigns is done by domestic actors who organize both nationally and regionally, often, but not always in the run-up to international women's conferences." See also Alvarez (2000) and Tripp (2004).
13. In its *Informe Nacional* to the 1995 Beijing conference of Women, Argentina presented a 159-page study that included general data concerning women, the establishment of national and provincial mechanisms to promote women's integration in society on an equal basis with men, the creation of NGOs with similar objectives, and the adoption of legislation and con-

stitutional provisions, including affirmative action. The report's Chapter Three deals more particularly with the adoption of the gender quota law and its effects at the national level. Accordingly, the *informe* asserts that the implementation of a 30 percent quota for national legislative candidates had opened up a new debate in the chamber around gender and other social questions that had not been previously part of the national legislative agenda (Consejo Nacional de La Mujer, 1995).

14. In addition, the UN Economic and Social Council (ECOSOC) requested governments to submit national action plans for review by the Commission on the Status of Women beginning in March 1997 (UNIFEM, 2001).
15. In Vargas' view (1998), the most important innovations at the Beijing conference were the call "for mainstreaming a gender perspective in all forms of policy-making." In addition, the mechanisms created by this conference to "follow up" and assess the "mapping progress" were critical in establishing an international framework that explicitly advocated gender equality legislation (Interview with Marcela Rodríguez: June 4, 2004).
16. See Rogers quote on this chapter (2003:2–3).
17. This subsection summarizes the major aspects of policy-adoption in eight Latin American countries. A more developed account of the "internal processes" of gender quota adoption in Latin America can be found in my Ph.D. dissertation: "Gender Quota Laws in Latin America: Analyzing Cross-national and Sub-national Diffusion," 2005. Also, see other chapters of this volume for more detailed accounts of Latin American countries adopting legislative quotas.
18. For reasons of brevity, this sub-section will not discuss the cases of Panama, Ecuador, and Uruguay. For information on Ecuador see; Maria Fernanda Cañete (2008), "Las mujeres y el déficit de Democracia en los partidos y los movimientos políticos independientes", in *Del Dicho al Hecho:Manual de Buenas Prácticas para la Participación de Mujeres en los Partidos Políticos Latinoamericanos*, eds. Beatriz Llanos and Kristen Sample. Stockholm: International IDEA; and on Uruguay, see Chapter Nine of this volume.
19. The regulation of Law 581, establishes the adequate and effective participation of women in all levels of decision-making positions and in all branches of government in accordance with articles 13, 40, and 43 of the national constitution.
20. According to Méndez and Montesdeoca (2002), the Collective of Women, an umbrella organization that included among others, the Centro de Estudios de la Mujer-Honduras, Centro de Derechos de Mujeres, CLADEM, Ciudadana para la Equidad de Género, and Comisión Cristiana de Desarrollo played a key role in the adoption of legislative quotas in Honduras. Another umbrella organization was the Convergence of women, which also included a plurality of women's organizations (p.25).
21. The pass of time seems to have benefited the election of women in the lower houses as seen in the table below. All eleven countries still enforcing gender quota legislation have increased the percentage of women in successive elections, though in some cases only slightly. A more modest increase of women senators may be also due to less favorable electoral rules.
22. As interpreted by extensive scholarship (Jones 1996, 2004, 2005; Htun and Jones 2002; Matland and Studlar 1996; Matland 2002; Rule 1994; Schmidt 2004) , the type of electoral system is one of the determining factors of whether a given gender quota legislation will be more or less effective. Whereas, proportional representation, high district and party magnitudes, and placement mandate mechanisms seem to influence the implementation of quotas more favorably, there is controversy on whether closed list systems are more beneficial than

open lists. For example, in 1997 Peru had only eleven percent of women in its Congress of the Republic (Congreso de La República) before the law was adopted, but by 2005 there were 29.7 percent of women in Peru's unicameral congress despite having a PR open list system (Schmidt, 2004).

23. In her book, *Quotas for Women in Politics* (2009), Krook discusses the cases of Argentina and France, both countries with legislative quotas. The author argues that in Argentina quotas were implemented more effectively due to "harmonizing consequences," whereas France's "disjointed sequences" led to less successful implementation of quotas. Further research should help shed light on whether harmonizing vs. disjointed sequences also played a role in Latin America, aside from Argentina.

Chapter Two: Candidate Selection as Political Barriers for Gender Quotas

1. Decree 1246/2000 states that: "Whenever TWO seats are to be renewed, a woman candidate should occupy one of the first two places on the list. Law 24.012 will not be considered to have been observed whenever, in cases where only one or two seats are to be renewed, only one woman candidate is included in the third position on the list. When more than TWO seats are to be renewed, there should be a minimum of one woman in one of the first THREE positions on the list" (article 4). "When ONE, TWO or more seats are to be renewed, the quota must always be calculated from the first position and the list should have at least ONE woman for every TWO men in order to respect the minimum percentage established by Law 24.012. Party lists cannot include three candidates of the same sex in successive positions if the requirement of THIRTY PERCENT (thirty percent) established by Law 24.012 (article 5) has not already been met."
2. To see the way this electoral formula operates, we recommend a study by Varani (2005) about the composition of the legislative bodies (*Concejos Deliberantes*) at municipal levels.
3. *Departamento*: the name of the local electoral/ administration units in which many Argentine provinces are divided.

Chapter Three: Gender Quotas and Equity Promotion in Mexico

1. Note that Mexico's three-party system also contains numerous smaller parties who play an important role in electoral and legislative politics. To keep the narration simple, however, these parties are not discussed here.
2. Imke Harbers. "Political Organization in Multi-level Settings: Mexican and Latin American Parties and Party Systems after Decentralization" (PhD diss., Leiden University, 2010), 124–125.
3. Guillermo Rosas, "The Ideological Organization of Latin American Political Parties: An Empirical Analysis of Elite Policy Preferences," *Comparative Political Studies* 38:7 (2005): 824–849.

4. María del Carmen Nava Polina and Jorge Yáñez López, "The Effects of Pluralism on Legislative Activity: the Mexican Chamber of Deputies, 1917–2000" (paper presented at the International Research Workshop, Saint Louis, Missouri, 2003).
5. Benito Nacif, "Para comprender la disciplina de partido en la Cámara de Diputados de México: El modelo del partido centralizado," *Foro Internacional* 40:1 (2002): 5–38; Jeffrey A. Weldon, "The Prohibition on Consecutive Reelection in the Mexican Congress," *Election Law Journal* 3:3 (2004): 574–579; Denise Dresser, "Mexico: From PRI Dominance to Divided Democracy," in *Constructing Democratic Governance in Latin America*, ed. Jorge I. Domínguez and Michael Shifter (Baltimore: The Johns Hopkins University Press, 2003).
6. Jeffrey A. Weldon, "The Prohibition on Consecutive Reelection in the Mexican Congress," *Election Law Journal* 3:3 (2004).
7. Joy Langston, "Legislative Recruitment in Mexico," in *Pathways to Power: Political Recruitment and Candidate Selection in Latin America,* ed. Peter Siavelis and Scott Morgenstern (University Park: Pennsylvania State University Press, 2008).
8. Linda S. Stevenson, "Gender Politics in the Mexican Democratization Process," in *Toward Mexico's Democratization: Parties, Campaigns, Elections, and Public Opinion,* ed. Jorge I. Domínguez and Alejandro Poiré (London: Routledge, 1999), 172.
9. María del Carmen Nava Polina and Jorge Yáñez López, "The Effects of Pluralism on Legislative Activity: the Mexican Chamber of Deputies, 1917–2000" (paper presented at the International Research Workshop, Saint Louis, Missouri, 2003).
10. Jennifer M. Piscopo, "Engineering Quotas in Latin America" (Working Paper, Center for Iberian and Latin American Studies, University of California, San Diego, 2006).
11. Joy Langston, "Legislative Recruitment in Mexico," in *Pathways to Power: Political Recruitment and Candidate Selection in Latin America,* ed. Peter Siavelis and Scott Morgenstern (University Park: Pennsylvania State University Press, 2008).
12. Linda S. Stevenson, "Gender Politics in the Mexican Democratization Process," in *Toward Mexico's Democratization: Parties, Campaigns, Elections, and Public Opinion,* ed. Jorge I. Domínguez and Alejandro Poiré (London: Routledge, 1999), 172; Kathleen Bruhn, "Whores and Lesbians: Political Activism, Party Strategies, and Gender Quotas in Mexico," *Electoral Studies* 22 (2003): 101–119.
13. Magda Hinojosa, " *¿Más Mujeres*? Mexico's Mixed-Member Electoral System," in *Women and Legislative Representation,* ed. Manon Tremblay (New York, Palgrave Macmillan., 2008), 184.
14. Kathleen Bruhn, "Whores and Lesbians: Political Activism, Party Strategies, and Gender Quotas in Mexico," *Electoral Studies* 22 (2003): 102.
15. Alma Rosa Sánchez Olvera, "El Feminismo en la construcción de la ciudadanía de las mujeres en México," *Itinerario de las Miradas* 63 (2006): 29.
16. Kathleen Bruhn, "Whores and Lesbians: Political Activism, Party Strategies, and Gender Quotas in Mexico," *Electoral Studies* 22 (2003): 108.
17. Kathleen Bruhn, "Whores and Lesbians: Political Activism, Party Strategies, and Gender Quotas in Mexico," *Electoral Studies* 22 (2003): 110.
18. "Las senadoras opinan: cuotas, ¿para qué?," *Milenio,* March 9, 2009.
19. Interview with PRI activist and former deputy and former senator, Mexico City, December 8, 2009. All interviews were conducted by the author in Spanish. All translations into English were completed by the author.
20. Ibid.

21. Ibid.
22. Kathleen Bruhn, "Whores and Lesbians: Political Activism, Party Strategies, and Gender Quotas in Mexico," *Electoral Studies* 22 (2003): 111–112.
23. Joy Langston, "Legislative Recruitment in Mexico," in *Pathways to Power: Political Recruitment and Candidate Selection in Latin America,* ed. Peter Siavelis and Scott Morgenstern (University Park: Pennsylvania State University Press, 2008), 149.
24. Interview with former PRI president, former federal deputy, and former and current senator, Mexico City, December 15, 2009.
25. Joy Langston, "Legislative Recruitment in Mexico," in *Pathways to Power: Political Recruitment and Candidate Selection in Latin America,* ed. Peter Siavelis and Scott Morgenstern (University Park: Pennsylvania State University Press, 2008).
26. Ibid.
27. Interview with member of the CEN of the PAN as well as former federal deputy and senator, Mexico City, December 10, 2009.
28. Lisa Baldez, "Primaries v. Quotas: Gender and Candidate Nominations in Mexico, 2003," *Latin American Politics and Society* 49:3 (2008): 69–96.
29. Lisa Baldez, "Elected Bodies: The Gender Quota Law for Legislative Candidates in Mexico," *Legislative Studies Quarterly* 24:2 (2004): 231–258; Richard E. Matland and Donald Studlar, "The Contagion of Women Candidates in Single-Member Districts and Proportional Representation Electoral Systems: Canada and Norway," *The Journal of Politics* 58:3 (1996): 707–33.
30. Kathleen Bruhn, "Whores and Lesbians: Political Activism, Party Strategies, and Gender Quotas in Mexico," *Electoral Studies* 22 (2003).
31. Miki Caul Kittilson, "Political Parties and the Adoption of Candidate Gender Quotas: A Cross-National Analysis," *Journal of Politics* 63:4 (2001): 1214–1229.
32. Kathleen Bruhn, "Whores and Lesbians: Political Activism, Party Strategies, and Gender Quotas in Mexico," *Electoral Studies* 22 (2003).
33. Victoria E Rodríguez, *Women in Contemporary Mexican Politics* (Austin, University of Texas Press, 2003); María Luisa Tarrés, "The Political Participation of Women in Contemporary Mexico, 1980–2000," in *Changing Structure of Mexico,* ed. Laura Randall (New York, M.E. Sharpe, 2006).
34. Interview with PRI leader, Mexico City, December 2, 2009.
35. Linda S. Stevenson, "Gender Politics in the Mexican Democratization Process," in *Toward Mexico's Democratization: Parties, Campaigns, Elections, and Public Opinion,* ed. Jorge I. Domínguez and Alejandro Poiré (London: Routledge, 1999), 176.
36. Lisa Baldez, "Elected Bodies: The Gender Quota Law for Legislative Candidates in Mexico," *Legislative Studies Quarterly* 24:2 (2004): 231–258.
37. Victoria E Rodríguez, *Women in Contemporary Mexican Politics* (Austin, University of Texas Press, 2003).
38. Ibid, 171.
39. Beatriz Magaloni, "The Demise of Mexico's One-Party Dominant Regime: Elite Choices and the Masses in the Establishment of Democracy," in *The Third Wave of Democratization in Latin America: Advances and Setbacks*, ed. Frances Hagopian and Scott P. Mainwaring (New York: Cambridge University Press, 2003).
40. Magdalena Huerta García and Eric Magar Meurs, *Mujeres legisladoras en México*(Mexico City: InMujeres, CONACYT, and Fundación FES, 2006), 53.

41. Paragraph 3, Article 175 of the 1993 COFIPE.
42. Diego Reynoso and Natalia D'Angelo, "Leyes de Cuotas y Elecciones de Mujeres en México: ¿Contribuyen a disminuir la brecha entre eligir y ser elegida," (paper presented at the Mexican Congress of Electoral Studies, Coahuila, Mexico, 2004), 5.
43. Lisa Baldez, "Elected Bodies: The Gender Quota Law for Legislative Candidates in Mexico," *Legislative Studies Quarterly* 24:2 (2004): 231–258.
44. Interview with former PRI president, former federal deputy, and former and current senator, Mexico City, December 2009.
45. Jennifer M. Piscopo, "Engineering Quotas in Latin America" (Working Paper, Center for Iberian and Latin American Studies, University of California, San Diego, 2006).
46. Anne Phillips, *The Politics of Presence* (New York: Oxford University Press, 1998). Victoria E Rodríguez, *Women in Contemporary Mexican Politics* (Austin, University of Texas Press, 2003), 182.
47. Ibid, 171; María Luisa Tarrés, "The Political Participation of Women in Contemporary Mexico, 1980–2000," in *Changing Structure of Mexico,* ed. Laura Randall (New York, M.E. Sharpe, 2006), 418.
48. Linda S. Stevenson, "Gender Politics in the Mexican Democratization Process," in *Toward Mexico's Democratization: Parties, Campaigns, Elections, and Public Opinion,* ed. Jorge I. Domínguez and Alejandro Poiré (London: Routledge, 1999).
49. Previous law had permitted civil courts to address inter-family violence through processes that promoted the reconciliation between the aggressor and the victim.
50. The following discussion is drawn from the following: *Consorcio para el Diálogo Parlamentario y la Equidad,*http://www.consorcio.org.mx/pactos.htm.
51. Chronicle of the Chamber of Deputies, Mexican Congress, Mexico City, October 10, 2000.
52. Author's interview with PRD leader who served in the 2000–2003 Congress. Mexico City, December 16, 2009.
53. Daily Agenda, Mexican Congress, Mexico City, January 12, 2001.
54. Text of the *Acuerdo Nacional para la Equidad Entre Mujeres y Hombres* (National Agreement for the Equality Between Men and Women), implemented as part of the PROEQUIDAD. Secretary of the Interior of Mexico, Mexico City, March 2002.
55. Author's interview with PRD leader who served in the 2000–2003 Congress. Mexico City, December 16, 2009.
56. Interview with member of the CEN of the PAN as well as former federal deputy, Mexico City, December 10, 2009.
57. Lisa Baldez, "Elected Bodies: The Gender Quota Law for Legislative Candidates in Mexico," *Legislative Studies Quarterly* 24:2 (2004), 247.
58. Ibid, 244–246.
59. Ibid, 247.
60. Author's interview with PRD leader who served in the 2000–2003 Congress. Mexico City, December 16, 2009. (Documented also by Baldez, 2004.)
61. Lisa Baldez, "Elected Bodies: The Gender Quota Law for Legislative Candidates in Mexico," *Legislative Studies Quarterly* 24:2 (2004), 243.
62. Victoria E Rodríguez, *Women in Contemporary Mexican Politics* (Austin, University of Texas Press, 2003), 180.

63. Jennifer M. Piscopo, "Engineering Quotas in Latin America" (Working Paper, Center for Iberian and Latin American Studies, University of California, San Diego, 2006).
64. Lisa Baldez, "Primaries v. Quotas: Gender and Candidate Nominations in Mexico, 2003," *Latin American Politics and Society* 49:3 (2008): 69–96.
65. Magdalena Huerta García and Eric Magar Meurs, *Mujeres legisladoras en México*(Mexico City: InMujeres, CONACYT, and Fundación FES, 2006), 15.
66. Lisa Baldez, "Primaries v. Quotas: Gender and Candidate Nominations in Mexico, 2003," *Latin American Politics and Society* 49:3 (2008): 69–96.
67. Ibid, 78.
68. Interview with current PRD senator, Mexico City, December 3, 2009.
69. Interview with current PRD deputy, Mexico City, December 15, 2009.
70. Interview with former PAN deputy and current senator, Mexico City, December 8, 2009.
71. Interview with former PRI deputy and current member of the CEN, Mexico City, December 16, 2009.
72. Lisa Baldez, "Primaries v. Quotas: Gender and Candidate Nominations in Mexico, 2003," *Latin American Politics and Society* 49:3 (2008): 69–96.
73. Interview with PRD founder and former deputy, Mexico City, December 8, 2009.
74. Interview with former PAN deputy and current CEN member, Mexico City, December 7, 2009.
75. Interview with former PRI deputy and current CEN member, Mexico City, December 2, 2009.
76. Interview with former PAN deputy and current CEN member, Mexico City, December, 7 2009.
77. Interview with former PRI deputy and current CEN member, Mexico City, December 2, 2009.
78. Text of the agreement, signed February 2007 in the Federal Congress.
79. Federal Electoral Institute, Mexico City, http://genero.ife.org.mx/mujeres_congreso.html.
80. Interview with former PAN deputy and current senator, Mexico City, December 8, 2009, and interview with former PRD deputy, Mexico City, December 8, 2009.
81. Interview with former PAN deputy and current CEN member, Mexico City, December 7, 2009.
82. Interview with PRD leader, San Diego, California, May 6, 2010.
83. Interview with member of the CEN of the PAN as well as former federal deputy and senator, Mexico City, December 10, 2009.
84. Interview with former PRD deputy, Mexico City, December 15, 2009.

Chapter Four: The Diffusion of Sub-National Gender Quotas in Mexico and Their Impacts

1. Three political parties, the PRI, the PRD, and the National Action Party (PAN), are the key players in Mexican politics. However, also a few smaller parties are represented in the Federal Congress as well as at lower levels of government.
2. This means, for instance, that I do not characterize the 1993 revision of COFIPE as a quota policy. The wording of the 1993 version of COFIPE implied that the political parties should promote an increased political participation of women in processes of electoral recruitment. However, it did not state a specific percentage.
3. In the federal quota law, as well as in many quota policies at the state level, it is said that the political parties do not have to comply with the quota if the candidates to majority seats are

selected by *voto directo*, or primary elections (see Baldez 2007 for a critical discussion about the *voto directo* clause).

4. Interview with María Luisa Sosa de la Torre, Zacatecas, November 2, 2006.
5. Interview with María Concepción Torres Zaragoza, Morelia, December 1, 2006.
6. Interview with Leodegario Varela González, Zacatecas, November 9, 2006.
7. Interview with María Luisa Sosa de la Torre, Zacatecas, November 2, 2006.
8. See for instance the quota laws of Tamaulipas and Zacatecas, which have similar (albeit not identical) ways to specify e.g. the sanctions for non-compliance and exception clauses as the federal quota law.

Chapter Five: Participation of Women in the Elections of 2002, 2006 and 2010

1. This article is the unfolding of a study published in *Dados* [online]. vol.50, n.3, 2007, pp. 535–577 ARAUJO, Clara and ALVES, José Eustáquio Diniz. Impacts of social indicators and the electoral system on women's chances in elections and their interactions with quotas. *Dados*. vol.50, n.3, 2007, pp. 535–577.
2. Voting is mandatory in Brazil, although the fine imposed on those that do not vote is paltry. All Brazilians, born or naturalized, over the age of 16 may vote.
3. In the elections held on October 3, 2010.
4. See, amongst others (Fundação Perseu Abramo, 2003 and Araújo & Scalon, 2007).
5. See also Araújo & Alves, 2007.
6. In Brazil, the constituencies correspond to geographical and administrative states.
7. Remembering that, in Brazil, the administrative and geographical states are also voting constituencies.
8. In other words, the electoral weight of a party, determined by the number of seats that it succeeds in winning, in relation to the remainder of the parties that disputed the same election in a particular ward.
9. The weighting of party size was ascertained in Brazil in an earlier study by Araújo (2009) in which a comparison was made of all of the states of the federation and it was ascertained that those parties with most weight in each state were those in which women were more likely to be elected.
10. The political culture would require a more qualitative study, which is not the case of the present article. Therefore, this item was not included in the analysis model that we built.
11. This rate, as employed by Schmidt (2002) and by Araújo & Schmidt (2004:10), merely seeks to evaluate the chances of being elected in the world of the dispute of men and women candidates, taking into account just the variable *candidacy*, and ignoring other factors. It is all to do with the percentage of women candidates that were elected, divided by the percentage of male candidates elected, multiplied by 100. Thus a Relative Success Rate (*TRS*) equal to 100 means that the candidates of each sex have the same chance of getting elected. When the number is lower than 100, this means that men obtained better results. When greater than 100, women got the best results, relative to the men in the universe that they were disputing.

What the Rate does is help to understand a little better the competitiveness of a group of rivals, of both sexes, in a particular universe. This might be the country, the state or the party. This competitiveness may vary according to the interaction of the various factors, whether systemic, linked to the electoral system, or personal factors or types of capital. As a result, it also serves to demonstrate the relative influence of the increase in candidacies and, when associated with other variables, the impact of this increase.

12. The constituencies were aggregated into small, medium and large based on the variance inside Brazil and on the literature that discusses electoral systems from a comparative point of view.
13. Definitions of left, center and right took the literature as a reference. It is a very generalized aggregation, for the purpose of understanding the analysis. The aggregation into the three large blocks also varies depending on party posturing and alignment throughout the period. There are some inflections that may redefine the allocation of a party to the center in one election and to the right or left in another, a fact which perhaps would not occur if the focus were more detailed and disaggregated.
14. This same relationship was analyzed in relation to 2002 and 2006 in another study (*Araújo e Alves, 2007).*
15 . In these elections, 21 of the 29 parties elected at least one deputy. This Federal Chamber is considered to be somewhat fragmented.
16. The same configuration as in 2002.
17. The *PFL* changed its name after the elections in 2006, becoming known as the *DEM* (Democrats) in 2007.
18. The Wald test is used to evaluate if the parameter is statistically significant. This test has a Normal distribution, its value being compared with values tabulated according to the defined level of significance.
19. In a sample survey of male and female candidates to the post of federal deputy in 2010, it was found that the majority of candidates who possessed more structured Blogs, capable of being regularly updated, were composed of individuals with legislative mandates.
20. Note that we are only taking into consideration the reelection of deputies that were in power at the time of the election. However there are many men who did not have mandates at the time of the elections, but had already taken part in other legislatures, a situation that was less common with women.
21. Rejuvenation in 1994 was 58%, 50.7% in 1998, 49.9% in 2002 and 47% in 2006 (*O Globo*, October 3, 2006, pg. 22). In 2010, rejuvenation stood at 44%. In this case, of the 513 deputies that comprised the Chamber of Deputies, 407 stood for reelection. Of these, 70.5% (287) were successful in the task. (*Diap* website – www.diap.org.br - accessed on November 26, 2010.
22. With regard to this concept and the three great plans which this injustice operates on, see Fraser (2007).
23. The Brasília Consensus recommends: *"Promoting the creation of mechanisms and supporting those already in place in order to assure the party political participation of women which, in addition to the parity in the registration of candidacies, assure parity of results, guarantee equal access to campaign funds and electoral advertising, as well as their insertion into the decision-making areas within the framework of the political parties. Similarly, creating mechanisms to ratify non-compliance with the laws in this regard"* (Cepal, 2010, pg. 8).

Chapter Six: Gender Quotas in Peru

1. The 1962–63 military *junta* tapped Anita Fernandini to be the capital's mayor. Women won eighteen percent of the seats on the Lima Provincial Council in 1983, twenty-one percent in 1989, and thirty-one percent in 1995, the last non-quota election (Blondet and Montero 1994, 23; JNE 1997).
2. Ten female cabinet ministers held six different portfolios under Fujimori (Tuesta Soldevilla 2001, 47–65).
3. See her comments during the floor debate in Congreso de la República (1997b).
4. Interview with Lourdes Flores Nano in Lima, June 7, 1999.
5. In an interview with the author on August 8, 2000 in Lima, Martha Chávez recalled that Hildebrandt and Salgado had both lobbied Fujimori on the quota issue. Chávez believes that Salgado's influence was decisive in winning the president's support.
6. Gonzáles Arica (1997). Subsequent legislation established a fifteen percent candidate quota for native communities in some provincial and regional elections, as well as a twenty percent quota for candidates younger than twenty-nine in municipal and regional elections (see Laws 27,683, 27,734, 28,869, and 29,470).
7. Congreso de la República (1997b) and interview with Ana María Yáñez in Lima, May 31, 1999.
8. The port city of Callao, which is adjacent to Lima, is both a region and a province. The Lima Region does not include metropolitan Lima.
9. Regions were created on the basis of departments, which had been administrative units since 1919. Various efforts to create regions encompassing more than one department have been short-lived or unsuccessful.
10. Or districts in the case of Callao Region.
11. In the 1998 municipal elections, runoffs between the top two lists were held when no list obtained at least twenty percent of the vote.
12. Prior to 1998, the winning list was sometimes awarded only a bare majority of the seats.
13. Interview with Jorge del Castillo in Lima, 8 August 8, 2000.
14. Excluding back-up candidates (*suplentes*), which are used in some other Latin American countries, but not in Peru before 2010 and then only at the regional level.
15. 10 divided by 39 = 25.64 percent.
16. 2 divided by 5 = 40 percent.
17. Back-up candidates (*suplentes*) were also elected at the regional level under this new system, but parties could not evade the quota by packing women into back-up slots (as in Bolivia).
18. A four percent national threshold for congressional representation was added for 2006; it was increased to five percent in 2011.
19. The CCD had eighty members. 120 members of Congress were elected in 1995, 2000, 2001, and 2006. The size of Congress was subsequently increased to 130, beginning with the 2011 election.
20. In the case of resignation or death, Peruvian legislators are replaced by the unelected candidate on their respective list with the highest number of preferential votes. Men replaced two congresswomen who resigned and another who died. One of four departing congressmen was replaced by a woman.
21. However, Gallo, Sample, and Schmidt (2008, 192) did not find a relationship between the use of the preferential vote and the election of women *across* regions. This is a topic that needs further research at the level of the electoral district (region).

22. Brazil has a gender quota; Chile does not.

Chapter Seven: From Temporary Measures to the Parity Principle

1. See Informe Latirobanometro (2005). Accordingly,only 20%of the people interviewed consider that laws are enforced in the region˙ Corporación Latinobarómetro,Informe 2005 (Santiago Corporación, 2005: 15–21.
2. INEC, Statistical estimates on population http://www.inec.go.cr/Web/Home/GeneradorPagina.aspx
3. See, among others: Robert Dahl, *On Democracy* (New Haven: Yale University Press, 1998).
4. IDD considers 31 indicators grouped in four dimensions: a) legality of democratic regimes, b) respect for political rights and civil liberties; c) institutional quality and degree of political efficiency and d) effective exercise of power to govern with two sub-dimensions: 1- capacity to generate policies that assure wellbeing and 2- capacity to generate policies ensuring economic efficiency).
5. Since December 2010, municipal elections take place one year after the national elections.
6. TSE. *Elecciones en cifras 1953–2010,* http://www.tse.go.cr/elecciones.htm.
7. ECLAC establishes three types of countries in the region, with Costa Rica categorized in the group with the highest GDP, lower demographic rates of dependency, less informal job markets, greater social security coverage, greater coverage of public health services, lower levels of poverty and indigence, and social spending greater that the total GDP per capita and as percent of GDP (primacy of social spending). ECLAC, *La hora de la igualdad* (Santiago: ECLAC, 2010), 202–203.
8. The UNDP's HDI is a composite indicator measuring average advances of a country in three measurable dimensions of human development: living a long and healthy life, availability of education and having a decent level of life, placing this country ninth in human development in the region (62nd in the world of a total of 169 countries), with a value of 0.725 (the highest percent possible is 1.000); in other words, considered a country with high human development. UNDP, *Informe sobre Desarrollo Humano 2010* (New York: UNDP, 2010), 162 http://hdr.undp.org/en/media/HDR_2010_ES_Complete_reprint.pdf.
9. UNDP, *Informe sobre Desarrollo Humano 2010* (New York: UNDP, 2010), data updated to September 2010 http://hdrstats.undp.org/es/indicadores/89106.html.
10. Based on data from: a) GESO, database; b) ECLA, Costa Rica, country profile http://www.cepal.org/cgi-bin/getProd.asp?xml=/mujer/noticias/paginas/0/29840/P29840.xml&xsl=/mujer/tpl/p18f-st.xsl&base=/mujer/tpl/top-bottom-estadistica.xsl b) INEC, Estimates on population statistics http://www.inec.go.cr/Web/Home/GeneradorPagina.aspx c) ILO, Gender equity in the world of work http://www.ilo.org/public/spanish/region/ampro/cinterfor/temas/gender/doc/cinter/equidad/cap1/v/index.htm and d) INAMU, Tendencias empleo femenino (San Jose: INAMU, 2006).
11. Ana Isabel García Q., *Estrategia para enfrentar la pobreza en Costa Rica* (San José: CEDAL, 2010, in press).
12. Ana Isabel García Q., *Conquista, compromiso y cambio* (San José: CMF, 1996).

13. Centro Nacional para el Desarrollo de la Mujer y la Familia (CMF) – Ana Isabel García (Directora), *La apuesta estratégica. Informe de Labores 1994–1998.* (San José: CMF/Government of Costa Rica, 1998).
14. Ana Isabel García and Carla Morales. *Módulo 3: Democracia, Ciudadanía y Participación Política* (San Jose: INAMU, 2010), 27.
15. In this context it is noteworthy that the last two governments have not granted the rank of "Minister without Portfolio" to the Executive President of INAMU, a prerogative that while unnecessary (as a power held by whoever occupies the position in the office of the Presidency of the Republic) is nevertheless established by Law on INAMU itself.
16. It should be added that in the decentralized sphere, institutional mechanisms have been created since 1997 in both the Executive Power and local government, which in Costa Rica's case are 81 municipalities. This means that several entities of the Executive Power have entities and specific institutional policies to promote women and gender equity, and that this occurs in at least half of the municipalities.
17. The purpose of the "Gender Equity Policy of the Judicial Power" (*Corte Plena* session No. 34-05) is to "foster the process of incorporation of gender perspective in institutional policies, to develop human potential and the elimination of any practice of inequality or discrimination, both for internal users and those outside the Judicial Power". In 2007, the Judicial Power approved the "policy of attention to victims of domestic violence who work in the Judicial Power " (session No. 64-07 of the Superior Council of the Judicial Power) and in 2008 approved "guidelines for attending cases of Judicial Power employees that face domestic violence (session No. 30-08 of the Superior Council of the Judicial Power). Cases of domestic violence are referred to the Gender Technical Unit, which must report to the Council once a year. With regard to TSE, its "Institutional Policy on Gender Equality and Equity" was first approved by the Gender Commission of that electoral body (extraordinary session No. 10-2008, Art. 2, of 25 August 2008) and then by the Tribunal (ordinary session No. 92-2008, Art. 4, of 16 October 2008).
18. There are four types of legislative commissions: two are permanent, one concerns specific projects and one has the power to meet as if it were comprised of the entire plenary. Currently there are 29 commissions, most (12) being the special Permanent Commissions, followed by the Special Commissions with a concrete and time-limited objective (9); the Regular Permanent Commissions (6); and those that have Full Legislative Power (3).
19. Ana Isabel García and Enrique Gomáriz. *Módulo: Políticas públicas nacionales y locales sobre género y ciudadanía.* (San Jose: GESO/FES/UCR, 2003).
20. Fundación Género y Sociedad, Database, consulted in December 2010.
21. See also, Eugenia Rodríguez Sáenz, "La lucha por el sufragio femenino en Costa Rica 1890–1949" (San Jose: Editorial de la Universidad de Costa Rica, 2002), 89–110. Sara Sharrat, "The Suffragist Movement in Costa Rica, 1889–1949. Centennial of Democracy?" (Pittsburgh, PA: University of Pittsburgh Press, 1997), 61–83.
22. Virginia Mora Carvajal, *Redefiniendo la política. La participación de las reformistas en la campaña electoral de 1923.* (San Jose: Editorial de la Universidad de Costa Rica, 2002), 111–130. Eugenia Rodríguez Sáenz states that "within this period in the evolution of the suffragist movement we can distinguish three large stages: 1890–1910, 1910–1923 and 1923–1949". Eugenia Rodríguez, *Dotar de voto político.* (San Jose: Escuela de Historia de la UCR, 2009).

23. Costa Rican electoral system is governed by a specialized electoral jurisdiction, the Supreme Electoral Tribunal (TSE), which is independent of other State bodies. The regimen is one of political parties. Suffrage is universal, with direct and secret vote. There is a permanent voter registration list updated automatically from the Civil Registry. Each voter is identified by a personal photo ID. Vote is made on an individual ballot for each election containing the lists of candidates presented by the political parties. Deputies and municipal offices are elected through a type of proportional representation (*cociente, subcociente* and *residuo mayor]* and for the President of the Republic by majority vote (but must be over 40% of total valid votes). Deputies are elected by electoral circumscription, which in Costa Rica's case is based on the political-administrative division of the country into seven provinces. Since 2002, in addition to the presidential formula (a president and two vice-presidents), the 57 deputies, and the regents and municipal representatives (*síndicos*), other municipal authorities are also elected: mayors (a principal and two alternates) and district councilpersons, municipal councilpersons, and intendants. The TSE's decisions on electoral matters cannot be appealed. The TSE is empowered to interpret the Constitution and laws under its exclusive competence, which means that it can create unwritten rules derived from its decisions. In addition, its opinions are binding within the procedure of the formation of electoral laws and it may also initiate the formulation laws in this area. Its independence includes the following: it prepares its own budget and the Executive Power may not object to expenditures made in relation to the effectiveness of suffrage; it can even establish regulations related to electoral laws and is empowered to make definitive declarations on elections. All TSE officials, including those of the Civil Registry, are banned from party partisanship (except in exercising the right to vote) including consultative processes such as referendums.
24. For more details see: Rosalía Camacho, Silvia Lara, Esther Serrano - CMF, *Las cuotas mínimas de participación de las* mujeres (San José: CMF, 1996). Rosalía Camacho. *Sintonizando la conciencia, el voto y los puestos de decisión* (San José: Fundación Arias, 1998). Ana Isabel García Q. *Mujeres, participación política y ciudadanía* (Washington: Diálogo Interamericano, 1999). Isabel Torres García, *La aplicación de la cuota mínima* (San José: Fundación Arias, 2001). Ana Isabel García Q., *Concretando el mandato: reforma jurídica en Costa Rica* (Lima: IDEA, 2003).
25. Women represent 87.7% of elected First Vice-Mayors and 17.7% of Second Vice-Mayors; 48.7% of District Council Members; 42.2% of District Municipal Council Members; 25% of Intendants; 75% of Vice-Intendants and 49.7% of Síndicos (but are only the 27.2% of those occupying that post as principals). TSE, http://www.tse.go.cr/elecciones.htm
26. In Latin America, a woman has only been elected president on five occasions: in 1990 in Nicaragua (Violeta Chamorro), 2006 in Chile (Michelle Bachelet), 2007 in Argentina (Cristina Fernández), 2010 in Costa Rica (Laura Chinchilla) and 2011 in Brazil (Delma Rousseff). On another three occasions a woman has been also been named President but without participating in electoral processes: 1973 in Argentina (María Estela Martínez), 1979 in Bolivia (Lydia Guelier) and 1999 in Haití (Ertha Pascal).
27. The IFED began operating in 2010 and has the following responsibilities: "plan and execute formation programs for the citizenry and political parties, that promote the effective exercise of political rights and the strengthening of civic culture, addressing the regional, socioeconomic and cultural diversity of the Costa Ricans". Its main objectives are to: 1) plan and execute training programs that develop electoral competencies, aimed at government officials, political parties and citizens involved in the management of elections; 2) generate proj-

ects toward an active citizenry that exercises its political rights effectively; 3) foster training programs for elected officials related with the electoral regimen, the exercise of the public function and practice of democratic values; 4) collaborate with the Ministry of Public Education in the formulation of civic education programs directed toward the student population; 5) support the political parties in their efforts to carry out citizenship formation projects; 6) foster spaces of debate and discussion in the context of electoral processes; 7) foment the development of investigations and publications in themes related to democracy and elections; 8) administer a documentation center specialized in democracy and elections, accessible to the citizenry and applying informatics technologies; and 9) provide information for the citizenry and population in general, about the democratic system and the role of popularly elected public officials." TSE http://www.tse.go.cr/organigrama/IFED.html

28. These reflections arose after the author participated in three events related to the theme between 2008 and 2010, for which print and audio documentation exists:1) Course for Women Leaders, given by INAMU during 2010, in which the author (along with Carla Morales) gave *Module 3: Democracy, Citizenship and Political Participation* (San José: INAMU, 2010); 2) Discussion board "Beyond parity: from rules to practices," organized by IFED-TSE and UNDP, 22 November 2010; 3) International seminar, "A Decrease of Feminine Quotas in Latin America: Balance and Perspectives on Women's Participation," organized by the Electoral Council of the Dominican Republic, Santo Domingo, 13–15 October 2008.
29. For more details,see Haydeé Hernández, "Aprobación del nuevo Código Electoral" (Revista Olimpia No 10, San José: INAMU, 2009).

Chapter Eight: Women's Quotas in the Dominican Republic

1. The author would like to express her sincere gratitude to Danielle Prichet (Rutgers University) and Josefina Arvelo (Participación Ciudadana) for generously reading and commenting on her paper and sharing current data and discussions about the topic.
2. The review of the Beijing PFA took place during the twenty-third special session of the UN General Assembly "Women 2000: Gender Equality, Development and Peace for the 21st Century", also known as Beijing +5.
3. United Nations. "Report of the Ad Hoc Committee of the Whole of the twenty-third special session of the General Assembly", also known as the Outcome document of Beijing+5, paragraph 23.
4. Beijing Platform for Action, Critical Area G, paragraph 181. http://www.un.org/womenwatch/daw/beijing/platform/decision.htm.
5. The United States first military occupation of the Dominican Republic in 1916–1924 led to the emergence of the Trujilloist regime. As a salient member of the National Guard created by the U.S. military government, Rafael Leonidas Trujillo Molina became the strong man to govern the impoverished rural Caribbean nation when the American troops ran off from the Dominican soil after the U.S. fail attempt at imposing a strict vertical political control over the regionally divided caudillo's system. After 31 years of absolute control of the nation, several factors contributed to the demise of his regime in the mid-late 1950's and his assassination on May 30 1961, such as the economic failure of the Free World Fair for Peace and

Confraternity (*Feria de la Paz y Confraternidad del Mundo Libre*), the SIM's (Military Intelligence Service) failed attempt to assassinate the Venezuela's president Rómulo Betancourt, and the SIM's assassination of the Columbia University's professor and former CIA spy and Trujillo's Ministry of Labor the Spaniard Manuel de Jesús Galíndez and the members of the June 14 Movement (1J4) Patria, Minerva and María Teresa Mirabal.

6. Balaguer occupied the presidency with the Reformist Party (PR) after triumphing over Juan Bosch in the 1966 non-competitive elections sponsored by the U.S. and the Organization of American States (OAS) that at the time was led by military Latin American regimes.
7. During the celebration of the International Women's Day in 2000 the United Nations World Food Program (WFP) acknowledged Mamá Tingó's daughter Jesús María de Paula, leader of the Dominican Republic's Rural Women Federation (*Federación de Mujeres Campesinas*) for her work to improve the conditions of farmers. José Gómez Cerda: *La Lucha Sindical Campesina: Mamá Tingó.*
8. Balaguer's former PR party, now known as the Reformist Social Christian Party after its merger with the petite Revolutionary Social Christian Party, allowed the PRSC's affiliation with the International Social Christian Democracy (ISCD) and provided him a newly-fashioned democratic appearance.
9. Balaguer triumphed over José Francisco Peña Gómez (PRD) in the fraudulent 1994 presidential elections in which the PRSC launched a nationalist/racist campaign against Balaguer's fervent rival and long-standing populist black leader whose parents had been assassinated during Trujillo's1937 massacre of black Haitian and Dominican families who lived in the border region. The sturdy controversy that followed Balaguer's electoral success over Peña Gómez led to an inter-party contingent agreement between the PRSC and the PRD known as the Pact for Democracy (*Pacto por la Democracia*), through which the now nonagenarian and sightless Balaguer complied with Peña Gómez to trim down his presidency to a two-year term that would end in 1996 and present to the Congress a constitutional reform forbidding the president's immediate reelection and, thus, would hold Balaguer's electoral aspirations until 2002.
10. The 1996 elections depicted the pervasive racial and political rivalry between the old enemies and now allies Juan Bosch (PLD) and Joaquín Balaguer (PRSC) —both Dominicans of mixed-European descent—and the Afro-Dominican José Francisco Peña Gómez. The old caudillos Balaguer and Bosch put an end to thirty years of political rivalry through the Patriotic Pact (Pacto Patriótico) that guaranteed the triumph of the PLD candidate the mulatto Leonel Fernández over the black Peña Gómez. Through his contingent electoral success Fernández inherited the presidential legacy of Balaguer and his inexorable influence in the political cuisine.
11. I witnessed Dr. Milagros Ortiz's education policies during my 2002–2006 tenure as a scholar and consultant at the UNESCO Latin American Social Sciences Faculty (FLACSO) during which I participated in the research project "Towards a National Plan in Education on Human Rights" that proposes the implementation of comprehensive ethnic, gender/sex programs in the elementary, higher, and technical education in public and private schools, universities, the judiciary, and non-governmental organizations.
12. Mejía's popularity vanished due to his unrelenting errors of judgment and several political and economic mistakes, such as his pledge to the US president George Bush's military politics through the envoy of Dominican militaries to the Middle East in exchange for a top-

heavy bilateral economic agreement that neglected the potential benefits of the Dominican Republic's participation in the Central American Free Trade Agreement (CAFTA). In addition, in 2004, the Dominican Monetary Board unveiled the biggest financial scandal in the nation's history equivalent to 67% of the national budget in 2003 (US$2,200 millions). The Dominican's largest commercial banks BANINTER (Inter-Continental Bank), *Bancrédito* and *Banco Mercantil* were involved in a colossal fourteen year-long fraud whose transactions also implicated the incumbent Mejía, former presidents Balaguer (deceased) and Fernández, former PRD leader Peña Gómez (deceased), the current leadership of the major parties (PRD, PLD and PRSC), social leaders, as well as parliamentary, military, police, religious and mass media hierarchs. (Jiménez Polanco 2006, 3).

13. Several PLD women candidates informed me of their flagrant deprivation of electorally won positions by the party cupola after I delivered a presentation as the official consultant and keynote speaker of the PLD first National Conference on Gender Equity on March 4, 2006. My speech, that did not include anything different from the draft I presented in advance to a small group of PLD women in the Women's State Ministry, provoked however the reaction of several members of the male-dominated party cupola who abruptly abandoned the stage as soon as I finished my presentation. In the huge audience of hundreds of national and international representatives, several women who said they have been long-standing PLD members took advantage of the Q and A section to raise their voice against the gender inequities and the need of changes at the interior of the party, which drove the tough female leader Alejandrina Guzmán (at the time a controversial Ministry of Education) to unexpectedly adjourn the event (although she was one of the women who signed the working paper), reminding the women in the audience the party rule that forbids "public criticism"– which actually astonished me since this was an internal party event and I was the only outsider working under a contract. That was the end of a long planned conference, the afternoon section with President Fernández was cancelled to avoid any other women's "dysfunctional" performance.
14. The constitutional reform was also rejected by other sectors such as the Sexual minorities that disapproved that Article 39 forbids all kinds of discrimination but does not prohibit discrimination for sexual identity/orientation, while Article 55 restricts the family rights to the heterosexual partnership, both of which neglect the constitutional protection to alternative LGBTI lesbian, gay, bisexual, transsexuals and intersex individuals and families. Environmentalists refused that Article 15 limits the state's protection to public areas through the recognition and protection of the private property of rivers, lakes, lagoons, beaches and coastal areas. Immigrant rights organizations said no to the *ius solis* that guarantees the citizenship rights to the Dominican children of immigrant (i.e. Haitian) descent only if their parents are legal residents. (Jiménez Polanco 2010).

Chapter Nine: From Vanguard to Straggler

1. Previously Ecuador (1929) and Chile (1931) had granted restricted voting rights to women. See Inter-Parliamentary Union, *Women in Parliaments, 1945–1995. A Worldwide Statistical Survey* (Geneva: IPU, 1995), 21.

2. See Charlotte Nicola Johnson, "'The Right to Have Rights': Gender Politics, Citizenship and the State in Uruguay" (PhD diss., University of London, 2000), 39–40.
3. Silvia Rodríguez Villamil and Graciela Sapriza, *Mujer, Estado y Política en el Uruguay del Siglo XX* (Montevideo: Ediciones de la Banda Oriental, 1984), 70.
4. Asunción Lavrin, *Women, Feminism, and Social Change in Argentina, Chile and Uruguay, 1890–1940* (Lincoln: University of Nebraska Press, 1995), 351.
5. See Alba G. Cassina de Nogara, *Hacia una Democracia Integral: Apuntes para una Historia del Feminismo en Uruguay* (Montevideo: CONAMU, 1990), 86.
6. See Mark P. Jones, "El Sistema de Cuotas y la Elección de las Mujeres en América Latina: El Papel Fundamental del Sistema Electoral," in *La Democracia Paritaria en la Construcción Europea* (Madrid: CELEM, 2000), accessed September 21, 2010, http://www.celem.org/prog_europeos/demo_paritaria2000/pdfs/capitulo01.pdf; Pippa Norris, "The Impact of Electoral Reform on Women's Representation," *Acta Politica* 41 (2006); Stina Larserud and Rita Taphorn, *Designing for Equality. Best-fit, Medium-fit and Non-favourable Combinations of Electoral Systems and Gender Quotas* (Stockholm: International Institute for Democracy and Electoral Assistance, 2007); Mona Lena Krook, *Quotas for Women in Politics: Gender and Candidate Selection Reform Worldwide* (New York: Oxford University Press, 2009); Drude Dahlerup and Lena Freidenvall, "Judging Gender Quotas: Predictions and Results," *Policy and Politics*, 38(3) (2010), accessed October 23, 2010, http://www.statsvet.su.se/homepages/archive/drude_dahlerup/dahlerup_freidenvall_Policy_Politics_38_3_2010.pdf.
7. Venezuela's 1997 quota law was declared unconstitutional in 1998 by the National Electoral Council, a decision later upheld by the Supreme Court of Justice. For an overview of quota laws adopted in Latin America, see Mala Htun and Mark Jones, "Engendering the Right to Participate in Decision-Making: Electoral Quotas and Women's Leadership in Latin America," in *Gender and the Politics of Rights and Democracy in Latin America*, edited by Nikki Craske and Maxine Molyneux (London: Palgrave, 2002); Beatriz Llanos and Kristen Sample, *30 Years of Democracy: Riding the Wave? Women's Political Participation in Latin America* (Stockholm: International Institute for Democracy and Electoral Assistance, 2008), chapter 4.
8. See Johnson "The Right to Have Rights", 135–6; Niki Johnson, "La Cuota: ¿Un Mecanismo Necesario y Efectivo para Incrementar la Representación de Mujeres en Cargos Políticos Electivos? El Caso Uruguayo," Paper presented at the Seminar *Estrategias Políticas de Género: Reformas Institucionales, Identidad y Acción Colectiva*, Instituto de Investigaciones Gino Germani, Universidad de Buenos Aires, August 2003.
9. See Johnson, "The Right to Have Rights", chapter 6.
10. Nélida Archenti and María Inés Tula, "Algunas Cuestiones Iniciales sobre las Leyes de Cuotas," in *Mujeres y Política en América Latina. Sistemas Electorales y Cuotas de Género*, edited by Nélida Archenti and María Inés Tula (Buenos Aires: Heliasta, 2008).
11. The RMP is a cross-party network, founded in 1992 to strengthen women's political participation and promote gender issues in party platforms and in public policy. See Johnson, "The Right to Have Rights", 176–8.
12. The previous year the RMP had unsuccessfully attempted to include an amendment on positive discrimination in the Constitutional reform that was passed in December 1996. See Johnson, "The Right to Have Rights", 141.
13. The BBF was created in 2000 by three women deputies from the three main political parties as a horizontal inter-party forum whose aim was to promote gender equality legislation and

monitor respect for women's human rights in public policy making. See Niki Johnson, "Actuación Parlamentaria y Diferencias de Género en Uruguay, 2000–2005", *Política. Revista de Ciencia Política* (Universidad de Chile), 46 (2006), 190–5.

14. The Gender Politics Area was formed in 2001 following the first in-depth research project into women's political participation and representation in Uruguay.
15. Both the NE (in 1998 and 2004) and the PI (in 2004) resolved to apply a minimum quota of 30% of candidates of the same sex to their electoral lists, but in both cases these were temporary measures, rather than a permanent criterion.
16. *Diario de Sesiones de la Cámara de Senadores* (*DS/CSS*), 452 (213) (May 21, 2008).
17. Comité para la Eliminación de la Discriminación contra la Mujer, *Observaciones Finales (Distr. General CEDAW/C/URY/CO/7)*, paragraphs 30–31.
18. Minutes 173, folio 2019, of the Chamber of Deputies Constitution Committee, (December 3, 2008).
19. *Distribuido* 1947 (transcript of the session of the Chamber of Deputies' Constitution Committee, March 11, 2009).
20. The electoral cycle starts in June, with presidential primaries held jointly with elections to party national and departmental conventions. Parliamentary and presidential elections follow in October (with a second-round ballotage for the presidency in November if no candidate wins by an outright majority in the first round). Finally, the cycle ends with elections to the 19 departmental executives and legislative bodies and to local municipal authorities in May of the following year. Apart from the June elections, voting is compulsory in all other ballots.
21. According to article 77, paragraph 7 of the Uruguayan Constitution, all electoral laws and reforms require the affirmative vote of two-thirds of the members of each House.
22. Agreement signed at the 10th Regional Conference on Women of the UN Economic Commission for Latin America and the Caribbean (Quito, Ecuador, August 6–9, 2007).
23. Quito Consensus, paragraph 17, and paragraph 1 (ii), 3 and 5.
24. Senator Alfie (PC), *DS/CSS*, 452 (214) (May 21, 2008), 340.
25. Senator Moreira (PN), Senate Constitution and Legislation Committee, *Distribuido* 1675 (May 22, 2007), emphasis added, 12.
26. Promoters of the bill responded to this hipothesis by citing the survey carried out in December 2007 by the Gender Politics Area, with support from IDEA International, which showed that 60% of respondents considered that there should be more women in parliament, close to 75% thought it would be a good thing were parties to include a woman candidate in their presidential formulas, and only 15% were against the quota. See Niki Johnson and Verónica Pérez, *Representación (S)electiva. Una Mirada Feminista a las Elecciones Uruguayas 2009* (Montevideo: Cotidiano Mujer-ICP-UNIFEM, 2010), 21–5.
27. Senator Penadés (PN), *DS/CSS*, 452 (213) (May 21, 2008), 304.
28. See International Institute for Democracy and Electoral Assistance, *The Implementation of Quotas: Latin American Experiences*, Workshop Report, Lima, Peru (February 23–24, 2003) (Stockholm: International IDEA, 2003); Clara Araújo and Ana Isabel García, "The experience and the impact of quotas in Latin America," in *Women, Quotas and Politics*, edited by Drude Dahlerup (London: Routledge, 2006); Marcela Ríos and Andrés Villar, *Cuotas de Género: Democracia y Representación* (Santiago de Chile: IDEA Internacional-FLACSO, 2006); Archenti and Tula, *Mujeres y Política*.

29. A total of 2,803 lists were registered by the electoral authorities, 1,000 of which corresponded to national conventions (*Órgano Deliberativo Nacional*), and the rest to departmental conventions (*Órgano Deliberativo Departamental*).
30. Eight parties took part in the June elections, five of which won a sufficient number of votes to go on to compete in the national elections in October. Of these, four won seats in parliament, but with important differences between them: the FA won 66 seats, the PN 39, the PC 22 and the PI just 2. In our analysis we refer to the FA, PN and PC as the three "main" or "principal" parties.
31. It should be noted that, since Uruguayan electoral laws allow candidates to appear on more than one list, certain *suplencias* in fact guarantee access to a seat, since it is known that the *titular* will occupy another one. However, it is impossible to establish a generalizable criterion which would enable us to assess whether *suplencias* should be regarded as "safe" positions.
32. Niki Johnson, "¿Democracia a Medias? La Representación de la Mujer en Cargos Políticos Electivos en Uruguay, 1984–1994," *Revista Uruguaya de Ciencia Política*, 12 (2001), and *La Política de la Ausencia: Las Elecciones Uruguayas 2004/2005, las Mujeres y la Equidad de Género* (Montevideo: CNS Mujeres-ICP, 2005); Verónica Pérez, "52% del Electorado, 11% del Parlamento. Factores Culturales y Representación Política Femenina en Uruguay." *Revista Uruguaya de Ciencia Política* 15 (2006); Verónica Pérez, "Variables Políticas y Representación Femenina: ¿Influencias de qué Tipo? Comentarios a partir del Caso Uruguayo," *Colección* 18–19 (2008).
33. See Pippa Norris, *Electoral Engineering: Voting Rules and Political Behavior* (Cambridge: Cambridge University Press, 2004).
34. The FA had a total of 23 women-headed lists. The 19 Space 609 (*Espacio 609*, E609, the largest sector of the FA) lists were headed by Senator Lucía Topolansky. While an important political figure in her own right, without a doubt her positioning at the top of these lists also had to do with the fact that she is the wife of José Mujica, historic leader of the E609, who in the 2009 primaries successfully competed for the FA's presidential candidacy, but did not appear as a candidate on any party convention list. Another three of the FA lists were also headed by a single female candidate, and one other woman occupied first place on another list.
35. In 2004 14 women *titulares* were elected to parliament, 3 senators and 11 deputies; in 2009 19 were elected, 4 senators and 15 deputies.
36. See, for Uruguay, Constanza Moreira and Niki Johnson, *Democracia, Género y Equidad: Aportes para el Debate sobre Mecanismos de Acción Afirmativa* (Montevideo: FESUR, 2003); Johnson, *Política de la Ausencia*, chapter 5. For Latin America see Archenti and Tula, *Mujeres y Política*; Jones, "El Sistema de Cuotas"; Jennifer M. Piscopo, "Engineering Quotas in Latin America", Center for Iberian and Latin American Studies Working Paper 23 (San Diego: University of California, 2006), accessed September 2, 2010, http://escholarship.org/uc/item/7j05q10b. For a broader comparative focus, see Larserud and Taphorn, *Designing for Equality*; Richard Matland, "Electoral Quotas: Frequency and Effectiveness," in Dahlerup, *Women, Quotas and Politics*.
37. While the Senate is elected in one large national district of 30 seats, deputies are elected in 19 districts, which correspond to the territorial division of the country in 19 departments. At each election the number of seats assigned per district is determined by the sum of the votes cast in that district in the previous election plus the number of new voters registered there,

with a minimum of two seats per department. Due to the unequal distribution of the population, there are significant differences in district magnitude: for the 2009 elections the only large district was Montevideo, with 41 seats, Canelones was medium-sized, with 14 seats, and the other 17 districts were all small, with four (3 departments), three (4 departments) or two (10 departments) seats.

38. For a more detailed discussion of this point, see; Niki Johnson, "Las Cuotas en Uruguay: Una Medida Resistida," in Archenti and Tula, *Mujeres y Política*; Pérez, "Variables Políticas".
39. See Johnson and Pérez, *Representación (S)electiva*, chapter 4.

Chapter Ten: Legislative Gender Quotas in Former Communist and Post-Conflict Societies

1. "Women in National Parliaments" as of 31 July 2010. Accessed September 1, 2010. http://www.ipu.org/wmn-e/world.htm ; http://www.ipu.org/wmn-e/arc/classif310710.htm
2. *Beijing Declaration and Platform for Action*, Fourth World Conference on Women, 15 September 1995, A/CONF.177/20 (1995) and A/CONF.177/20/Add.1 (1995). Accessed August 30, 2010. http://www.un.org/womenwatch/daw/beijing/platform/ .
3. M. Sawer, M. Tremblay and L. Trimble, "Introduction. Patterns and Practice in the Parliamentary representation of Women," in *Representing Women in Parliament. A Comparative Study*, ed. M. Sawer, M. Tremblay and L. Trimble New York, NY: Routledge, 2006); A. M. Goetz, "Women's Political Effectiveness: A Conceptual Framework," in *No Shortcuts to Power. African Women in Politics and Policy Making*, ed. A. M. Goerts and S. Hassim (London: Zed Books, 2003).
4. One of the oldest arguments goes back to E. Haavio-Mannila et al. *Unfinished Democracy: Women in Nordic Politics* (New York: Pergamon, 1985). For more recent arguments see Anne Philips, "Quotas for Women," in *Women, Gender, and Politics*, ed. M.L. Krooks and S. Childs (Oxford, NY: Oxford University Press, 2006).
5. L. Krook "Promoting Gender-balanced Decision-making: The Role of International Fora and Transnational Networks," in C*rossing Borders: Re-Mapping Women's Movements at the Turn of the 21st Century*, ed. H. Roemer Christensen, B. Halsaa, and A. Saarinen (Odense: University Press of Southern Denmark, 2004), 205–220.
6. *Beijing Declaration and Platform for Action* .
7. D. Dahlerup "Introduction," in *Women, Quotas and Politics*, ed. D. Dahlerup (London, New York: Rutledge, 2006).
8. United Nations Development Program, Human Development. Accessed September 1, 2010, http://hdr.undp.org/en/humandev/hdi/ ; Human *Development Report 2009. Readers' Guide.* Accessed September 1, 2009, http://hdr.undp.org/en/media/HDR_2009_EN_Readers.pdf
9. *Women and Elections. Guide to Promoting the Participation of Women in Elections.* United Nations 2005. Accessed September 20, 2010 http://www.un.org/womenwatch/osagi/wps/publication/WomenAndElections.pdf
10. Full text of the *Security Council Resolution 1325* is available from http://www.peacewomen.org/themes_page.php?id=15&subtheme=true&adhoc=53 or http://www.un.org/events/res_1325e.pdf (accessed September 15, 2010). On history and background of the Res-

olution 1325 (2000) see http://www.un.org/womenwatch/ianwge/taskforces/wps/history.html Accessed September 16, 2010

11. M. Butler, K. Mader and R. Kean. *Women, Peace and Security Handbook: Compilation and Analysis of United Nations Security Council Resolution Language 2000–2010*. PeaceWomen Project of Women's International League for Peace and Freedom, October 2010. Accessed September 15, 2010 http://www.peacewomen.org/assets/file/peacewomen_schandbook_2010.pdf
12. United Nations Security Council S/2005/636 *Report of the Secretary-General on Women and Peace and Security*. 10 October 2005. http://www.un.org/womenwatch/ods/S-2005-636-E.pdf Accessed September 16, 2010
13. *National implementation of Security Council Resolution 1325 (2000)* http://www.un.org/womenwatch/ianwge/taskforces/wps/national_level_impl.html Accessed September 16, 2010.
14. For more information about implementation of the Resolution 1325 (2000) please visit a webpage titled *10th Anniversary of SCR 1325 (October 2010)* prepared by the WomenPeace project of the Women's International League for Peace and Freedom, at http://www.peacewomen.org/publications_enews_issue.php?id=148 Accessed September 16, 2010.
15. Moser, and F.C. Clark, eds. *Victims, Perpetrators or Actors? Gender, Armed Conflict and Political Violence* (London and New York Zed Books, 2001); *Women and Elections. Guide to Promoting the Participation of Women in Elections*; *Women, Peace and Security*. Study submitted by the Secretary-General pursuant to Security Council resolution 1325 (2000)United Nations 2002 Accessed September 20, 2010 http://un.org/womenwatch/daw/public/eWPS.pdf; T. Bouta, G. Freks, I. Bannon, *Gender, Conflict and Development*, The World Bank Washington DC 2005.
16. T. von Gienanth, "Elections in Post-Conflict Societies—Lessons Learned from Liberia, Sierra Leone, DR Congo, and Kosov," Report of a ZIF/KATPIC Seminar, June 12–14, 2008, Accra / Ghana. Accessed September 15, 2010 http://www.zif-berlin.org/fileadmin/uploads/analyse/dokumente/veroeffentlichungen/ZIF_KAIPTC_Elections__Report_02_09.pdf; T. Debiel and U. Terlinden, "Promoting Good Governance in Post-Conflict Societies. Discussion Paper" Deutsche Gesselschaft fur Technische Zusammenarbeit (Eschborn, 2005)
17. Electoral system data from http://www.ipu.org/parline/reports/2013_B.htm Accessed September 15, 2010; "Women's Political Participation in the 2007 Parliamentary Elections in the Republic of Armenia. Analytical Overview." Gender Studies Center of the Association of Women with University Education Organization for Security and Co-operation in Europe OSCE Office in Yerevan. Yerevan 2007 http://www.osce.org/documents/oy/2007/11/27913_en.pdf
18. *CEDAW Assessment Tool Report for Armenia* (July 2002) A Report by the Central European and Eurasian Law Institute www.abanet.org/ceeli . Accessed September 14, 2010; S. Payaslian, *History of Armenia: From the Origins to the Present* (New York: Palgrave Macmillan), 186. International Women's Rights Action Watch Armenia Initial Report (Addendum) Dated 5 December 1998 (E/1990/5/Add. 36) Accessed September 15, 2010 http://www1.umn.edu/humanrts/iwraw/cescrarmenia.htm
19. N. Itano, "Quota Law Puts More Women in Armenia's Election"; S. Nelson, B. Katilus, USAID/Armenia *Armenia Political Party Assessment Final Report* May 2005. Accessed September 14, 2010 http://www.usaid.gov/locations/europe_eurasia/countries/am/docs/political_party_assessment.pdf

20. N. Itano, "Quota Law Puts More Women in Armenia's Election," *We News*, May 10, 2007. Accessed September 14, 2010 http://www.womensenews.org/story/the-world/070510/quota-law-puts-more-women-armenias-election
21. Full text of the CEDAW is available from http://www.un.org/womenwatch/daw/cedaw/text/econvention.htm Accessed September 14, 2010.
22. See, for example, CEDAW/C/ARM/2 dated September 9, 1999, Second Periodic Reports of State Parties on Armenia at http://www2.ohchr.org/english/bodies/cedaw/cedaws_exceptional.htm Accessed September 14, 2010, and CEDAW/C/CR.672 dated January 14, 2003, *Second periodic report of Armenia* from the 572nd meeting held at headquarters, New York, on Wednesday, 7 August 2002 at http://www.unhchr.ch/tbs/doc.nsf/898586b1dc7b4043c1256a450044f331/069c54c12687b321c125729f003b5a7a/$FILE/N0251487.pdf Accessed September 14, 2010; CEDAW/C/SR.52 issued on January 14, 2003 Committee on the Elimination of Discrimination against Women Exceptional session Summary record of the 571st meeting Held at Headquarters, New York, on 7 August, 2002. *Second periodic report of Armenia.* Accessed September 15, 2010 http://www2.ohchr.org/english/bodies/cedaw/cedaws_exceptional.htm.
23. There is a vast literature on this conflict. For brief summary see, for example, C. Migdalovitz, "Armenia-Azerbaijan Conflict," *CRS Issue Brief for Congress* August 8, 2003. Accessed September 15, 2010 http://pards.org/crs_country/CRSReportArmenia-AzerbaijanConflict (August8,2003) Updated.pdf.
24. O. Tranca , "What Causes Ethnic Conflict Diffusion? A Study of Ethnic Conflicts in Azerbaijan and Macedonia," *Journal of Peace, Conflict & Development Issue* 12, May 2008. Accessed September 15, 2010.www.peacestudiesjournal.org.uk
25. C.H. Enloe, *The Morning After: Sexual Politics at the End of the Cold War* (Berkeley, Los Angeles: University of California Press, 1993); C.H. Enloe, *Maneuvers: the International Politics of Militarizing Women's Lives* (Berkeley, Los Angeles: University of California Press, 2000).
26. CEDAW/C/ARM/4 Combined Third and Fourth Periodic Reports of States Parties Armenia, December 28, 2007. Accessed September 15, 2010 http://www.unhcr.org/refworld/pdfid/48c7c25e2.pdf
27. *Armenia Questionnaire to Governments on Implementation of the Beijing Platform for Action (1995) and the Outcome of the Twenty-Third Special Session of the General Assembly (2000)* http://www.un.org/womenwatch/daw/Review/responses/ARMENIA-English.pdf Accessed September 15, 2010.
28. R. Panossian, "Armenia: Nationalism and its (Dis)Content, in *After Independence: Making and Protecting the Nation in Postcolonial and Postcommunist States*, ed. Lowell W. Barrington (USA: University of Michigan Press, 2006).
29. *Electoral Code of the Republic of Armenia*. Passed on February 5, 1999. HO-284. Unofficial Publication. Accessed September 14, 2010 http://www.venice.coe.int/docs/2007/CDL-EL(2007)010-e.pdf.
30. *Armenia. Parliamentary Chamber: Azgayin Joghov. Elections Held In 1999.* Accessed September 14, 2010. http://www.ipu.org/parline-e/reports/arc/2013_99.htm ; Office *Republic of Armenia. Parliamentary Election. 30 May 1999. Final Report.* Warsaw 30 July 1999. ODIHR Election Observation http://www.osce.org/documents/odihr/1999/07/1217_en.pdf Accessed September 14, 2010.
31. *Armenia. Parliamentary Chamber: Azgayin Joghov. Elections Held In 1999.* Accessed September 14, 2010. http://www.ipu.org/parline-e/reports/arc/2013_99.htm ; Office *Republic of Ar-*

menia. Parliamentary Election. 30 May 1999. Final Report. Warsaw 30 July 1999. ODIHR Election Observation http://www.osce.org/documents/odihr/1999/07/1217_en.pdf Accessed September 14, 2010.

32. OSCE Office for Democratic Institutions and Human Rights. Republic of Armenia. *Parliamentary Elections May 25, 2003 Final Report.* Warsaw 31 July 2003. Accessed September 15, 2010 http://www.osce.org/documents/odihr/2003/07/533_en.pdf ; *Armenia Questionnaire to Governments on Implementation of the Beijing Platform for Action (1995) and the Outcome of the Twenty-Third Special Session of the General Assembly (2000)* Accessed September 15, 2010 http://www.un.org/womenwatch/daw/Review/responses/ARMENIA-English.pdf .
33. J. Nichols, "Armenia's Legislative Election: Outcome and Implication for U.S. Interests," *CRS Report* for Congress RL 33453. Accessed September 15, 2010 http://www.fas.org/sgp/crs/row/RS22675.pdf ; OSCE/ODIHR Election Observation Mission Republic Of Armenia Parliamentary Elections 2007 Interim Report No. 2 29 March – 17 April 2007 Accessed September 14, 2010 http://www.osce.org/documents/odihr/2007/04/24101_en.pdf
34. *Armenia. Last Elections.* Inter-Parliamentary Union. Accessed September 15, 2010. http://www.ipu.org/parline/reports/2013_E.htm
35. For more information please visit http://www.womenforum.org/; http://www.ndi.org/Armenia Accessed September 14, 2010
36. "Women's Political Participation in the 2007 Parliamentary Elections in the Republic of Armenia. Analytical Overview." Gender Studies Center of the Association of Women with University Education Organization for Security and Co-operation in Europe OSCE Office in Yerevan. Yerevan 2007 http://www.osce.org/documents/oy/2007/11/27913_en.pdf
37. "Women's Political Participation in the 2007 Parliamentary Elections in the Republic of Armenia. Analytical Overview"; N. Itano, "Quota Law Puts More Women in Armenia's Election"
38. A. Stiglmayer, M.Faber (eds.), *Mass Rape: The War against Women in Bosnia-Herzegovina* (Lincoln: University of Nebraska Press, 1994). Look also at the Case Study: Bosnia and Herzegovina at www.gendercide.org Accessed September 14, 2010. There is a vast literature on the war in Bosnia Herzegovina and collapse of Yugoslavia. For example, see Sabrina P. Ramet, *The Three Yugoslavias: A State-Building and Legitimation, 1918–2005* (Bloomington, IN: Indiana University Press, 2006); C. Rogels, *The Breakup of Yugoslavia and its Aftermath* (Westport, Conn.: Greenwood Press, 2004).
39. B. Borić, "Application of Quotas: Legal Reforms and Implementation in Bosnia and Herzegovina," a paper presented at the International Institute for Democracy and Electoral Assistance (IDEA)/CEE Network for Gender Issues Conference *The Implementation of Quotas: European Experiences* Budapest, Hungary, 22–23 October 2004 Accessed September 15, 2010 http://www.legislationline.org/userdocuments/cat/5 ; S. Meznaric and M.Ule, "In Pursuit of a Framework. Delayed Modernization and Emancipation of Women in the Balkans," in *Gender Politics in the Western Balkans: Women and Society in Yugoslavia and the Yugoslav successor States*, ed. S. Ramet (U Park, Pa.: Pennsylvania State University Press, 1999); Y. Galligan, C. Clavero, *Gender Politics and Democracy in Post-Socialist Europe* (Opladen, Germany; Farmington Hills, MI: Barbara Budrich Publishers, 2007)
40. H.Sander, "Prologue"
41. H.Sander, "Prologue"; "Women, Peace and Security Get Renewed Commitment From Parliamentarians in the Region", UNDP Gender in Europe and CIS, June 28, 2010 Accessed

September 16, 2010 http://europeandcis.undp.org/gender/show/833ED8B9-F203-1EE9-BF9C4197015D45F2

42. Full text is available from http://www.state.gov/www/regions/eur/bosnia/bosagree.html
43. L. Effron, F.S. O'Brien, *Bosnia and Herzegovina: Post-Conflict Reconstruction and the Transition to the Market Economy: an OEO Evaluation of World Bank Support* (Washington, DC: World Bank, 2004), chapter 1; S. Rose, "The Bosnia State a Decade After Dayton," *International Peacekeeping* 12 (5), Autumn 2005
44. J. Blanc, A. Hylland, K. Vollan, *State Structure and Electoral Systems in Post-Conflict Situations* (Washington, DC: IFES, 2006), pp. 26–28; Detailed information about mandate of the OHR is available from its website http://www.ohr.int Accessed September 15, 2010. The OHR was supposed to close in 2008, but its mandate as extended indefinitely.
45. This information is from ElectionGuide at http://www.electionguide.org/election.php?ID=1506 Accessed September 15, 2010
46. B. Borić, "Application of Quotas: Legal Reforms and Implementation in Bosnia and Herzegovina"; see also report on Bosnia Herzegovina by Women's Campaign International at http://www.womenscampaigninternational.org/countries/bosnia-herzegovina. Accessed September 15, 2010
47. *USAID/Bosnia-Herzegovina Gender Assessment* May 2005 http://pdf.usaid.gov/pdf_docs/PDACG120.pdf Accessed September 15, 2010
48. *USAID/Bosnia-Herzegovina Gender Assessment*
49. M. Sahadzic, "The Electoral System of Bosnia and Herzegovina," *Contemporary Issues* 2 (1), 2009.
50. R. Belloni, "Peacebuilding and Consociational Electoral Engineering in Bosnia and Herzegovina," *International Peacekeeping* 11 (2), 2004
51. Only 4.7 percent of women were elected to the House of Representatives of the Parliamentary Assembly. See *USAID/Bosnia-Herzegovina Gender Assessment*
52. OSCE Office for Democratic Institutions and Human Rights. *Bosnia and Herzegovina, General Elections October 1, 2006.* OSCE/ODIHR Election Observation Mission. Final Report (Warsaw February 6, 2007). Accessed September 15, 2010 http://www.osce.org/documents/odihr/2007/02/23206_en.pdf
53. *Bosnia and Herzegovina. Elections in 2005.* Accessed September 15, 2010. http://www.ipu.org/parline-e/reports/arc/2039_06.htm
54. OSCE Office for Democratic Institutions and Human Rights. *Bosnia and Herzegovina, General Elections October 1, 2006.*
55. *Bosnia and Herzegovina. Elections in 2005.*
56. *Human Rights in Bosnia And Herzegovina. Legal Provisions, Practice and International Human Rights Standards In The Bosnia And Herzegovina With Public Opinion Survey.* (Sarajevo: Human Rights Center. University of Sarajevo, 2008) Accessed September 15, 2010 http://www.hrc.unsa.ba/hrr2008/PDFS/humanrightsinbih2008.pdf; *Shadow Report on the Implementation of CEDAW and Women's Human Rights in Bosnia and Herzegovina. Presented to the United Nation's Committee on the Elimination of Discrimination Against Women (CEDAW).* Global Rights Partners in cooperation with Non-Governmental Organizations in Bosnia and Herzegovina, January 2004. Accessed September 15, 2010 http://www.iwraw-ap.org/resources/pdf/Bosnia&Herzegovina_SR.pdf

57. *Yugoslavia. Elections held in 1982.* http://www.ipu.org/parline-e/reports/arc/YUGOSLAVIA_1982_E.PDF ; *Yugoslavia. Elections held in 1986.* http://www.ipu.org/parline-e/reports/arc/YUGOSLAVIA_1986_E.PDF Both links were accessed on September 15, 2010
58. *Serbia. Elections held in 1992* http://www.ipu.org/parline-e/reports/arc/2355b_92.htm Accessed September 15, 2010.
59. *Yugoslavia. Elections held in 1992.*
60. There is a vast literature on the ethnic wars in former Yugoslavia. See, among many other, Sabrina P. Ramet, *The Three Yugoslavias: A State-Building and Legitimation, 1918–2005* and C. Rogels, *The Breakup of Yugoslavia and its Aftermath.*
61. L. Silber, "The 'Hero' of Dayton: Slobodan Milosevic and The Politics of War and Peace," *World Policy Journal* 13 (1), Spring 1996; D. Doder and L. Branson, *Milosevic: Portrait of a Tyrant* (New York, NY: The Free Press, 1999), p. 7; L. Sell, *Slobodan Milosevic and The Destruction of Yugoslavia* (Durham, NC: Duke University Press, 2002), pp. 223–261.
62. B. Bijelic, "Nationalism, Motherhood, and the Reordering of Women's Power," in *Serbia since 1989: Politics and Society under Milosevic and After*, ed. Sabrina P. Ramet and V. Pavlakovic (Seattle: University of Washington Press, 2005)
63. Figures about internally displaced people at http://www.internal-displacement.org/8025708F004CE90B/(httpPages)/22FB1D4E2B196DAA802570BB005E787C?OpenDocument&count=1000 Accessed September 15, 2010. On Serbian Women Refugees see *Refugees and Internally Displaced Women and Children in Serbia and Montenegro* (New York: Women's Commission for Refugees and Children, September 2001); V. Nikolic-Ristanovic, "Refugee Women in Serbia – Invisible Victims of War in Former Yugoslavia," *Feminist Review* 73, 2003
64. M. Blagojevic, "Belgrade Protests 1996/1997: From Women in the Movement to Women's Movement," in *Women and Citizenship in Central and Eastern Europe,* ed. J. Lukić, J. Regulska, D. Zaviršek, (Aldershot: Ashgate, 2006)
65. M. Blagojevic, "Belgrade Protests 1996/1997: From Women in the Movement to Women's Movement"; M. Pajvančić, "Summary. Serbia's European Perspective From Women's Point Of View" Published in Serbian language in the book titled Pravo na Ravnopravnost Polova [Right for Gender Equality] (Novi Sad, 2008) http://www.zenskavlada.org.rs/downloads/eng-gender-izbori-2007.pdf Accessed September 15, 2010
66. More information about Gender Task Force of the Stability Pact for South Eastern Europe is available from its website at http://www.stabilitypact.org/gender/default.asp Accessed September 15, 2010; *About the Stability Pact* http://www.stabilitypact.org/about/default.asp Accessed September 15, 2010
67. Gender Task Force. Spot Report. *Women's Activism Prior to Serbia Elections September 24, 2000* http://www.stabilitypact.org/gender/000901-report.asp Accessed September 2010
68. M. Pajvančić, "Summary. Serbia's European Perspective From Women's Point Of View"
69. *Law on The Election Of Representatives*, Official Gazette of The Republic of Serbia, No. 35/2000, http://www.legislationline.org/documents/action/popup/id/3873 Accessed September 15, 2010
70. *Elections Held in 2000,* http://www.ipu.org/parline-e/reports/arc/2355_00.htm
71. OSCE Office for Democratic Institutions and Human Rights *Final Report on the Parliamentary Elections in the Republic of Serbia*, 23 December 2000 published on 20 February 2001 http://www.osce.org/documents/odihr/2001/02/1330_en.pdf Accessed September 15, 2010

72. OSCE Office for Democratic Institutions and Human Rights. *Final Report on the Parliamentary Elections in the Republic of Serbia (Serbia and Montenegro)*, 28 December 2003 published on 27 February 2004 http://www.osce.org/documents/odihr/2004/02/2177_en.pdf
73. M. Pajvančić, "Summary. Serbia's European Perspective From Women's Point Of View"
74. *Law on Local Elections of the Republic of Serbia*, Official Gazette of the Republic of Serbia" No. 33 of 13 June 2002 http://www.venice.coe.int/docs/2005/CDL-EL(2005)027-e.pdf Accessed September 16, 2010
75. *Law on the Election of Representatives* (2000, updated in 2004) http://www.legislationline.org/documents/action/popup/id/3871 Accessed September 16, 2010
76. M. Pajvančić, "Summary. Serbia's European Perspective From Women's Point Of View"
77. M. Dokmanović, "Constitutional and Political Analyses," in *Engendering Constitutions: Gender Equality Provisions in Selected Constitutions. A Comparative Study Accompanied with Case Studies in Bosnia and Herzegovina, Kosovo, Montenegro, Serbia*, ed. K. Van der Leest (November 2007). http://www.unifem.sk/uploads/doc/Constitutional%20publication%20Nov%2020071.pdf Accessed September 15, 2010
78. "Montenegro Gets Serb Recognition," *BBC News*, June 15, 2006
79. M. Dokmanović, "Constitutional and Political Analyses"
80. M. Dokmanović, "Constitutional and Political Analyses"
81. S. Orlovic, "Parties and Party System of Serbia and European Integration," *Journal of Balkan and Near Eastern Studies* 10 (2), August 2008
82. M. Dokmanović, "Constitutional and Political Analyses"
83. *Serbia. Elections in 2007.* http://www.ipu.org/parline-e/reports/arc/2355_07.htm Accessed September 2010
84. OSCE Office for Democratic Institutions and Human Rights. *Final Report on the 21 January 2007 Parliamentary Elections in Serbia* published on 26 April 2007. Accessed September 16, 2010 http://www.osce.org/documents/odihr/2007/04/24171_en.pdf
85. OSCE Office for Democratic Institutions and Human Rights. *Final Report on the 11 May 2008 Early Parliamentary Elections in the Republic of Serbia* published on 29 August 2008 http://www.osce.org/documents/odihr/2008/08/32769_en.pdf Accessed September 16, 2010. *Serbia. Elections Held in 2008.* http://www.ipu.org/parline-e/reports/2355.htm Accessed September 16, 2010
86. S. Orlovic, "Parties and Party System of Serbia and European Integration."

Chapter Eleven: Diffusion of Gender Quotas in Latin America and Beyond

1. Cited in Michael Mintrom and Marta Vergari (1998, February). Policy networks and Innovation Diffusion: The Case of State Education Reforms. *The Journal of Politics*, 60(1):128
2. William Alves and Richard Morril. 1975, July. " Diffusion Theory and Planning. Studies in Spatial Diffusion Processes: II. Conceptual." *Economic Geography*, *51*(3):290–304.
3. Homophily, according to Rogers (2003), is the degree to which pairs of individuals or groups who interact are similar in certain attributes such as beliefs, values, education, social status and the like.

4. These "three stages of development," are not necessarily present in all cases nor they are easily discoverable; they serve as a means to simplify an otherwise complex reality.
5. Further research in other organizations' resolutions, meetings, and conferences including such organizations as the IBD and PROLEAD may provide a better understanding of this trend.
6. Chile's congressional elections are governed by a unique binomial system that rewards coalition slates. Each coalition can present two candidates for the two Senate and two lower-chamber seats apportioned to each chamber's electoral districts. One of the possible obstacles for Chilean women is the country's electoral system because of its small district magnitude. (see Matland, 2002). According to Siavelis(2008, 192) this system was incorporated to benefit Chile's center-right coalition and despite some efforts, the system has remained in place since the Pinochet years.

References

Introduction

Bacchi, Carol. 2006. "Arguing for and Against Quotas." In *Women, Quotas, and Politics*, ed. Dahlreup, Drude. 32–52. Routledge: New York.

Baldez, Lisa.2004. "Elected Bodies: The Gender Quota Law for Legislative Candidates in Mexico." *Legislative Studies Quarterly 24* (2):231–58.

Beckwith, Karen .2003. "The Gendering Ways of States: Women's Representation and State's Configuration in France, Great Britain, and the United States." In *Women's Movement Facing the Reconfigurated State*, ed. Lee Ann Banaszak, Karen Beckwith, and Dieter Rucht, 169–202.. New York, Cambridge University Press.

Bell, James and Lynn Staeheli. 2001, February. "Discourses of diffusion and democratization." *Political Geography,* 20(2), 175–195.

Berry Frances and William Berry.1990, June. "State Lottery Adoptions as Policy Innovations: An Event History Analysis." *The American Political Science Review,* 84 (2) 389–401.

Crocker, Adriana.2007. "Gender Quota Laws in Latin America: Innovation, Diffusion, and the End of a Wave?" *Cena Internacional* 9 (2): 95–124.

____________ and Daniel Kempton .2008. *Gender Quotas in Afghanistan: Solution or Problem?* Georgetown University Institute for the Study of Diplomacy.GUISD.

Dahlerup, Drude and Anja Thorup Nordlund. 2004. Gender Quotas a Key to Equality? A Case Study of Iraq and Afghanistan." *European Political Science 3*(3): 91–98.

Dahlerup, Drude. 2006. *Women, Quotas, and Politics.* New York: Routledge.

Diehl, Paul. and John Vasquez. 2008. "The ConflictSpace Project: Testing Complex Models of the Diffusion of War." Paper prepared for presentation at the annual meeting of the American Political Science Association, Boston, Massachusetts, August 28, 2008

Groshek, Jacob. 2010. "A Time–Series, Multinational Analysis of Democratic Forecasts and Internet Diffusion." *International Journal of Communication 4:* 142–174

Htun, Mala and Mark Jones.2002. "Engendering the Rights to Participate in Decision-Making Electoral Quotas and Women's leadership in Latin America." In *Gender and the Politics of Rights and Democracy in Latin America*, eds. Nikki Craske and Maxine Molyneux, 32–56. New York: Palgrave.

Huntington, Samuel. 1991. T*he Third Wave: Democratizaton in the Late Twentieth Century.* Norman and London: University of Oklahoma Press

Florini, Anne. 1996. "The Evolution of International Norms." *International Studies Quarterly. 40*, 363–390.

Kittilson, Miki Caul. 2006. *Challenging Parties Changing Parliaments: Women and Elected Office in Contemporary Western Europe.* Columbus Ohio: Ohio State University Press.

Krook, Mona Lena. 2006. "Reforming Representation: The Diffusion of Candidate Gender Quotas Worldwide."*Politics & Gender* 2 (3):367–94.

____________. 2009 . *Quotas For Women in Politics: Gender and Candidate Selection Reform Worldwide.* Oxford University Press, Oxford and London.

Mintrom, Michael and Sarah Vergari. 1998. "Policy Networks and Innovation Diffusion: The Case of State Education Reforms." *Journal of Politics 60* .:126–148.

Murray, Rainbow. 2010, March. "Second Among Unequals? A Study of Whether France's "Quota Women" are Up to the Job." *Politics & Gender. 6(1)*: 93–118.

Most, Benjamin. 1980. "Diffusion, Reinforcement, Geopolitics and the Spread of War." *American Political Science Review*, 74: 932–946.

Pitlik, Hans. 2007. "A race to liberalization? Diffusion of economic policy reform among OECD-economies." *Public Choice,* 132: 1–2.

Quota Project. 2010. Global Database of Quotas For Women. http://www.quotaproject.org/ (Accessed May 23, 2010).

Ross, Marc and Ernst Homer. 1976, October. "Problems in Cross-National Research." *World Politics*, 29 (1): 2–16.

Schedler, Andreas.1998. "What is Democratic Consolidation?" *Journal of Democracy*, 9 (2): 91–107.

Schmidt Gregory and Kyle Saunders.2004. "Effective Quotas, Relative Party Magnitude, and the Success of Female Candidates: Peruvian Municipal Elections in Comparative perspective." *Comparative Political Studies*, 37 (6): 704–34.

Simnowitz, Rosyln. 1998. "Evaluating Conflict Research on the Diffusion of War." *Journal of Peace Research. 35(2):* 211–230

Simmons Beth, Frank Dobbin and Geoffrey Garret. Eds. 2003. *The Global Diffusion of Markets and Democracy.* Cambridge University Press: Cambridge, UK.

Siverson Randolph and Harvey Starr. 1991. "The Diffusion of Wars: A Study of Opportunity and Willngness."University of Michigan Press, Ann Arbor.

Starr, Harvey. 1991, June. "Democratic Dominoes: Diffusion Approaches and the Spread of Democracy in the International System." *The Journal of Conflict Resolution*, 35(2): 356–381.

True, Jaqui and Michael Mintrom. 2001. "Transnational Networks and Policy Diffusion: The Case of Gender Mainstreaming." *International Studies Quarterly, 45:* 27–57

Chapter One: Jumping on the Bandwagon

Adler, Emmanuel. 1991. "Cognitive Evolution: A Dynamic Approach for the Study of International Relations and their Progress,"in *Progress in Postwar International Relations*, eds. Adler & B. Crawford. New York: Columbia University Press, 15–51.

Alvarez, Sonia. 1998. "Latin American Feminisms Go Global: Trends of the 1990s and Challenges of the New Millennium." In *Cultures of Politics/Politics of Cultures: Revising Latin American Social Movements*, eds. Sonia Álvarez, E. Dagnino, & A. Escobar, 51–89. Boulder, Colorado: Westview Press.

Amado, A. 1993, April. "Las Consejeras del Presidente." *Red de Comunicación Alternativa de La Mujer, 138,* 2. Santiago, Chile: Fempress

Auth, Janice (ed). 1998. *To Beijing and Beyond.* Pittsburgh, Pennsylvania: University of Pittsburgh Press.

Aschtul, Monique, Interview by author. Tape recording. Buenos Aires, Argentina. May 21, 2003.

Baldez, Lisa. 2004. "The Adoption of Gender Quotas for Legislative Candidates in Mexico." *Legislative Studies Quarterly 29 (2):231–258.*

Beckwith, Karen .2003. "The Gendering Ways of States: Women's Representation and State's Configuration in France, Great Britain, and the United States." In *Women's Movement Facing the Reconfigurated State*, ed. Lee Ann Banaszak, Karen Beckwith, and Dieter Rucht, 169–202. New York, Cambridge University Press.

Bernard, Russell and Peter Killworth. (1973). "On the Social Structure of an Ocean-Going Research Vessel and Other Important Things." *Social Science Research, 2*:145–184

Brown Alice et al. 2002. "Women and Constitutional Change in Scotland and Northern Ireland." In *Women, Politics, and Change* ed. Karen Ross. New York, Oxford University Press: 71–84.

Calleya, Stephen. 1996. "Post-Cold War Regional Dynamics in the Mediterranean Area", *Mediterranean Quarterly* 3(7): 42–54.

Camacho-Granados, Rosalía et al. 1997. *Las Cuotas Mínimas de Participación de las Mujeres. Un Mecanismo de Acción Afirmativa para la Discusión*. 2nd. Ed. San José. Costa Rica. Centro Nacional para el Desarrollo de la Mujer y la Familia.

Cerva Cerna, Daniela (2008), "Los partidos políticos frente a la equidad de género." In *Del dicho al Hecho: Manual de Buenas Prácticas para la Participación de Mujeres en los Partidos Políticos Latinoamericanos*, Beatriz Llanos & Kristen Sample (eds.), Stockholm: International IDEA

Checkel, Jeffrey. 1998. "The Constructivist Turn in International Relations," *World Politics* 50 (1): 324–48.

Choi, Young Jong and James. Caporaso. 2002. "Comparative Regional Integration," in *Handbook of International Relations* eds. Walter Carlsnaes, Thomas Risse, and Beth A. Simmons. London: Sage: 480–99.

Commission on the Status of Women. 2004. Forty-Eight Session. "Development Efforts, Peace Process Require Women's Equal Participation." United Nations, 3-3-2004.

Consejo Nacional de la Mujer (CNM). 1995. *Mujeres en la Política: Reflexiones Acerca de la Sanción y Aplicación de la Ley de Cupos en Argentina.* Buenos Aires, Argentina: CNM Publications.

Cox, Gary.1997. *Making Votes Count: Strategic Coordination in the World's Electoral Systems.* Cambridge: Cambridge University press.

Crocker, Adriana. 2005. " Gender Quotas in Latin America: Explaining Cross-national and Subnational Diffusion." Ph.D. dissertation http://www.iadb.org/sds/doc/gedcrockerdissertation.pdf. (Accessed May 5, 2009).

__________. 2010. "Constructing Policy Innovation in Argentina: From Gender Quotas to Same-Sex Marriage." In *Same-Sex Marriage in the Americas: Policy Innovation for Same-Sex Relationships.* Jason Pierceson, Adriana Piatti-Crocker and Shawn Schulenberg ed. Lexington Books: Boulder, Co

Dadhlerup, Drude. 1997. *Women and Mainstreaming: Political Strategies and Theories Concerning the Gender Issue.* http//:www.quotaproject.org. (Accessed September 6, 2005).

Dorsey, Ellen. 1997. "The Global Women's Movement." In *The Politics of Global Governance: International Organizations in an Interdependent World*, ed. Paul Diehl Boulder, 335–360. New York: Lynne Rienner.

Economic Commission for Latin America and the Caribbean (ECLAC). 2000. *Gender Indicators for Follow-up and Evaluation of the Regional Program of Action for the Women in Latin America and the Caribbean, 1995–2001, and the Beijing Platform for Action.* Retrieved May 12, 2002 from http://www.eclac.cl.

Estrada, Daniela. 2006. Latin America: Progress Towards Gender Parity in Politics. http://peacewomen.org/news/International. (Accessed December 16, 2006).

Facultad Latinoamericana de Ciencias Sociales (FLACSO). 1997. *Mujeres en Cifras.* Retrieved May 20, 2003 from http://www.eurosur.org/FLACSO.

Franganillo, Virginia. 1999, October. *Ley de Cupos: Balance y Memoria de la Ley de Cupos a Pocos Días de las Elecciones Presidenciales, 33:* 215. Santiago, Chile: Mujer/Fempress. Santiago, Chile.

Franganillo, Virginia. Interview by author. Tape recording. Buenos Aires, Argentina May 30, 2003.

Freedom House. 1991–2005. *Freedom in the World.* http://www.freedomhouse.org. (Accessed June 10, 2003).

Friedman, Elisabeth. 2000. *Unfinished Transitions: Women and the Gendered Development of Democracy in Venezuela, 1936–1996.* Pennsylvania: The Pennsylvania State University Press.

Fundación Fredrich Ebert. 1991, October. *Seminario: Mujer y Participación Política.* Programa, Buenos Aires, Argentina: Centro de Documentación y Estudios.

__________ . 1990. *Cuota Mínima de Participación de Mujeres: el Debate en el Partido Socialdemócrata Federal de Alemania.* Asunción, Paraguay: Centro de Documentación y Estudios.

__________. 1991. *Cuota Mínima de Participación de Mujeres: Discusión y Resoluciones del Partido Socialista Obrero Español.* Asunción, Paraguay: Centro de Documentación y Estudios.

__________. 2002. *Rumbo a la Igualdad de Oportunidades: Transversalidad de Género en el Trabajo de Cooperación Internacional para el Desarrollo.* Bonn, Germany.

Fundación Mujeres en Igualdad. 1999. *Mujeres en Política, 6* (14). Buenos Aires, Argentina.

Gallo, Edit and Carlos Giacobone. 2001. *Cupo Femenino en la Política Argentina: Ley Nacional-Leyes Provinciales, Debates Parlamentarios, Normativa Internacional,* Jurisprudencia. Buenos Aires, Argentina: Eudeba.

García Quesada, Ana Isabel. 2003. "Putting the Mandate into Practice: Legal Reform in Costa Rica." Paper presented at the International IDEA Workshop. "The Implementation of Quotas: Latin American Experiences," Lima, Peru, February 23–24.

Htun, Mala. 2000. "Women's Leadership in Latin America: Trends and Challenges." *Politics Matters: A Dialogue of Women Political Leaders*, Washington: Inter-American Development Bank, Inter-American Dialogue, and International Center for Research on Women, 13-26.

Htun, Mala and Mark Jones. 2002. "Engineering the Right to participate in Decision-Making: Electoral Quotas and Women's leadership in Latin America." In *Gender, Rights, and Justice in Latin America,* eds. Nikki Craske and Maxine Molyneux, 32-68. Basinsgtoke, England: Macmillan.

Inter-Parliamentary Union. 1997. *Towards Partnership Between Men and Women in Politics.* Geneva: IPU Press.

International Idea. "Global Database of Quotas for Women." http://www.quotaproject.org. (Accessed, May 12, 2009).

Jones, Mark. 1996. "Increasing Women's Representation Via Gender Quotas: The Argentine Ley de Cupos." *Women and Politics 16* (4): 75-98.

Jones, Mark. 2004, November. "Quota Legislation and the Election of Women: Learning from the Costa Rican Experience." *Journal of Politics 66*: 1203-23

Jones, Mark. 2005, December . "The Desirability of Gender Quotas: Considering Context and Design." *Politics & Gender 1* (4):645-652

Knight, Silvia. Interview by author. Tape recording. Buenos Aires, Argentina. June 14, 2003.

Katzenstein, Peter. 1996. "Regionalism in Comparative Perspective," *Cooperation and Conflict 31(2)*: 123-59.

Kingdon, John. 1995. "Agendas, Alternatives, and Public Policies." (2nd ed.). Boston: Little Brown.

Krook, Mona. 2006, September. "Reforming Representations: The Difusión of Candidate Gender Quotas Worldwide." *Politics & Gender 2* (3): 303-328.

Lipsciz, Cecilia. Interview by author. Tape recording. Buenos Aires, Argentina. May 23, 2003.

Lozano Eljure, Nora.2003, November 28. *En Colombia, el Gobierno Aún no Permite Mayor Presencia de las Mujeres en la Política.* http//:Cimacnoticias.com. (Accessed September 20, 2003).

Lubertino, Maria Jose. *Female Citizenship, Legal Instruments, and Constitutional Reforms.* http//www.ispm.org.ar. (Accessed June 20, 2002).

Lubertino, Maria. Interview by author. Tape recording. Buenos Aires, Argentina. May 13, 2003.

Matland, Richard. 2002. "Enhancing Women's Political Participation: Legitimate Recruitment and Electoral Systems." In *Women in Parliament: Beyond Numbers* , A. Karam, ed. Stockholm: International IDEA: 32-45.

Matland, Richard and Studlar, Donley. 1996. "The Contagion of Women Candidates in Single-Member District and Proportional Representation Systems: Canada and Norway." *Journal of Politics, 58 (3)*: 707-733.

Menéndez, Maria and Montesdeoca, Elba. 2003. "La Ley de Igualdad de Oportunidades Para la Mujer en Honduras: Luces, Sombras, y Desafíos." *Colección de Cuadernos de Desarrollo Humano Sostenible, 19.* Tegucigalpa, Honduras: PNUD Press.

Meyer, Mary and Elizabeth Prugl. 1999. *Gender Politics in Global Governance,* eds. Maryland: Rowman and Littlefield.

Mintrom, Michael and Sarah Vergari. 1998. "Policy Networks and Innovation Diffusion: The Case of State Education Reforms. *Journal of Politics 60*, 126-148.

Mintrom, Michael. 2000. "Policy Entrepreneurs and Social Change." Washington D.C: Georgetown University Press.

Molyneux, Maxine. Ed. 2001. *Women's Movement in International Perspective*. Institute of Latin American Studies, University of London Press.

Norris, Pippa. 2000. "Women: Representation and Electoral Systems." *International Encyclopedia of Elections*, Richard Rose, ed. Washington: CQ Press, 348-351.

PARLATINO. 1995. *Declaración de la Comisión de la Mujer del Parlamento. Latinoamericano hacia Beijing '95 IV Conferencia de la Mujer*. São Paolo, Brazil: Parlatino Publications.

Peschard, Jacqueline.2003. "Quota Implementation in Mexico", in the *Implementation of Quotas: Latin American Experiences*, Quotas Report Series no. 2, And Stockholm: International IDEA

Red Nacional de Mujeres- Regional Bogotá. 1998, September. *Garantizando la Participación Política de las Mujeres en Colombia: Ley de Cuotas.* http://colnodo.apc.org . (Accessed May 23, 2003).

Reyes, Socorro. 2002. "Quotas for Women for Legislative Seats at the Local Level in Pakistan." Stockholm, International IDEA. Bahasa-Indonesia Version.

Reynolds, Andrew. 1999. "Women in Legislatures and Executives of the World: Knocking at the Highest Glass Ceiling." *World Politics 51* (4), 547-572.

Rigat Pflaum, María. Interview by author. Tape recording. Buenos Aires, Argentina. May 24, 2003.

Rodríguez, Marcela. Interview by author. Tape recording. Buenos Aires, Argentina. June 4, 2003.

Rogers, Everett. 5 ed. 2003. *Diffusion of Innovations.* New York: Free Press.

Rogers, Everett. 1981. *Communication Networks: Toward a New Paradigm of Research.* New York: The Free Press.

Rule, Wilma and Joseph Zimmerman. 1994. *Electoral Systems in Comparative Perspective: Their Impact on Women and Minorities.* Westport CT: Greenwood Press

Saint-Germain, Michelle. 1994. "Equality: Costa Rican Women Demand the Real Thing." *Women and Politics, 11*(3): 23-75

Schmidt, Gregory.2004. *Unanticipated Successes: Lessons from Peru's Experiences with Gender Quotas in Majoritarian Closed List and Open List PR Systems.* http://www.quotaproject.org/CS/CS_Schmidt2.pdf. (Accessed March 16, 2005).

Skidmore, Thomas and Smith, Peter. 5th ed. 2001. *Modern Latin America.* Oxford: Oxford University Press.

Staudt, Kathleen. 1997. *Women, International Development and Politics: the Bureaucratic Mire.* Temple: University press, Philadelphia.

Starr, Harvey. 1991, June. "Democratic Dominoes: Diffusion Approaches and the Spread of Democracy in the International System." *The Journal of Conflict Resolution*. 356-381.

Storani, Maria Luisa. Interview by author. Tape recording. Buenos Aires, Argentina. May 21, 2003.

Taagapera, Ross and Martin Shugart. 1989. *Seats and Votes: The Effects and Determinants of Electoral Systems.* New Haven: Yale University press.

Taylor-Robinson, Mary and Roseanna Heath. 2003. "Do Women Legislators Have Different Policy Priorities than Their Male Colleagues?" *Women and Politics, 24 (4)*: 77-101.

Tenewicki, Ines and DiegoRossi. 1995. *Participación Política de la Mujer: La Mirada del Legislador Desde el Sufragio Hasta la ley de Cupos*. Buenos Aires, Argentina: Cámara de Diputados de la Nación.

True, Jaqui and Michael Mintrom. 2001. "Transnational Networks and Policy Diffusion: The Case of Gender Mainstreaming." *International Studies Quarterly, 45*, 27-57.
Tripp, Aili Mari. 2004. *Transnational Feminisms and Political Representation in Africa.* Paper Presented at the American Political Science Association Annual Meeting, September.
Lycklama a Nijeholt, Geertje, Virginia Vargas, and Saskia Wieringa. Ed. 1998. *Women's Movements and Public Policy in Europe, Latin America and the Caribbean.* New York, NY: Garland.
West, Lois. 1999. "The United Nations Women's Conferences and Feminist Politics." In *Gender politics in Global Governance, eds.* Mary K. Meyer and Elizabeth Prugl, 35-82. Boulder, Co: Rowman & Littlefield Publications.
Winslow, Anne. 1995. *Women, Politics, and the United Nations.* Westport: Greenwood Press.
Zabal Canedo, Maria. 1998. *Mujeres, Cuotas, y Ciudadanía en Bolivia.* La Paz, Bolivia: Coordinadora de la Mujer.

Chapter Two: Candidate Selection as Political Barriers for Gender Quotas

Araujo, Clara. 2006. "Condicionantes Institucionais das políticas de cotas" in Gláucio Soares y Lúcio Rennó (eds), *Reforma Política: Lições da História Recente.* Río de Janeiro: Fundação Getúlio Vargas.
Archenti, Nélida. 2002. "Los caminos de la inclusión política. Acciones afirmativas de género." In. *Hombres públicos, Mujeres públicas.* Silvia Vazquez, ed. Buenos Aires: Friedrich Ebert Stiftung.
________. 2004. "Representación política, género y reformas institucionales en Argentina." In *Igualdad de Derechos, Igualdad de Oportunidades, Igualdad de Ejercicio,* eds. Kathya Araujo, Nélida Archenti, Rocío Villanueva Flores; Bérèngere Marques-Pereira. Santiago de Chile: Fundación Instituto de la Mujer.
Archenti, Nélida and María Inés Tula. 2007. "Cuotas de género y tipo de lista en América Latina". Revista Opinião Pública *Universidad Nacional de Campinas (UNICAMP) Vol.13, Nº1,* June: 2007, 185-218.
_________. 2007. "Los límites institucionales de las cuotas de género en América Latina". Revista Iberoamericana, *Instituto Iberoamericano Berlín/ Instituto de Estudios Latinoamericanos.* Hamburgo: Nueva Época, Año VII, Nª27, September: 184-190.
__________(Eds.). 2008. *Mujeres y Política en América Latina. Sistemas Electorales y Cuotas de Género.* Buenos Aires: Heliasta.
Ashiagbor, Stefakor. 2009. *Partidos políticos y democracia en perspectivas teóricas y prácticas. Selección de candidatos para cargos legislativos.* NDI.
Baldez, Lisa. 2007. "Primaries vs. Quotas: Gender and Candidate Nominations in Mexico, 2003". *Latin American and Society*, V. 49, N3, Miami: University of Miami, 69-96.
Billie, Lars. 2001. "Democratizing a Democratic Procedure: myth or reality? Candidate Selection in Western European Parties, 1960-1990". *Party Politics*, V.7, N3, London: Sage Publication.
Buquet, Daniel. 2001. "Selección de candidatos y fraccionalización partidaria en Uruguay (1942-1999)". XXIII International Meeting of Latin American Studies Association. Washington, September.

Caul, Miki. 2002. "Political Parties and the Adoption of Candidate Gender Quotas: A Cross-National Analysis". *The Journal of Politics* N° 63, November, 1214-1229.

Colotta, Mariana. 2010. *La ¿nueva? Inclusión de las mujeres al mundo político. Los discursos y prácticas de las concejalas bonaerenses".* PH D Thesis, Buenos Aires: Universidad del Salvador.

Dahlerup, Drude. 1998. "Using Quotas to Increase Women's Political Representation" in Karam, Azza (Ed.): *Women in Parliament: Beyond Numbers.* Stockholm: International IDEA.

De Luca, Miguel; Jones, Mark P. and Tula, María Inés. 2000. *Partidos políticos y selección de candidatos en Argentina (1983-1999). XXII* International Meeting of Latin American Studies Association. Miami, March.

__________. 2002. "Buenos Aires: The evolution of local governance" in Myers and Dietz (Eds.) *Capital City Politics in Latin America. Democratization and Empowerment*, Lynne Rienner Publishers.

__________. 2002. "Back rooms o ballot boxes? Candidate Nomination in Argentina". 2002. *Comparative Political Studies*, N 35. 413-433.

__________. 2009. "De internas, aparatos y punteros. La selección de candidatos a diputados nacionales en Argentina, 1983-2005." In *Selección de Candidatos, Política Partidista y Rendimiento democrático*, eds. Freidenberg, Flavia y Alcántara Sáez, Manuel. México: Tribunal Electoral del Distrito Federal.

Epstein, Leon. 1967. *Political Parties in Western Democracies.* New York: Praeger.

Freidenberg, Flavia and Alcántara, Manuel (Eds.) *Selección de Candidatos, Política Partidista y Rendimiento democrático.* 2009. México: Tribunal Electoral del Distrito Federal.

Freidenberg, Flavia. 2003. *Selección de candidatos y democracia interna en los partidos de América Latina.* Ágora democrática- Lima: IDEA- Transparencia.

Freidenberg, Flavia and Francisco Sánchez López. 2001. *Partidos políticos y métodos de selección de candidatos en América Latina. Una discusión sobre reglas y prácticas.* XXIII International Meeting of Latin American Studies Association. Washington, September.

Gallagher, Michael and Michael Marsh (Eds.). 1988. *Candidate selection in comparative perspective. The secret garden of politic,* London: Sage.

Hazan, Reuven and Rahat, Gideon. 2009. "Selección de candidates: Métodos y Consecuencias". In *Selección de Candidatos, Política Partidista y Rendimiento democrático,* eds. Freidenberg, Flavia y Alcántara Sáez, Manuel. México: Tribunal Electoral del Distrito Federal.

Htun, Mala and Mark Jones. 2002. "Engendering the right to participate in decision-making: electoral quotas en women´s leadership in Latin America."In *Gender and the politics of rights and democracy in Latin America.* eds. Nikki Craske and Maxine Molineux. London: Palgrave.

International Institute for Democracy and Electoral Assistance (IDEA). 2003. The Implementation of Quotas: Latin American Experiences. Stockholm: IDEA.

Jones, Mark P. 1997. "Cupos de Género, leyes electorales y elección de legisladoras en las Américas" *Revista Argentina de Ciencia Política*, N° 1, Noviembre. 57-72.

________. 2000. "El sistema de cuotas y la elección de las mujeres en América Latina: El papel fundamental del sistema electoral" in Saavedra Ruiz, Paloma, (ed.). In *La Democracia Paritaria en la Construcción Europea, 35-46.* Madrid: CELEM.

__________. 2004. "The recruitment and selection of legislative candidates in Argentina. "In *Pathways to power: political recruitment and democracy in Latin America.* Conference. Wake Forest University, Winston-Salem, April.

Katz, Richard. 2001. "The problem of Candidate Selection and Models of Party Democracy". *Party Politics*, V7, N3, London: Sage Publications.

Kirchheimer, Otto. 1965. "El camino hacia el partido de todo el mundo." In *Teoría y sociología críticas de los partidos políticos*, Lenk, eds. Kurt y Neumann, Franz. Barcelona: Editorial Anagrama, 1980, 328-347.

Krook, Mona Lena. 2006. 'Reforming Representation: the Diffusion of Candidate Gender Quotas Worldwide". *Politics and Gender 2*. 303-327.

__________. 2008. "La adopción e impacto de leyes de cuotas de género: una perspectiva global." In *Mujer y política. El impacto de las cuotas de género en América Latina,* ed. Marcela Ríos Tobar. Santiago de Chile: FLACSO-Chile/IDEA.

__________. 2009. "Beyond supply and demand. A feminist-institucionalist theory of candidate selection". *Political Research Quarterly*, June 17 (Sage Journals on line: DOI: 10.1177/1065912909336275)

__________. 2009. *Quotas for women in politics: gender and candidate selection reform worldwide*, Oxford University Press.

Martinez Ten, Carmen. 1998. "Políticas para la Igualdad, un proyecto de izquierda", *Revista Leviatan*, N 71 (Spring).

Lovenduski, Joni. 1986. *Women and European Politics: Contemporary Feminism and Public Policy*. Brighton: Wheatsheaf Books ltd.

__________. 1993. "Introduction: The Dynamics of Gender and Party." In *Gender and Party Politics,* eds. Joni Lovenduskii and Pippa Norris. London: Sage Publications.

__________. 1994. "The Rules of the Political Game: Feminism and Politics in Great Britain." In *Women and Politics Worldwide, eds.* Barbara J. Nelson and Najma Chowdhhury . New Haven & London: Yale University Press.

__________. 1995. "An Emerging Advocate: The Equal Opportunities Commission in Great Britain." In *Comparative State Feminism,* eds. Dorothy McBride Stetson and Amy G. Mazur. London: Sage Publications.

Lovenduski, Joni and Pippa Norris (Eds.). 1993. *Gender and Party Politics*. London: Sage.

Martín, María Elena. 2010. "Parlamento y género. El caso de la provincia de Misiones (1983-2001" PH D Thesis, Buenos Aires: Universidad del Salvador.

Marx, Jutta; Borner, Jutta y Caminotti, Mariana (2007). *Las legisladoras. Cupos de género y política en Argentina y Brasil.* Buenos Aires: Siglo XXI

Marx, Jutta et al. 2009. "Gender quotas, candidate selection and electoral Campaigns: Comparing Argentina and Brazil." In *Feminist Agendas and Democracy in Latin America,* ed. Jean Jaquette. Duke University Press.

Matland, Richard. 2002. "*Estrategias* para ampliar la participación femenina en el parlamento. El proceso de selección de candidatos legislativos y los sistemas electorales." In *Mujeres en el Parlamento-más allá de los números,* eds. M. Montalvo y J. Ballington. Stockholm: IDEA.

Nohlen, Dieter. 1994. *Sistemas electorales y partidos políticos*, México: Fondo de Cultura Económica.

Norris, Pippa. 1993. "Conclusion: Comparing Legislative Recruitment." In *Gender and Party Politics*, eds. Jomi Lovenduski and Pippa Norris. London: Sage Publications.

__________. 1996. "Legislative Recruitment." In, *Comparing Democracies*, eds. Lawrence Le Duc, Richard Niemi,and Pippa Norris. Thousand Oaks: Sage.

__________. (Ed.). 1997. *Passsages to power: Legislative recruitment in advanced democracies*. Cambridge University Press.

_________. 2001. 'Breaking the Barriers: Positive Discrimination Policies for Women." In.), *Has Liberalism Failed Women?: Assuring Equal Representation in Europe and the United State,* eds. Jytte Klausen and Charles S. Maier. New York: Palgrave.

_________. 2001. "Gender and Contemporary British Politics" in Hay, Colin (Ed.), *British Politics Today*, Cambridge: Polity Press.

_________. 2006. "The Impact of Electoral Reform on Women´s Representation". *Acta Política (Special Issue)* 41. 197-213.

Norris, Pippa and Lovenduski, Joni. 1993. *Gender and Party Politics in Britain*. Pennings, Paul and Reuven Y. Hazan. 2001.

Rae, Douglas, 1971. *The political consequences of electoral laws*, New Haven: Yale University Press.

Rahat, Gideon and Reuven Y. Hazan. 2001. "Candidate Selection Methods: An Analytical Framework," *Party Politics* 7. 297-322.

Ramos, Alicia y Verónica Spaventa. 2010. "De derechos y participación política de las mujeres en Salta" in María Sivia Varg (coord.) *Las mujeres y el bicentenario*, Salta: Mundo Gráfico Salta Editorial.

Ranney, Austin. 1981. "Candidate Selection" In *Democracy at the Polls: A comparative study of competitive national elections,* eds. David Butler, Howard Penniman, and Austin Ranney. Washington, DC: American Enterprise Institute for Public Policy Research.

Rule, Wilma. 1987. "Electoral Systems, contextual factors and women's opportunity for election to parliament in twenty-three democracies" *Western Political Quarterly* Vol. XL, N° 3, September. 477–498.

Shattschneider, Elmer. 1941. *Party Government*. New York : Holt, Rinehart and Winston.

Siavelis, Peter and Scott Morgenstern (Eds.). 2008. *Pathways to Power: Political Recruitment and Candidate Selection in Latin America*. The Pennsylvania State University Press. 440.

Taylor, Steven. 2000. *Towards a detailed discussion of candidate selection in Latin America*. XXXII International Meeting of Latin American Studies Association. Miami, Marzo.

Tula, María Inés. 2002. "La ley de cupo en la Argentina: la participación de las mujeres en los órganos representativos de gobierno" in Silvia Vázquez (comp.) *Hombres públicos, Mujeres públicas.* Buenos Aires: Friedrich Ebert Stiftung.

Varani, Javier. 2005. 'La imprescindible reforma de la Ley Electoral bonaerense: El caso de la integración de los Concejos Deliberantes", in Tula, María Inés (Ed.) *Aportes para la discusión de la Reforma Política bonaerense*, Buenos Aires: Prometeo.

Zimmerman, Joseph and Wilma Rule (Eds.). 1994. *Electoral systems in Comparative Perspective: Their Impact on Woman and Minorities.* Westport: Greenwood.

Chapter Three: Gender Quotas and Equity Promotion in Mexico

Baldez, Lisa. 2008. "Primaries v. Quotas: Gender and Candidate Nominations in Mexico, 2003." *Latin American Politics and Society 49(*3): 69-96.

Baldez, Lisa. 2004. "Elected Bodies: The Gender Quota Law for Legislative Candidates in Mexico." *Legislative Studies Quarterly 24(*2): 231-258.

Bruhn, Kathleen. 2003. "Whores and Lesbians: Political Activism, Party Strategies, and Gender Quotas in Mexico." *Electoral Studies 22:*: 101-119.

Caul Kittilson, Miki. 2001. "Political Parties and the Adoption of Candidate Gender Quotas: A Cross-National Analysis." *Journal of Politics 63 (*4):1214-1229.

Dresser, Denise. 2003. "Mexico: From PRI Dominance to Divided Democracy." In *Constructing Democratic Governance in Latin America*, edited by Jorge I. Domínguez and Michael Shifter, 321–347. Baltimore: The Johns Hopkins University Press..

Harbers, Imke. 2010. *Political Organization in Multi-level Settings: Mexican and Latin American Parties and Party Systems after Decentralization*. Ph.D. Diss., Leiden University.

Hinojosa, Magda. 2008. "¿Más Mujeres? Mexico's Mixed-Member Electoral System?" In *Women and Legislative Representation*, edited by Manon Tremblay, 177-190. New York: Palgrave Macmillan.

Huerta García, Magdalena and Eric Magar Meurs. 2006. *Mujeres legisladoras en México.* Mexico City: InMujeres, CONACYT, and Fundación FES.

Langston, Joy. 2008. "Legislative Recruitment in Mexico." In *Pathways to Power: Political Recruitment and Candidate Selection in Latin America*, edited by Peter Siavelis and Scott Morgenstern,143-163. University Park: Pennsylvania State University Press.

Magaloni, Beatriz. 2003. "The Demise of Mexico's One-Party Dominant Regime: Elite Choices and the Masses in the Establishment of Democracy." *In The Third Wave of Democratization in Latin America: Advances and Setbacks*, edited by Frances Hagopian and Scott P. Mainwaring, 121-146. New York: Cambridge University Press.

Matland, Richard E., and Donald Studlar. 1996. "The Contagion of Women Candidates in Single-Member Districts and Proportional Representation Electoral Systems: Canada and Norway." *The Journal of Politics 58* (30): 707-33.

Nacif, Benito. 2001. "Para comprender la disciplina de partido en la Cámara de Diputados de México: El modelo del partido centralizado." *Foro Internacional* 40 (1): 5-38.

Nava Polina, María del Carmen and Jorge Yáñez López. 2003. "The Effects of Pluralism on Legislative Activity: the Mexican Chamber of Deputies, 1917-2000." *Paper Presented at the International Research Workshop*, Saint Louis, Missouri.

Phillips, Anne. 1998. *The Politics of Presence*. New York: Oxford University Press.

Piscopo, Jennifer M. 2006. "Engineering Quotas in Latin America." *CILAS Working Paper Series, #23*. San Diego, Center for Iberian and Latin American Studies, University of California.

Reynoso, Diego and Natalia D'Angelo. 2004. "Leyes de Cuotas y Elecciones de Mujeres en México: ¿Contribuyen a disminuir la brecha entre eligir y ser elegida." *Paper presented at the Mexican Congress of Electoral Studies*, Coahuila, Mexico.

Rosas, Guillermo. 2005. "The Ideological Organization of Latin American Political Parties: An Empirical Analysis of Elite Policy Preferences." *Comparative Political Studies* 38 (7): 824-849.

Rodríguez, Victoria E. 2003. *Women in Contemporary Mexican Politics.* Austin: University of Texas Press.

Sánchez Olvera, Ama Rosa. 2006. "El Feminismo en la construcción de la ciudadanía de las mujeres en México." *Itinerario de las Miradas 63*: 1-35.

Stevenson, Linda S. 1999. "Gender Politics in the Mexican Democratization Process." In *Toward Mexico's Democratization: Parties, Campaigns, Elections, and Public Opinion*, edited Jorge I. Domínguez and Alejandro Poiré, 57-87. London: Routledge.

Tarrés, María Luisa. 2006. "The Political Participation of Women in Contemporary Mexico, 1980-2000." In *Changing Structure of Mexico*, edited by Laura Randall, 406-423. New York, M.E. Sharpe.

Weldon, Jeffrey A. 2004. "The Prohibition on Consecutive Reelection in the Mexican Congress." *Election Law Journal 3* (3): 574-579.

Chapter Four: The Diffusion of Sub-National Gender Quotas in Mexico and Their Impacts

Bacchi, Carol. 2006. "Arguing for and against quotas: theoretical issues." In *Women, Quotas, and Politics*, ed. Drude Dahlerup. London and New York: Routledge.

Baldez, Lisa. 2004. "Elected Bodies: The Gender Quota Law for Legislative Candidates in Mexico." *Legislative Studies Quarterly* XXIX (2):231-58.

———. 2006. "The Pros and Cons of Gender Quota Laws: What Happens When You Kick Men Out and Let Women In?" *Politics & Gender* 2 (1):102-9.

———. 2007. "Primaries vs. Quotas: Gender and Candidate Nominations in Mexico, 2003." *Latin American Politics and Society* 49 (3):69-96.

Bruhn, Kathleen. 2003. "Whores and lesbians: political activism, party strategies, and gender quotas in Mexico." *Electoral Studies* 22 (1):101-19.

Dahlerup, Drude. 2007. "Electoral gender quotas: Between equality of opportunity and equality of result." *Representation* 43 (2):73-92.

Dahlerup, Drude, and Lenita Freidenvall. 2005. "Quotas as a 'Fast Track' to Equal Representation for Women: Why Scandinavia is no longer the model." *International Feminist Journal of Politics* 7 (1):26-48.

Franceschet, Susan. Forthcoming. "Gender Policy and State Architecture in Latin America." *Politics & Gender.*

Goodin, Robert E. 1977. "Convention Quotas and Communal Representation." *British Journal of Political Science* 7 (2):255-61.

Hecock, R. Douglas. 2006. "Electoral Competition, Globalization, and Subnational Education Spending in Mexico, 1999-2004." *American Journal of Political Science* 50 (4):950-61.

Hughes, Melanie M, and Pamela Paxton. 2008. "Continuous Change, Episodes, and Critical Periods: A Framework for Understanding Women's Political Representation over Time." *Politics & Gender* 4 (2):233-64.

INMUJERES. 2010. "Análisis de los códigos y/o leyes electorales estatales en materia de género." (Accessed September 1, 2010). http://enlamira.inmujeres.gob.mx/index.php?option=com_content&view=article&id=111&Itemid=187

Jones, Mark P. 1998. "Gender quotas, electoral laws, and the election of women. Lessons from the Argentine Provinces." *Comparative Political Studies* 31 (1):3-21.

Krook, Mona Lena, Susan Franceschet, and Jennifer M Piscopo. 2009. "The Impact of Gender Quotas: A Research Agenda." Paper presented at the First European Conference on Politics and Gender, Belfast, United Kingdom, January 21-23.

Murray, Rainbow. 2010. "Second Among Unequals? A Study of Whether France's "Quota Women" are Up to the Job." *Politics & Gender* 6 (1):93-118.

Pitkin, Hanna. 1967. *The Concept of Representation*. Berkeley: University of California Press.

Reynoso, Diego, and Natalia D'Angelo. 2006. "Las leyes de cuota y su impacto en la elección de mujeres en México." *Política y Gobierno* XIII (2):279-313.

Román, José Antonio. 2010. "Pide magistrada respeto a cuotas de género." *La Jornada*, September 8.

Sacchet, Teresa. 2008. "Beyond Numbers: The Impact of Gender Quotas in Latin America." *International Feminist Journal of Politics* 10 (3):369-86.

Salinas, Muriel. 2009. "Renuncia de diputadas y cuotas de género." *La Jornada Guerrero*, September 13.

Zapata Morales, Isabel. 2008. "Representación femenina en los congresos locales mexicanos. El impacto de las cuotas de género." Paper presented at El II Congreso Internacional de la Asociación Mexicana de Estudios Parlamentarios, Puebla, September 24-26.

Zaremberg, Gisela. 2009. "Cuánto y para qué? Los derechos políticos de las mujeres desde la óptica de la representación descriptiva y sustantiva." In *Género y derechos políticos. La protección jurisdiccional de los derechos político-electorales de las mujeres en México*, ed. Karina Ansolabehere Sesti and Daniela Cerva Cerna. México D.F.: Tribunal Electoral del Poder Judicial de la Federación.

Zetterberg, Pär. 2008. "The Downside of Gender Quotas? Institutional Constraints on Women in Mexican State Legislatures." *Parliamentary Affairs* 61 (3):442-60.

_________. 2009a. Engineering Equality? Assessing the Multiple Impacts of Electoral Gender Quotas, PhD dissertation, Uppsala University, Uppsala

_________. 2009b. "Quotas and Women's Symbolic Representation: Lessons from Mexico." Paper presented at the Annual Meeting of the American Political Science Association, Toronto, Canada, September 3-6.

Chapter Five: Participation of Women in the Elections of 2002, 2006 and 2010

Alcântara, A. 2006. *A Participação Feminina nas Eleições de 2004 no Brasil*. Masters Dissertation, ENCE

Alvares, L. 2004. *Mulheres na Competição Eleitoral, Seleção de Candidaturas e o Padrão de Carreira Política no Brasil*. Doctorate Thesis, Rio de Janeiro, IUPERJ.

Alvares, M. Luzia M. 2008. "Mulheres brasileiras em tempo de competição eleitoral: seleção de candidaturas e degraus de acesso aos cargos parlamentares." *Dados, 51*(4): 895-939.

Alves, J.E.D, Correa, S. 2009." Igualdade e desigualdade de gênero no Brasil: um panorama preliminar, 15 anos depois do Cairo." In: ABEP, Brasil, 15 años após a Conferência do Cairo, ABEP/UNFPA, Campinas. ttp://www.abep.nepo.unicamp.br/docs/outraspub/cairo15/Cairo15_3alvescorrea.pdf

Alves, J. E. D. 2010. "Eleições: O poder das mulheres em 2010." Presença da Mulher, 23, Encarte teórico.

Alves, J.E.D.2003. "Mulheres em movimento: voto, education e trabalho." Ouro Preto, REM.

Alves, J.E.D. et al.2005. A mulher nas eleições de 2004: avaliação da política de quotas no Brasil. XXV° Congreso de la Asociación Latinoamericana de Sociología, Porto Alegre – Brasil, 22 to 26 August 2005

Araujo, Clara, Alves, José Eustáquio Diniz. 2007. "Impactos de indicadores sociais e do sistema eleitoral sobre as chances das mulheres nas eleições e suas interações com as quotas." *Dados.* 50 (3):535-577.

Araujo, Clara . 1999. Cidadania Incompleta: o Impacto da Lei de Quotas sobre a Representação Política das Mulheres no Brasil. Tese de Doutorado, IFCS/UFRJ.

________. 2003. Quotas for Women in the Brazilian Legislative System. In: The Implementation of Quotas: Latin American Experiences, pp 72-86. Stockholm: International Institute for Democracy and Electoral Assistance (IDEA).

________.2006. "Women and Electoral System in Brazil.," In Women and Electoral System, ed. R TREMBLAY. At press.

________ .2006ª. *Condicionantes Institucionais das políticas de quotas, In: Gláucio Soares e Lúcio Rennó (orgs),* Reforma Política. Rio de Janeiro: Fundação Getúlio Vargas.

________.2009. "Gênero e o acesso ao poder legislativo no Brasil: as quotas entre as instituições e a cultura." *Revista Brasileira de Ciência Política,* 2 :23-60.

Avelar, Lúcia. 2001." Mulheres na elite política brasileira." *2ª. Edição revista. São Paulo*: Fundação Konrad Adenauer.

Beltrão, K.I., Alves, J.E.D. 2004. *A reversão do hiato de gênero na education brasileira no século XX. Anais do XIV Encontro da Associação Brasileira de Estudos Populacionais da ABEP,* Caxambu.

Bohn, Simone.2006. "Ainda o velho problema da distorção da representação dos estados na Câmara dos Deputados." In Gláucio Soares and Lúcio Rennó (eds), *Reforma Política: Lições da História Recente,* Rio de Janeiro: FGV

Bruschini, M.C. 2007. "Trabalho e Gênero no Brasil nos Últimos Dez Anos." *Cadernos de Pesquisa.* 37(132):537-572.

CEPAL.2010. "XI Conferencia Regional sobre la Mujer de América Latina y el Caribe." Brasilia 13 to 16 Jul. http://www.eclac.cl/mujer/conferencia/default.asp

Diaz, Mercedes Mateo.2002. *Are Women in Parliament representing Women?From Descriptive to Substantive representation...and Back Again.* Louvain: Université Catholique de Louvain.

Duverger, Maurice. 1955. *Lês roles politiques dês femmes,* UNESCO.

Fraser, Nancy. 2007. "Mapping the Feminist Imagination: from redistribution to recognition to representation." In *The Future of Gender..*, ed. Jude Browne. Cambridge: Cambridge University Press.

Htun, Mala and Mark Jones.2002. "Engendering the Right to Participate in Decision-Making: Electoral Gender Quotas: electoral quotas and Women´s Leadership in Latin America." In *Gender and the Politics of Rights and Democracy in Latin America,* eds. Nikki Craske and Maxime Molyneux. New York: Palgrave;

IDEA. 2009. Global Database of Quotas for Women. http://www.quotaproject.org. (Accessed April 20, 2009).

IBGE.2002. "Tabulação avançada do censo demográfico. " *IBGE,* Rio de Janeiro.

IBGE. 2007. Síntese de Indicadores Sociais. http://www.ibge.gov.br/home/estatistica/populacao/condicaodevida/indicadoresminimos/sinteseindicsociais2007/indic_sociais2007 .pdf. (Accessed on January 24, 2009)

Matland, Richard.2002. "Estrategias para ampliar la participación femenina en el parlamento. El proceso de selección de candidatos legislativos y los sistemas electorales." In *Mujeres en el Parlamento - más allá de los números,* eds. In M. Montalvo and J. Ballington. Stockholm: IDEA;

Melo, Carlos Ranulfo.2006. "Sistema Partidário, presidencialismo e reformas políticas no Brasil," In *Reforma Política: Lições da História Recente*, eds. Gláucio Soares and Lúcio Rennó, Rio de Janeiro: FGV

Nicolau, J. 2006. "Voto personalizado e reforma eleitoral no Brasil. In *Reforma Política: Lições da História Recente*, eds. Gláucio Soares and Lúcio Rennó, Rio de Janeiro: FGV

Norris, Pippa.1993. "Conclusion."In *Gender and Party Politics*, eds. Pippa Norris & Joni Lovenduski. London, Sage Publications;

__________. 2003. "Electoral Enginering: voting rules and political behavior." Preliminaty version - www.pippanorris.com

Santos, André.2006. "Regras eleitorais, deputados e fidelidade partidária." In *Reforma Política: Lições da História Recente*, eds. Gláucio Soares and Lúcio Rennó. Rio de Janeiro: FGV

PNUD.2004.*Relatório do Desenvolvimento Humano*" Liberdade Cultural num Mundo Diversificado, Lisbon.

Schmidt, Greg. 2006. "Is Closed-List PR Really Optimal for the Election of Women?: A Cross-National Analysis" (manuscript)

Schmidt, Greg and Clara Araújo. 2004. "The Devil's in the Details: Open List Voting and Gender Quotas in Brazil and Peru." Paper presented at the XXV International Congress of Latin American Studies Association, Las Vegas, October 7-9.

Shuttz, J., Caminoti, M and Borner, J. 2006., "Cuotas de género y accesso femenino al Parlamento: los congresos nacionales de Argentina y Brasil". Final Report, Buenos Aires: Instituto Torcuato di tella.

Soares, Gláucio and Lúcio Rennó. 2006. "Projetos de Reforma Política na Câmara dos Deputados." In *Reforma Política: Lições da História Recente*, eds. Gláucio Soares and Lúcio Rennó. Rio de Janeiro: FGV

SPM. Política de quotas para mulheres na política tem 75% de aprovação, Mais Mulheres no Poder. Available at: http://www.maiswomennopoderbrasil.com.br/_estudos.html (Accessed April 20, 2009).

Therborn, Göran. 2007. "Familias en el mundo. Historia y futuro en el umbral del siglo XXI." In Arriagada, Irma (org). *Familias y políticas públicas en América Latina: Una historia de desencuentros*, CEPAL, Santiago, Chile.

TSE. Tribunal Superior Eleitoral, www.tse.gov.br, 2002, 2006 and 2010

Chapter Six: Gender Quotas in Peru

Ballington, Julie.2005. "Ten Years of Progress: Enhancing Women's Political Participation." In *Ten Years of Supporting Democracy Worldwide*, 113-124. Stockholm: International IDEA.

Bermúdez Valdivia, Violeta. 1998. "Mecanismos legales de promoción de la participación política de la mujer en la región andina." In *Memorias de la cumbre parlamentaria andina sobre la mujer*, 25-55. Guayaquil: Fondo de la Comisión Europea para ONGs Latinoamericanas.

Blondet, Cecilia and Carmen Montero. 1994. *La situación de la mujer en el Perú 1980-1994*, Lima: Instituto de Estudios Peruanos.

Calandria (Asociación de Comunicadores Sociales Calandria). 2000. *Buscando la equidad en el Congreso: Encuesta sobre participación política de la mujer*. Lima: Calandria.

Congreso de la República.1997(a). *Diario de los Debates, Primera Legislatura Ordinaria de 1997, 12a Sesión, (Matinal) y 12a A Sesión (Vespertina)* Miércoles, 17 de Setiembre de 1997. Lima.

Congreso de la República. 1997(b). *Transcripciones magnetofónicas, Segunda Legislatura Ordinaria de 1996, 24a Sesión (Matinal) y 24a A Sesión (Vespertina), Miércoles, 18 de Junio de 1997*. Lima.

El Comercio and Movimiento Manuela Ramos. *Mujeres en el Poder y el poder de las mujeres. El Comercio* (Lima), March 8, 1999, Suplemento especial sobre el Día Internacional de la Mujer.

Farrell, David M. 2001. *Electoral Systems: A Comparative Introduction*. Houndmills, Basingstoke, Hampshire, England: Palgrave.

Gallo, Máximo, Kristen Sample, and Gregory Schmidt. 2008. "Las elecciones legislativas peruanas en 2006: Un caso exitoso de cuotas con voto preferencial." *In Mujer y Política: El impacto de las cuotas de género en América Latina*, edited by Marcela Ríos, 179-200. Santiago, Chile: Facultad Latinoamericana de Ciencias Sociales (FLACSO) and International IDEA.

Gonzáles Arica, Guillermo. "Cuota obligatoria." *Caretas*, 1457, March 20, 1997, 78-79.

Gonzáles Arica, Guillermo. 1998. "La cuota que faltaba: Cómo se hizo la ley electoral que dispone laparticipación política de la mujer en cuotas parlamentarias y de regidores." *In Poder político con perfume de mujer: Las cuotas en el Perú*, edited by Ana María Yáñez and Lisbeth Guillén, 21–27. Lima: Movimiento Manuela Ramos and Instituto de Estudios Peruanos.

Htun, Mala N. 2002. "Mujeres y poder político en Latinoamérica." In *Mujeres en el parlamento: más allá de los números*, edited by Myriam Méndez-Montalvo and Julie Ballington, 18-43. Stockholm: International IDEA.

Htun, Mala N., and Mark P. Jones.2002. "Engendering the Right to Participate in Decision-making: Electoral Quotas and Women's Leadership in Latin America." *In Gender and the Politics of Rights and Democracy in Latin America*, edited by Nikki Craske and Maxine Molyneux, 32-56. Houndmills, Basingstoke, Hampshire, England: Palgrave.

Inter-Parliamentary Union. "Women in National Parliaments: Situation as of 30 June 2010." http://www.ipu.org/wmn-e/world.htm (accessed July 17, 2010)

JNE (Jurado Nacional de Elecciones). 1997. *Elecciones Municipales: Resultados de las Elecciones Municipales Generales de 1995*. Resultados de las Elecciones Municipales Parciales de 1996. Lima: JNE, Fundación Internacional para Sistemas Electorales (IFES), and Agencia para el Desarrollo Internacional (USAID).

JNE. 1999. Elecciones Municipales 1998 y Complementarias 1999. *Resultados Generales*. Lima.

JNE. 2006(a). Elecciones Generales. *Elección Presidencial, Congresal y al Parlamento Andino. Resultados*. Lima.

JNE. 2006 (b). Elecciones Municipales 2006: *Resultados y Estadísticas*. Lima.

JNE. 2006(c) Elecciones Municipales en Lima y Callao 1998-2006. Lima, 2006.

JNE. 2006(d). Elecciones Regionales 2006: *Resultados Generales*. Lima.

JNE. 2006(e). Elecciones Regionales y Municipales 2002: *Estadísticas Generales*. Lima.

JNE. 2010. Cuotas electorales en elecciones regionales (Aprobadas por Resoluciones N° 254-2010-JNE, N° 292-2010-JNE y N° 370-2010-JNE). Lima.

Matland, Richard E. 2005. "Enhancing Women's Political Participation: Legislative Recruitment and Electoral Systems." In *Women in Parliament: Beyond Numbers*, revised edition, edited by Julie Ballington and Azza Karam, 93-111. Stockholm: International Institute for Democracy and Electoral Assistance (IDEA).

Norris, Pippa. 2004. *Electoral Engineering: Voting Rules and Political Behavior*. New York: Cambridge University Press.

PROMUJER (Proyecto de "Promoción de la Participación Política de la Mujer").1998. *Poder político con perfume de mujer: Las cuotas en el Perú.* Lima: Movimiento Manuela Ramos and Instituto de Estudios Peruanos.

Schmidt, Gregory D. 1996. "Fujimori's 1990 Upset Victory in Peru: Electoral Rules, Contingencies, and Adaptive Strategies." *Comparative Politics*, 28 (3): 321-354.

Schmidt, Gregory D. 2003(a) "The Implementation of Gender Quotas in Peru: Legal Reform, Discourses, and Impacts." In *The Implementation of Quotas: Latin American Experiences*, 42-50. Stockholm: International Institute for Democracy and Electoral Assistance (IDEA).

Schmidt, Gregory D. 2003(b) "Unanticipated Successes: Lessons from Peru's Experiences with Gender Quotas in Majoritarian Closed List and Open List PR Systems." *In The Implementation of Quotas: Latin American Experiences*, 120-133. Stockholm: International Institute for Democracy and Electoral Assistance (IDEA).

Schmidt, Gregory D. 2005. "Is Closed List PR Really Optimal for the Election of Women?: A Cross-National Analysis." *Paper presented at the annual meeting of the American Political Science Association*, Washington D.C., September 2, 2005.

Schmidt, Gregory D. 2006. "All the President's Women: Fujimori and Gender Equity in Peruvian Politics." In *The Fujimori Legacy: The Rise of Electoral Authoritarianism in Latin America*, edited by Julio Carrión, 150-177. University Park: The Pennsylvania State Press.

Schmidt, Gregory D. 2010. "Accounting for Gender Disparities in Re-Election: The 2002-2006 Electoral Cycle in Peru." Lima: *Paper Prepared for International IDEA.*

Schmidt, Gregory D. and Kyle L. Saunders. 2004. "Effective Quotas, Relative Party Magnitude, and the Success of Female Candidates: Peruvian Municipal Elections in Comparative Perspective." Comparative Political Studies 37 (6):704-734.

Tuesta Soldevilla, Fernando.(2001) "Perú político en cifras, 1821-2001." 3a edición. Lima: Friedrich Ebert Stiftung.

Villanueva Flores, Rocío. 1998. "¿Están justificadas las cuotas de mujeres en las listas electorales?" In *Poder político con perfume de mujer: Las cuotas en el Perú*, edited by Ana María Yáñez and Lisbeth Guillén, 28-41. Lima: Movimiento Manuela Ramos and Instituto de Estudios Peruanos.

Webb, Richard and Graciela Fernández Baca. 2000. "Perú en Números 2000," Lima: Cuánto S.A.

Yáñez, Ana María. 1998. "Lo que hizo el movimiento de mujeres por las cuotas políticas: Un caminoque tomó siete años." In *Poder político con perfume de mujer: Las cuotas en el Perú*, edited by Ana María Yáñez and Lisbeth Guillén, 15-20.Lima: Movimiento Manuela Ramos and Instituto de Estudios Peruanos.

Yañez, Ana María. 1999. "Participación política y liderazgo de la mujer." *Socialismo y Participación*, *85*: 107–114.

Zárate, Patricia. 2008. "¿Las mujeres se presentan a la re-elección en menor medida que los hombres?: Un análisis cuantitativo de los dos últimos procesos electorales." Lima: *Paper Prepared for International IDEA.*

Chapter Eight: Women's Quotas in the Dominican Republic

Alvarez, Virtudes. 1996. *Tiempo Vivido.* Santo Domingo: Editora Taller.

Gómez Cerda, José. 2010. *La lucha sindical campesina: Mamá Tingó*. http://www.acedaasociado.com/mamatingo.html. (Accessed September 20, 2010).

Instraw. 2006. *Women in Power and Decision-Making: New Challenges. Beijing at 10: Putting Policy into Practice*. Santo Domingo:AECI.

Inter-Parliamentary Union (IPU). http://www.ipu.org/wmn-e/classif.htm. (Accessed December 15,1995 and December 31, 1999).

Inter-Parlamentary Union (IPU). http://www.ipu.org/english/home.htm. (Accessed November 15, 2010).

Jiménez Polanco, Jacqueline. 2010. "República Dominicana: Crecimiento macroeconómico y estabilidad política versus desigualdad social e insatisfacción popular". *Revista de Ciencia Política, 30* (2): 479-498.

Jiménez Polanco, Jacqueline. 2008. "La representación política de las Mujeres en la República dominicana: Obstáculos y potencialidades." In *Mujeres y Política: Sistemas Electorales y Cuotas de Género en América Latina*, eds. Nélida Archenti and María Inés Tula, 165-189. Buenos Aires: Heliasta.

Jiménez Polanco, Jacqueline. 2006. "Crisis de legitimidad y de legitimación de los partidos políticos en América Latina y el Caribe". Clavedigital. http://www.clavedigital.com/App_Pages/opinion/Firmas.aspx?Id_Articulo=6718&Id_ClassArticulista=150). (Accessed August 15, 2010).

Jiménez Polanco, Jacqueline. 2005. "La representación política de las mujeres en la República Dominicana: Obstáculos institucionales a su incorporación en los espacios de poder. Un análisis de las elecciones de 1998 y 2002." In *Miradas desencadenantes: Los estudios de género en la República Dominicana al inicio del tercer milenio*, ed. Ginetta E.B. Candelario, 305-318. Santo Domingo: INTEC.

Jiménez Polanco, Jacqueline. 2004. "Las mujeres y otros sectores subordinados en el espacio público nacional". In *Desde la orilla: Hacia una nacionalidad sin desalojos*, ed. Silvio Torres-Saillant, Ramona Hernández and Blas Jiménez. Santo Domingo, Editora Librería La Trinitaria.

Jiménez Polanco, Jacqueline. 2002. *Efectos nocivos del voto preferencial en la cuota femenina, la representación proporcional de las minorías y la estabilidad del sistema de partidos*. Santo Domingo: Secretaría de Estado de la Mujer, Dirección de Políticas Públicas: Género y Reformas. http://www.sem.gov.do/pdffiles/votopreferencial.pdf.

Jiménez Polanco, Jacqueline. 2001. "La représentation politique des femmes en Amérique Latine". In *La Représentation Politique des Femmes en Amérique Latine*, edited by Berengere Marques-Pereira and Patricio Nolasco, 27-81. Bruselas: UNESCO and L'Harmattan.

Jiménez Polanco, Jacqueline. 1999. "La representación política de las mujeres en América Latina". *América Latina Hoy, 22*:69-92.

Jiménez Polanco, Jacqueline. 1999a. "El pactado ascenso al poder de Leonel Fernández en la elección presidencial de 1996: La emergencia del liderazgo contigente y la construcción de una poliarquía consultiva". In *La República Dominicana en el Umbral del Siglo XXI*, ed. Ramonina Brea, 331-357. Santo Domingo: Pontificia Universidad Católica Madre y Maestra.

Jiménez Polanco, Jacqueline. 1999b. *Los Partidos Políticos en la República Dominicana: Actividad Electoral y Desarrollo Organizativo*. Santo Domingo: Editora Centenario.

Jiménez Polanco, Jacqueline. 1994. "Las elecciones de 1994 en la República Dominicana: El último clivaje de una cuasipoliarquía gerontocrática y delegativa". *América Latina Hoy*, 13. http://campus.usal.es/~iberoame/americalatinahoy/ALH-PDF-TIFF/ALHvol13/ALHvol13jimenez.pdf. Retrieved on August 10, 2010.

Junta Central Electoral. 2006. "Resolución Cuota Femenina." *Listín Diario*, February 24.
Liriano, Alejandra et al. 2003. *Hacia un Plan Nacional de Educación en Derechos Humanos. Santo Domingo.* UNESCO, PNUD, the Dominican State Secretariat of Education.
PLD. 2006. *Conferencia Nacional sobre Equidad de Género.* Documento de Trabajo. Santo Domingo.
United Nations. *Beijing Platform for Action.* http://www.un.org/womenwatch/daw/beijing/platform/decision.htm. (Accessed on September 15, 2010).
United Nations. *Report of the Ad Hoc Committee of the Whole of the twenty-third special session of the General Assembly.* http://www.un.org.womenwatch/daw/followup/as2310rev1.pdf. (Accessed August 30, 2010)
United Nations. *Women 2000: Gender Equality, Development and Peace for the 21st Century.* http://www.un.org/womenwatch/asp/user/list.asp?ParentID=4002. Retrieved on August 25, 2010.

Chapter Nine: From Vanguard to Straggler

Araújo, Clara and Ana Isabel García. 2006. "The experience and the impact of quotas in Latin America." In *Women, Quotas and Politics*, ed. Drude Dahlerup, 83-111. London: Routledge.
Archenti, Nélida, and María Inés Tula. 2008. "Algunas Cuestiones Iniciales sobre las Leyes de Cuotas." In *Mujeres y Política en América Latina.* Sistemas Electorales y Cuotas de Género, ed. Nélida Archenti and María Inés Tula, 9-29. Buenos Aires: Heliasta, 2008.
Archenti, Nélida and María Inés Tula. 2008. Mujeres y Política en América Latina. Sistemas Electorales y Cuotas de Género. Buenos Aires: Heliasta.
Cassina de Nogara, Alba G. 1990. *Hacia una Democracia Integral: Apuntes para una Historia del Feminismo en Uruguay.* Montevideo: CONAMU.
Dahlerup, Drude, and Lena Freidenvall. "Judging Gender Quotas: Predictions and Results." *Policy and Politics, 38*(3) (2010): 407-25. Accessed October 23, 2010, http://www.statsvet.su.se/homepages/archive/drude_dahlerup/dahlerup_freidenvall_Policy_Politics_38_3_2010.pdf.
Dahlerup, Drude. Ed. 2006. *Women, Quotas and Politics.* London: Routledge.
Htun, Mala and Mark Jones. 2002. "Engendering the Right to Participate in Decision-Making: Electoral Quotas and Women's Leadership in Latin America." In *Gender and the Politics of Rights and Democracy in Latin America,* eds. Nikki Craske and Maxine Molyneux, 32-56. London: Palgrave.
International Institute for Democracy and Electoral Assistance. 2003. *The Implementation of Quotas: Latin American Experiences, Workshop Rep*ort. Lima, Peru, February 23-24, 2003. Stockholm: International Institute for Democracy and Electoral Assistance.
Inter-Parliamentary Union. 1995. "Women in Parliaments, 1945-1995. A Worldwide Statistical Survey, Series "Reports and Documents" 23. Geneva.
Johnson, Charlotte Nicola. 2000. "'The Right to Have Rights': Gender Politics, Citizenship and the State in Uruguay". PhD diss., University of London.
Johnson, Niki. 2006. "Actuación Parlamentaria y Diferencias de Género en Uruguay, 2000-2005." *Revista de Ciencia Política*, 46: 173-98. Universidad de Chile.
Johnson Niki. 2001. "¿Democracia a Medias? La Representación de la Mujer en Cargos Políticos Electivos en Uruguay, 1984-1994." *Revista Uruguaya de Ciencia Política, 12:* 69-97.

Johnson, Niki. 2003, August. "La Cuota: ¿Un Mecanismo Necesario y Efectivo para Incrementar la Representación de Mujeres en Cargos Políticos Electivos? El Caso Uruguayo." Paper presented at the Seminar Estrategias Políticas de Género: Reformas Institucionales, Identidad y Acción Colectiva, Instituto de Investigaciones Gino Germani, Universidad de Buenos Aires.

Johnson, Niki. 2008. "Las Cuotas en Uruguay: Una Medida Resistida." In *Mujeres y Política en América Latina. Sistemas Electorales y Cuotas de Género*, eds. Nelida Archenti and María Inés Tula, 211-32. Buenos Aires: Heliasta.

Johnson, Niki. 2005. *La Política de la Ausencia: Las Elecciones Uruguayas 2004/2005, las Mujeres y la Equidad de Género*. Montevideo: CNS Mujeres-ICP.

Johnson, Niki, and Verónica Pérez. 2010. *Representación (S)electiva. Una Mirada Feminista a las Elecciones Uruguayas 2009*. Montevideo: Cotidiano Mujer-ICP-UNIFEM.

Jones, Mark P. 2000. "El Sistema de Cuotas y la Elección de las Mujeres en América Latina: El Papel Fundamental del Sistema Electoral". In La Democracia Paritaria en la Construcción Europea. Madrid: CELEM. Accessed September 21, 2010 http://www.celem.org/prog_europeos/demo_paritaria2000/pdfs/capitulo01.pdf.

Krook, Mona Lena. 2009. *Quotas for Women in Politics: Gender and Candidate Selection Reform Worldwide*. New York: Oxford University Press.

Larserud, Stina and Rita Taphorn. 2007. *Designing for Equality. Best-fit, medium-fit and non-favourable combinations of electoral systems and gender quotas*. Stockholm: International Institute for Democracy and Electoral Assistance.

Lavrin, Asunción. 1995. *Women, Feminism, and Social Change in Argentina, Chile and Uruguay, 1890-1940*. Lincoln: University of Nebraska Press.

Llanos, Beatriz and Kristen Sample. 2008. *30 Years of Democracy: Riding the Wave? Women's Political Participation in Latin America*. Stockholm: International Institute for Democracy and Electoral Assistance.

Matland, Richard. 2006. "Electoral quotas: frequency and effectiveness." In *Women, Quotas and Politics*, ed. Drude Dahlerup, 275–92. London: Routledge.

Moreira, Constanza and Niki Johnson. 2003. *Democracia, Género y Equidad: Aportes para el Debate sobre Mecanismos de Acción Afirmativa*. Montevideo: FESUR.

Norris, Pippa. 2006."The Impact of Electoral Reform on Women's Representation." *Acta Politica, 41*: 197-213.

Norris, Pippa. 2004. *Electoral Engineering: Voting Rules and Political Behavior*. Cambridge University Press: Cambridge.

Pérez, Verónica. 2006. "52% del Electorado, 11% del Parlamento. Factores Culturales y Representación Política Femenina en Uruguay." *Revista Uruguaya de Ciencia Política, 15*: 57-81.

Pérez, Verónica. 2008. "Variables Políticas y Representación Femenina: ¿Influencias de qué Tipo? Comentarios a partir del Caso Uruguayo." *Colección 18-19*: 119-42.

Piscopo, Jennifer M. 2006. "Engineering Quotas in Latin America." *Center for Iberian and Latin American Studies Working Paper 23*, San Diego: University of California. Accessed September 2, 2010 http://escholarship.org/uc/item/7j05q10b.

Ríos, Marcela and Andrés Villar. 2006. C*uotas de Género: Democracia y Representación. Santiago de Chile.* Instituto Internacional para la Democracia y Asistencia Electoral-FLACSO.

Rodríguez Villamil, Silvia and Graciela Sapriza. 1984. *Mujer, Estado y Política en el Uruguay del Siglo XX*. Montevideo: Ediciones de la Banda Oriental.

Chapter Ten: Legislative Gender Quotas in Former Communist and Post-Conflict Societies

Azgayin Joghov. 1999. *Armenia-Parliamentary Chamber:*. http://www.ipu.org/parline-e/reports/arc/2013_99.htm (Accessed September 14, 2010).

Beijing Declaration and Platform for Action. 1995. *Fourth World Conference on Women, 15 September 1995*, A/CONF.177/20 (1995) and A/CONF.177/20/Add.1. http://www.un.org/womenwatch/daw/beijing/platform/ (Accessed August 30, 2010).

Belloni, Roberto. 2004. "Peacebuilding and Consociational Electoral Engineering in Bosnia and Herzegovina," *International Peacekeeping* 11 (2).

Bijelic, Biljana. 2005. "Nationalism, Motherhood, and the Reordering of Women's Power." In *Serbia since 1989: Politics and Society under Milosevic and After*, ed. Sabrina P. Ramet and V. Pavlakovic. Seattle: University of Washington Press: 286-308.

Blagojevic, Marina. 2006. "Belgrade Protests 1996/1997: From Women in the Movement to Women's Movement." In *Women and Citizenship in Central and Eastern Europe,* ed. Jasmina Lukić, Joanna Regulska, Darja Zaviršek. Aldershot: Ashgate: 147-164

Blanc, Jarrett; Aarund Hylland, Kare Vollan. 2006. *State Structure and Electoral Systems in Post-Conflict Situations*. Washington, DC: IFES.

Borić, Besima. 2004. "Application of Quotas: Legal Reforms and Implementation in Bosnia and Herzegovina." a Paper presented at the International Institute for Democracy and Electoral Assistance (IDEA)/CEE Network for Gender Issues Conference *The Implementation of Quotas: European Experiences* Budapest, Hungary, 22–23 October 2004. http://www.legislationline.org/userdocuments/cat/5 (Accessed September 15, 2010)

Bose, Sumantra. 2005. "The Bosnian State a Decade After Dayton," *International Peacekeeping* 12 (3), Autumn: 322-335.

Bouta, Tsjeard, Georg Freks, Ian Bannon. 2005. *Gender, Conflict and Development*. Washington DC: The World Bank.

Butler, Maria, Kristina Mader and Rachel Kean. 2010. *Women, Peace and Security Handbook: Compilation and Analysis of United Nations Security Council Resolution Language 2000-2010*. PeaceWomen Project of Women's International League for Peace and Freedom, October 2010. http://www.peacewomen.org/assets/file/peacewomen_schandbook_2010.pdf (Accessed September 15, 2010)

CEDAW Assessment Tool Report for Armenia. 2002, July. A Report by the Central European and Eurasian Law Institute. www.abanet.org/ceeli. (Accessed September 14, 2010)

CEDAW/C/ARM/2.1999. Second Periodic Reports of State Parties on Armenia at http://www2.ohchr.org/english/bodies/cedaw/cedaws_exceptional.htm (Accessed September 14, 2010)

CEDAW/C/ARM/4. 2007. Combined Third and Fourth Periodic Reports of States Parties Armenia. http://www.unhcr.org/refworld/pdfid/48c7c25e2.pdf (Accessed September 15, 2010)

CEDAW/C/CR.672 .2003. *Second periodic report of Armenia* from the 572nd meeting held at headquarters, New York. .http://www.unhchr.ch/tbs/doc.nsf/898586b1dc7b4043c1256a450044f331/069c54c12687b321c125729f003b5a7a/$FILE/N0251487.pdf (Accessed September 14, 2010).

CEDAW/C/SCG/1. 2006, October. Convention on the Elimination of All Forms of Discrimination against Women. Consideration of Reports submitted by States Parties under article

18 of the Convention on the Elimination of All Forms of Discrimination against Women. *Initial report of States Parties. Serbia* http://www.un.org/womenwatch/daw/cedaw/cedaw38/reports/serbiaE.pdf (Accessed September 16, 2010).

CEDAW. 2003. Committee on the Elimination of Discrimination against Women Exceptional session Summary record of the 571st meeting. *Second periodic report of Armenia.* http://www2.ohchr.org/english/bodies/cedaw/cedaws_exceptional.htm (Accessed September 15, 2010).

Dahlerup, Drude. 2006. "Introduction." In *Women, Quotas and Politics*, ed. Drude Dahlerup. London, New York: Rutledge: 1-3.

Debiel, Tobias and Ulf Terlinden, 2005. "Promoting Good Governance in Post-Conflict Societies. Discussion Paper" Eschborn: Deutsche Gesselschaft fur Technische Zusammenarbeit. http://www2.gtz.de/dokumente/bib/05-0032.pdf (Accessed September 15, 2010).

Doder, Dusko and Louise Branson, 1999. *Milosevic: Portrait of a Tyrant.* New York, NY: The Free Press.

Dokmanović, Mirjana. 2007. "Constitutional and Political Analyses." In *Engendering Constitutions: Gender Equality Provisions in Selected Constitutions. A Comparative Study Accompanied with Case Studies in Bosnia and Herzegovina, Kosovo, Montenegro, Serbia*, ed. K. Van der Leest (November 2007). http://www.unifem.sk/uploads/doc/Constitutional%20publication%20Nov%2020071.pdf (Accessed September 15, 2010).

Effron, Laurie, F. Stephen O'Brien, 2004. *Bosnia and Herzegovina: Post-Conflict Reconstruction and the Transition to the Market Economy: an OED Evaluation of World Bank Support.* Washington, DC: World Bank.

Electoral Code of the Republic of Armenia. 1999. HO-284. Unofficial Publication. http://www.venice.coe.int/docs/2007/CDL-EL(2007)010-e.pdf (Accessed September 14, 2010).

Enloe, Cynthia H. 1993. *The Morning After: Sexual Politics at the End of the Cold War.* Berkeley, Los Angeles: University of California Press.

_______________. 2000. *Maneuvers: the International Politics of Militarizing Women's Lives.* Berkeley, Los Angeles: University of California Press.

Haavio-Mannila, Elina et al. 1985. *Unfinished Democracy: Women in Nordic Politics.* New York: PergamonC.H. Enloe. 2000. *Maneuvers: the International Politics of Militarizing Women's Lives.* Berkeley, Los Angeles: University of California Press.

Human Rights Center. 2008. *Legal Provisions, Practice And International Human Rights Standards In The Bosnia And Herzegovina With Public Opinion Survey.* Sarajevo http://www.hrc.unsa.ba/hrr2008/PDFS/humanrightsinbih2008.pdf (. Accessed September 15, 2010)

Galligan, Yvonne, Sara Clavero, Marina Calooni. 2007. *Gender Politics and Democracy in Post-Socialist Europe.* Opladen, Germany; Farmington Hills, MI: Barbara Budrich Publishers.

Gender Task Force. 2000. *Women's Activism Prior to Serbia Elections.* http://www.stabilitypact.org/gender/000901-report.asp. (Accessed September 15, 2010)

Global Rights Partners in cooperation with Non-Governmental Organizations in Bosnia and Herzegovina. *2004. Shadow Report on the Implementation of CEDAW and Women's Human Rights in Bosnia and Herzegovina. Presented to the United Nation's Committee on the Elimination of Discrimination Against Women (CEDAW).* http://www.iwraw-ap.org/resources/pdf/Bosnia&Herzegovina_SR.pdf (Accessed September 15, 2010).

Goetz, Anne Marie .2003. "Women's Political Effectiveness: A Conceptual Framework." In *No Shortcuts to Power. African Women in Politics and Policy Making*, ed. Anne Marie Goerts and Shireen Hassim. London: Zed Books: 29-80.

International Women's Rights Action Watch. 1998. *Armenia Initial Report* (Addendum). http://www1.umn.edu/humanrts/iwraw/cescrarmenia.htm (Accessed September 15, 2010).

Inter-Parliamentary Union. 2002. *Bosnia and Herzegovina, Elections held in 2002.* http://www.ipu.org/parline-e/reports/arc/2039_02.htm (Accessed September 15, 2010).

Inter-Parliamentary Union. 2005. *Bosnia and Herzegovina. Elections held in 2005.* http://www.ipu.org/parline-e/reports/arc/2039_06.htm Accessed September 15, 2010).

Inter-Parliamentary Union. 1993. *Serbia. Elections.* http://www.ipu.org/parline-e/reports/arc/2355b_92.htm (Accessed September 15, 2010).

Inter-Parliamentary Union. 2002. *Serbia. Elections.* http://www.ipu.org/parline-e/reports/arc/2355_00.htm (Accessed September 15, 2010).

Inter-Parliamentary Union. 2007. *Serbia. Elections..* http://www.ipu.org/parline-e/reports/arc/2355_07.htm (Accessed September 2010).

Inter-Parliamentary Union. 2008. *Serbia, Elections.* http://www.ipu.org/parline-e/reports/2355.htm (Accessed September 16, 2010).

Inter-Parliamentary Union. 2010. *Last Elections.* http://www.ipu.org/parline/reports/2013_E.htm. (Accessed September 15, 2010).

Inter-Parliamentary Union. 1992. *Yugoslavia. Elections held in 1992.* http://www.ipu.org/parline-e/reports/arc/2355_92.htm (Accessed September 15, 2010).

Inter-Parliamentary Union. 1992. *Yugoslavia. Elections in 1982.* http://www.ipu.org/parline-e/reports/arc/YUGOSLAVIA_1982_E.PDF (Accessed September 15, 2010).

Inter-Parliamentary Union. 1992. *Yugoslavia. Elections in 1986.* http://www.ipu.org/parline-e/reports/arc/YUGOSLAVIA_1986_E.PDF (Accessed September 15, 2010).

Itano, Nicole. 2007. "Quota Law Puts More Women in Armenia's Election." *We News*, May 10, 2007. http://www.womensenews.org/story/the-world/070510/quota-law-puts-more-women-armenias-election (Accessed September 14, 2010).

Krook, Mona Lena. 2004. "Promoting Gender-balanced Decision-making: The Role of International Fora and Transnational Networks." In Crossing Borders: Re-Mapping Women's Movements at the Turn of the 21st Century, ed. Hilda Roemer Christensen, Beatrice Halsaa, and Aino Saarinen. Odense: University Press of Southern Denmark: 205-220

Law on the Election of Representatives. 2004. http://www.legislationline.org/documents/action/popup/id/3871 (Accessed September 16, 2010)

Meznaric, Silva and Mirjana Ule, 1999. "In Pursuit of a Framework. Delayed Modernization and Emancipation of Women in the Balkans." In *Women in the Politics of Postcommunist Eastern Europe,* ed. Marylin Rueschemeyer. New York: M.E. Sharpe: 196-202.

Migdalovitz, Carol. 2003. "Armenia-Azerbaijan Conflict." *CRS Issue Brief for Congress* August 8, 2003. http://pards.org/crs_country/CRSReportArmenia-AzerbaijanConflict (August 8, 2003) Updated.pdf (Accessed September 15, 2010).

Moser, Caroline N.O. and Fiona Clark, eds. 2001. *Victims, Perpetrators or Actors? Gender, Armed Conflict and Political Violence.* London and New York Zed Books.

N/A "Montenegro Gets Serb Recognition," *BBC News*, June 15, 2006

N/A.2001. September. *Refugees and Internally Displaced Women and Children in Serbia and Montenegro.* New York: Women's Commission for Refugees and Children.

Nelson, Sue Brian Katilus, 2005. USAID/Armenia *Armenia Political Party Assessment Final Report* May 2005. http://www.usaid.gov/locations/europe_eurasia/countries/am/docs/political_party_assessment.pdf (Accessed September 14, 2010)

Nikolic-Ristanovic, Vesna. 2003. "Refugee Women in Serbia – Invisible Victims of War in Former Yugoslavia." *Feminist Review* 73.

Nichols, Jim. 2007. "Armenia's Legislative Election: Outcome and Implication for U.S. Interests." *CRS Report for Congress* RL 33453. http://www.fas.org/sgp/crs/row/RS22675.pdf (Accessed September 15, 2010)

Official Gazette. 2002. *Law on Local Elections of the Republic of Serbia,* No. 33. 2002 http://www.venice.coe.int/docs/2005/CDL-EL(2005)027-e.pdf (Accessed September 16, 2010)

Official Gazette. 2007. *Official Gazette of the Republic of Serbia, no. 129.* http://www.legislationline.org/documents/action/popup/id/4326 (Accessed September 16, 2007).

Official Gazette. 2000. *Law on the Election of Representatives,* Official Gazette of The Republic of Serbia, No. 35/2000, http://www.legislationline.org/documents/action/popup/id/3873 (Accessed September 15, 2010)

Official Gazette. *Election Law of Bosnia And Herzegovina.* http://www.legislationline.org/documents/action/popup/id/6274 or http://www.oscebih.org/documents/25-eng.pdf (Accessed September 15, 2010)

Orlović, Slaviša. 2008. "Parties and Party System of Serbia and European Integration." *Journal of Balkan and Near Eastern Studies* 10 (2), August.

OSCE Office for Democratic Institutions and Human Rights. 2003. *Republic of Armenia. Parliamentary Elections. Final Report.* http://www.osce.org/documents/odihr/2003/07/533_en.pdf (Accessed September 15, 2010)

OSCE/ODIHR. 2007. *Election Observation Mission Republic Of Armenia Parliamentary Elections 2007 Interim Report No. 2 29.* http://www.osce.org/documents/odihr/2007/04/24101_en.pdf (Accessed September 14, 2010)

OSCE Office for Democratic Institutions and Human Rights. 2007. *Bosnia and Herzegovina, General Elections October 1, 2006. OSCE/ODIHR Election Observation Mission. Final Report.* http://www.osce.org/documents/odihr/2007/02/23206_en.pdf (Accessed September 15, 2010)

OSCE Office for Democratic Institutions and Human Rights. 2007. Bosnia and Herzegovina, General Elections October 1, 2006. OSCE/ODIHR Election Observation Mission. Final Report. http://www.osce.org/documents/odihr/2007/02/23206_en.pdf (Accessed September 15, 2010)

OSCE Office for Democratic Institutions and Human Rights. 2001. *Final report on the parliamentary elections in the Republic of Serbia, 23 December 2000* http://www.osce.org/documents/odihr/2001/02/1330_en.pdf, (Accessed September 15, 2010)

OSCE Office for Democratic Institutions and Human Rights. 2004. *Final report on the parliamentary elections in the Republic of Serbia (Serbia and Montenegro)*, 28 December 2003. http://www.osce.org/documents/odihr/2004/02/2177_en.pdf (Accessed September 16, 2010).

OSCE Office for Democratic Institutions and Human Rights. 2007. *Final Report on the 21 January 2007 Parliamentary Elections in Serbia.* http://www.osce.org/documents/odihr/2007/04/24171_en.pdf (Accessed September 16, 2010)

OSCE Office for Democratic Institutions and Human Rights. 2008. *Final Report on the 11 May 2008 early parliamentary elections in the Republic of Serbia.* http://www.osce.org/documents/odihr/2008/08/32769_en.pdf (Accessed September 16, 2010)

OSCE. 1999. *Republic of Armenia. Parliamentary Election. 30 May 1999. Final Report.* Warsaw.ODIHR Election Observation. http://www.osce.org/documents/odihr/1999/07/1217_en.pdf (Accessed September 14, 2010).

OSCE. 2007. "Women's Political Participation in the 2007 Parliamentary Elections in the Republic of Armenia. Analytical Overview." *Gender Studies Center of the Association of Women with University Education Organization for Security and Co-operation in Europe OSCE Office in Yerevan.* http://www.osce.org/documents/oy/2007/11/27913_en.pdf (Accessed September 14, 2010)

Pajvančić, Marijana. 2008. "Summary. Serbia's European Perspective From Women's Point Of View" Published in Serbian language in the book titled Pravona Ravnopravnost Polova [Right for Gender Equality] (Novi Sad, 2008) http://www.zenskavlada.org.rs/downloads/eng-gender-izbori-2007.pdf (Accessed September 15, 2010).

Panossian, Razmik. 2006. "Armenia: Nationalism and its (Dis)Content." In *After Independence: Making and Protecting the Nation in Postcolonial and Postcommunist States*, ed. Lowell W. Barrington. USA: University of Michigan Press.

Payaslian, Simon. 2007. *History of Armenia: From the Origins to the Present.* New York: Palgrave Macmillan.

Phillips, Anne. 2006. "Quotas for Women." In *Women, Gender, and Politics*, ed. Mona Lena Krook and Sarah Childs. Oxford, NY: Oxford University Press: 185-193.

Ramet, Sabrina P. 2006. *The Three Yugoslavias: A State-Building and Legitimation, 1918-2005.* Bloomington, IN: Indiana University Press.

Rogels, Carole. 2004. *The Breakup of Yugoslavia and its Aftermath.* Westport, Conn.: Greenwood Press.

Sahadzic, Maja. 2009. "The Electoral System of Bosnia and Herzegovina." *Contemporary Issues* 2 (1).

Sander, Helke. 1994. "Prologue." In *Mass Rape: The War against Women in Bosnia-Herzegovina* ed. Alexandra Stiglmayer. Lincoln: University of Nebraska Press: xvii-1.

Sawer, Marian, Manon Tremblay and Linda Trimble, 2006. "Introduction. Patterns and Practice in the Parliamentary representation of Women." In *Representing Women in Parliament. A Comparative Study*, ed. Marian Sawer, Manon Tremblay and Linda Trimble. New York, NY: Routledge: 103-119.

Sell, Louis. 2002. *Slobodan Milosevic and the Destruction of Yugoslavia.* Durham, NC: Duke University Press.

Silber, Laura. 1996. "The 'Hero' of Dayton: Slobodan Milosevic and the Politics of War and Peace" *World Policy Journal* 13 (1), Spring.

Stiglmayer, Alexandra (ed.) 1994. *Mass Rape: The War against Women in Bosnia-Herzegovina.* Lincoln: University of Nebraska Press.

Tranca, Oana. 2008 "What Causes Ethnic Conflict Diffusion? A Study of Ethnic Conflicts in Azerbaijan and Macedonia." *Journal of Peace, Conflict & Development Issue* 12, May. www.peacestudiesjournal.org.uk (Accessed September 15, 2010).

UNDP 2010. Women, Peace and Security, Get Renewed Commitment From Parliamentarians in the Region. http://europeandcis.undp.org/gender/show/833ED8B9-F203-1EE9-BF9C4197015D45F2 (Accessed September 16, 2010)

UNSC- National Implementation of Security Council Resolution 1325. *2000*. http://www.un.org/womenwatch/ianwge/taskforces/wps/national_level_impl.html (Accessed September 16, 2010).

United Nations Development Program, Human Development. 2009. http://hdr.undp.org/en/humandev/hdi/. (Accessed September 1, 2010).

USAID. 2005 May./*Bosnia-Herzegovina Gender Assessment.* http://pdf.usaid.gov/pdf_docs/PDACG120.pdf. (Accessed September 15, 2010).

Von Gienanth,Tobias. 2008. "Elections in Post-Conflict Societies- Lessons Learned from Liberia, Sierra Leone, DR Congo, and Kosov." Report of a ZIF/KATPIC Seminar, June 12-14, 2008, Accra / Ghana. http://www.zif-berlin.org/fileadmin/uploads/analyse/dokumente/veroeffentlichungen/ZIF_KAIPTC_Elections__Report_02_09.pdf (Accessed September 15, 2010)

Women, Peace and Security. 2002. Study submitted by the Secretary-General pursuant to Security Council resolution 1325. http://un.org/womenwatch/daw/public/eWPS.pdf (Accessed September 20, 2010).

Women's Campaign International. *Bosnia-Herzegovina. Background.* http://www.womenscampaigninternational.org/countries/bosnia-herzegovina. (Accessed September 15, 2010).

Women Watch. 2005. *Women and Elections. Guide to Promoting the Participation of Women in Elections.* http://www.un.org/womenwatch/osagi/wps/publication/WomenAndElections.pdf (Accessed September 20, 2010).

Women Watch. 2000. *Questionnaire to Governments on Implementation of the Beijing Platform for Action (1995) and the Outcome of the Twenty-Third Special Session of the General Assembly (*2000). http://www.un.org/womenwatch/daw/Review/responses/ARMENIA-English.pdf Accessed September 15, 2010

WomenPeace. *2010. 10th Anniversary of SCR 1325.* http://www.peacewomen.org/publications_enews_issue.php?id=148 (Accessed September 16, 2010)

Chapter Eleven: Diffusion of Gender Quotas in Latin America and Beyond

Bernard, Russell and Peter Killworth. 1973. "On the Social Structure of an Ocean-Going Research Vessel and Other Important Things." *Social Science Research, 2*:145-184.

Berry, Frances, and William D. Berry. 1990. "State Lottery Adoptions as Policy Innovations:An Event History Analysis." American Political Science Review 84(2):395–415

Berry, Frances Stokes and William D. Berry. 1999. "Innovation and Diffusion Models in Policy Research." In *Theories of the Policy Process*, ed. Paul Sabatier. Boulder CO: Westview Press.

Camacho Granados, Rosalía et al. 1997. *Las Cuotas Mínimas de Participación de las Mujeres: Un mecanismode acción afirmativa. Aportes para la Discusión*. 2nd ed. San José: CentroNacional para el Desarrollo de la Mujer y la Familia.

Crocker, Adriana. 2005. *Gender Quotas in Latin America: Explaining Cross-national and Sub-national Diffusion*. Ph.D. dissertation http://www.iadb.org/sds/doc/gedcrocker dissertation.pdf. (Accessed June 3, 2009).

_________. 2007."*Gender Quotas in Latin America, Innovation, Diffusion, and the End of a Wave?" Cena Internacional, vol.9 n2: 95–124.*

_________ and Kempton, Daniel. 2008.*Gender Quotas in Afghanistan: Solution or Problem?* Pew Case Study #296. Institute of Diplomacy Edmund A. Walsh School of Foreign Services, Georgetown University: Washington D.C.

_________. 2010. "Constructing Social Change in Argentina, from Gender Quotas to Same-Sex Marriage." In *Same-Sex Marriage in the Americas*, eds. Jason Pierceson, Adriana Piatti-Crocker, and Shawn Shulenberg, 37-72. Lexington Publishers

Daley, Dorothy M. 2007. "Voluntary Approaches to Environmental Problems: Exploring the Rise of Non-traditional Public Policy." *The Policy Studies Journal* 35,2: 165-80.

Dolowitz, D. and Marsh, D. 1996. "Who Learns What from Whom: a Review of the Policy Transfer Literature," *Political Studies*, 44, 343–57.

Estrada, Daniela. 2006. Latin America: Progress Towards Gender Parity in Politics. http:/ce-women.org/news/International. (Accessed December 16, 2006).

Escobar-Lemmon, Maria and Michelle Taylor-Robinson. 2005, October. "Women Ministers in Latin American Government: When, Where, and Why?" A*merican Journal of Political Science* 49(4): 822-44.

Guenther, Katja M. 2006. "'A Bastion of Sanity in a Crazy World'": A Local Feminist Movement and the Re-constitution of Scale, Space, and Place in an Eastern German City." *Social Politics* 13,4: 551-75

International Idea. 2010. "Global Database of Quotas for Women." http://www.qaproject.org. (Accessed May 23, 20010).

Htun, Mala and Jones, Mark. 2002. "Engineering the Right to participate in Decision-Making: Electoral Quotas and Women's leadership in Latin America." In *Gender, Rights, and Justice in Latin America,* eds. Nikki Craske and Maxine Molyneux. Basinsgtoke, England: Macmillan, 32-68.

Krook, Mona Lena. 2006. "Reforming Representation: The Diffusion of Candidate Gender Quotas World-wide." *Politics & Gender,* 2: 303-27.

Insituto Nacional de las Mujeres. 2010. "Cuotificacion entre resistencias y Vacios Legales." http://www.inmujeres.gub.uy/mides/colgado.jsp?contentid=1949&site=1&channel=inmujeres . (Accessed June 29, 2010).

Mintrom, Michael and Vergari, Sara. 1998. "Policy Networks and Innovation Diffusion: The Case of State Education Reforms.*Journal of Politics, 60:* 126-148.

_________. 2000. "Policy Entrepreneurs and Social Change." Washington D.C: Georgetown University Press.

PARLATINO. 2009. *XII Reunion de la Comision de Equidad de Genero, Ninez y Juventud.* http://www.parlatino.org/es/comisiones-permanentes/equidad-de-genero-ninez-y-juventud.html. (Accessed June 29, 2010).

Rogers, Everett. 1981. *Communication Networks: Toward a New Paradigm of Research*. New York: The Free Press.

_________. 5 ed. 2003. *Diffusion of Innovations.* New York: Free Press.

True, Jaqui and Michael Mintrom. 2001. "Transnational Networks and Policy Diffusion: The Case of Gender Mainstreaming." *International Studies Quarterly, 45,* 27-57

Siavelis, Peter. 2008. " Chile: The End of the Unifinished Transition ." In *Constructing Democratic Governance in Latin America,* eds. Jorge Dominguez and Michael Shifter, ed. Johns Hopkins: Baltimore: 177-208.

Simmons Beth ,Frank Dobbin and Geoffrey Garrett.2006. "The International Diffusion of Liberalism." *International Organizations, 60 (4)*:781-810 Cambridge University Press.

UNFPA. 2002. http://www.unfpa.org/about/report/2002. (Accessed June 21, 2009).

UN-ECLAC. 2010. Division on Gender. http://www.eclac.org/mdg/proyectos/default.asp?idioma=IN. (Accesed March 18, 2010).

UN-Women. 2004 .Commission on the Status of Women. Follow-Up to Beijing and Beijing + 5. http://www.un.org/womenwatch/daw/csw/48sess.htm.. (Accessed April 3,2008).

About the Contributors

José Eustáquio Diniz Alves, is a Ph.D. in demography from the Center for Development and Planning (CEDEPLAR) at the Federal University of Minas Gerais (UFMG), with post-doctoral studies at the Center for Population Studies–NEPO/UNICAMP. He is a professor at the National School of Statistical Sciences (ENCE) at the Brazilian Census Bureau (IBGE). His areas of research include: population and development, fertility, gender and women in politics.

Clara Araújo is a professor and researcher in the Post-Graduate Program in Social Sciences at the State University of Rio de Janeiro-Brazil. She also coordinates the Center of Studies on Contemporary Inequalities and Gender Relations. Her main areas of research are Gender and Political Participation and Gender and Family.

Nélida Archenti is a Ph.D. from the University of Buenos Aires, Argentina. She is a Professor of Political Science at the University of Buenos Aires, Argentina. Dr. Archenti has published numerous articles and her research interests include; political representation, gender and politics, gender and electoral Systems and public opinion.

Ana Isabel García Quesada is a Journalist and sociologist with a master's degree from the University of Costa Rica. On two occasions she held public posts in the government of Costa Rica; in 1994–1998, as Executive Director of the Instituto Nacional de las Mujeres (INAMU) and in 2006–2008, as Viceminister of Social Development. García Quesada is author and co-author of more than twenty books, has a similar number of articles published in books and magazines, as well as technical reports. Her main areas of work and experience are related to design and management of social policies, strategic planning, political participation of women, gender mainstreaming in systems, institutions and policies.

Niki Johnson has a PhD in Politics and an MA in Latin American Area Studies from the University of London. She is a lecturer and Coordinator of the Gender Politics Research Area at the Institute of Political Science, Faculty of Social Sciences, and Universidad de la República in Montevideo, Uruguay. Her research covers issues of gender politics (political representation, citizenship, legislative and public policy agendas) in relation to both institutional and women's movement politics in Uruguay and other Latin American countries.

Verónica Pérez has a BA in Political Science from the Faculty of Social Sciences, Universidad de la República, in Montevideo, Uruguay. She is an assistant in the Gender Politics Research Area at the Institute of Political Science, Universidad de la República, and Montevideo, Uruguay. Her teaching and research focus on gender politics, electoral politics and democracy in Uruguay and Latin America.

Adriana Piatti-Crocker is Associate Professor of political science at the University of Illinois, at Springfield. She holds a J.D. from the University of La Plata (Argentina) and a Ph.D. in Political Science from Northern Illinois University. She specializes in Latin American politics, gender and politics, and international and regional organizations with particular emphasis on gender. Dr. Piatti-Crocker has written several journal articles and co-edited a book.

Jennifer M. Piscopo is Assistant Professor of Public Policy at Salem College. Her work on women and politics in Latin America has been published in Politics & Gender, Parliamentary Affairs, and several edited volumes. She is the co-editor (with Susan Franceschet and Mona Lena Krook) of *The Impact of Gender Quotas: Women's Descriptive, Substantive, and Symbolic Representation* (forthcoming from

Oxford University Press). She received her Ph.D. in Political Science from the University of California, San Diego in 2011.

Jacqueline Jiménez Polanco is a Ph.D. in Political Science and Sociology, Complutense University (Madrid-Spain) and a J.D. in Law, Pontifical Catholic University Madre y Maestra (Santiago, Dominican Republic) and Complutense University (Madrid-Spain). Polanco is Assistant Professor of Sociology, Department of Social Sciences at Bronx Community College of the City University of New York. Her research interests include Dominican/Latin American Politics, Women in Politics, Sexual Minorities, and Migration.

Gregory D. Schmidt is a professor of political science at the University of Texas at El Paso, where he serves as chair of the department. He also has taught at Northern Illinois University and several leading Peruvian universities. Professor Schmidt has published extensively on Peru in leading journals and for prestigious presses, focusing on development, decentralization, electoral rules and administration, executive-legislative relations, and gender.

Laman Tasch was born and grew up in Azerbaijan. She received her bachelor and master's degrees in sociology from the Middle East technical University (Ankara, Turkey) and a Ph.D. in political science from the Northern Illinois University (DeKalb, Illinois). Currently she teaches at Columbia College (Chicago, Illinois). Her research interests include the issues of identity politics, minorities and human rights in Russia, Turkey, and their neighbors.

María Inés Tula is Licensed in Political Science and a J.D. from the University of Buenos Aires, Argentina. She published a number of journal articles on elections, electoral systems and political parties. She is currently a professor in the Political Science Department at the University of Buenos Aires and a researcher at the National Council of Scientific and Technical Research (CONICET).

Pär Zetterberg is Assistant Professor at the Department of Government at Uppsala University (Sweden). His doctoral dissertation, entitled *Engineering Equality? Assessing the Multiple Impacts of Electoral Gender Quotas* (2009), focused on the likelihood for gender quotas to serve as a tool to disrupt gender inequalities in politics, with an empirical focus in Latin America and particularly Mexico. He is also interested in research on political inequalities more broadly and the challenges to political integration of traditionally excluded groups (such as women, youth, immigrants, and indigenous peoples). He has published his research in journals such as *Political Research Quarterly*, *Parliamentary Affairs*, *Representation*, and *Development and Change*.

Index

A

B

C

D

E

F

M

N

O

P

R

S

T

U

V

W

Z

LATIN AMERICA

Interdisciplinary Studies

Gladys M. Varona-Lacey
General Editor

Latin America: Interdisciplinary Studies serves as a forum for scholars in the field of Latin American Studies, as well as an educational resource for anyone interested in this region of the world. Themes and topics encompass social, political, historical, and economic issues, in addition to literature, music, art, and architecture.

For additional information about this series or for the submission of manuscripts, please contact:

Dr. Gladys M. Varona-Lacey
Ithaca College
Department of Modern Languages & Literatures
Ithaca, NY 14859

To order other books in this series, please contact our Customer Service Department at:

(800) 770-LANG (within the U.S.)
(212) 647-7706 (outside the U.S.)
(212) 647-7707 FAX

Or browse online by series at:

WWW.PETERLANG.COM

www.ingramcontent.com/pod-product-compliance
Ingram Content Group UK Ltd.
Pitfield, Milton Keynes, MK11 3LW, UK
UKHW021828100926
8556IPUK00003B/220